# Using Microsoft® Works: Macintosh® Version

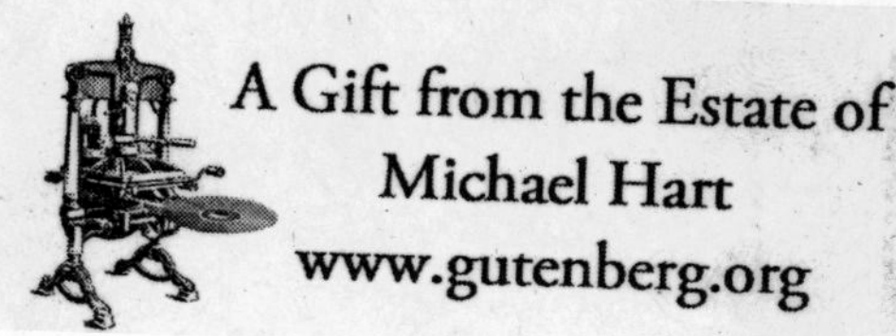


## 2nd Edition

Ron Mansfield

Revised by Barrie A. Sosinsky

# Using Microsoft® Works: Macintosh® Version

## 2nd Edition



Library of Congress Catalog No.: 89-62806

ISBN 0-88022-461-4



92 91 8 7 6

Interpretation of the printing code: the rightmost double-digit number is the year of the book's printing; the rightmost single-digit number, the number of the book's printing. For example, a printing code of 89-1 shows that the first printing of the book occurred in 1989.

*Using Microsoft Works*, 2nd Edition is based on Version 2.0 and the earlier Versions 1.0 and 1.1.

# Dedication

To my best friend
and wonderful wife,
Nancy

—R.M.

***Publishing Manager***

Lloyd J. Short

***Production Editor***

Gregory Robertson

***Editors***

Jo Anna Arnott
Fran Blauw
Kelly Currie

***Technical Editors***

Gene Klein
Daniel Zoller

***Editorial Assistant***

Stacie Lamborne

***Indexer***

Sherry Massey

***Book Design and Production***

Dan Armstrong
Brad Chinn
Dave Kline
Lori A. Lyons
Jennifer Matthews
Jon Ogle
Joe Ramon
Dennis Sheehan

*Composed in Garamond and Excellent No. 47*
by Que Corporation

# About the Author

Ron Mansfield

Ron Mansfield is president of Mansfield and Associates, a California-based consulting firm that helps businesses select, install, and learn how to use microcomputer systems. Mansfield and Associates also prepares technical documentation. Ron writes monthly computer columns and feature articles for a number of national magazines. He also is the author of the *1987 Computer Buying Guide*.

# Contents at a Glance

## Part VII Integrating Applications

# Table of Contents

# II Word Processing

## IV Spreadsheets and Graphs

# V Databases

## VI Additional Works Capabilities

## VII Integrating Applications

# Acknowledgments

I want to thank my sister, Gina Sosinsky, for all the help she gave me while this work was in progress.

Thanks also go to Glenn Hoffman, Director of the Boston Macintosh Users Group of the Boston Computer Society.

The Boston Computer Society made possible much of the needed perspective for this work, and the Macintosh Users Group is a great resource for learning.

Thanks are due also to everyone who helped produce this book: Lloyd Short, publishing manager; Karen Bluestein, acquisitions editor; Greg Robertson, production editor; Jo Anna Arnott, Fran Blauw, and Kelly Currie, editors; Gene Klein and Daniel Zoller, technical editors; and the production department of Que Corporation.

—B.A.S.

# Trademark Acknowledgments

Que Corporation has made every effort to supply trademark information about company names, products, and services mentioned in this book. Trademarks indicated below were derived from various sources. Que Corporation cannot attest to the accuracy of this information.

1-2-3 and Lotus are registered trademarks of Lotus Development Corporation.

4th Dimension is a trademark of ACIUS.

CompuServe is a registered trademark of CompuServe, Inc. and H&R Block, Inc.

Cricket Draw and Cricket Graph are trademarks of Cricket Software, Inc.

dBASE is a registered trademark and Ashton-Tate, FullWrite Professional, and Full Impact are trademarks of Ashton-Tate Corporation.

Encapsulated PostScript is a registered trademark of Adobe Systems, Inc.

FullPaint is a trademark of Ann Arbor Softworks, Inc.

GEnie is a trademark of General Electric Co.

HP is a registered trademark of Hewlett-Packard Company.

IBM is a registered trademark of International Business Machines, Inc.

LaserWriter, ImageWriter, AppleTalk, AppleWorks, Apple IIc, Apple IIe, Apple IIGS, HyperCard, MacPaint, Macintosh, MacWrite, and MacDraw are registered trademarks and AppleShare is a trademark of Apple Computer, Inc.

Microsoft and Multiplan are registered trademarks of Microsoft, Inc.

PageMaker is a registered trademark of Aldus Corporation.

Radio Shack is a registered trademark of Tandy Corporation.

Smartcom II is a registered trademark of Hayes Microcomputer Products, Inc.

The Source is a service mark of Source Telecomputing Corporation.

SuperLaserSpool is a trademark of SuperMac Software, Inc.

SuperPaint is a trademark of Silicon Beach Software, Inc.

Telenet is a registered trademark of GTE Telenet Communications Corporation.

Tempo is a trademark of Affinity Microsystems, Ltd.

ThunderScan is a registered trademark of ThunderWare, Inc.

TOPS is a registered trademark of Centram Systems West, Inc.

Tymnet is a registered trademark of Tymnet, Inc.

VAX is a trademark of Digital Equipment Corporation.

Wingz is a trademark of Informix Software, Inc.

WordPerfect is a registered trademark of WordPerfect Corporation.

WorksPlus Spell is a trademark of Lundeen & Associates.

# Conventions Used in This Book

The conventions used in this book have been established to help you learn to use the program quickly and easily. As much as possible, the conventions correspond with those used in the Microsoft Works: Macintosh Version documentation.

Commands and menu names are written with initial capital letters (the Set Cell Attributes command on the Format menu).

Dialog boxes are called by the name of the command used to display that box.

Buttons in dialog boxes are written as they appear on-screen: the Yes button, the Date Long button.

File names are written with initial capital letters. Keys are written with an initial capital: Option key, Shift key. The command key is indicated by ⌘. Key combinations are hyphenated: Shift-Return, ⌘-V.

Material you are to type is in italic (type *$332.21*). Messages that appear on-screen are in a `special typeface`.

# Preface

Perhaps you are looking at this book and wondering, "Is Microsoft Works 2.0 a program I should spend some time with?" Many people do use Microsoft Works; Works on the Macintosh has been a bestseller since its introduction. Many people buy Works as their very first computer program; some people use it to run a small business, and other people use it for their general personal and family computing needs.

Works is an integrated program containing a word processor, spreadsheet, database, and draw and communications programs. By using the Works interface, any combination of these programs can be available to you when you need them. Few basic tasks you may want to accomplish on your Macintosh cannot be done in Works. Microsoft Works is easy to use and has advanced features that you can grow into. Many experienced Macintosh owners continue to use Works long past the point at which they master more powerful stand-alone programs. These users continue to use Works because the important features they want are contained in Works; they are not distracted by scores of "convenience" features they will never use.

Maybe you have used a previous version of Works and you know what I mean. You are thinking of upgrading and wonder what's been added to this new version. Works 2.0 contains several important new features, including a spell checker, a full-featured draw function, color support, and a macro recorder. This second edition of *Using Microsoft Works: Macintosh Version* has several new chapters to cover these additional features of the program. Perhaps you have just purchased Works 2.0 and read the documentation, but you still have questions and want to master the possibilities Works offers. This book is for you. Contained within this book is a hands-on approach to this program, with many examples that you can use. I have discussed resources and tricks that you will not find in the manual.

*Using Microsoft Works: Macintosh Version* is not like other books that teach you how to use a particular program. This book takes you from the basics of point-and-click to some advanced concepts that you will use indefinitely. With Works, you can automate your letter writing, organize your data, do desktop publishing, and communicate with others. As you can see, Microsoft has made Works for business and personal use. Read this book, learn Microsoft Works, and you will be on your way to using not only Works, but all your other Macintosh programs to fullest advantage as well.

As the revision author of a good book, I attempted to keep to the spirit of the first edition. I tried to be clear, concise, and accessible to most readers. If mistakes or inaccuracies have crept in, however, I take responsibility for them.

Barrie A. Sosinsky

# Preface to the First Edition

I distrust long book prefaces and seldom read them, so I'll keep this one brief. After all, if information is both introductory and important, it should be in the first chapter, right?

As a working member of the computer press, I review software. In addition, the people in my consulting firm deal with both new and experienced computer users daily. We help people select, install, and learn how to use business micros. Obviously, we use computers in our own business, too. As a result of my experience with computers over the past ten years, I have seen many ugly software programs and frustrated users, so I'm skeptical of new software.

In my experience, software is rarely as good as the brochures describe it. I brought that skepticism to my first tour of the Microsoft Works program. How could something that costs so little do so much? Where's the catch? Anything this big with so many features must have bugs. Where are they?

The Works program was already a bestseller when I started writing *Using Microsoft Works*. After living with the evolving manuscript night and day for about eight months, I know why Works is a bestseller. Works is good software. It "feels" right. Programs work as you'd expect. You don't need to master a host of new skills for each different function. Once you've learned how to insert and delete text, for example, you can use those same skills when creating database and spreadsheet entries. You are not distracted by dozens of illogical rules, so you are free to concentrate on the creative aspects of computing. The program has enough power to help you effectively communicate, file, and compute, but it does not have scores of "Hey lookit" features that do little but complicate matters and confuse you.

Yes, I did find compromises and even a few bugs—they're described in this book—but my skepticism is gone. You can easily work around the few problems and shortcomings, and many of them have been eliminated altogether in the recently released Works Version 1.1. The power and easy use of the Works program far outweigh its shortcomings. It is a reliable "Swiss army knife" for business and family computing. Works may be the only application software you'll ever need for your Mac, with the exception of a paint program.

Many of the examples you will see in this book are from actual business and home applications. I wrote *Using Microsoft Works* while using Works Versions 1.0 and 1.1 on a Macintosh Plus, a Macintosh SE, and a Macintosh II.

It's a rare piece of software that stays on my computer after a project is completed. Works is a "keeper." Once you've read this book and used Works for a while, I think you'll agree.

Ron Mansfield

# Introduction

## An Overview of Microsoft Works

Microsoft Works was designed to take advantage of the power and standard interface of the Macintosh. If you have used programs such as MacWrite or MacDraw, you will feel right at home with Works.

## *What is Microsoft Works?*

An important difference between Works and the stand-alone software programs you may have used is that Works performs five major functions: word processing, drawing (object-oriented graphics), database management and reporting, spreadsheets and graphs, and data communications. You can perform all these functions with stand-alone programs, such as MacWrite or Microsoft Word, Microsoft Excel, FileMaker II, and Red Ryder, but Works ties all these functions together and integrates them.

You can, for example, create spreadsheets with related pie graphs and include them in a word processing document. You can personalize the resulting document for selected people from your computerized mailing list and send the document to them either on paper or through a modem, all with the same program.

### *The Word Processor*

Works includes a full-featured word processor with a spell checker that enables you to create simple correspondence or complex reports and proposals. You can create a letterhead in the form of a template (which Works calls Stationery) for your correspondence, business cards, and memos (see figs. I.1 and I.2). A typical word processing screen is shown in figure I.3.

**Fig. I.1**

*Letterhead created in Works.*

THE PUBLIC WORKS

Macintosh TEMPS: Word Processing, Graphics, Spreadsheets, Databases, & Communications

45 Lexington Street, Suite 2, Newton, MA 02154 • (617)244-9078

**Fig. I.2**

*Sample memo from Works.*

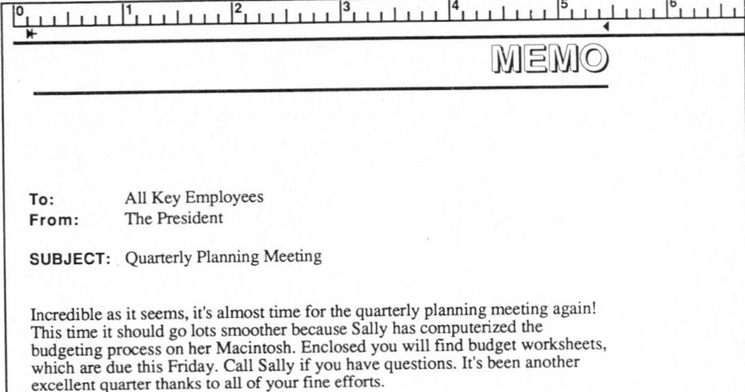

MEMO

**To:** All Key Employees
**From:** The President

**SUBJECT:** Quarterly Planning Meeting

Incredible as it seems, it's almost time for the quarterly planning meeting again! This time it should go lots smoother because Sally has computerized the budgeting process on her Macintosh. Enclosed you will find budget worksheets, which are due this Friday. Call Sally if you have questions. It's been another excellent quarter thanks to all of your fine efforts.

**Fig. I.3**

*Typical Works word processing window.*

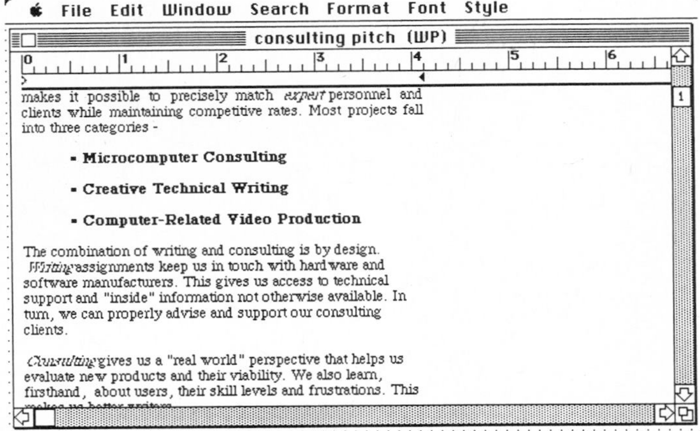



makes it possible to precisely match *expert* personnel and clients while maintaining competitive rates. Most projects fall into three categories -

- **Microcomputer Consulting**
- **Creative Technical Writing**
- **Computer-Related Video Production**

The combination of writing and consulting is by design. *Writing* assignments keep us in touch with hardware and software manufacturers. This gives us access to technical support and "inside" information not otherwise available. In turn, we can properly advise and support our consulting clients.

*Consulting* gives us a "real world" perspective that helps us evaluate new products and their viability. We also learn, firsthand, about users, their skill levels and frustrations. This

Works provides the features you expect from any good Macintosh word processing program. With the Clipboard and Scrapbook, you can move, duplicate, and store text temporarily. You can place up to 14 documents in windows simultaneously (memory permitting), and you easily can move text from one window to another. A search-and-replace feature is provided, as well as a way to move quickly to any page in your document.

Rulers and page setup capabilities enable you to control completely the formatting of your documents. You can define margins, page size, indentation, set various types of tabs and line spacing, change justification, and more, and you can do this for individual paragraphs or for a whole document. You also can add a line of header information, along with a line of footer information.

Headers and footers can include titles, automatic date and time insertions, and automatic page numbers. You also can define title pages, control starting page numbers, and force manual page breaks. (Works does not produce automatic footnotes, however.) You can use any font in your system file or any font accessible through a suitcase file. You can print in bold, italic, outline, or shadow type styles. You also can underline words or sentences, and use superscripts and subscripts in whatever sizes of fonts you want to use. By combining these fonts, and changing formats, attributes, or font point sizes, you can create professional-looking documents.

Works includes a 50,000-word spell checker. The spell checker adds new words with a variety of suffixes and checks homonyms (words that sound alike). You can create or buy multiple dictionaries and change the basis for many of the search parameters.

## Graphics and Design

Unlike many other word processors, Works has a full-featured drawing program. In draw, you can create text objects with full word processing features and link the text objects together to do layout work and create multicolumn text.

Unlike paint programs in which the graphics you create on-screen are *bit-mapped*, the Works draw module generates object-oriented graphics. In bit-mapped paint programs, each pixel or pixel element is turned on or off individually. A picture of the screen is kept in memory and updated to your monitor. A pixel can be white or black (on or off), or it can be a collection of red, blue, and green spots blended to give colors (on a color monitor). In an object-oriented program, you can create lines, boxes, shapes, and a variety of advanced special effects (see fig. I.4).

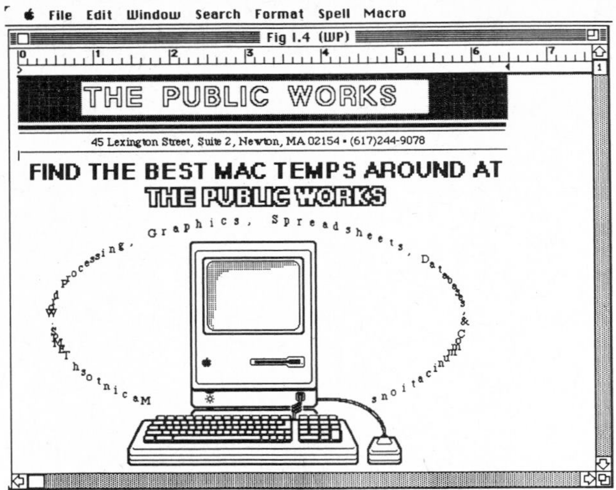


**Fig. I.4**

*A flier created by using draw and text. Notice the different formats of text.*

In object-oriented graphics, on-screen objects are described by mathematical formulas and are clean, crisp images when printed. You can group objects, move them, align them to a grid (if you want), and combine them with your documents. Each on-screen object can have various fills and lines. The draw module also supports color objects that print on an ImageWriter II or other color output device. With draw, you can use Works as desktop publishing software for many projects.

You can import graphics from MacPaint-compatible programs by using the Clipboard and Scrapbook. You can use the data in a Works spreadsheet to create graphs, and you can enhance your spreadsheet and graphs with all the power of the Works draw module. You can paste the results into your document to clarify important points.

Works also provides a print merge capability. Print merging enables you to combine database information with word processing documents. You can use the powerful draw capabilities to create personalized form letters, forms, mailing labels, and more. With draw, you can create invoices, statements, purchase orders, and receipts—any kind of form—and automate the procedure for running a business.

## Databases

*Databases* are organized collections of information. A phone book is a database, as are recipe collections, inventory records, mailing lists, and shoe boxes filled with receipts for tax-deductible expenses. Works can help you organize many kinds of information into useful computerized databases. Once you have designed a Works database, you can enter information and quickly organize it for easy retrieval and report generation.

Think of a Works database as the electronic equivalent of a box of file cards. Each *record* in your computerized database is the computer's equivalent of a card in a file box or a rotary card file. You can have as many as 6,000 records in a Works database, depending on factors described in Chapter 9. The individual entries in a record are placed in *fields*. A field contains one item of data—the ZIP code, for instance. Basic database concepts are explored in more detail at the beginning of Chapter 9, "Creating Databases."

When you first set up a database, Works helps you create an on-screen form containing blanks and labels for each field (see fig. I.5). If you design your form properly, Works tries to prevent you from entering the wrong type of information in a blank.

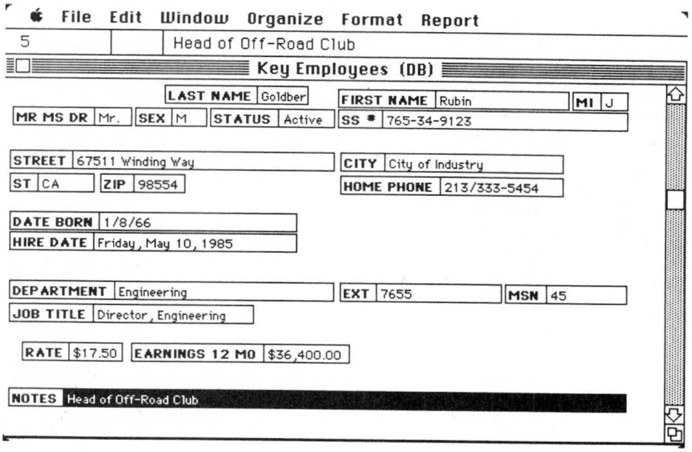

**Fig. I.5**

*A typical Works form window, which holds a database record.*

After designing a database and entering the data (an employee list, for example), you can use Works to get information. For example, you can scroll through all employee records, sorted by hire date, or you can display a list of managers making more than $35,000 a year.

You also can have calculated fields in a Works database. For example, the EARNINGS 12 MO field in figure I.5 is computed by Works, based on the RATE entry and some assumptions about hours worked. Whenever the employee's rate changes for a record, Works automatically computes a new annual earnings amount and places that number in the EARNINGS 12 MO field.

Works can display single records or lists of records. The list window, shown in figure I.6, makes viewing multiple records easy.

File Edit Window Organize Format Report

cc (DB)

| FIRM | PHONE | FN | LN | PFX | S |
|---|---|---|---|---|---|
| Auto Club of Southern California | 818-795-0601 | Hugh | Singer | Mr. | |
| Automated Systems Program | 818-355-4013 | Carrie | Joseph | Ms. | |
| Avera B Lewis Jr. | 213-792-5224 | B. Lewis | Avera | Mr. | Jr |
| Avery International | 818-304-2000 | Diane | Dixon | Ms. | |
| Avis Rent A Car | 818-449-6122 | Rick | Simonson | Mr. | |
| Avon Products, Inc. | 818-578-8000 | William | Roy | Mr. | |
| B & J Janitorial Service | (?)794-0746 | Norman | Taylor | Mr. | |
| B W & C Investments, The dba The Bral | 213-624-1001 | Tony | Canzoneri | Mr. | |
| B.C.D. Software Services | 818-796-1764 | Chris | Leu | Mr. | |
| Babaeian Transportation Co. Inc. | 818-956-2227 | Masood | Babaeian | Mr. | |
| Badger-Carmichael | 818-793-7910 | Gary | Badger | Mr. | |
| Bahama Bowling Lanes | 818-351-8858 | Billy | Meyers | Mr. | |
| Bailey, Soleno & Associates | 818-304-0555 | Lucinda | Bailey | Ms. | |
| Bank of America | 818-578-5091 | Jim Fang | Ding | Mr. | |
| Bank of America | 818-578-5163 | Alan | Hancock | Mr. | |
| Barker Brothers | 818-796-0133 | Don | Glasgow | Mr. | |
| Barnes, Edwin A (Ned) | 818-799-6201 | Ron | Barnes | Mr. | |

**Fig. I.6**

*Displaying multiple records in the list window.*

With Works, you easily can redesign databases. You can add, delete, resize, or move fields, and inserting, deleting, and editing records is just as easy. Because Works adheres closely to most Macintosh conventions, you can use the Clipboard and Scrapbook in the usual Macintosh manner to maintain your databases and to import information from and export information to other places.

Search and selection features (similar to those found in the word processing module) enable you to find quickly records containing specific items. The search criteria can be simple (find Smith) or complex (find Smith or Smyth or Smythe with a salary greater than $20,000 but less than $40,000). You can sort your data many different ways. When you are finished sorting and searching, you can save as a separate database the sets of records that have special relevance for your needs.

You can print the results of these information requests, as well as see them on-screen. You can sum fields in various ways, and you can control page layout, report titles, type styles, headers, footers, margins, and so on (see fig. I.7). You also can pass selected data to a spreadsheet for further analysis and graphing. Using the word processor and database information, you can create personalized documents such as form letters or mailing labels (see fig. I.8).

KEY EMPLOYEE PAY BY DEPARTMENT

July 14, 1987

| LAST NAME | FIRST NAME | JOB TITLE | DEPARTMENT | EARNINGS 12 M |
|---|---|---|---|---|
| Baxter | James | Director Personnel | Personnel | $41,600.00 |
| Baxter | Tammy | Assistant Director | Personnel | $37,440.00 |
| | | | | $79,040.00 |
| Berfel | Ferd | Pull Tab Inspector | Test Lab | $18,470.40 |
| | | | | $18,470.40 |
| Flusher | Johnathon | Cleaning Associate | Maintenance | $10,400.00 |
| | | | | $10,400.00 |
| Goldberg | Rubin | Director, Engineering | Engineering | $36,400.00 |
| | | | | $36,400.00 |
| Goldsmith | Ray | President | Corporate | $83,200.00 |
| Goldsmith | Nancy Rae | Assistant to the President | Corporate | $81,120.00 |
| | | | | $164,320.00 |
| Makit | Willie | Production Supervisor | Production | $26,520.00 |
| | | | | $26,520.00 |
| Mi | Sue | New Product Development | Engineering | $58,240.00 |
| | | | | $58,240.00 |
| West | George | Sales | Sales | $62,400.00 |
| Quickcloser | John | Inside Sales | Sales | $52,000.00 |
| So | Mi | Inside Sales | Sales | $52,000.00 |
| | | | | $166,400.00 |
| Winston | Doc | Sr. Sardine Eye Closer | Production | $16,536.00 |
| | | | | $16,536.00 |
| | | | | $576,326.40 |

**Fig. I.7**

*Printed report from a Works database.*

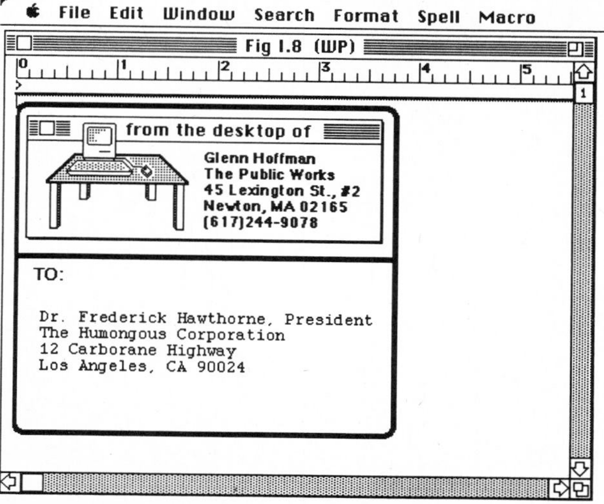


**Fig. I.8**

*Sample mailing label created from a Works database.*

The Works database is a *nonrelational* database (sometimes called a *flat file* database). In a nonrelational database, you can work with only one database file at a time. You cannot, for example, use one database (containing names, addresses, and client numbers) and a second database (containing only client numbers and expenses) to create (with one operation) invoices containing the names and addresses from the first database and the expense details from the second. For most applications, this restriction can be overcome with some careful planning.

The Works database has many uses at home, too. For example, you can use Works to aid your shopping or to organize your phonograph or compact disc collection. Databases make great address books. The Works database module can meet the needs of most business and home computer users, particularly when combined with the other Works modules.

## Spreadsheets and Graphs

Spreadsheets consist of *cells* that contain labels or titles, numbers, and equations (see fig. I.9). If you have ever set up a budget, you know what a simple spreadsheet is. A spreadsheet is to a calculator what a word processor is to a typewriter. The Works spreadsheet module enables you to set up simple or complex spreadsheets and see the results of changes in your assumptions. You can see the results of different income estimates, for example. This capability is very helpful in managing a business. You can play "what-if" games by changing a number and watching Works do all the math.

File Edit Window Select Format Options Chart

A48 -EXPENSES-

PL87 WORKS (SS)

| | A | B | C | D | E | F |
|---|---|---|---|---|---|---|
| 47 | | JAN | FEB | MAR | APR | MAY |
| 48 | -EXPENSES- | | | | | |
| 49 | | | | | | |
| 50 | (6) Advertising | $1225 | $299 | $1348 | $0 | $100 |
| 51 | (8) Bank Svc. Charges | $33 | $2 | $29 | $1 | $0 |
| 52 | (9) Car Expenses | $462 | $429 | $512 | $422 | $0 |
| 53 | (13) Dues & Publications | $15 | $23 | $36 | $0 | $0 |
| 54 | (16) Insurance | $579 | $296 | $414 | $0 | $116 |
| 55 | (18) Legal & Prof. Fees | $320 | $320 | $319 | $0 | $0 |
| 56 | (20) Office Supplies | $50 | $0 | $116 | $0 | $528 |
| 57 | (22) Rent/Util - Office | $1450 | $1454 | $1462 | $1647 | $1437 |
| 58 | (24) Repairs and Parts | $0 | $0 | $0 | $0 | $0 |
| 59 | (25) Supplies (other) | $1450 | $1454 | $1462 | $1647 | $1437 |
| 60 | (27) Travel/Entertain | $377 | $101 | $95 | $13 | $0 |
| 61 | (28) Phone Equip & lines | $0 | $816 | $407 | $508 | $351 |
| 62 | (29.1) Salaries | $1663 | $1584 | $1584 | $1584 | $0 |
| 63 | (31.1) Delivery | $106 | $23 | $183 | $34 | $0 |

**Fig. I.9**

*A typical Works spreadsheet window.*

Works has a wide range of mathematical, statistical, trigonometric, logarithmic, time and date, location, and financial functions. You can use the 64 functions in Works to build equations and relationships just by clicking the mouse.

Once you have designed and tested your spreadsheets, you can perform what-if calculations quickly and accurately. Recalculation can occur automatically or only when requested. To prevent important parts of the spreadsheet from being changed accidentally, you can protect cells.

The spreadsheet also contains a feature that enables you to attach a note to any cell to help you remember how the spreadsheet was constructed or to remind you of something you need to know or do. Theoretically, a Macintosh with 1M of memory can hold spreadsheets with as many as 22,500 cells, which is plenty for most projects.

Works enables you to set up professional-looking spreadsheets with a useful variety of type styles and formats. You can display and print numbers and labels in boldface (with or without underscores to add emphasis), center or align cell contents to the left or to the right, create various cell borders, turn grid lines on or off, display numbers with dollar signs and commas, define the number of decimal places, and print and display in color.

To copy and move things around, you use the Clipboard and the Scrapbook. You can quickly locate cells and edit them. New rows and columns can be inserted easily, and the information in rows or columns can be sorted using three levels of sorts. Suppose that you have a list of customers, their purchases, and the dates of purchase. Works helps you quickly rearrange their order of appearance on the spreadsheet, based on the size of their expenditures, chronology, and by the spelling of their names—all this with just one command. You choose the sort criterion you want to use.

You can print spreadsheets vertically (portrait mode) or horizontally (landscape mode), and you can reduce them to fit your page. You also can display and print the results graphically by using the Works graphing feature (see fig. I.10).

You can spruce up graphs by using the draw feature, add lines with arrows to point out an element of the graph, and use labels made with the text tool. Graphs are dynamically linked to a spreadsheet; change a cell value and the graph automatically changes to show you the effect. The graphs, with or without their corresponding spreadsheets, can be pasted into word processing documents or transferred to other Works users by means of the data communications module.

**Fig. I.10**

*The types of graphs that Works can produce.*

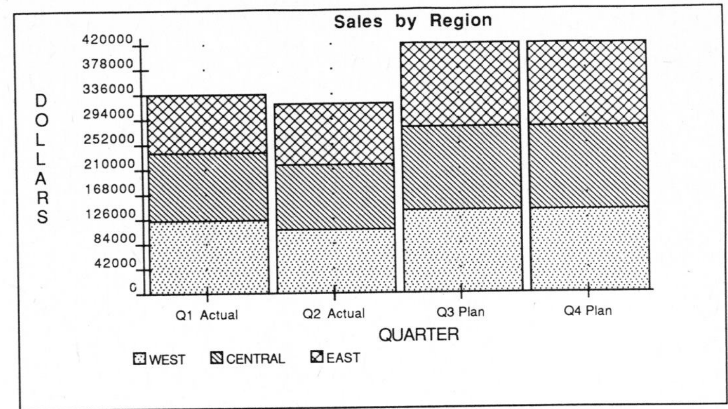


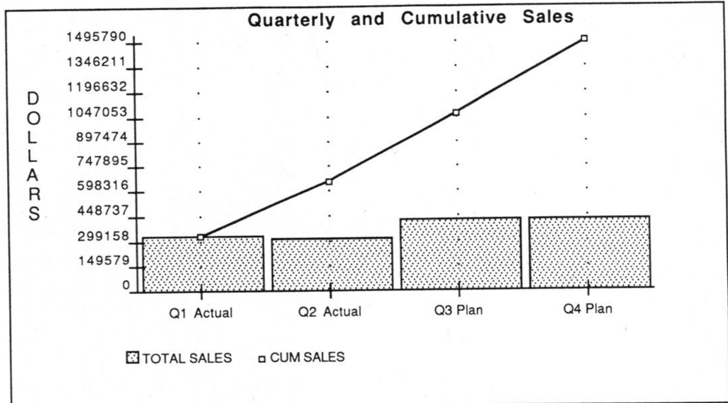


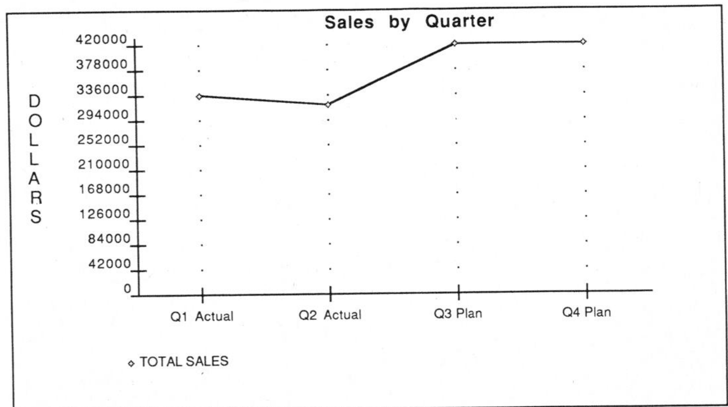

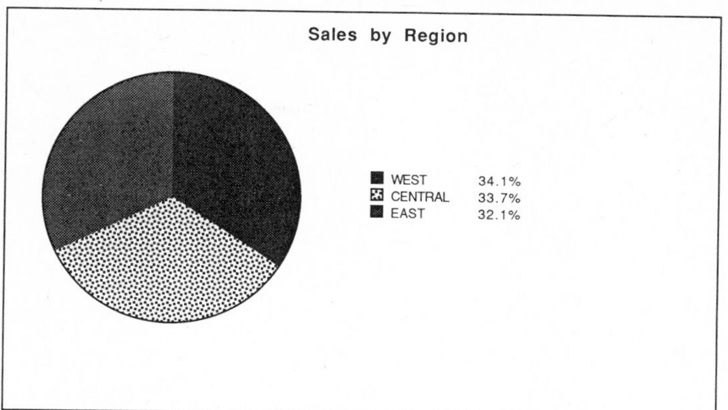


**Fig. I.10**

*Continued.*

Works spreadsheets are compatible with others, such as Excel and FileMaker II (only 64 of the approximately 125 Excel functions are supported, however). Chapter 14 discusses exporting and importing data when using other spreadsheets. Considering that the Works spreadsheet is only one part of a fully integrated package, the spreadsheet is surprisingly powerful and feature-packed. You can find most of the functions you need in the Works spreadsheet module.

Works 2.0 contains a keystroke click-and-drag recorder module. This feature, new to Version 2.0, is similar in design to the Apple system software program MacroMaker. With the macro module, you can save miniature programs called *macros*, which enable you to perform simple functions in far fewer keystrokes. You can assign keystrokes to actions like typing a text string, choosing a set of menu commands to format a paragraph, sorting a database or spreadsheet, and so on. Macros are described more fully in Chapter 11.

## *Data Communications*

The Works data communications capability enables you to connect your computer with others, near or far. Works, an Apple- or Hayes-compatible modem, and normal telephone lines are your keys to subscription information services such as CompuServe, Delphi, The Source, and GEnie (see fig. I.11). You also can dial free bulletin board systems (BBSs) and exchange files of all types with other computer users. Appendix B lists some of the many hundreds of BBSs available.

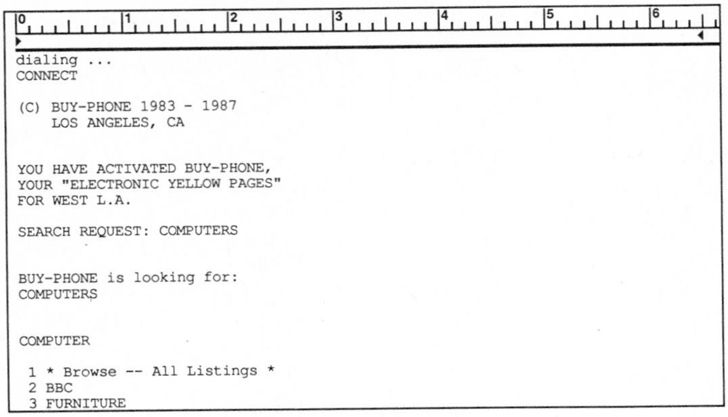

```
dialing ...
CONNECT

(C) BUY-PHONE 1983 - 1987
    LOS ANGELES, CA


YOU HAVE ACTIVATED BUY-PHONE,
YOUR "ELECTRONIC YELLOW PAGES"
FOR WEST L.A.

SEARCH REQUEST: COMPUTERS


BUY-PHONE is looking for:
COMPUTERS


COMPUTER

 1 * Browse -- All Listings *
 2 BBC
 3 FURNITURE
```

**Fig. I.11**

*A typical Works communications screen.*

Works captures incoming data on disk for later review and printing. You also can send files from your computer or converse with another user by using the keyboard. Works supports a wide range of data communications speeds and protocols (communication methods). A simple but effective "phone book" is provided in which you can store 10 phone numbers for automatic dialing. The current Works communications module provides no automatic log-on or script feature, but you can add this feature with third-party products. With a modem, Works can answer the phone unattended, and send and receive data in the background while you're doing other things, such as working on a word processing document.

You can use the communications feature without a modem to exchange data with another computer located nearby. This direct-connection capability makes possible the exchange of information with dissimilar computers, such as Apple IIs, IBM PCs, Commodore Amigas, Toshiba laptops, and so forth.

# Getting Help

Works provides on-line help for all its commands and many of the program features. Choose the Help command in the Window menu and your cursor turns into a question mark. If you choose a command such as Hide Ruler, the Help window appears below your word processing window, as shown in figure I.12. Either scroll for additional help or use the cursor (in the shape of a question mark) to pull down other commands from the menu and receive additional information.

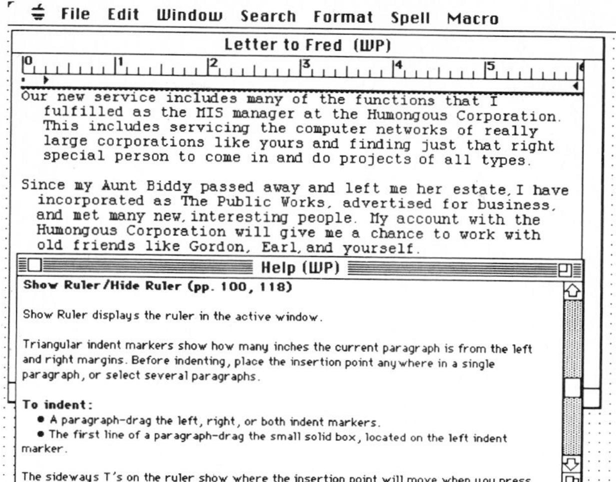


**Fig. I.12**

*The Help window for the word processor ruler.*

# *Who Should Use This Book?*

*Using Microsoft Works: Macintosh Version* is for beginners and pros alike. If you already own Microsoft Works, this book will be a valuable addition to your Works owner's manual. This book contains information that you will not find in your Works manual or in other books about Works. You learn about the hardware and software required by Works, as well as shortcuts and tips to help you get the most out of the program. This book contains information about Version 2.0 (the latest release of Works), and how to update from a previous version. *Using Microsoft Works: Macintosh Version* helps you discover the strengths and weaknesses of Works and shows you how to get the most from one of today's best integrated software packages for the Apple Macintosh.

In this book you learn basic operating skills and advanced techniques. Information about third-party software that can add features such as automatic hyphenation, a full macro language, low-cost templates, purchased databases, financial systems, and automated computer log-on files also is included. You can do your payroll, balance your checkbook, get information on all the American presidents, and do your taxes by using third-party software.

# *How To Use This Book*

For Macintosh newcomers, this book teaches how to cut and paste, click and drag, open and close, and much more. Included in Chapter 1 are explanations of the hardware and software you need to run Works. Even experienced users learn important details like memory requirements, available utilities, and shortcuts.

This book presents information about Works in a logical order. Most people use the word processor first, and then the draw feature, which is explained after word processing. Spreadsheets and databases have many shared features, especially functions for calculating values, and those chapters should be read as a unit. Most users find that the communications section becomes of interest later on. Finally, the book ties together all the Works modules and explains how to integrate Works with other programs.

Part I, "Learning About and Starting Works," tells you just that: how to get started with Microsoft Works. This part of the book is for users new to Microsoft Works, as well as for those who need to review Macintosh techniques.

Chapter 1, "Getting Started," offers a brief review of Macintosh basics for those who need to brush up on concepts such as clicking, dragging, using Finder and MultiFinder, making backup copies, configuring your system, and so on. This chapter amplifies topics covered in the Macintosh manual, discussing in more detail basic concepts you need to get started. Chapter 1 contains many helpful suggestions to improve your efficiency and mentions special products to help you with your work.

Part II, "Word Processing," tells you how to use the word processing module of Microsoft Works. Word Processing is one of the most common uses for computers, and Works comes with a full-featured word processor.

Chapter 2, "Entering, Editing, Saving, and Printing Text," is a guide to using Microsoft Works for your writing chores. This chapter tells you how to open the word processing module, enter and edit text, use the spell checker, save the text you create, and print your document.

Chapter 3, "Formatting Text and Adding Style," teaches you more about using the word processor and files. You learn how to format paragraphs and pages (set margins, and indent, tab, center and justify text, and so forth). The techniques learned in this chapter can help you improve your efficiency and the appearance of your documents.

Part III, "Graphics and Design," consists of two chapters that show you how to use the draw module of Microsoft Works to create object-oriented graphics. You learn how to import graphics from other programs, and how to create visually appealing documents.

Chapter 4, "Drawing," explains the drawing features in the draw module. You can use these draw tools to create high-quality desktop published materials.

Chapter 5, "Graphics and Design," is a special chapter that describes how to carry out projects, work with color, and make your projects more attractive. This chapter contains tips that can be useful in creating newsletters, brochures, business forms, and many other kinds of projects.

Part IV, "Spreadsheets and Graphs," tells you how to use Works to make financial calculations. In addition, you can create graphs of the results of these calculations. These features are very useful in running a business, for example.

Chapter 6, "Spreadsheet Concepts," discusses the basics of spreadsheets. You learn what spreadsheets are, what functions are included in the Works spreadsheet module, and how to use these functions.

Chapter 7, "Graphs," shows how to create graphs of the spreadsheet calculations. Putting calculations into a visual format often makes the differences between financial conditions more apparent than just numbers on a page do.

Chapter 8, "Spreadsheet and Database Functions," discusses the functions used in spreadsheets and databases. These functions are an integral part of Works spreadsheet and database modules. Be sure to read this chapter before you read about databases.

Part V, "Databases," consists of two chapters that explain how to use the database module of Works. Databases are an important part of almost all businesses.

Chapter 9, "Creating Databases," describes how to use Works to create databases and how to use them in conjunction with word processing documents. You can use this combination for many time-saving tasks, such as creating personalized form letters and mailing labels.

Chapter 10, "Database Reports," explains how to generate reports from the information contained in a database. Businesses often need printed reports of data.

Part VI, "Additional Works Capabilities," tells you how to use two features of Works that are valuable in helping you work more efficiently and compile and distribute information more quickly.

Chapter 11, "Creating and Using Macros," describes a feature new to Works: the macro recorder. Because the macro recorder is always available, you can read this chapter at any time.

Chapter 12, "Communications," describes the communications module, discusses all the terms you need to know, and tells how to download (copy and save files from another source) files safely and how to protect your computer from viruses. The capability to communicate between computers opens up a vast world of information to the computer user.

Part VII, "Integrating Applications," teaches you how to use Microsoft Works as a package, and in conjunction with other software, to get the most out of your investment.

Chapter 13, "Tying It All Together," discusses how to use the Works modules together. Each module is valuable by itself, but using them together offers even more power.

Chapter 14, "Using Works with Other Products," is a chapter that shows you how to augment Microsoft Works with software packages such as MacPaint, MacDraw, MultiFinder, SuperGlue II, Capture, WorksPlus Command, and others. You learn how to import and export data between modules, between programs, and between Microsoft Works files and from other computers.

Appendix A gives the names and addresses of hardware makers and software developers whose products are mentioned in this book.

Appendix B is a list of commercial and low-cost electronic bulletin boards.

Finally, this book contains an index, designed to help you find whatever you need. After you have finished using *Using Microsoft Works: Macintosh Version* as a tutorial, the index turns the book into a powerful reference tool.

## *Microsoft Works Target Users*

Microsoft Works was designed for both personal and business use. Not only is Works an excellent first program for beginners, but some people find that it's the only program they ever need for their Macintosh. Running a multimillion-dollar business with Works is possible.

Some "power" users, however, may outgrow Works, particularly if their applications are very demanding. For example, the spreadsheet portion of Works is not as full-featured as Excel, Microsoft's stand-alone spreadsheet. Usually, this limitation is not a problem unless you need features like a macro language, specialized statistical functions, or complex formatting. In many cases, you can work around missing features by using the techniques described in this book or by adding to your system the compatible software suggested throughout the book and in Chapter 14.

# Part I

# Learning About and Starting Works

## Includes

1

# Getting Started

This chapter is intended for persons who want to brush up on the basics of Microsoft Works. To get the most from your investment in Works, you need to know the techniques and terms described in this chapter. This information is not meant to replace that provided in your Apple Macintosh manuals, however. Included in this chapter are the minimum memory requirements for Works, procedures for starting the program, and techniques backing up your original disks. The importance of making a backup copy of your original Works disks cannot be overstated.

## *Reviewing Basic Macintosh Techniques*

The developers of the Macintosh created a series of standards and simple techniques often referred to as the *Macintosh interface*. This interface provides standardized ways to perform tasks. For example, the use of pull-down menus is a part of the interface, as are the mouse and the procedures performed with it (clicking, double-clicking, dragging, and so on). The use of symbols (called *icons*) such as the Trash or disk symbol (shown when the machine starts, or *boots up*—see fig. 1.1) creates what is called a graphical interface. In a graphical interface, actions are represented by items (icons or menu commands) on-screen. Because these items (actions) can be found on-screen, most users find this interface intuitive and easy to learn.

Apple has provided these tools and rules to all software developers. You can learn a new program more easily when you see symbols whose meanings are familiar to you. For the most part, Microsoft Works adheres to the Macintosh interface. Works differs from the basic Apple procedures sometimes, however, and the interface itself continues to

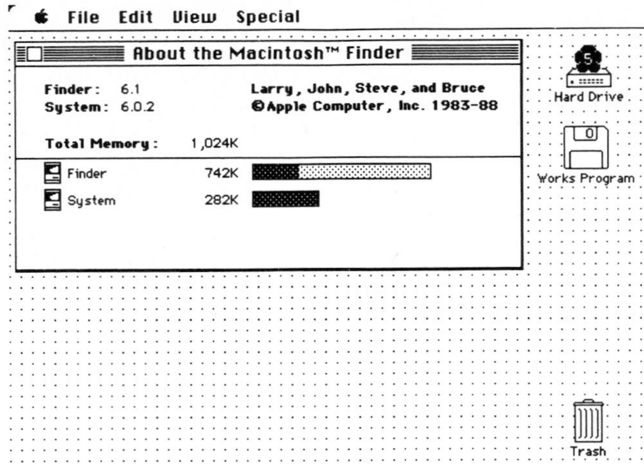


**Fig. 1.1**

*A desktop with the About window.*

evolve. Even if you are an experienced Macintosh user, then, the information that follows is useful.

An understanding of the following information is critical to understanding Works and most other Macintosh software. This chapter uses examples from Works and gives you a sufficient understanding of the Macintosh interface for successful Works operation. For additional information, consult your Apple manuals.

## *Understanding the Macintosh Desktop and Icons*

When you turn on your Macintosh, instructions encoded in the read-only memory (ROM) of the microprocessor look for System in your system folder. System is assumed to be on your start-up disk, which can be either a floppy disk or a hard disk drive. System contains information concerning where your Macintosh can find various resources, such as instructions on how to print, how to use the Clipboard, and how to behave on a network. One program you load at start-up is called Finder. Finder is a display program that creates the familiar Macintosh desktop shown in figure 1.1, but Finder is not essential to your Macintosh. Other display programs can tell your Macintosh how to display your desktop and organize your commands: MultiFinder (discussed later in this chapter) and the commercial product PowerStation are two examples of other display programs.

In Finder (see fig. 1.1), an icon representing your start-up disk—in this case your hard disk drive—always appears at the upper right corner of the screen. An icon for your Works program floppy disk in the internal drive appears below the start-up disk, and a Trash icon for items you want to throw away is displayed at the lower right corner of the screen. A *menu bar* is displayed across the top of the screen. You can use your mouse or, in most cases, your keyboard to pull down commands hidden under each word in the menu bar. By pulling down the Apple menu (on the far left under the Apple icon) the About Finder command is issued and a dialog box is displayed. This box tells you the version of System and Finder that you are using and how much *random access memory*, or *RAM*, is in your machine and in use.

A set of miscellaneous icons is shown in figure 1.2: the Finder program, a folder that contains files, the Trash for deleting items, and the ImageWriter printer driver file. The programs or features these icons represent are explained in this chapter. Refer to figure 1.3 to see all the Microsoft Works icons.

**Fig. 1.2**

*Some Works icons.*

# *Using the Mouse*

Your mouse is an input device that you use to tell your programs to perform specific functions. You can select text or data that you want to move, delete, or modify, and you can use the mouse to rearrange things (icons, for example) on your desktop. You also can choose from a variety of options by using the mouse with pull-down menus and dialog boxes, which are explained in subsequent sections.

When you move the mouse across a surface, a pointer on-screen moves a corresponding distance in the same direction as the mouse. The size and shape of the pointer are under software control and change at times (see fig. 1.4). The shape of the cursor indicates what type of operation you are performing.

You use the button on the mouse to select items. The process of pressing and releasing the mouse button is called *clicking*. Clicking usually initiates an action or tells Works what you want to do. Sometimes you *double-click* the mouse button (press and release the mouse button

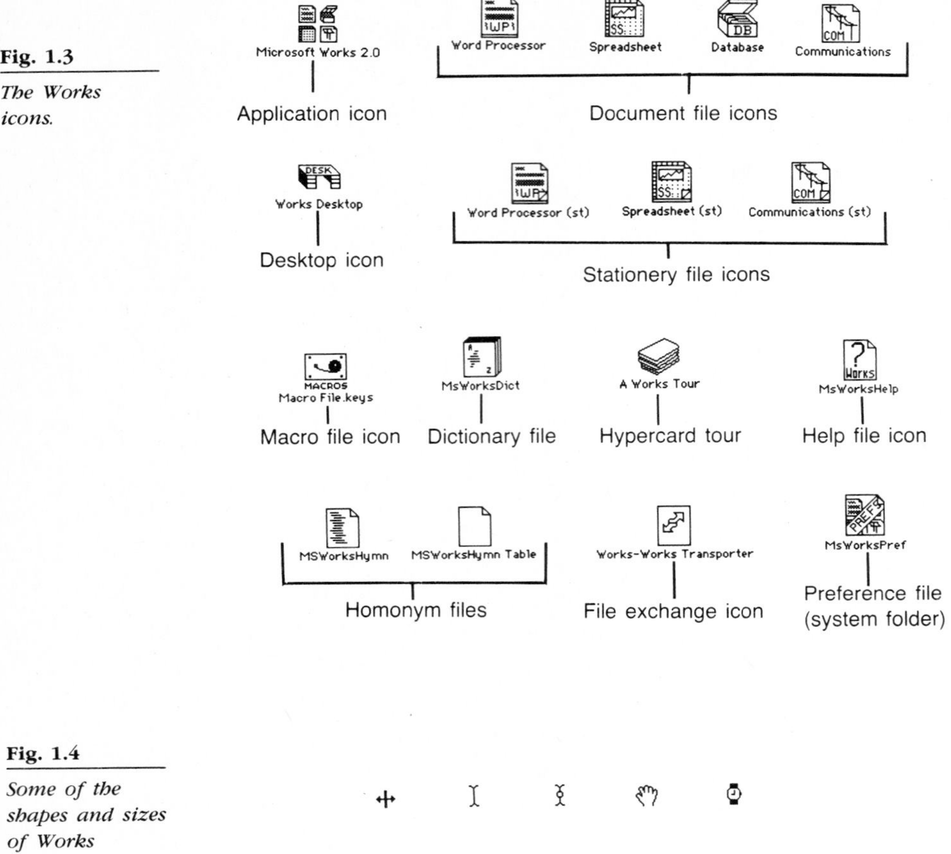


**Fig. 1.3**

*The Works icons.*

**Fig. 1.4**

*Some of the shapes and sizes of Works pointers.*

twice in rapid succession). Double-clicking is a shortcut for many commonly used procedures, and requires some practice. If you wait too long between clicks, your Macintosh "thinks" that you made two regular clicks rather than one double-click. You adjust the double-click time delay in the General settings on your Control Panel (see fig. 1.5).

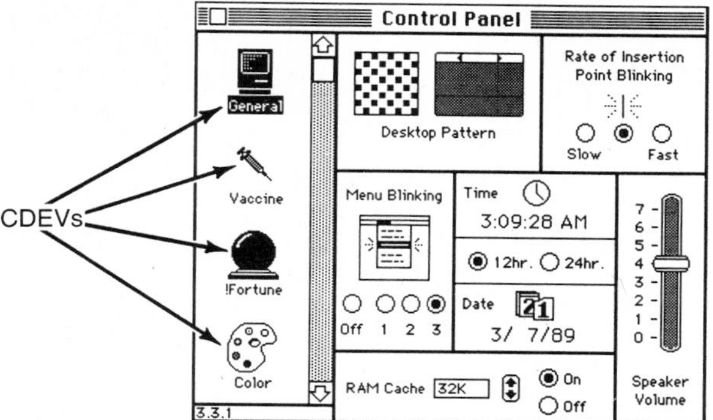


**Fig. 1.5**

*The Control Panel showing General program settings.*

Moving the mouse while holding down the mouse button is called *dragging*. This technique enables you to move things on-screen, perform multiple selections, highlight text for editing, or pull down menus from the menu bar. Sometimes dragging is done while pressing another key. For example, dragging while pressing the Shift key sometimes produces different results than does regular dragging. Keys that change operations are called *modifier keys*. The most common modifier keys are Shift, Ctrl, Option, and the command (or cloverleaf—⌘) key.

## Working with Menus and Menu Shortcuts

Macintosh programs have a menu bar at the top of the screen (see fig. 1.6). The menu bar lists categories of commands you can issue with the program. These commands are logically grouped as sets under menu headings. Frequently, items appear and disappear, or are "grayed out," indicating their availability based on what you are doing or where you are in the program. Figure 1.6 shows the File menu pulled down in a database document; the arrow cursor was used to select the Quit command by dragging down from the menu bar. If you release the mouse button at this point, the program will quit, or close down.

You tell the computer what you want to do by selecting the appropriate choice on the menu. Pull down a menu by putting the pointer on the menu title and then dragging the pointer down from the menu bar. As the pointer passes over the available choices in the menu, Works highlights your choices (the letters turn white, and the background becomes black). If you release the mouse button on a highlighted

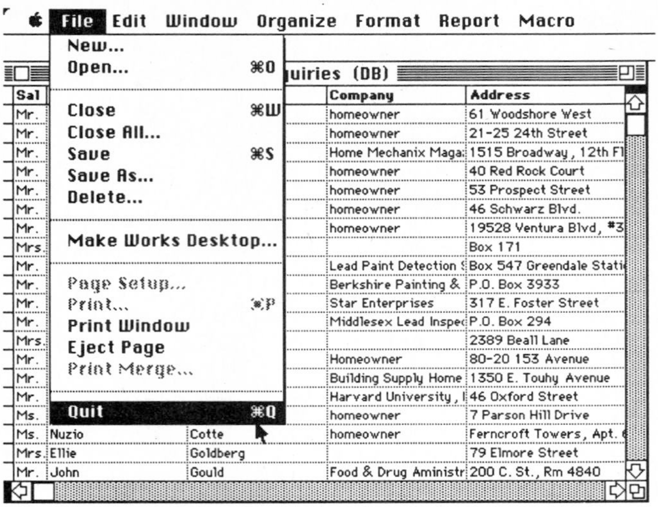

**Fig. 1.6**

*A Works menu bar with the File menu pulled down.*

choice, Works executes your request. If you change your mind, you can slide the pointer off the choice before releasing the mouse button. The menu then disappears without any choice being activated. If you make a mistake, the Undo command on the Edit menu *usually* (but not always) reverses your last command.

Frequently, some menu choices are dimmed, which indicates that they are not available at that moment, probably because you need to do something else first. In figure 1.6, for example, the Print Merge command currently is not available.

You can invoke some frequently used Works menu items without pulling down the menu. Listed in the menu next to some of the command names are sets of keys that you can type to perform the same function as the corresponding menu commands. Key combinations that do the same thing as a menu command are called *keystroke equivalents* or *keyboard shortcuts*. For instance, if you press ⌘-Q (fig. 1.6), the program will quit. To press ⌘-Q, hold down the ⌘ and press the letter Q at the same time. For example, the shortcut for accessing the Print dialog box involves holding down the ⌘ key and then pressing the P key at the same time. As you gain experience you will find that you remember many keyboard equivalents and that using them is generally faster than using the mouse.

If you choose a menu option that is followed by three dots (the dots are called an *ellipsis*), you see a dialog box from which you then must make more choices. For instance, the three dots after Save As on the

File menu indicate that you must answer additional questions about saving before saving actually occurs. The dialog box for Save As is shown in figure 1.7.

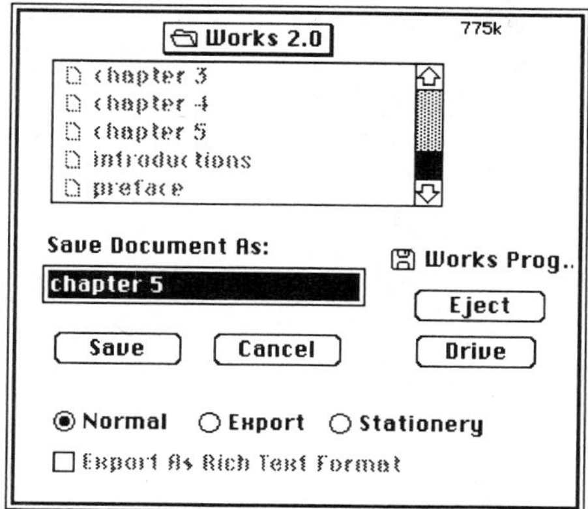


**Fig. 1.7**

*The Save As dialog box.*

## *Moving, Activating, and Changing Sizes of Windows*

Just like a regular desktop, your Macintosh's desktop can contain several items at once. For example, you can have two word processor documents, a spreadsheet, a database, and a communications window open at the same time. Each project occupies its own window. Microsoft Works Version 2.0 supports up to 14 windows, or as many as your computer's memory allows. Figure 1.8 has windows displayed so that they overlap, but you can tile or stack windows and arrange them as you like. You only work in one window at a time; the window in which you currently are working is called the *active window*, and can be recognized by a title bar with six lines running through it.

You can move windows by positioning the cursor on the window's title bar and dragging the window. To move a window without making it the active window, hold down the ⌘ key while you drag the window's title bar.

To activate a window, click anywhere within the desired window. If you cover the window in which you want to work with another window, you can bring the one you want to the top of your desktop and activate it by choosing its name from the Window menu that is in any of the Works modules. If you drag a window off the screen you will not

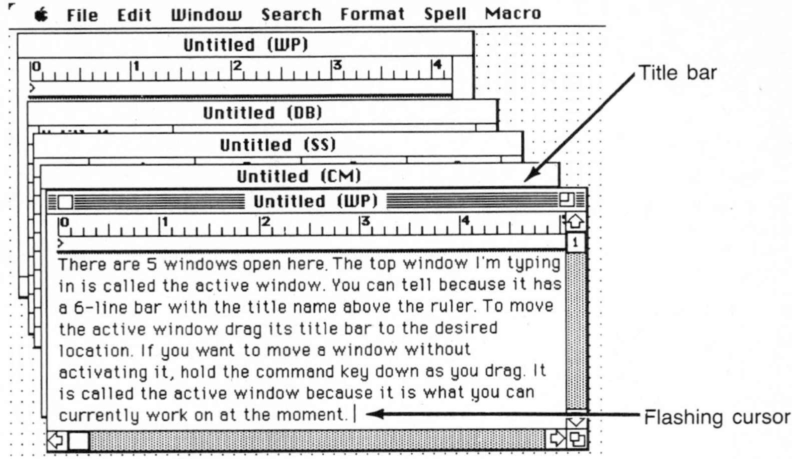


**Fig. 1.8**

*Desktop with several windows open.*

be able to use size boxes, scroll bars, and close boxes (discussed below) with that window.

If you attempt to perform an operation that requires more memory than your computer currently has, your Macintosh warns you by displaying a dialog box. Available memory and document size may reduce the number of windows you can have open at one time. To learn more about the memory requirements for using Works with other programs, read "Finder and MultiFinder" elsewhere in this chapter.

Figure 1.9 shows you the elements of a Macintosh window. Scroll bars, size boxes, title bars, zoom boxes, and close boxes are actually written into the Macintosh operating system (ROM), embedded as instructions in the microprocessor chip (also called a central processing unit, or CPU) in your computer. All Macintosh programs use these elements in the same manner. Earlier you learned how to move the window by using the title bar. To resize a window, drag the *size box* to the desired location, as shown in figure 1.9. To switch (or toggle) between the window size on-screen and the window size that fills your monitor, click the *zoom box*. To close a window, click the *close box*. Version 2.0 does not have a Full/Small Window command in the window menu as did previous versions. Instead, Version 2.0 has the zoom box, which is used to expand the window to fill the entire screen or to shrink the expanded window to its size before expansion. Works 2.0 supports any size monitor.

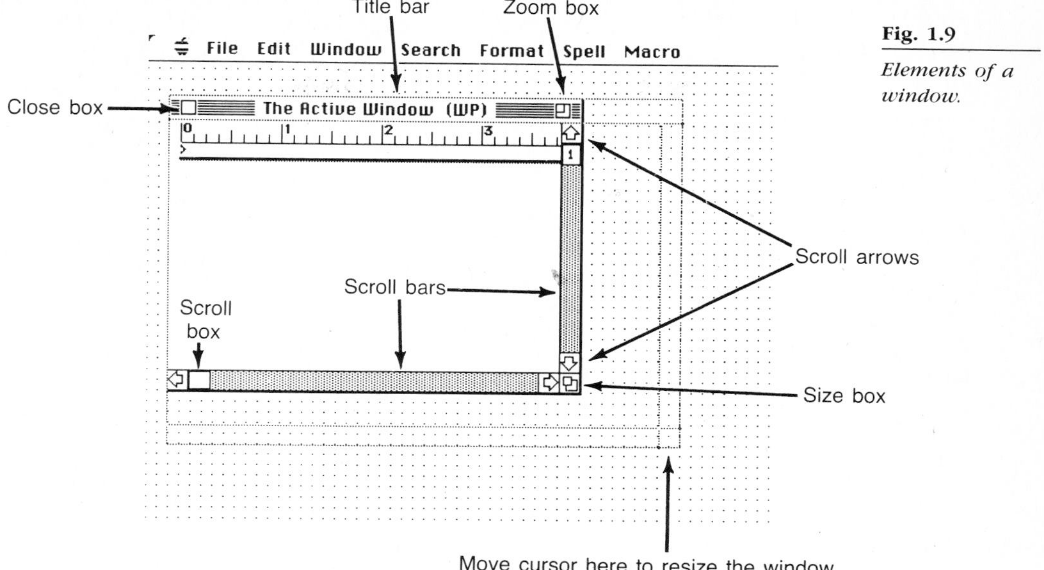


**Fig. 1.9**

*Elements of a window.*

# *Using Scroll Bars and Scroll Boxes*

Some Macintosh windows, including most Works windows, have horizontal and vertical *scroll bars*. These bars, found on the right side and along the bottom of a window, are used to display things that otherwise will not fit in a window. Because many documents are too big to be displayed in their entirety, you use the scroll bars to move around in your window (see fig. 1.9). The horizontal scroll bar at the bottom of the window moves things left or right; the vertical scroll bar on the right side of the window moves your document up or down.

Clicking the arrows in the scroll bars moves the screen contents in one-inch increments. If you press the mouse button while pointing at a scroll arrow, the screen movement continues until you release the mouse button. For faster moves, point at either scroll box, and while pressing the mouse button, drag the box in the desired direction. Inside the scroll bar is the scroll box, a tiny square whose location on the scroll bar gives the relative position of the screen display within the document. If the scroll box is in the middle of the scroll bar, for instance, the portion of the document displayed on-screen is in the middle of the document. If you click the scroll bar on either side of the scroll box you will advance the document one screen size for each click.

# *Using the Boxes and Buttons*

From time to time, your Macintosh needs information from you in order to make a decision. In such cases, Works displays a dialog box (see fig. 1.7 for an example of a dialog box), and sometimes your computer beeps. Recent Macintosh computers make a variety of sounds (from boings to chimes) to tell you when you have made a mistake. Most dialog boxes contain one or more buttons and check boxes (see fig. 1.10); some also contain edit or text boxes. Buttons are of two types: push buttons and radio buttons. *Push buttons* contain words or command choices. To indicate your choice, you can point and click anywhere inside the button. *Radio buttons* are circles next to choices on-screen; to select or deselect a choice, point and click the circle. When a choice is selected, the center of the radio button is black. Check boxes are selected and deselected like radio buttons.

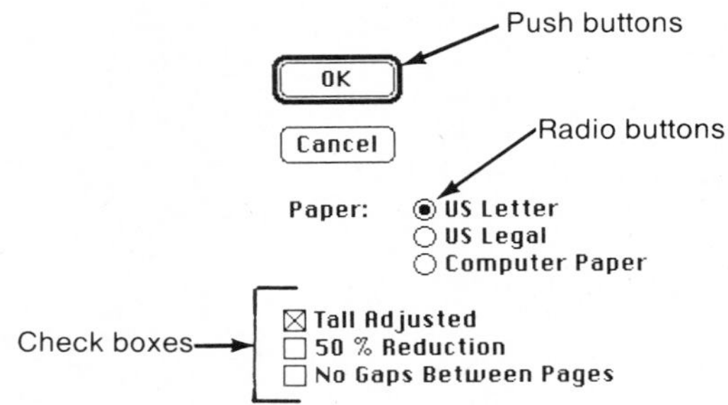


**Fig. 1.10**

*Buttons and check boxes come in a variety of shapes and sizes.*

Sometimes one of the buttons on-screen is darker than the rest (and has a double line around it, like the OK button in fig. 1.10), indicating that the option is the default. Usually, you can press the Return key to accept the default choice. If `Cancel` is displayed, often you can use the ⌘-.(period) keystroke instead of clicking it with the mouse button.

*Text boxes* appear when you need to enter or modify information by using the keyboard (see fig. 1.11). For example, when you want to print you must tell Works how the output should look. Issuing the Page Setup command displays the Page Setup dialog box. The dialog box for an ImageWriter printer is shown in figure 1.11. You can select a different Page Setup box by changing your printer type (to a LaserWriter

NTX, for example). You can do this by selecting Chooser in the Apple menu (see "Using the Apple Menu and Desk Accessories").

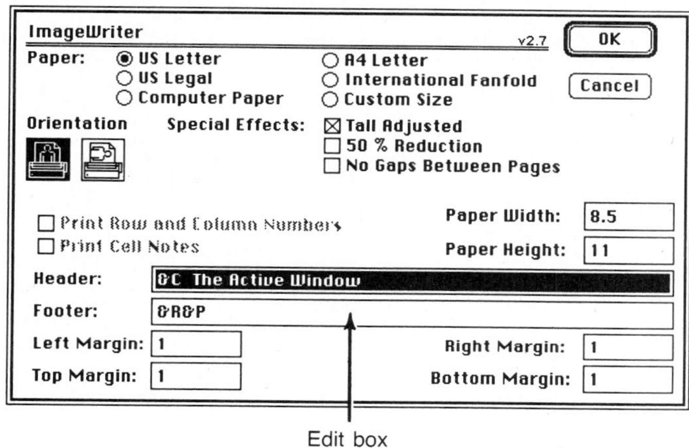


**Fig. 1.11**

*Page Setup dialog box and its editing choices.*

Text boxes usually are highlighted and you can indicate your choice by typing any information you want. To make a change to another text box, you can click that box or press the tab button until that box is highlighted. Tabbing to move between boxes is a general Macintosh convention for all dialog boxes that contain multiple text boxes.

*Alert boxes* usually contain warnings or alert you to mistakes that you have made (see fig. 1.12). You must acknowledge the alert by clicking the OK button, although sometimes you can press the Return key instead.

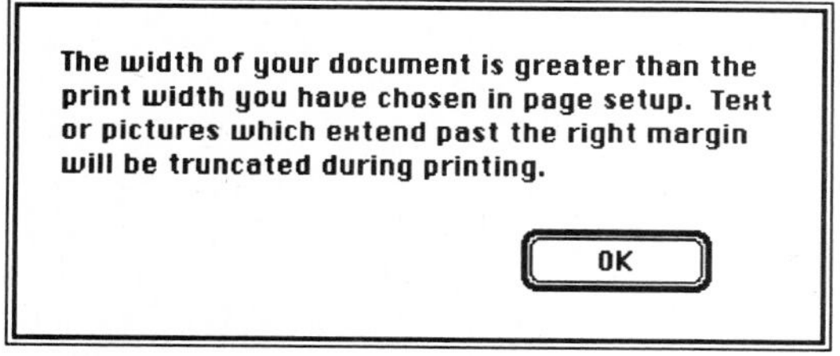


**Fig. 1.12**

*An Alert box.*

# *Navigating the Hierarchical File System*

After you put a new floppy disk into the disk drive of your Macintosh, an on-screen message tells you that the disk needs to be initialized. The computer then asks whether you want one or two sides to be formatted. When your computer formats a disk, it establishes a pattern of markings called *sectors* that separate areas of the disk. These sectors contain pieces of rings called *tracks*, where data may be written. When your computer is finished marking your floppy disk, it creates a Desktop file on your disk, which is similar to a table of contents for your disk. The Desktop file is invisible in Finder (it has no icon) but it shows up in certain dialog boxes. Your hard drive contains bigger disks (and sometimes more than one) but goes through a similar formatting procedure by the manufacturer.

A computer collects information in the form of *bits* (binary digits 1 or 0) and forms groups of bits into *bytes*. A byte is similar to a word or a collection of letters. A *kilobyte* (K) is a thousand bytes, and a megabyte (M) is a million bytes. (A gigabyte, abbreviated by the letter G, is a billion bytes, but you rarely encounter mention of gigabytes.) These terms are used to describe memory size, either the amount available in a computer or the amount required by a program. Current Macintosh disks can be formatted with 400K on one side or 800K on two sides of a floppy. A new drive (called super drive) in the Macintosh IIcx, Macintosh IIx, and Macintosh SE/30 also formats your floppies at 1.4M.

When you save a file, Macintosh writes the data onto the disk sectors and creates an entry in your Desktop file. Conceivably, you could have thousands of files on a hard drive, but they should not be scattered at random. You need a reliable method to organize these files and eliminate clutter. The Macintosh Finder uses folder icons. Folders can be stored inside other folders, and these folders can be stored inside other folders, and so on. This system is called the *Hierarchical File System* (HFS) and has been supported with all versions of Finder with which you can run Works 2.0 (see the section on software requirements). A previous method, the Macintosh File System (MFS), wrote files only on one level. Because this earlier method is not as practical as the Hierarchical File System, it will not be discussed further.

You can navigate the HFS in two ways. The first method uses Finder, the Macintosh desktop. Double-click your disk icon and open the first window. Anything in your first window is at the highest level in the hierarchical file system and is called your *root directory*. Double-clicking a folder opens a second window, and if you double-click the second window, a third window opens, and so on. A newly opened disk or folder has a dotted black background. If the window for a folder is hidden, you can bring it to the top of your desktop simply by double-clicking its icon. Figure 1.13 shows several open windows created this way.

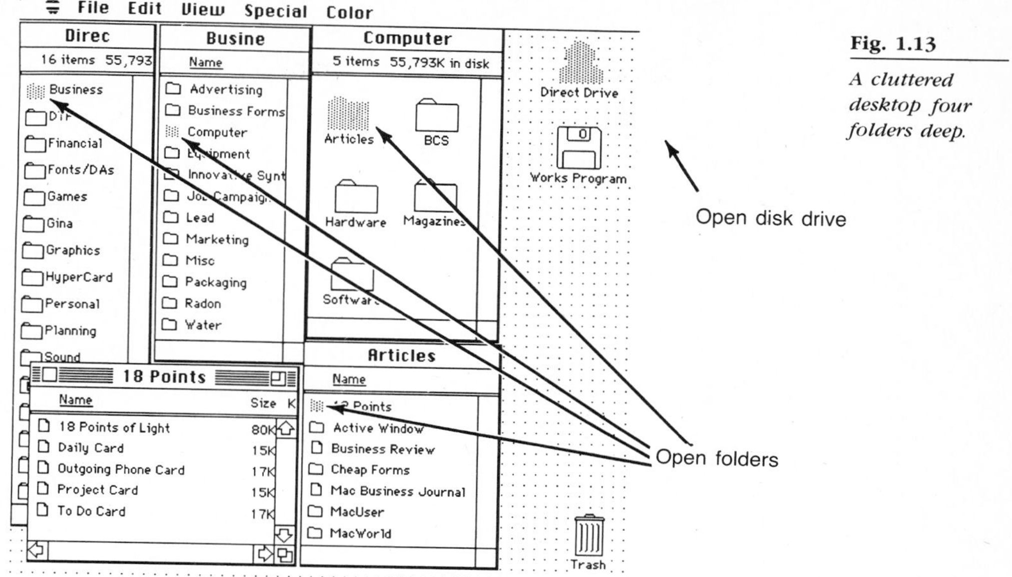


**Fig. 1.13**
*A cluttered desktop four folders deep.*

**NOTE:** The Open and Close commands in the File menu are common to all Works modules. You can find information on creating, saving, opening, and closing files in the "Working with Word Processing Text and Files" section in Chapter 2.

If you have folders buried several layers deep in your HFS, opening windows to get at files becomes very cumbersome. The second way to navigate the HFS while in Works involves using dialog boxes. Finder (and MultiFinder) creates a dialog box, called the Standard File Put (SF Put) box, after you issue the Save or Save As command (see fig. 1.7). A dialog box called the Standard File Get (SF Get) box is created after you issue the Open command to retrieve a file. Often these two boxes are referred to as the Save (Save As) or Open dialog boxes, respectively. Figure 1.14 shows an SF Get Box with a display of folders several layers deep, inside a scrolling window.

You can use two methods to move up or down the HFS within the SF Put or SF Get boxes to the file you want to open. First, select the desired disk drive by clicking the Drive button until the correct drive is named. Dragging down the folder name as shown in figure 1.14 moves you up the HFS tree of folders. You also can use the ⌘-Up arrow keyboard shortcut or click the disk drive name to move up in one-

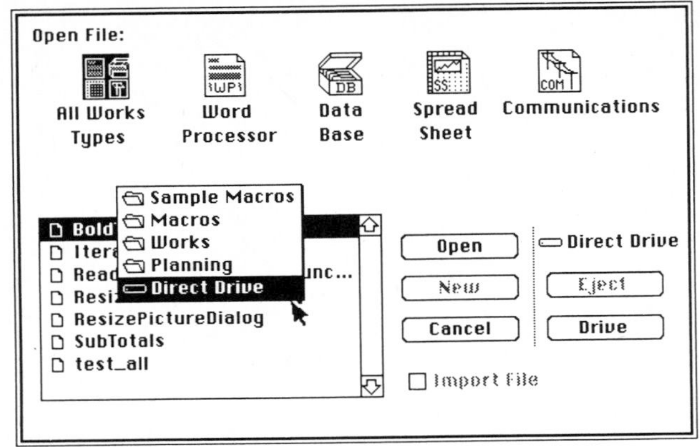


**Fig. 1.14**

*The Open command dialog box.*

folder jumps. When you want to locate a file in the scrolling box, type the first letter(s) of the file name to move you to that file. You also can click the file name and then the Open button, or simply double-click the file name to open the file. File names shown are from previously saved work.

**NOTE:** In Works, when you click an icon like the spreadsheet icon (see fig. 1.3 for a chart of Works icons), only files of a similar type (in this case, spreadsheets) are shown.

The Find File command in the Apple menu opens a window like the one shown in figure 1.15. To use the Search function, type the name of the file (or part of the name) you want to find, press Return, or click the jogger icon. When the search "stops," the computer tells you where the file is located. Click the file name, and the path route needed to open the file is displayed. Find File is a desk accessory (DA). Other more sophisticated HFS search and modification DAs include DiskTools II and DiskTop. For more information on desk accessories read the section "Using the Apple Menu and Desk Accessories." Findswell (an invaluable utility) is a control panel device (see "Control Panel") that also serves the Search function by placing a button in the Open (SF Get) or Close (SF Put) dialog box.

**NOTE:** When you open or close a file through the HFS system, you are left in the same position in the directory (desktop file) until you quit the program or move around the file tree again.

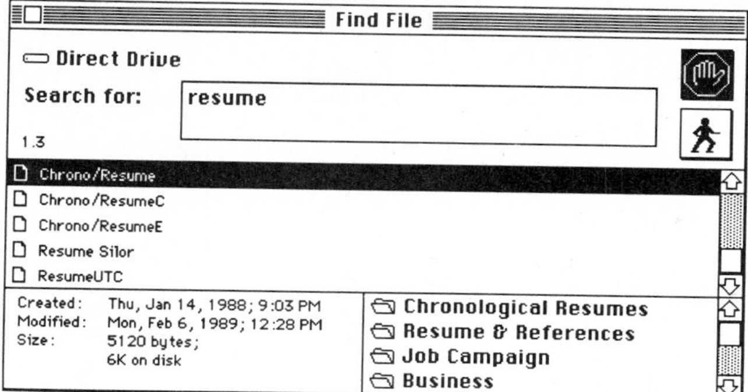


**Fig. 1.15**

*Find File desk accessory.*

## *Deleting and Recovering Files*

You can delete files in any of the Works modules in either of two ways. The first way uses the Trash, which is a temporary storage area. There is no limit to the size of items placed in it because only the names of the files and the locations of their sectors on disk are stored there. In the Finder you delete files by dragging them to the Trash icon in the lower right corner of the screen (see fig. 1.1). When the Trash is emptied, file names are deleted from the Desktop file. The Trash has files in it when the icon looks as if it is bulging, and the file name is deleted by issuing the Empty Trash command from the Special menu. The Trash automatically empties when you launch programs and perform other operations. A second way to delete Works files is to use the Delete command from the Works File menu. (*Note:* The Delete command in the File menu is common to all Works modules.) This command brings up the Open (SF Get) dialog box, and you can select the file to delete by navigating the file system as explained previously in the section "Navigating the Hierarchical File System."

**NOTE:** It is very important to realize that when you delete a file that was stored to disk you have not erased the data from the disk; you have erased only the name and address of written sectors in the Desktop file. In later operations, the Macintosh will write over these sectors.

If you accidentally erase an important file you want to retrieve, you should investigate Symantec Utilities for the Macintosh or HFS 1st Aid. These programs are called file recovery utilities, and they are used to do just that: recover accidentally erased files. The procedure is simple, but requires that you not overwrite the data by saving additional files to disk. This point is critical to successful data recovery. You must immediately stop working with the disk and use these utilities. When a file name is deleted from the directory, your Macintosh allows subsequent operations to write data to those sectors that are not assigned. A full discussion of this topic falls outside the scope of this book. Consult a book on Apple hard disk management for more information.

At this point, you may want to jump ahead to Chapter 2 for information on creating a new file in "Closing and Opening Files," and saving files to disk in "Saving Your Work." All the commands to accomplish these tasks are common to all Works modules.

## Working with the Clipboard

The *Clipboard* is a set of addresses in memory within the Macintosh operating system. When you want to move selected text or graphics within a document, or from a source document to a target document (even while you change programs) you must issue the Cut or Copy commands from the Edit menu. The Cut command removes the selection and places it in the Clipboard. The Copy command leaves the selection in your source document and places a copy in the Clipboard. You can view what is currently in the Clipboard by choosing the Show Clipboard command on the Windows menu, which places the current contents of the Clipboard inside a window (fig. 1.16).

**Fig. 1.16**

*The Clipboard, a temporary storage area.*

To insert the contents of the Clipboard into your destination document, you position the cursor in the document, click the insertion point (indicated by a flashing vertical line) and select the Paste command on the Edit menu. Paste copies the Clipboard to the document and leaves the contents of the Clipboard unchanged. The Clipboard can contain text, graphics, or some combination of the two, and in the Cut and Paste operations some documents can accept one or both parts of the text or graphics. Remember, to issue a command, you point the arrow cursor to the menu title, click the mouse, and drag straight down to the command name. The command name is highlighted and when you release the mouse button the command is carried out. The uses of the Clipboard are discussed throughout the book, because it is a central feature of the Macintosh operating system. For further information, refer to "Importing and Exporting Graphics" in Chapter 4, "Drawing."

You can cause selected text in your document to disappear (be deleted) by pressing the Backspace key. This approach leaves the contents of your Clipboard intact. The Undo command returns deleted text or graphics if you have not performed any subsequent operations. For more information, refer to "Editing Your Text" in Chapter 2. Use the Backspace or Delete key if you have something important in your Clipboard.

Remember that the Clipboard is a temporary storage area in your computer's RAM. The Clipboard can hold only one item at a time, and only while the computer is turned on.

When first installed, your Macintosh has only one Clipboard in the system folder. If a power failure occurs, if you turn off the computer's power, or if you copy something new to the Clipboard, you lose the contents of the Clipboard.

## *Working with the Scrapbook*

If there is an item you want to keep and use again (for example, a letterhead or a logo), use the *Scrapbook*, which is a part of the Macintosh operating system. The Scrapbook contents are written to permanent memory and are not affected by shutdown or power loss. Select the Scrapbook command in the Apple menu to open the Scrapbook. Scrapbook is a desk accessory, which are discussed subsequently in this chapter. The Scrapbook works almost identically to the Clipboard; you cut or copy selected items from a source file to your Clipboard, open a page in the Scrapbook, and then paste your selection into the Scrapbook from the Clipboard. Use the scroll bar in the Scrapbook to see other images. Figure 1.17 shows a Scrapbook image. With the Scrapbook, you can copy or cut the image, and paste that image into your target document at any time.

To remove an item from the Scrapbook, open the Scrapbook, display the item by using the scroll bar (if needed), and use the Cut option on the Edit menu. You can use the Clear command from the Edit menu instead, if you want to remove items from the Scrapbook.

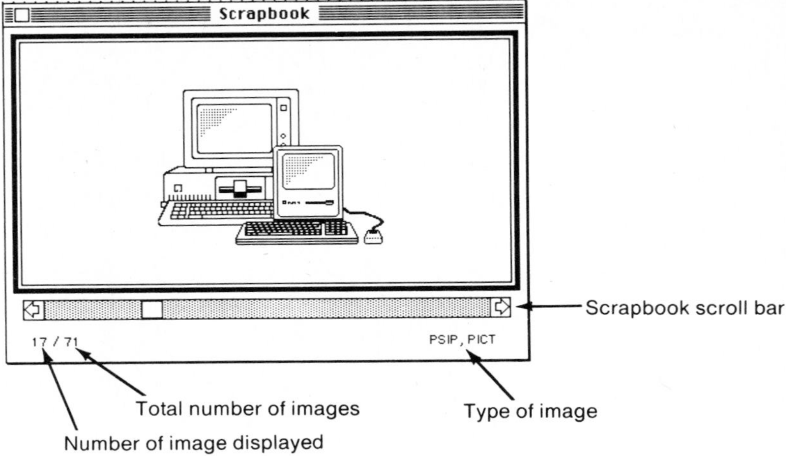


**Fig. 1.17**

*Use the Scrapbook to store things you want to reuse frequently.*

Normally, a Macintosh system contains only one Clipboard and one Scrapbook. These functions are so useful, however, that software developers have created enhanced versions of these programs. Two such programs, the SmartScrap and the Clipper and Open It!, are discussed in Chapter 4 in the "Importing and Exporting Graphics" section.

# *Modifier Keys and Other Special Characters on the Macintosh*

As you use Works, you become familiar with special modifier keys on the Macintosh, such as Shift, Ctrl, Option, and ⌘. The uses of these modifier keys are discussed throughout the book; they often perform unique functions not accessible with a mouse. In the pull-down menus you find time-saving keyboard shortcuts that use these keys. For example, to execute the Save command, hold down the ⌘ key while pressing the S key, instead of using the drag method with your mouse.

Macintosh supports many type faces, known as *fonts*, as well as many type sizes and styles. The section "Fonts, Printers, and Networks," later in this chapter, provides further information on this topic.

In addition to the usual numbers, punctuation marks, and letters shown on the keyboard of your Macintosh, you can use your computer to produce special characters for certain fonts. You can access these special characters by using a modifier key or modifier key combinations. By selecting the Key Caps option on the Apple menu (see fig. 1.18), you can press the modifier keys and change the characters on your keyboard. The Key Caps in figure 1.18 uses the Chicago font (the same font used in the Menu bar, and a proprietary Apple font). Changing fonts changes the available characters. Experiment with different combinations of modifier keys. You can type short entries in the entry bar of the Key Caps window and then select that text and copy it to your other Works windows.

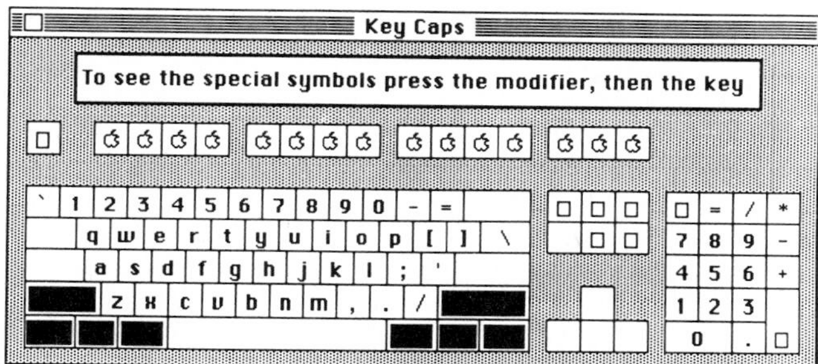


Modifier keys are shaded black

**Fig. 1.18**

*Key Caps with the Chicago font.*

# *Using the Apple Menu and Desk Accessories*

Works, like most Macintosh programs, has an Apple menu (see fig. 1.19) on the left side of the menu bar. The first line below the menu bar displays information about the program at the top, and desk accessories are below the dotted line. A *desk accessory* (DA) is a small program written to operate within any application, such as Works. You can have several DAs open at a time, but close the DAs when you are finished with them. If the DA is well-written and well-behaved, when you quit an application the DA closes behind it, except under MultiFinder, where the DA remains open. Apple includes a desk accessory feature to enhance the functionality of the Macintosh operating system. Desk accessories have been a great success.

The contents of the Apple menu vary depending on the program you are in, or on how you have set up your Macintosh. At a minimum, the menu contains the following: About (with the name of the program being run, such About MS-Works), Chooser, Control Panel, Key Caps, and Scrapbook. The Macintosh has an artificial limit of 15 desk accesso-

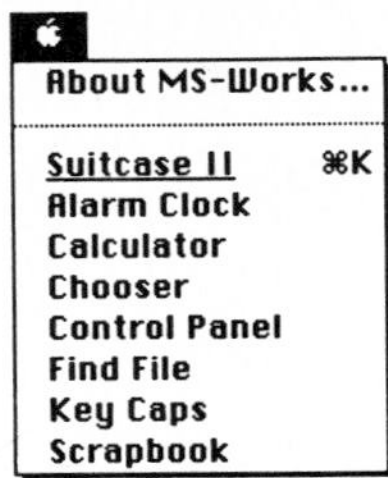


**Fig. 1.19**

*A typical Apple menu (yours may have more or fewer choices).*

ries that you can have in your system file (program), and a similar limit on the number of fonts. Suitcase II and Master Juggler, however, remove this artificial limit. Other programs open up other areas of RAM for DA use. You can add and remove fonts and DAs by using the Font/DA Mover (an Apple utility). Refer to your Macintosh manual for more information. The use of Font/DA Mover is discussed briefly in the section on "Fonts, Printers, and Networks" later in this chapter, and in the section on "Choosing Fonts" in Chapter 3.

Desk accessories are so popular that developers have written programs like Suitcase II and Font/DA Juggler to let you access hundreds of DAs in the Apple menu; these programs also operate with font groups. You should not own a hard drive without owning one of these remarkable utilities, which are examples of programs called *INITs*, or *initiated programs*. INITs are placed in your system folder and are what programmers call *patches*: they add instructions to your system file, giving it additional capabilities. There are many INITs on the market; some are commercial, some are free, and some are distributed under a shareware program. Figure 1.19 shows the desk accessory associated with Suitcase II.

## *The About MS-Works Screen*

The About MS-Works choice in the Apple menu brings up a screen that tells you which program version you are using and how much memory is available, along with information about copyrights (see fig. 1.20). If you're using memory-resident software such as WorksPlus Spell (see "Using WorksPlus Spell" in Chapter 2) or WorksPlus Command (see "Works-Plus Command" in Chapter 11), you may see information about that software as well. With Works Version 2.0, About MS-Works shows your name and your company name as you entered them at installation.

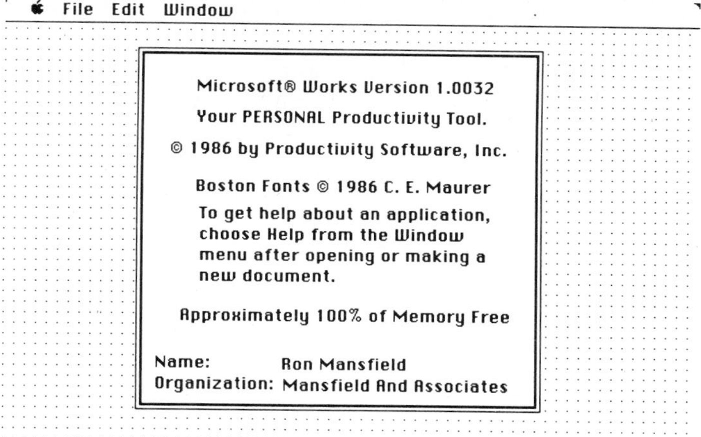


**Fig. 1.20**

*The About MS-Works screen.*

# *The Control Panel*

The Control Panel is another desk accessory in your system folder. The Control Panel (shown in fig. 1.21) enables you to configure (set up) your computer system to meet your needs and preferences. You can change your desktop pattern, adjust the speaker volume, change keyboard parameters, and so on. The Control Panel sets the amount of RAM used for the *cache*, a part of memory reserved for recent operations. Caching allows faster operation. You may want to consult your Macintosh manual about all the options available to you through the Control Panel.

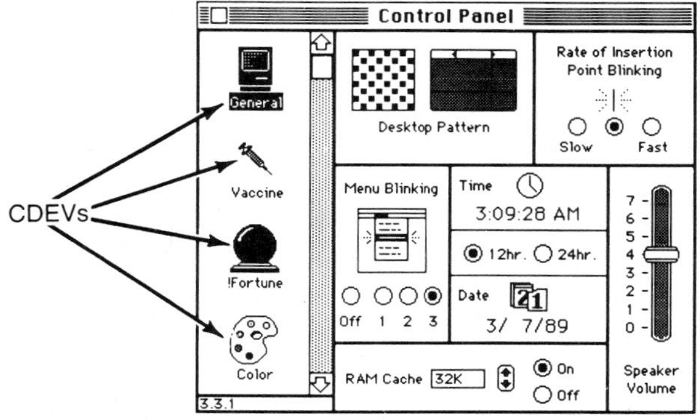


**Fig. 1.21**

*The Control Panel showing General program settings.*

Recent Macintosh system software operating versions (later than system Version 3.2) support a new type of program called *Control Panel Devices* or *CDEVs*. CDEVs are programs like INITs that are placed in your system folder and initiated at start-up. You may have to reboot in order to activate these programs for the first time. Unlike INITs, CDEVs can be configured with the Control Panel. Scroll the window, click the CDEVs icon and make the changes you want. When the Control Panel is closed, those changes are written to your system file and executed. If you remove your Control Panel (by Font/DA Mover), the settings in place at the time of removal remain behind. CDEVs, like INITs, serve all manner of useful functions, including macro programs, screen savers, menu clocks, menu modifiers, file search utilities, and a host of others.

## Other Desk Accessories

This book discusses many useful desk accessories. Three other desk accessories supplied by Apple for the basic system are Chooser, Alarm Clock, and Calculator. Chooser is discussed in the section "Fonts, Printers, and Networks" elsewhere in this chapter. Alarm Clock enables you to adjust your Macintosh's internal clock and calendar and set an alarm. The Calculator is another popular desk accessory. Many useful commercial products and public domain utilities, such as time-delayed screen grabbers, paint/draw programs, HFS file aids, and print spoolers, are installed as desk accessories.

## Finder and MultiFinder

Finder runs one program at a time. If you want to work in another program, you must close the first and open the second. To return, you must reverse the procedure. Opening and closing applications takes time and is inefficient. Larger, more sophisticated computers use an operating system in which several programs can be active and running in windows at the same time. This capability is called *multitasking*. MultiFinder is the beginning of the evolution toward the goal of multitasking for all Macintosh operating systems. Under MultiFinder, generally only one program runs, but memory is reserved for other opened programs. Clicking the windows of these opened programs or choosing them from the bottom of the Apple menu instantly activates them.

To run MultiFinder, choose the Set Startup command in Finder. The dialog box shown in figure 1.22 is displayed. If you select a program such as Works, this dialog box enables you to launch Works instantly at start-up. To change from Finder to MultiFinder (or from MultiFinder to Finder), you need to reboot your Macintosh. Keep in mind that each additional program requires additional installed RAM. As a rule of thumb, you need 2M of RAM to run two major applications, and an additional 400K to 750K of RAM for every additional application.

Works requires 768K of RAM in MultiFinder. To do sophisticated graphics, 4M or 5M normally are required, and some high-end computer-aided design (CAD) or digital image manipulations require the full 8M now accessible by the Macintosh operating system. (The standard Macintosh, however, comes with 1 or 2M of RAM, depending on the model. You pay extra for any other RAM you want.) The current Macintosh system limit of 8M increases substantially in system 7.0. In System 7.0, a feature called *virtual memory* writes to disk instructions meant for RAM and retrieves those instructions when needed. With virtual memory you can work with large file sizes, even with smaller quantities of RAM.

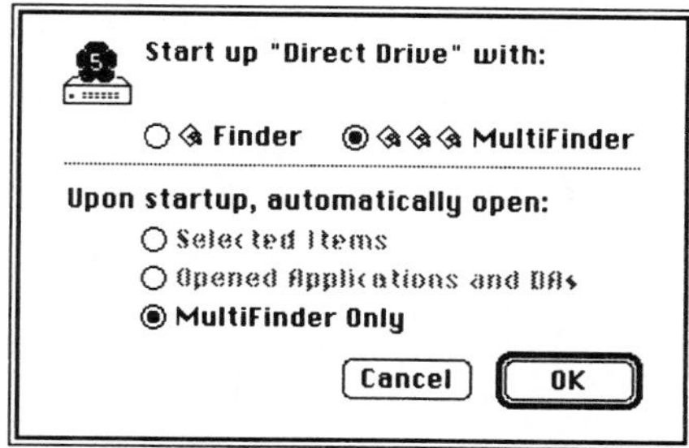


**Fig. 1.22**

*The Set Startup dialog box.*

To find out how much memory your application is using, choose the Get Info command in the File menu. You can change the suggested memory size allocated to an application by typing the desired amount of memory in the dialog box as shown in figure 1.23. If you use Works under MultiFinder and add fonts or DAs to the program, you may want to increase the amount of memory you enter. Lowering available memory below the suggested amounts may get you through a certain operation, but it also may have strange and unexpected results, such as a system freeze-up. Consult your manual for more information on MultiFinder.

# *Minimum Requirements for Running Works*

Works was designed to function with all of today's most popular Macintosh configurations. Version 2.0 even supports oversized display

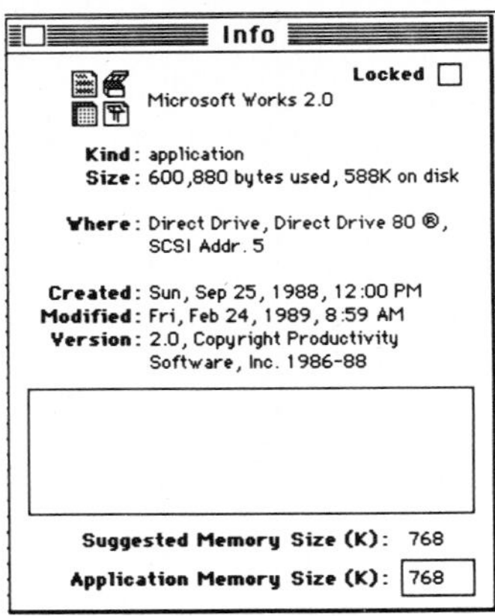


**Fig. 1.23**

*Application size in the Get Info command dialog box.*

screens and runs on networks like AppleShare. The minimum requirements for running Works on a simple system are discussed in the following sections.

# *Hardware Requirements*

Two basic Macintosh configurations can be used to run Works. The preferred configuration is a computer with a hard drive. If you are using Works at home, you should consider 40M of memory as a minimum hard drive requirement. If you are running a small business, that number should increase to 80M. Undoubtedly, you will find that no matter how much storage you buy, eventually you will run out. You should have enough memory to fully configure your system, to add DAs and fonts as you want, to have no real limitations on what can be saved to disk, to create an HFS structure, and to create a personalized work environment.

You can use Works with two floppy disk drives by using the two Works program disks supplied by Microsoft. A two-floppy system enables you to have a basic system and save a reasonable number of files to disk. If you have a Macintosh with one disk drive, you must swap disks into and out of your disk drive. Disk swapping is impractical and not recommended. When working with a two-drive system that formats disks at 800K, you can load the system and the dictionary on one disk, and the program and the help file on a second. If you can delete the help file, you will be left with nearly 200K of storage space to save files. If you are using a Macintosh with an FDHD drive that formats floppies at

1.4M, these storage limitations do not apply. Remember, however, that 1.4M floppies do not run on the older 800K drives.

Works 2.0 requires a computer with at least 1M of RAM. Versions 1.0 and 1.1 can be used with a 512K Macintosh. Works runs on any Macintosh Plus, SE, SE/30, II, IIx, or IIcx, because these computers come with a minimum of 1M of RAM. To use Works under the Finder program, 1M normally is sufficient, but you need at least 2M of memory to use Works in MultiFinder (see "Finder and MultiFinder" elsewhere in this chapter).

You can increase memory by adding single in-line memory module (SIMM) boards containing dynamic random access memory chips (DRAMs). Only certain configurations are possible, and in general you should have SIMMs installed by a competent technician. You also can increase memory by installing the INIT Virtual, which swaps instructions for RAM out to your disk and retrieves those instructions when needed. To use virtual memory, you need to have a Macintosh with a 68030 CPU (Macintosh SE/30, IIx, or IIcx) or one with a 68020 CPU (Macintosh II) and a Paged Memory Management Unit (PMMU) chip installed. The Macintosh Plus and Macintosh SE (but not the SE/30) have 68000 CPU chips and cannot use virtual memory. System 7.0 includes virtual memory also.

Several factors reduce the amount of RAM available to Works. Additional DAs and fonts you load, as well as the size of the RAM cache, reduce the amount of RAM available for creating Works documents. If you include graphics in your word processing documents or if you frequently change fonts, you may find that the maximum page count is reduced. If you copy a large graphic to the Clipboard, for example, Works requires twice the memory of the graphic to paste it. You may need to close windows or DAs to accomplish this paste. To increase the memory available, purge the Clipboard by overwriting it with a selected amount of space or other character, by cutting it, or by copying it.

With 1M RAM, Works should be capable of handling word processing documents of 180 to 240 pages. The maximum database capacity is about 6,000 records at 100 characters per record. The spreadsheet size limit varies with the complexity of the spreadsheet, but averages around 22,500 filled cells. A draw object (text or graphics) has a maximum size of 32K (which is the same as about 10 pages of character-only based text).

## Software Requirements

Works requires system software Version 5.0 or later. The current version is Macintosh Version 6.0, the recommended current Version release is 6.02 (6.03 for the Macintosh SE/30). Apple releases new versions of software every 6 to 12 months; System 7.0 is scheduled for release in the first quarter of 1990. In general, you should use the most recent system software. If you want to update Works, you should use the Installer program so that you do not lose your installed fonts and DAs or any other customization (such as network information) currently in your system. You may want to have this done by a competent technician, or consult your Macintosh manual if you decide to do it yourself.

If you have a new system or if you have not installed any custom features in your system file, you can copy and replace all of the system files from your Works disk. For information about moving Fonts and DAs see the section on "Fonts, Printers, and Networks" later in this chapter. You may want to retain a copy of your current System and Finder programs (with customization) on a floppy disk. If you perform any operation that corrupts your system file, you will be able to replace it simply by copying it from your backup copy.

> ***Caution:*** Because each program disk normally comes with its own system, it is easy to copy an extra system file onto another disk. Make sure that you do not have more than one system on your start-up disk, however, because having two or more can cause a system error and unexpected results. See the section on "Backup Procedures" elsewhere in this chapter.

## Fonts, Printers, and Networks

*Fonts* are collections of type face families. Fonts are of two types: bit-mapped and outline. *Bit-mapped* fonts are displayed and printed in a pixel-on/pixel-off manner and are programmed by using Apple's QuickDraw language. On your Macintosh screen, this results in resolution of 72 dots per inch (dpi). When you print to an ImageWriter II at 160 dpi you still can see the dots in each character. When printing large point sizes with a LaserWriter at 300 dpi, the dots are very noticeable. *Outline* fonts are described by mathematical equations and print to the full resolution of the printer (this can be 2400 dpi—typographic quality—to a Linotronic printer). The most common outline fonts are written in the PostScript programming language developed by Adobe Corporation. Adobe fonts are proprietary and can be purchased. The LaserWriter NT and NTX printers are PostScript output devices, but the LaserWriter SC is a QuickDraw printer. All previous versions of LaserWriters were PostScript devices.

You can use the Apple Font/DA Mover utility that comes with your system tools to add fonts and DAs to your system file, your applications, or to files you can create called *suitcase files* (the icon is a suitcase shape). To use the Font/DA Mover, double-click its icon. The dialog box shown in figure 1.24 appears. Navigate the HFS to the appropriate source and target files and copy or remove the fonts you want. To open and attach Fonts or DAs to an application, you need to press the Option key while clicking the Open button. Refer to your Macintosh manual for further details.

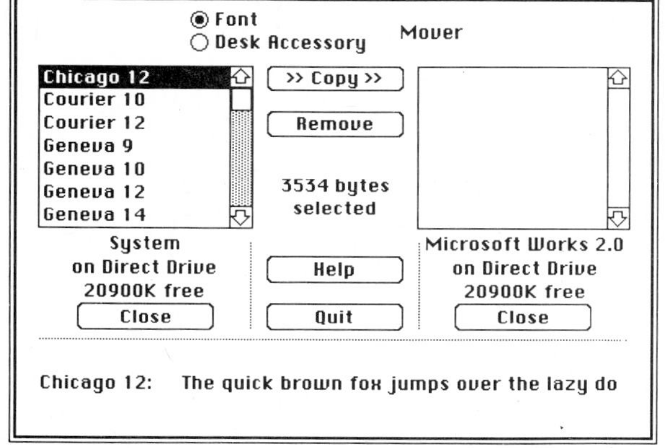


**Fig. 1.24**

*Font/DA Mover dialog box and related icons.*

PostScript fonts require both screen display fonts (which draw fonts on your monitor and that you move and load with Font/DA Mover) and printer fonts. If you have either of the utilities Suitcase II or Font/DA Juggler, you can access suitcase files of your choice and hundreds of fonts can appear in the Font submenu of the Works Format menu. Suitcase II and Font/DA Juggler enable you to place suitcases and printer driver files in any folder of your choice, and store the paths (or address of the file in the Desktop) needed to access them.

The ImageWriter II and ImageWriter LQ (letter quality) printers are *dot matrix* printers (sometimes called impact printers). Printing takes place when pins in the print head strike the ribbon against the paper. When you look closely at the output from an ImageWriter you can see individual dots. To improve resolution, the ImageWriter is driven by the QuickDraw program and uses fonts twice the size of those in your document for the ImageWriter II, and three times the document font's size for the ImageWriter LQ. The larger sizes are used to generate fractional sizes mathematically, which leads to enhanced resolution. If you use these larger font sizes, you get better print quality.

The ImageWriter II offers three print modes: best, faster, and draft. The best mode delivers output at 160 dpi for the ImageWriter II and 216 dpi for the ImageWriter LQ. Your screen has images at 72 dpi. Best modes makes two passes of the print head (one in each direction). As a result, the best mode is significantly slower than the other print modes, but it delivers near letter-quality output for the ImageWriter II, and letter-quality for the LQ. If you are printing graphics you should use the best mode. The faster mode is sufficient for most jobs, even though its resolution is somewhat lower. The draft mode normally is not used. You select the print mode you want in the Print dialog box, and you should remember that the select button on the ImageWriter II printer must be properly set up to correspond to your choice.

The ImageWriter II can use tractor-fed paper or can be loaded from a sheet feeder. The tractor feed is preferred by many users, because the sheet feeder often jams. At times, however, the paper on which you want to print will be available only in sheet form. Note also that the ImageWriter II is available in a narrow- or wide-carriage model, and the ImageWriter LQ is available only in a wide-carriage model.

LaserWriter printers print near typographic quality output at 300 dpi. The laser printing process is similar to that of a photocopier, using toner from a cartridge and a light source. Laser output is superior to other printing methods for type and graphics output, but not for satisfactory photograph reproduction. (For photograph reproduction, you should use the traditional photograph and halftone methods. Go to a commercial printer for this service.) LaserWriters offer you the option of precisely scaling your work. For more information on scaling, see "Fonts, Printers, and Networks" elsewhere in this chapter.

Works supports any printer for which a Macintosh-compatible printer driver has been written. The Apple-family printers (ImageWriter II, ImageWriter LQ, LaserWriter SC, NT, and NTX) have printer drivers supplied with Apple system software. A host of other fine third-party printers can be attached to your Macintosh and come with their own printer drivers. Some printers require a hardware connector like The Grappler.

You select your printer by using the Chooser desk accessory from the Apple menu, which brings up the dialog box shown in figure 1.25.

With Chooser you can select the printer, modem, scanner, print utility, or other output device to which you want to send data. Chooser also enables you to select the network (when you have more than one attached), and to choose your output port. Refer to Chapter 2, "Entering, Editing, Saving, and Printing Text," for specific information on printing.

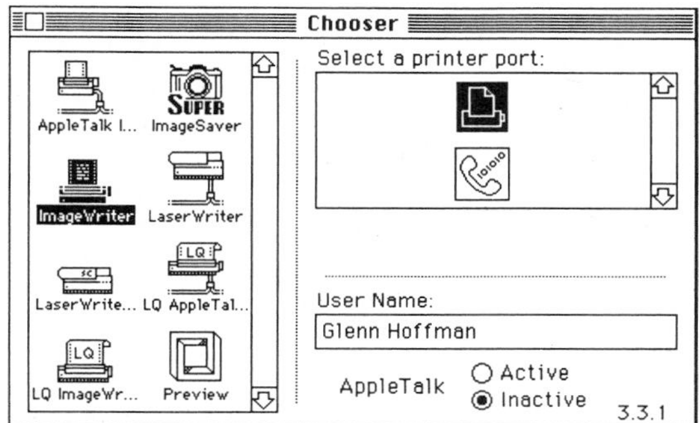


**Fig. 1.25**
*Chooser desk accessory.*

Network files are placed in your system folder, and AppleTalk network files for an ImageWriter, an ImageWriter LQ, and a LaserWriter are supplied with your system software. ImageWriters can be connected directly to your computer or your modem. LaserWriters are always used with an AppleTalk network. To choose a network, you select it in the scrolling box of Chooser. The choice of printer affects the Page Setup dialog box (see fig. 1.11) and the Print command dialog box; each printer driver creates its own dialog box. When you use Works with a file server (on a network, normally a separate computer that acts as a controller of the network), Works files are created when the Works folder and the local system folder are on the same volume. When they are on different folders (as in AppleShare) files are placed as shown in table 1.1.

**Table 1.1**
**Placement of Works Files**

| *File name* | *On same volume* | *On different volumes* |
|---|---|---|
| MS Works(keys) | Works folder | System folder |
| Works Desktop | Works folder | Root directory of system file |
| MSWorksPref | System folder | System folder |

Figure 1.11 shows the dialog box displayed when you select the ImageWriter from Chooser and give the Page Setup command in the File menu. This box gives choices for what type of paper you want to use, the orientation of the output (vertical orientation is *portrait mode*; horizontal orientation is *landscape mode*), some special effects, and the margins that apply to all printed output. Six preset paper types have preset sizes, or you can type your own custom size in the Paper Width and Paper Height text boxes. You can set special margins of your choice or accept the defaults. Choosing settings in this box is discussed in Chapter 3, in the section called "The Page Setup Dialog Box." Select the Tall Adjusted button to print in portrait mode and to scale graphics correctly. Choose the 50% Reduction button to print at one-half the original size. Select No Gaps Between Pages to print up to the perforation without leaving a space. Headers and footers are discussed in Chapter 3, under "Headers and Footers." The Print Rows and Column Numbers refer to Spreadsheet and Database documents. Print Cell Notes is a spreadsheet feature.

The Page Setup command dialog box for a LaserWriter is shown in figure 1.26. LaserWriters can scale text or graphics perfectly to any size you choose. Just type the amount (percentage) in the Reduce or Enlarge box. LaserWriters contain built-in fonts that speed up printing or can download fonts from your computer. There are smoothing options and a faster bit-mapped printing option (consult your printer manual for further information on these options).

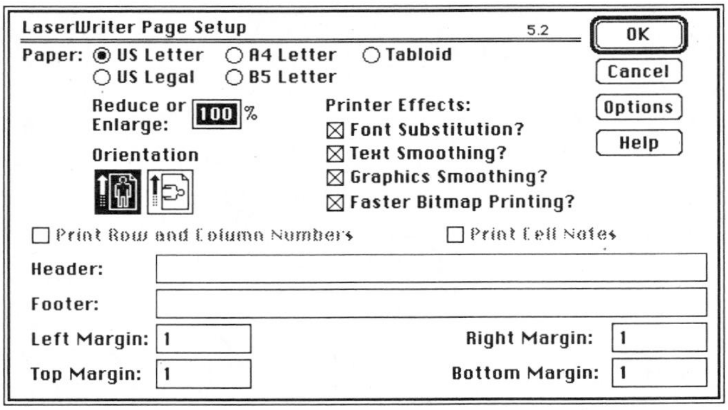

**Fig. 1.26**

*The Page Setup dialog box for a LaserWriter printer.*

The Print command in the File menu is common to all modes of Works and can apply to a file on disk (which must be open to print) or a document on-screen. If you want to print the active window, choose the Print Window command in the File menu. Only the visible portion of the active window is printed. Use ⌘-Shift-4 to print the current contents of your screen to your printer. When the Print command is chosen, a dialog box appears that is similar to one of those shown in figure 1.27. The dialog boxes for the ImageWriter and LaserWriter printers enable you to configure the output according to your needs. You can print all pages, a range of pages, or a single page, and you can print one or more copies.

ImageWriter v2.7 OK
Quality: ◉ Best ○ Faster ○ Draft
Page Range: ◉ All ○ From: [ ] To: [ ] Cancel
Copies: [1]
Paper Feed: ◉ Automatic ○ Hand Feed
☐ Print Preview

LaserWriter "LaserWriter" 5.2 OK
Copies: [1] Pages: ◉ All ○ From: [ ] To: [ ] Cancel
Cover Page: ◉ No ○ First Page ○ Last Page Help
Paper Source: ◉ Paper Cassette ○ Manual Feed
☐ Print Preview

**Fig. 1.27**

*The Print command dialog boxes for ImageWriter and LaserWriter printers.*

A feature new to Works 2.0, and common to Excel and Word, is the Print Preview command. This command is available by putting a check in the Print Preview button in the Print dialog box (click the Print Preview button once for the check to appear). Clicking OK or pressing Return brings you to the second dialog box (shown in fig. 1.28), which shows a miniature version of your document. You can examine your document by clicking the page when you see a magnifier cursor. You may go to a preview of the next page, cancel the dialog box and go back to your document to make changes, or print your document. A good practice is to leave the Print Preview option on, because checking your work before printing it saves you paper and time.

**NOTE:** The Page Setup, Print, and Print Window commands in the File menu are common to all modules of Works.

Works files can be passed around most local area networks, including AppleTalk, AppleShare, and TOPS. Each network user is required to purchase his or her own copy of Works, and the program should be installed on each Macintosh on a network. Users then share documents that may be stored on the server or on each user's disk.

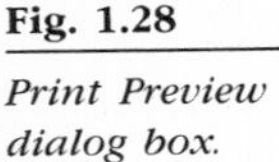

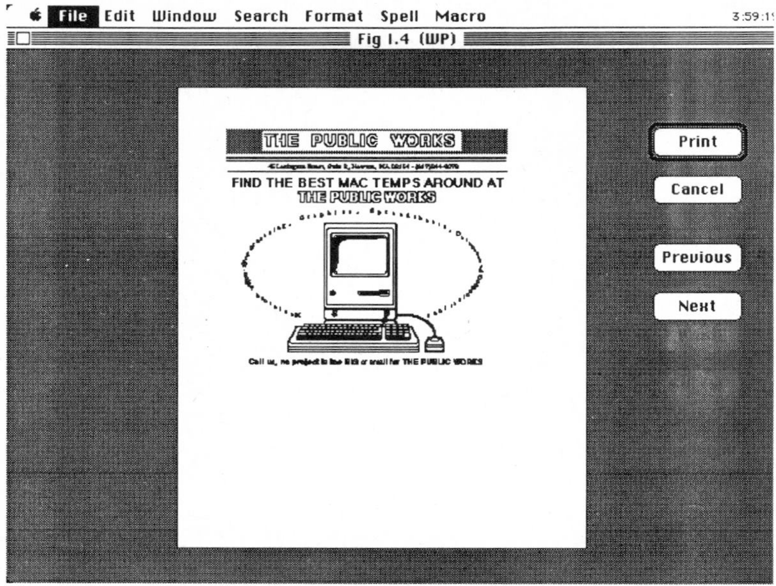


**Fig. 1.28**

*Print Preview dialog box.*

If Works is installed on a file server, only one user at a time may open the application. AppleShare allows shared Works documents from a file server; the first person to open a document has read/write privileges, all others have read-only privileges until the document is closed by the first user. The subsequent users (who have only read privileges) can use the Save As command (see Chapter 2) to create additional files to which they can write.

# Backup Procedures

Sometimes a sector on your disk can be damaged if your hard drive is shaken, or if you leave your floppy near a magnet (the magnet in your telephone, for example). You then must reformat your disk, which causes loss of all data. Your files also could be damaged if a virus infects your computer's hard disk (see "Protecting Your Computer From Viruses" in Chapter 12). A virus is a program that disrupts or corrupts your programs or data. A system malfunction due to incompatible DAs also can damage files, and even corrupt your system file.

You can back up your hard drive in a number of ways. The least expensive and most common is to copy the files and programs from your hard drive to floppy disks. Apple supplies the utility called HD Backup with its system software, which allows you to back up and restore a hard drive globally (everything on it), or restore selected files. Backup utilities write your files to disk in a continuous manner so that no space on the floppy goes unused. Other developers have written enhanced backup programs that also do incremental backups; these programs write to a separate set of disks all the files that have changed since the last global backup. Some backup programs worth considering include HFS Backup, DiskFit, and Fastback.

---

**WARNING:** You *must* back up your files. Remember that you do not have a copy of what is shown on-screen until you save it to disk, and you cannot count on being able to replace it in the event of a catastrophe unless you have made a backup copy (two backup copies is an even better idea).

---

A second way to back up a hard drive is by the use of magnetic tape. The utilities mentioned previously also perform this function, and some of them even do timed backups. In a timed backup, the utility program copies files you specify to another storage device at a particular date and time.

A third procedure is to copy your hard disk drive onto another disk drive. It is unlikely that two disk drives will go bad at the same time. The problem with this method is that most people do not have a second hard disk drive.

Still another procedure you may want to consider is the use of removable disk drive cartridges. Backup technology seems to change daily, but whichever method you use, the importance of a regular backup cannot be overemphasized.

## *Copying Your Works Disks*

When using Microsoft Works, *never use your original Works program disks*. Make backup copies the first time you put the disks into your drive. (*Note:* Works is not copy-protected, but don't abuse that fact and give away or sell copies of the program. Make copies strictly for your own use.) Your three Works disks contain the files shown in figure 1.29. You can use the following procedures to copy files from other disks as well, not just the Works program disks.

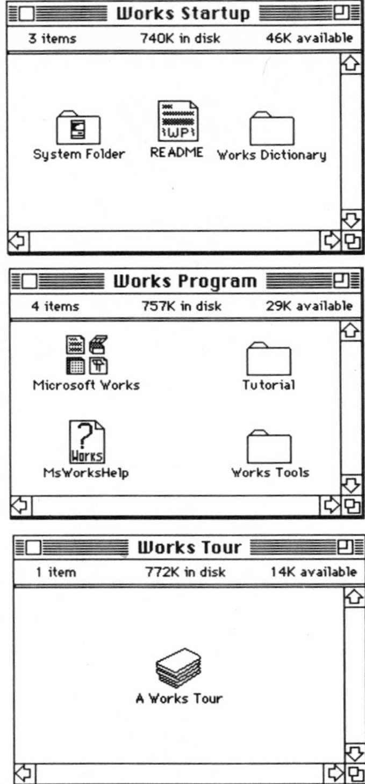


**Fig. 1.29**

*Contents of the three Works disks.*

To make copies of your Works disks when using a one floppy drive system, perform the following steps:

1. Insert a labeled, blank disk. (Be sure to label it like the original so that you will know which disk it is.) If it is not initialized (formatted), your Macintosh will ask you to initialize it.
2. Press ⌘-E for eject and the disk is ejected. A dimmed disk icon remains.
3. Insert the program disk you want to copy into the disk drive.
4. Drag the program disk icon onto the blank disk icon.
5. Your Macintosh prompts you (as necessary) to switch disks for the disk-to-disk copy.
6. When you are finished, drag the disk icons (one at a time) to the Trash to eject them.

To copy Works disks when using a two-drive system, follow these steps:

1. Insert one of the original program disks into one drive, and insert a labeled, blank disk into the second drive. If the blank disk requires initialization your Macintosh will tell you to initialize it.
2. Drag the program icon onto the blank disk icon.
3. Your Macintosh proceeds to do a disk-to-disk copy and informs you of its progress with a dialog box.
4. Eject the disks by dragging their icons to the Trash.
5. Repeat this procedure until you have copied all the Works disks.

To copy your Works disks to a hard disk drive, perform the following steps:

1. Insert one of the original program disks into the disk drive.

> ***Caution:*** Do not copy the Works system file to your hard drive (see "Software Requirements" earlier in this chapter for further information).

2. Select files you want to copy by double-clicking the desk icon to open its window. Click the desired folder's icon and shift-click additional files and folders, as desired.
3. Drag the files into the window or folder on your hard drive to which you want the files copied. The computer will tell you when it is finished copying the files.

# *Personalizing Microsoft Works Version 2.0*

The first time you double-click the Works icon (or any Works icon) the personalization screen appears. You must enter your name and your organization's name (if any) before Works will let you continue (see fig. 1.30). If you don't have an organization name, you can just press Return. Afterwards, your name and organization appear on-screen whenever you use the disk you personalized or any copies made from it.

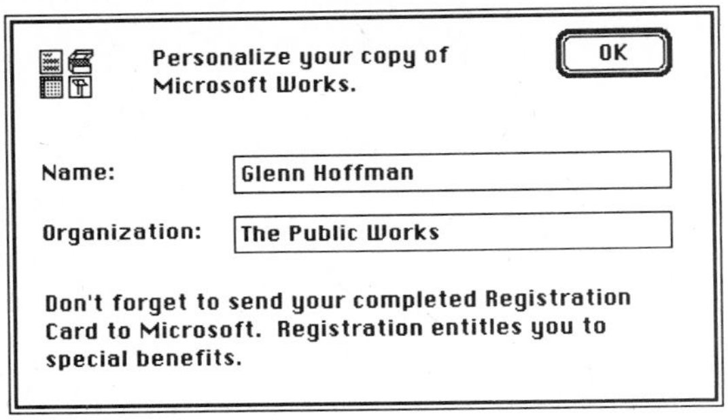

Personalize your copy of Microsoft Works.

OK

Name: Glenn Hoffman

Organization: The Public Works

Don't forget to send your completed Registration Card to Microsoft. Registration entitles you to special benefits.

**Fig. 1.30**

*The Works personalization screen.*

# *Starting Works*

Works starts automatically when you turn on your computer with the Works start-up disk in a drive, because the Set Start-up command has been programmed that way. You can change this setup so that the computer goes directly into Finder. See "Finder and MultiFinder" earlier in this chapter for more information. If you have Works installed on a hard drive, you start Works from the hard drive itself. To start Works from the hard drive, you double-click the Works icon, or any Works icon. See "Navigating the Hierarchical File System" elsewhere in this chapter if you need to learn how to get to the Works icon within folders. If you double-click a Works file made with a previous version of Works, your Macintosh will tell you that the `Application is busy or unavailable`. You must open the previously created document by launching the Works program from its icon, opening the file, and saving it. Thereafter Works launches from this file directly. Documents created with Version 2.0 launch Works directly.

Works comes with a file called MSWorksPref, which contains all the settings Works uses to configure itself. MSWorksPref is found in the system file on the disks supplied with the program. If you forget to copy the MSWorksPref file, or lose your system file, Works writes a new version of MSWorksPref automatically when you next open the application.

# Part II

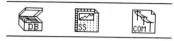

# Word Processing

## Includes

Entering, Editing, Saving, and Printing Text

Formatting Text and Adding Style

2

# Entering, Editing, Saving, and Printing Text

How many times have you been ready to send an important letter, only to find an error in your final copy? Just a single mistake can force you to retype the entire letter or article. A word processor eliminates the tedious retyping to make corrections. You can enter and change (edit) text, check spelling, save your document to disk, and retrieve it later. You also can print your documents in many different ways; for example, with different type styles and scaled to different sizes, and you can use tables with different kinds of tabs. Once you learn to write on a word processor, you find it difficult to go back to writing with a pen or a typewriter.

In this chapter, you learn how to open a word processing window, type text, make corrections, move things around, save your work to disk, and print your document. Much of this chapter describes text-selection shortcuts and other useful techniques. You should understand these techniques fully before you move on. The Quick Reference Summary at the end of this chapter quickly guides you through the basic tasks needed for word processing.

## *Opening a Word Processing Window*

The first step in any new Works word processing project is to open a new (untitled) document and enter some text. Even if you have never used a typewriter before, Works makes you look like a professional. The nice thing about word processing is that you can type as fast as you want; your mistakes happen on-screen, and you can correct them before they get to paper. You also can save your document as a file on a disk for later revision if you want to polish your work later.

The quickest way to begin a new typing project is either to double-click the word processor icon in the Open File dialog box or to click the word processor icon once and then click the Open button (see fig. 2.1). If you need help with choosing commands and working with pull-down menus, reread Chapter 1.

**Fig. 2.1**

*Selecting the word processor icon.*

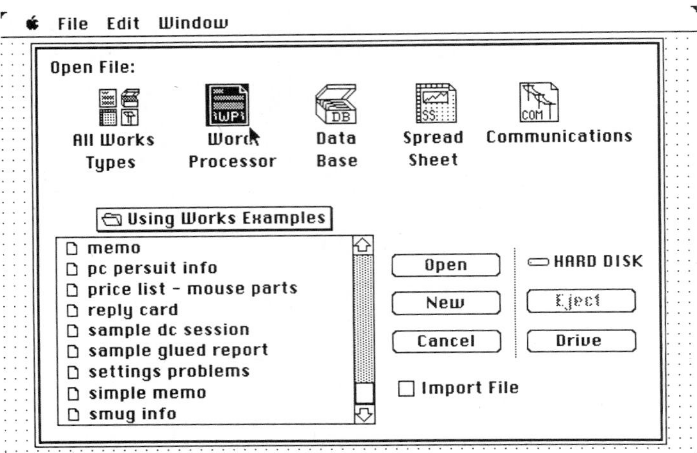


If you cancel the Open File dialog box or encounter a blank screen (as you might if you cancel the Open File dialog box and click the About MS Works screen), you can use an alternative method to create a new document. Select the New command from the Edit menu to bring up the Create New Document dialog box shown in figure 2.2. To open a new, "untitled" document, click the word processor icon, and then click the OK button (or press Return). You also can double-click the word processor icon to open a new document.

**Fig. 2.2**

*The Create New Document dialog box.*

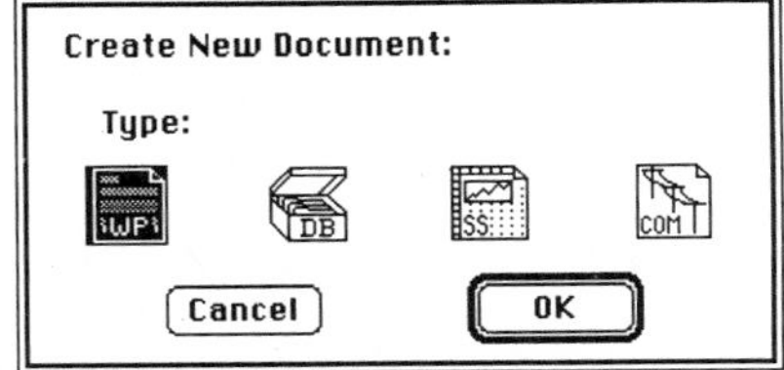

Your new document will be named "Untitled" (see fig. 2.3). A window named Untitled usually means that you are using an unsaved word processing document (rather than a previously saved and opened file). The letters WP indicate that you're working with a word processing window. A cursor bar blinks at the top left corner of the page. When you begin typing, the first character is positioned at this cursor point, which is often called the insertion point.

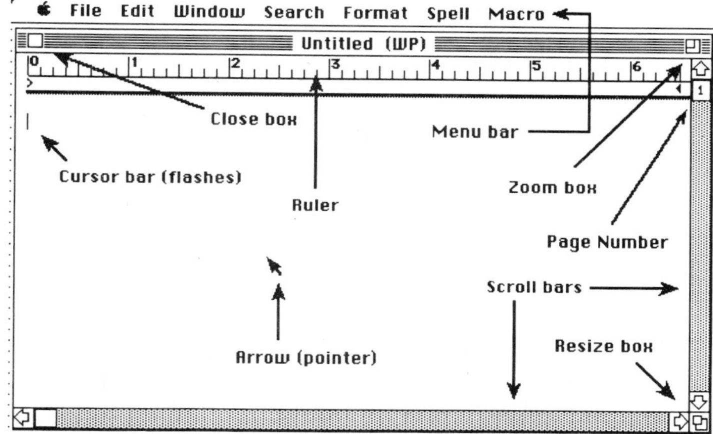


**Fig. 2.3**

*A new, untitled word processing window.*

We discussed the elements of a window in Chapter 1: scroll bars, close boxes, title bars, and zoom boxes. Zoom boxes are a new feature in Works 2.0. For help, see the "Moving, Activating, and Changing Sizes of Windows" and "Using Scroll Bars and Scroll Boxes" sections in Chapter 1.

The ruler is a special feature of a word processing window and is discussed more fully in the next chapter. In figure 2.3, you can see that the ruler scale is marked in 1/8-inch segments.

# Typing Text

You enter text as you would with a typewriter, with one exception. When you near the end of a line, you don't press the Return key to move to the next line. Works takes care of that task for you by "wrapping" words automatically; words that don't fit entirely on a line are moved to the line below. You press Return only when you want to force a line ending or end a paragraph (see the "Formatting Document Pages" section in Chapter 3).

If you don't want the Works wordwrap feature to break up words separated by spaces (such as names, titles, telephone numbers, part numbers, and so on) you can enter hard, or required, spaces. Hard spaces keep words on the same line despite the automatic wordwrap feature. To create a hard space, hold down the Option key and press the space bar. On-screen, hard spaces appear larger than normal spaces.

When you want short lines (when typing an address or formatting poetry, for example), you should use a forced line ending. Press Return to end a paragraph or to insert a blank line. Return places an invisible character on-screen that inserts a blank line. If you accidentally press Return, you can remove the invisible return character the same way you would any other. These invisible characters are called *formatting marks* (they store formatting information for the paragraph they define); on advanced word processors like Microsoft Word, you can choose a command to make them visible.

Whenever you make a change to a document, inserting a word or line, for example, Works immediately adjusts the remaining text to accommodate your changes. If your changes affect the *page breaks* (where one page ends and the next one begins), a process called *automatic repagination* adjusts the page breaks for you. You also can force a page break to place a break exactly where you want it. The entire wordwrap and repagination process is automatic and very fast.

## *Using the Backspace (Delete) Key To Correct as You Type*

If you make a mistake, you can correct your error right away by using the Backspace, or Delete, key. This key is in the upper right corner of the main keyboard (newer Macintosh keyboards label the key Delete instead of Backspace). Whenever you use the Backspace key to delete something, that item is gone forever.

The Backspace key deletes one character at a time. Like most of the keys on your Macintosh, however, the Backspace key is a repeating key. If you hold it down, the cursor moves to the left, deleting characters until you release it.

# Editing Your Text

As you write, you will want to add more text, correct errors, rearrange text, remove portions of text, and copy text to other documents. Works provides a number of selection tools and keyboard shortcuts to accomplish these tasks easily. Dragging is the only selection technique you really *need* to know, but you will find the shortcuts quite helpful.

## Selecting Text

Selection is the first step in many operations, including striking over old text. One way to select text is to click the mouse and drag the cursor to select the area to be affected. This method was used in figure 2.4 to select the words `microcomputer projects on the Macintosh`. You can select any amount of text using this method. Works highlights the selected text so that it appears in white letters against a black background. If you want to change the amount of text selected, click again to deselect the highlighted text and try again.

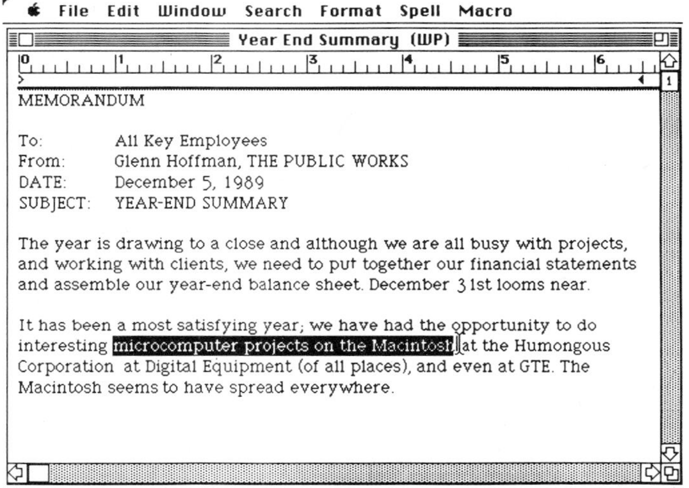


**Fig. 2.4**

*The insertion process.*

Sometimes when you use the dragging method, you may select too much or too little text and notice the error only after you have released the mouse button. Rather than begin the selection process over, you can alter the selection by holding down the Shift key and moving the mouse cursor to the end of your desired selection. Pressing

Shift "freezes" your starting position as you adjust your selection. When you click (still holding down the Shift key) your new text selection is highlighted.

You can select whole words rather than single characters by double-clicking to select a word and then holding down the Shift key while dragging. This technique is a quick way to select several words.

The methods shown in figure 2.5 are ways to select text that are faster than dragging a selection. To select a single word, move the I-beam cursor anywhere within the word, and double-click. Punctuation enclosing words, however, cannot be selected this way (for example, quotation marks or parentheses, dollar signs, or decimal points). If you double-click the 20 in $20.00, for example, Works highlights only the 20. Double-clicking the 00 (cents) portion selects only the 00. To deselect a selected word, click once anywhere in the document.

**Fig. 2.5**

*Four ways to select text.*

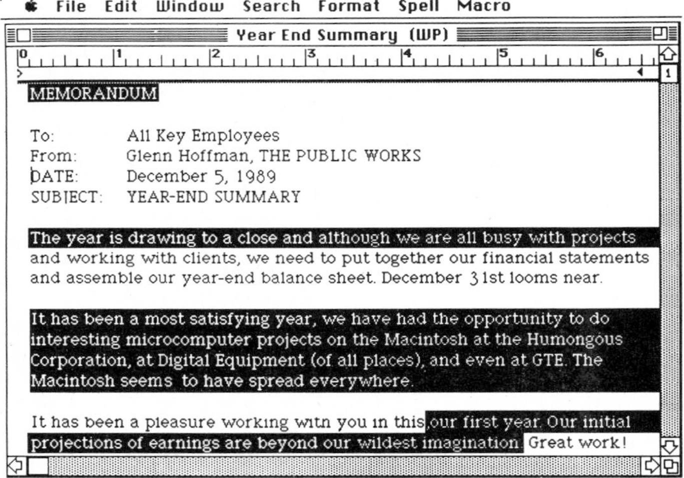


If you want to extend a selection, hold down the Shift key and double-click the word you want as the end of your selection. That word and all the words between them become selected. Shift-clicking is a Macintosh system shortcut; it increases the range of a selection in all the modules of Works and in most other Macintosh programs.

The Works word processor contains some additional shortcuts for selecting lines and paragraphs. To select a single line, place the cursor in the left margin (it changes shape from an I-beam to an arrow) and click (the second operation in fig. 2.5). To select a paragraph, double-click in the left margin (the third operation in fig. 2.5). To select text over an irregular area, use the dragging method (the fourth operation in fig. 2.5).

To select your entire document, choose the Select All command in the Edit menu. Your entire word processing window is selected, as shown in figure 2.6. To deselect the document, click anywhere in the document.

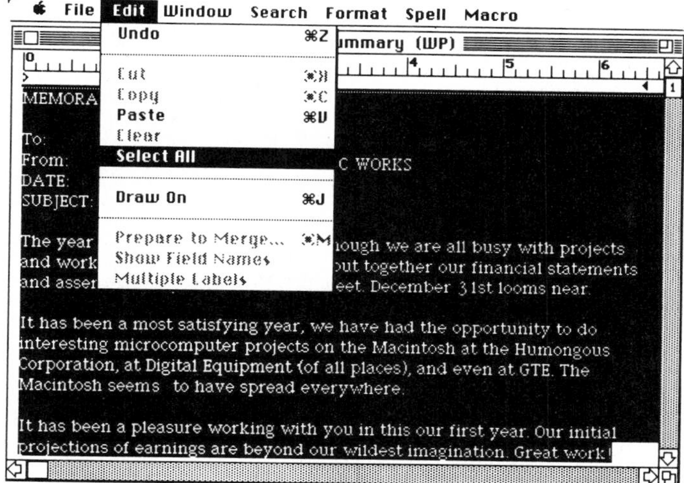


**Fig. 2.6**

*The Select All command and its effect on a window.*

## Selecting Graphics

You select graphics differently from text. Works has a Draw command in the word processor mode that is discussed in detail in Chapters 4 and 5.

## Inserting Text

Suppose that you want to add a word or a paragraph somewhere in a document. In the memo shown in figure 2.4 you want to add the word *computer* after the word *Macintosh*. Move the cursor (in the form of an I-beam) to the left of where you want the insertion to occur and click. When you click, a flashing vertical line cursor (|) appears to the left of the I-beam cursor.

You can move the I-beam cursor and click again to move the flashing bar to a new location, or you can begin typing. As you type, the new letters appear to the left of the flashing bar, and everything to the right of the insertion point moves to the right, then down when the line becomes too long for the margin. This movement is the wordwrap feature at work. At the end of a line, the flashing cursor moves to the next line.

In large documents, you may notice that the I-beam bulges (contains a small circle) in the center from time to time. This bulge means that Works is reformatting or wrapping the information. You can continue typing while Works performs these chores; your keyboard has a buffer that remembers keystrokes for four or five seconds.

## Deleting Text

What if you want to delete or add a lot of text? Works enables you to select text you want to delete or replace by using your mouse, by clicking, or by dragging. These methods are shown in figure 2.5. When you select a word, a line, a paragraph, or even your whole document, you can delete it to make it disappear forever, or you can choose the Cut command in the Edit window to move your selected text to the Clipboard for use elsewhere. When you select an item, anything you type, even a space character, replaces the selected item.

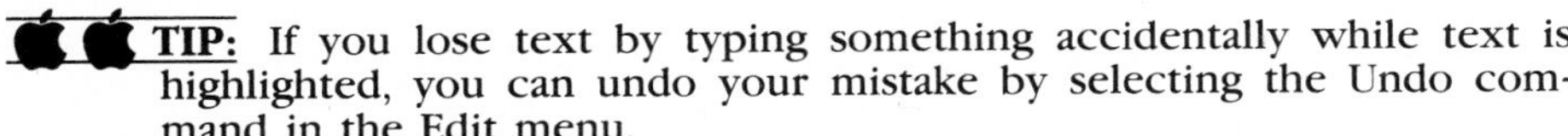

**TIP:** If you lose text by typing something accidentally while text is highlighted, you can undo your mistake by selecting the Undo command in the Edit menu.

# Undoing Mistakes

If you make a mistake when you delete a word or type over a selection, you can retype the selection, of course, but you may be able to undo the damage. Pull down the Edit menu and select the Undo command; you can restore your selection, provided that deleting it was the last thing you did. The Undo command cannot replace characters if you erased them by backspacing. The keyboard equivalent of the Undo command is the ⌘-Z key combination.

To return to the last saved version of your document, close the document you're working on without saving changes (by clicking the No button in the dialog box) and reopen your document. If your document was never previously saved, it is still named "Untitled," and you cannot use this procedure. For information about saving files, see the "Saving Your Work" section later in this chapter.

# *Copying, Cutting, and Pasting*

After selecting text or graphics, you can copy the item to the Clipboard by choosing the Copy command on the Edit menu, or by using the ⌘-C keystroke. When you use Copy command, Works duplicates the selected item (placing a copy on the Clipboard), without altering the document. The Clipboard can hold only one thing at a time, however, so when you copy something else to the Clipboard, the new item replaces the Clipboard's previous contents.

Selected text or graphics also can be cut (removed from the document). The Cut command on the Edit menu moves selected items from the document to the Clipboard. By using the Undo command, you can return to the document items that were cut accidentally (if you catch your mistake soon enough), but the Clipboard cannot be restored to its previous condition.

Items can be pasted from the Clipboard to the document you're working on or to another document. You also can move things to the Scrapbook this way. *Pasting* is a method of inserting copies of the Clipboard's contents into your document. Place the pointer where you want a copy of the Clipboard's contents to go, click to create an insertion point, and select the Paste command on the Edit menu, or use the ⌘-V keystroke. Paste leaves the contents of the Clipboard unchanged.

If you forget what's on the Clipboard, you can select the Show Clipboard command on the Window menu (see fig. 2.7). The contents of the Clipboard appear on-screen inside a scrolling window. You close the Clipboard window with the close box, or you can click in your document.

To move text or graphics safely, follow these steps:

1. Copy the selected item to the Clipboard (rather than cut it).
2. Point to the desired destination.
3. Click to position the pointer at the desired insertion point.

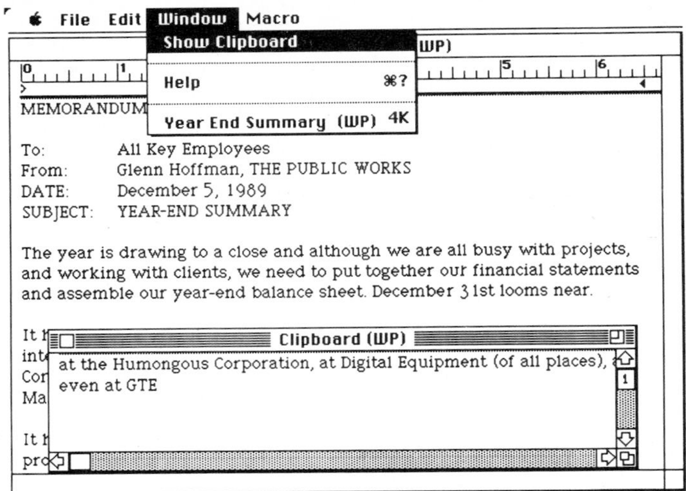


**Fig. 2.7**

*The Show Clipboard command and the Clipboard window.*

4. Press ⌘-V or select the Paste command from the Edit menu.
5. Delete the original item from the source, if desired.

Cutting and pasting is faster than copying, but you can lose cut items if you are interrupted, or if you forget to paste the items before using the Clipboard for something else.

You can use the Scrapbook as a more secure home for items in transit, although this process is more time-consuming. Remember that if you make a mistake, you may be able to recover by using the Undo command. In the worst case, you always can reload a copy of the saved file from the disk (if you have been saving your work as you go).

# Finding and Replacing Text

To find a word embedded in the text of your document, choose the Find command (or press ⌘-F) from the Search menu to bring up the Find dialog box (see fig. 2.8). Enter into the text box any word or set of characters (up to 80 characters long), and Works will scan your document and highlight the first occurrence of the search string. Click the Find Next button (or press Return), and Works highlights the next occurrence of the characters.

Find What:

Match Whole Words Only  Check Upper/Lowercase

Cancel  Find Next

**Fig. 2.8**

*The Find dialog box.*

You can use the Find command to search for tabs and carriage returns (remember that these are invisible on your screen) by clicking the appropriate boxes located in the upper left of the Find What dialog box. You can search for character strings as whole words by clicking the Match Whole Words Only box. Whole words have spaces, tabs, or punctuation both before and after alphanumeric character strings. If you want to find words containing special characters, you must enter the special characters for the search as they were entered originally in the text. Required, or hard, spaces also are special characters.

You also can make your search case-sensitive by clicking the Check Upper/Lowercase box. If you search for "work," for example, Works locates "Works," "working," and "worked," in addition to "work." If you are interested in only the name "Works," a case-sensitive search is quicker. When Works gets to the end of a document, it presents a dialog box with the message `All occurrences of the search have been found`. Click OK or press Return to continue editing your document.

If you search for the string " ton", Works locates the word `tons` but not the letters in "button"; the space is a required character.

If you hyphenate words manually to make line endings more attractive, you should search for portions of those words rather than the whole words. Otherwise, you risk missing the hyphenated versions of those words. Good automatic hyphenation features like the one found in WorksPlus Spell do not confuse the Find feature (see "Using WorksPlus Spell" later in this chapter).

The Replace command (⌘-R) works identically to the Find command and brings up the dialog box shown in figure 2.9. In the Replace With text box, you enter the characters you want substituted for those in the Find What box. You can perform a global Replace All, or you can check each occurrence. To check each occurrence, use the Find Next box followed by either Replace or Replace then Find.

Works has a Go To Page # command that scrolls your document and places the insertion point at the beginning of the first line of that page. When you use the Go To Page # command (⌘-G), you see the dialog box shown in figure 2.10. The default page number is the page you are on currently. Enter the page desired and click the OK box.

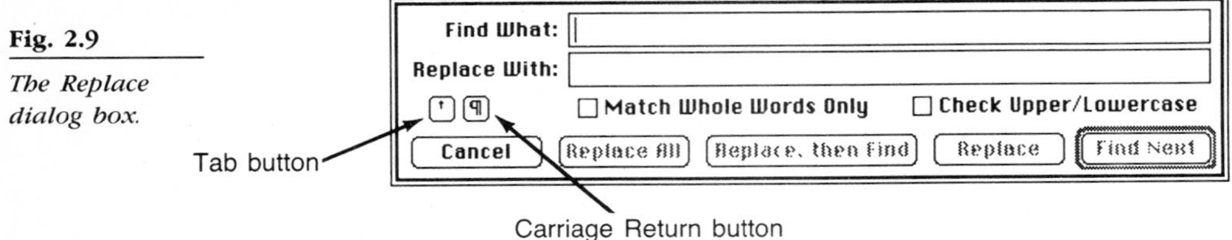


**Fig. 2.9**

*The Replace dialog box.*

**Fig. 2.10**

*The Go To Page # dialog box.*

# *Checking Your Spelling*

Works 2.0 has a 60,000-word spell checker to help you correct your work. The spell checker is a very flexible feature because it enables you not only to correct typing errors and misspelled words, but to correct misused homonyms (words that sound alike, such as *sight*, *site*, and *cite*), add words to a dictionary, check spacing, find double word errors, and even use other dictionaries or create your own.

The spell checker does not work on text objects created with the draw module (discussed in Chapter 4). If you need to correct the spelling of words in a text object, do so while in the word processor, then cut and paste the words into your text object. You always should check spelling before you finalize your work. Spell checking is another way the Works word processor helps you improve your writing.

All the options for the spell checker are found in the Spell menu. You can check the spelling of the whole document or of selected text. Choose the Correct Spelling command from the Spell menu to load a dictionary that you select and to bring up the Correct Spelling dialog box (see fig. 2.11). The first time you select the Correct Spelling command you are asked to locate the dictionary (one is provided for you in the Dictionary folder on your Works start-up disk). Works stores in memory the path you indicate and automatically loads this dictionary the next time it is called for, unless the dictionary is moved to a new place.

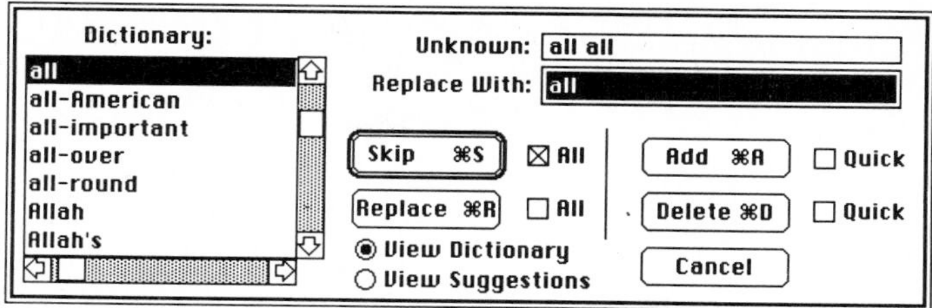


**Fig. 2.11**

*The Correct Spelling dialog box.*

When you use the spell checker, Works highlights an unknown word in your document, places it in the Unknown box, and suggests alternatives in the Replace With box. You can leave the word unchanged by clicking the Skip button (or by pressing ⌘-S or Return) and go on to the next questioned word (see fig. 2.11). If you click the Skip All box, Works skips all other occurrences of the word in the document.

You can click Replace (⌘-R) if you want to use the word suggested in the Replace With box. If you click Replace All, Works replaces all occurrences of the word in question with what you have entered in the Replace With box. As another method to replace a word, you can type the correct word in the Replace With box and click the Replace button. As you type, Works scrolls new suggestions in the Dictionary scroll box, any one of which you can choose by clicking it; double-clicking a word in the dictionary causes an automatic replacement in your text.

Use the View Dictionary box to match your word with others in the dictionary. The View Suggestions box lists similarly spelled and sounding words. To add your word to the dictionary, click the Add button (or press ⌘-A) to display the Adding Word to Dictionary dialog box (see fig. 2.12). When your word is unknown to the Works dictionary, this dialog box enables you to add many variations of the word at once. Use the mouse to select all the words with correct suffixes, then click Add Word Now (or press Return). You also can add your own variation by typing your word in the Unknown box and clicking Add Word Now (or press Return); you can add words up to 31 characters long.

**TIP:** If you have clicked the Add Quick box in the Correct Spelling dialog box (see fig. 2.11), you can add the selected word to your dictionary just by choosing the Add box (also in the Correct Spelling dialog box). Using this method bypasses the dialog box shown in fig. 2.12.

To delete a word from the dictionary, while in the Correct Spelling dialog box, select the word from the list in the dictionary text box and

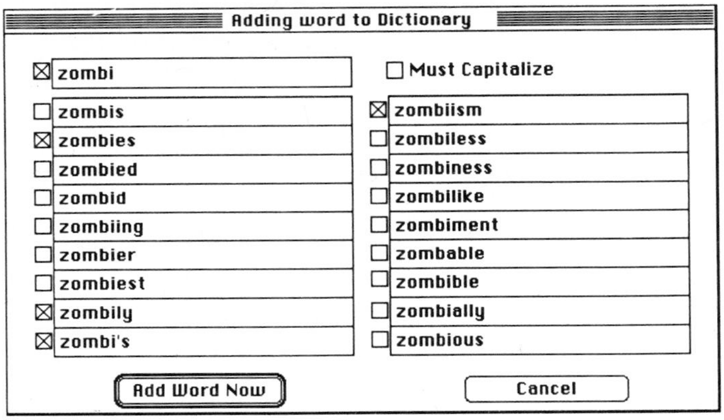

**Fig. 2.12**

*The Adding Word to Dictionary dialog box.*

click the Delete button (⌘-D). If you have clicked the Quick box next to the Delete box, the deletion occurs automatically; otherwise, Works prompts you for a confirmation of the deletion.

You can select one or more of the options before you check your spelling. Choose Options from the Spell menu to bring up the Options dialog box shown in figure 2.13. The options are as follows:

- ❑ `Must capitalize after period`. If this option is selected, Works questions any period, question mark, or exclamation point that occurs before a word that is uncapitalized. Works also questions abbreviations.
- ❑ `Proper noun capitalization`. Works questions all nouns not capitalized.
- ❑ `Mix numbers and letters`. Works checks for items like BAS52.
- ❑ `Double word errors`. Works checks for word repetitions.
- ❑ `Two spaces after period`. When checked, Works highlights words that follow a period, question mark, or exclamation point with only one space in-between. (You usually should leave this option unchecked and use only one space after a period.)
- ❑ `Homonyms`. Works highlights all words in a homonym file and displays the dialog box shown in figure 2.14.
- ❑ `Treat hyphens as spaces`. Works treats each half of a hyphenated word separately and not as a whole word.

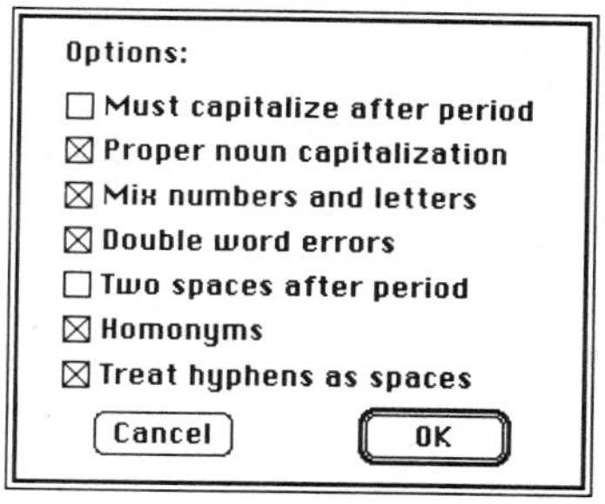

Options:

☐ Must capitalize after period
☒ Proper noun capitalization
☒ Mix numbers and letters
☒ Double word errors
☐ Two spaces after period
☒ Homonyms
☒ Treat hyphens as spaces

Cancel OK

**Fig. 2.13**

*The Spelling Options dialog box.*

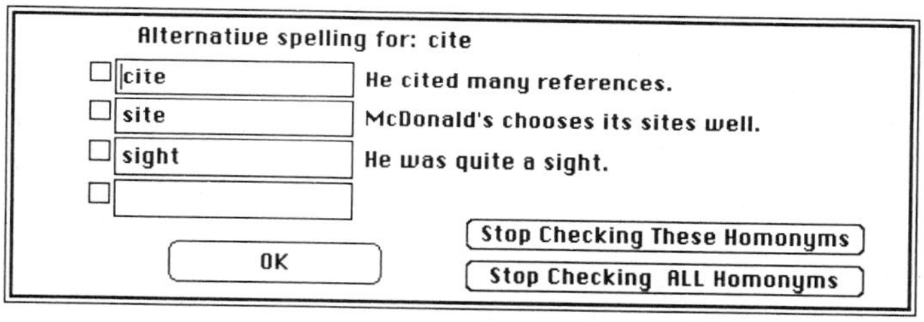

Alternative spelling for: cite

☐ cite — He cited many references.
☐ site — McDonald's chooses its sites well.
☐ sight — He was quite a sight.
☐

OK
Stop Checking These Homonyms
Stop Checking ALL Homonyms

**Fig. 2.14**

*The Homonym dialog box.*

When Works is finished checking the spelling of your document, it leaves selected the last highlighted word. To continue spell checking (which you need to do if you started spell checking in the middle of the document), you must deselect this word. Works also tells you how many words were checked and how many words were skipped (words that Works flagged but which you indicated were correct). Works asks if you would like to create a dictionary of skipped words for your the document. If you indicate yes, Works creates a file with the same name as your document file plus the file extension .DICT. The next time you spell check this document, Works will not check previously checked words (provided that you have both the document file and its .DICT file in the same folder). This feature is particularly handy when you're working on a long document that requires many work sessions.

## *Using the Homonyms Option*

When you select the Homonyms option on the Options menu, Works may ask you (the first time) to find the MSWORKSHYMN file (if it isn't already open). This file originally was contained in the Works dictionary folder.

If the word in question is correct, click OK (or press Return) to continue spell checking. If the word is incorrect, you can choose any of the suggestions, or type your own replacement in the blank text box. Click the box next to your selection, and click OK. If you select the Stop Checking These Homonyms option, Works will not question this group of homonyms again. Choosing the Stop Checking All Homonyms option is the same as canceling this feature in the Options dialog box (see fig. 2.13).

All homonyms are saved to a separate file called MSWORKSHYMN. To add or delete groups of words from this file, you must open that file. Choose the Open command from the Edit menu (or press ⌘-O). In the resulting Open File dialog box, select the Word Processor icon by clicking it, check the Import File option, and navigate to the MSWORKSHYMN file. Open that file by double-clicking the name, or click it once and press Return.

When you have opened the homonym file, you see a word processor document with groups of homonyms separated by asterisks. Each homonym is followed by examples:

```
**
sight, sights, sighted He has excellent sight
site, sites We chose a level site
cite, cites, cited Cite a reference
**
```

To delete a group of homonyms, select and delete the text (don't forget to remove a line of asterisks, if necessary). Do not remove the first line of the document. Add your own homonyms by using the same data structure.

When you're finished adding or deleting words, use the Save As command to save the new homonym file by using the Export File option (see the "Saving Your Work" section later in the chapter). Works stores a smaller copy of your homonym file in a file named MSWORKSHYMN TABLE. Works prompts you to replace the TABLE file; check the Yes button. If you close the untitled document, your changes are not saved.

Works uses the smaller homonym table to save time when checking your document. This file contains an old copy of your homonym file. When you make changes to the MSWORKSHYMN file, you must delete the MSWORKSHYMN TABLE file; Works will create a new copy of MSWORKSHYMN TABLE when you restart the program.

# *Using WorksPlus Spell*

Several other spell checkers are compatible with Microsoft Works 2.0. One notable third-party checker is WorksPlus Spell 2.0, a product you install directly into Works, and which loads with the program.

WorksPlus Spell replaces the Works Spell menu with its own. WorksPlus Spell contains a larger (90,000-word) dictionary and is much faster than the spell checker that comes bundled with Works. All the features found in the Works spell checker are contained in WorksPlus Spell.

WorksPlus Spell enables you to add words with a variety of suffixes by using a command directly from the menu, and you can change many of the search parameters. The program has an automatic hyphenation feature, and it allows you to set the hyphenation parameters, which is valuable, particularly with long documents. You also can choose text justification. This feature is illustrated in figure 2.15.

WorksPlus Spell also contains a glossary feature, which allows you to build a custom list of words. If you are a chemist, for example, you may want Works to recognize the spelling of unusual compounds you are working with. This glossary feature allows you to customize WorksPlus Spell so that it recognizes these unusual words.

Other worthwhile spell checkers are Thunder II, Lookup, and Spellswell, all of which are desk accessories.

If you do extensive writing with the word processor, you may want to consider adding a thesaurus to your Macintosh. A thesaurus lists synonyms for a selected word. (Synonyms are words with the same or similar meaning.) The two programs currently on the market that are compatible with Works are Word Finder and Big Thesaurus.

# *Saving Your Work*

Whenever you create a new document, it resides in your computer's RAM; the document isn't stored on disk until you tell Works to store it. If you turn off the computer without saving your document, or if a power failure or computer malfunction occurs, your work is lost forever. For these reasons, you should save your work regularly. In fact, many experienced computer users save their work (with the Save command) about every 15 minutes, and anytime they are interrupted, such

**Fig. 2.15**

*Text before and after hyphenation when using WorksPlus Spell.*

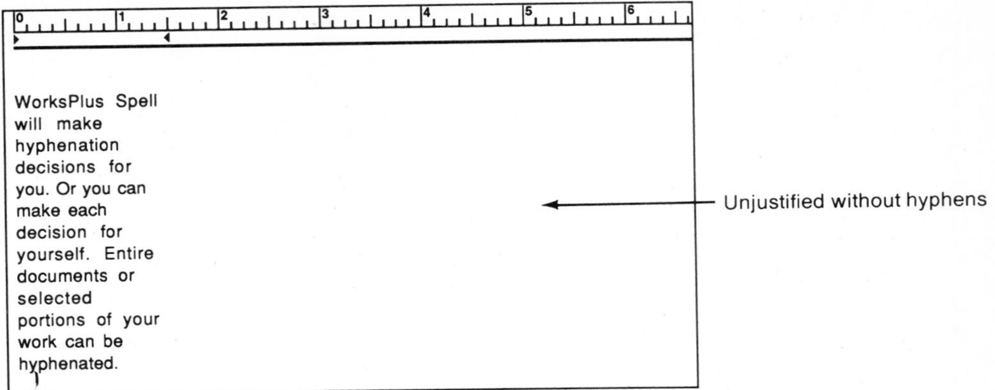


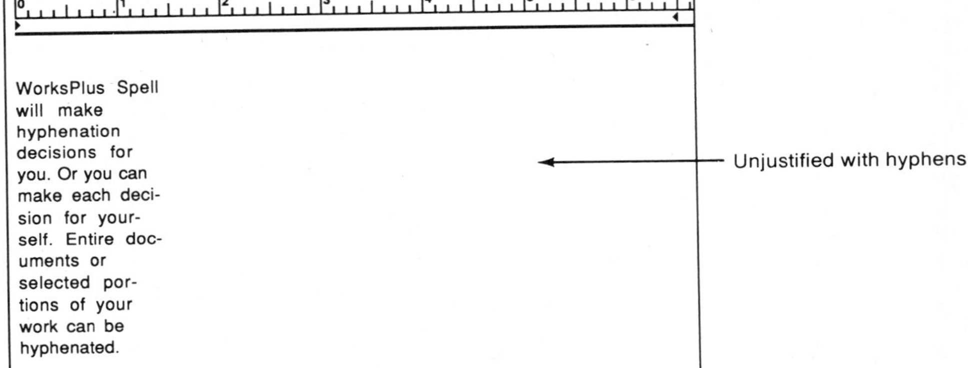


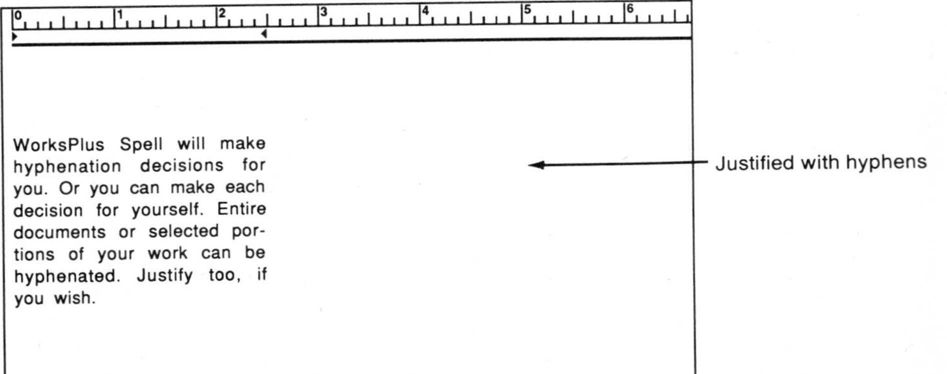

as by a telephone call or a visitor. This habit is a good one because you keep the current document on disk.

To write an untitled file to disk for the first time, use either the Save or Save Document As command on the File menu. In this case, the two commands are equivalent. (The Save and Save Document As commands are common to all Works modules.) Works displays the Save dialog box, which is shown in figure 2.16. (This dialog box also is called the Standard File Put, or SF Put, dialog box.)

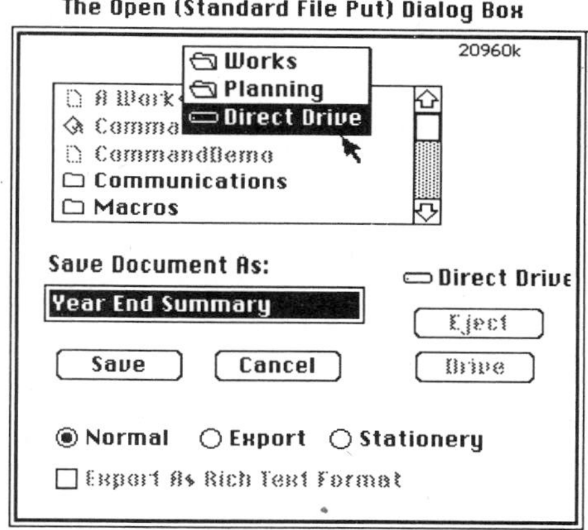


**Fig. 2.16**

*The Save/Save As dialog box.*

The SF Put dialog box options enable you to examine a disk, eject a disk, and navigate a disk's HFS with the scroll box and pull-down folder menu (this process is discussed in the Chapter 1 section "Navigating the Hierarchical File System"). The disk icon tells you what kind of disk is in use (hard disk or floppy).

Navigate through the hierarchical file system to get to the disk folder in which you want to store your document. After you have chosen the appropriate options (also discussed in Chapter 1), click the Save button to write your file to disk and place the file name in the correct place in your Desktop directory file.

You are prompted to type a file name in the SF Put text box. File names can be up to 32 characters long and can contain any keyboard character except a colon (:). When you're assigning file names and requesting files by name from the keyboard, capitalization is not important, but spaces are considered the same as any other character. If you save your file as "Untitled," Works will open this document whenever you issue the New command on the Edit menu.

If you decide not to save your work in its current form and would like to return to your last active window, click the Cancel button. Works takes you back to your document without saving.

Works 2.0 offers additional options for saving your file that previous versions did not. These options are the Normal, Export, Stationery, and Export as Rich Text Format.

When you create a document, it contains text and formatting information. Each text character is represented by an ASCII symbol, and formatting information includes type styles, tabs, justification, and so on. (Formatting is discussed in Chapter 3.) Saving your document with the Normal box highlighted preserves all this information, and usually you leave this box highlighted. But when you want to export a file to another computer or to a program that can read only text characters, click the Export box; a text file that doesn't contain the formatting information is written to disk.

The Stationery saving option creates a template document. The Rich Text Format (RTF) option is a format supported by Microsoft both on the Macintosh and on the IBM PC, and is supported by some other manufacturers—notably, page layout programs. In RTF, text and embedded formatting commands are saved together. With a file saved in RTF, you can place formatted text into other appropriate applications. (These options are discussed in detail in Chapter 14.)

Once you save the document to disk, the Save and Save As commands are no longer equivalent. When you make changes to a previously saved document, selecting the Save command (⌘-S) writes your changes to disk without first displaying the SF Put dialog box. If you use the Save As command, Works displays the SF Put dialog box and prompts you for a new document title. Then, if you try to save your file using the same name as before, Works asks if you want to replace the previous version. The most common use for the Save As command is to write to disk a copy of a file with a new name.

The Stationery option creates a template file that substitutes for the Save As command. Opening a Stationery document places into your active word processing window an untitled document with all the previously saved information, formatting, and settings. Icons for Stationery documents have the lower right corner turned up (see fig. 1.3). The Stationery option is most useful for files that you have set up and want to add to: a letterhead, business form, or page layout template. The Stationery option prevents you from accidentally altering your previous work.

# Closing and Opening Files

You can close a file on your Works desktop or close all the open files on your desktop by using the Close or Close All commands in the Edit menu. These two commands are common to all modules in Works.

If you have made changes to a file since it was first opened, the Close command prompts you with the dialog box shown in figure 2.17. (If you have not made any changes, this dialog box does not appear.) Click Yes (or press Return) to save your changes to disk, click No to keep your previously saved version, or click Cancel ⌘-. (period) if you prefer to continue working with the document on-screen. Note that the triangle with the exclamation point indicates that this operation is a potentially "dangerous" one. If you click No instead of yes, for instance, you would lose a lot of work, because you would not be saving changes you have made. Make sure that you make the correct choice in dialog boxes that contain the triangle and exclamation point alert icon.

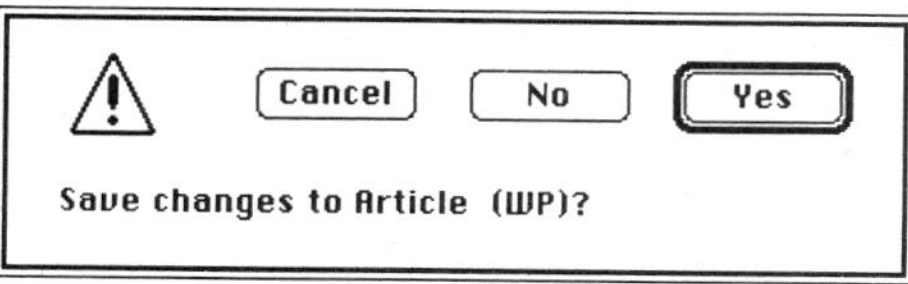


**Fig. 2.17**

*The Save Changes dialog box.*

The Close All command, new to Works 2.0, enables you to close all your files and return to the Open (SF Get) dialog box to open additional files. Choose the Close All command to see the dialog box shown in figure 2.18. You can choose to save all changed files, without further prompting, by clicking the appropriate box. To close files without saving changes, leave this box unchecked. In all other aspects, the Close All dialog box is identical to the Close dialog box.

Close All:

Are you sure you want to close all open windows on the Desktop?

☐ Save all changed files without further prompting

Cancel

OK

**Fig. 2.18**

*The Close All dialog box.*

The Close All command is most useful for a set of Works files that you commonly use together—using a database and a word processing document to do mail merges, for example. (Mail merging is covered in Chapters 9 and 10.) If you use a set of documents together, you should create desktop files for them (see Chapter 13, "Tying It All Together") and use the Close All command as a convenience feature to speed your work. Clicking a Works desktop file opens all the documents in the condition they were in when the Works desktop file was created.

In Chapter 1, you learned about opening files using the Open command. Figure 1.14 showed the Open (SF Get) dialog box, and Chapter 1 discussed how to find a file. This discussion also applies to opening word processor files (and all other Works files), except that clicking the word processor icon in the Open File dialog box lists only word processor documents in the scroll box. When you click a file type icon, you see only that type of file in the scroll box.

Depending on the amount of memory available, you can have up to 14 files open at a time. You open them sequentially by using the Open command in the File menu. The word processor has a Window menu (as do all modules), and any opened file is listed at the bottom of this menu. You can drag down to select a file from the Window menu, or you can click any window to activate that window, bring it to the top of your desktop, and change your working file.

## *Printing Your Work*

To print your document, you must determine what output device you want to use and what you want the output to look like. To select the output device, you use the Chooser DA to make your hardware and network choices. For controlling the appearance of your output, use the Page Setup command and set options in the Page Setup dialog box (see fig. 1.11 for an example of options for an ImageWriter, and fig. 1.26 for an example of options for a LaserWriter).

You can print a file stored on disk, print the document currently onscreen, or print the contents of the active window.

Specific options are available for each printer, and these are provided for by its printer driver. Some printers, for example, require 1/2-inch margins on all edges of the pages, and some printers can take large paper sizes. When creating documents, you should consider the capabilities and restrictions of your printer.

Most advanced Works users use the Page Setup feature. For new users, the default Page Setup is fine for most standard typing jobs on Apple printers. Learn what your printer's capabilities and limitations are. Consult your printer manual before you begin printing—especially if you are having trouble.

After you have selected your printer type in Chooser and your Page Setup options, select the Print command (⌘-P) on the File menu to bring up the Print dialog box. If you selected the Print Preview option, you see the Print Preview screen (see fig. 1.28). Otherwise your document begins printing immediately.

To print a single window of a document, use the Print Window option on the File menu. The printout shown in figure 2.19 is the result of applying the Print Window command to the Year End Summary Memo shown in figure 2.4. Works prints the contents of the window and the ruler but does not print scroll bars or the cursor.

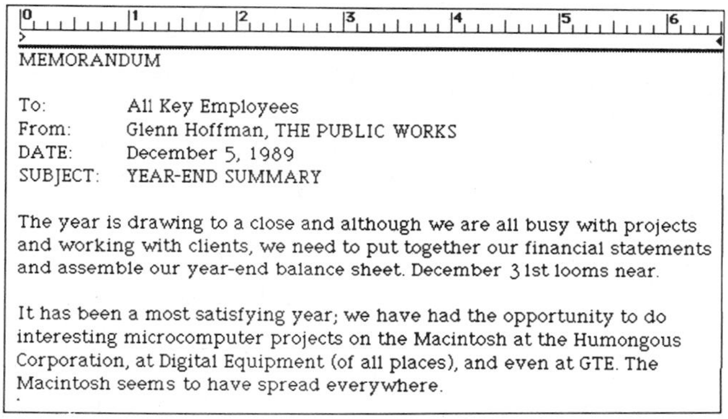

```
0      1      2      3      4      5      6
MEMORANDUM

To:        All Key Employees
From:      Glenn Hoffman, THE PUBLIC WORKS
DATE:      December 5, 1989
SUBJECT:   YEAR-END SUMMARY

The year is drawing to a close and although we are all busy with projects
and working with clients, we need to put together our financial statements
and assemble our year-end balance sheet. December 31st looms near.

It has been a most satisfying year; we have had the opportunity to do
interesting microcomputer projects on the Macintosh at the Humongous
Corporation, at Digital Equipment (of all places), and even at GTE. The
Macintosh seems to have spread everywhere.
```

**Fig. 2.19**

*The Print Window command applied to figure 2.4.*

Don't confuse the Print Window option with the Apple Print Screen feature, which you invoke by pressing ⌘-Shift-4 keys. The Works Print Window command works with laser printers; the Apple command doesn't. Moreover, the appearance of the output differs. The Print Window command eliminates scroll bars, menus, and other clutter. The Print Screen keystroke performs what is commonly called a *screen dump*—everything on-screen that is within the size of your Page Setup constraints is sent to your printer. When you use the Print Window command on the File menu with a laser printer, text is printed using cleaner, clearer laser fonts rather than the fuzzier screen fonts. Experiment to find the feature you prefer.

The ⌘-Shift-3 keyboard command sends to disk a screen dump in MacPaint (bit-map) file format. If you have ever wondered how the figures in books such as this one were produced, that's your answer. Screen dump utilities are discussed in Chapter 14.

**NOTE:** The ⌘-Shift-number keyboard commands are called *FKeys*. They perform a simple function or convenience. Many FKeys are available as freeware or shareware, and they can be installed by utilities such as Suitcase II, Font/DA Juggler, or shareware installers such as FKey Mover, among others.

# *Quick Reference Summary*

In order to use this Quick Reference Summary, you must be able to perform some basic Macintosh operations. You must be able to start your computer, use the mouse to select menu items, icons, and dialog box options. You must be able to work with windows, resize, and scroll them. All these techniques are discussed in the first four sections of Chapter 1; you should review these techniques if they are unfamiliar.

To begin Microsoft Works, follow these steps:

1. Double-click the Works (or application) program icon. All the Works icons are shown in figure 1.3.
2. After the About MS-Works screen appears, you see the Open File dialog box.

To create a new file, follow these steps:

1. Click the word processor icon and the New button (or press ⌘-N). Alternatively, you can double-click the word processor icon.
2. A window named "Untitled" opens. You can use this window to create a new file. A new file is created when you save your file under a different file name.

To save a file, use the following steps:

1. Select the Save command in the File menu, and you see the Save File (SF Put) dialog box.
2. Give your file a name by typing the name in the Save Document As box.

3. Click the Save button (or press Return), and the "Untitled" name in the title bar of the window is replaced with the new name you typed.

If you have previously saved a file to disk and you have reopened it, you can use the Save As command in the File menu to create a copy of your document. The Save As dialog box results.

To open an existing document, use the following procedure:

1. Select the Open command from the File menu. You see the Open File (SF Get) dialog box.
2. If the file you want is located in the scroll box, either click it and press the Open button, or double-click the file name.
3. If you need to change folders to locate your file, use the mouse to drag open the folder names above the scroll box to go to a higher folder. To go to a lower folder (a folder further away from the root directory), click the folder name in the scroll box, and then click the Open box (or double-click the folder name).

Alternatively, you can press ⌘-up arrow to go to higher folders, press ⌘-down arrow to open a lower folder. Press the up- and down-arrows to move around in the scroll box, or type the first letters of the file name to highlight the file you want.

To type a word processing document, do the following:

1. Click the top line of the document.
2. Type your text into the window. Works has automatic wordwrap to move text to the next line. Press Return when you want to move to the next line at the end of a short sentence, or when you have completed a paragraph.

To move text, follow these steps:

1. Select the text you want to move by clicking and dragging over it.

   You can select a word by double-clicking it. You can select a line by clicking once in the left margin (when the cursor is an arrow), and you can select a paragraph by double-clicking in the left margin.

2. Choose Cut from the Edit menu.
3. Position the cursor where you want to move the text, then click to create an insertion point.

4. Choose the Paste command from the Edit menu.

To copy text, follow these steps:

1. Select the text to be copied.
2. Choose the Copy command in the Edit menu.
3. Position the cursor where you want the selected text copied, then click to create an insertion point.
4. Select the Paste command from the Edit menu.

Use the following steps to delete text:

1. Select the text to be removed.
2. Press the Delete key (on some keyboards this is called the Backspace key).

To print your work, follow these steps:

1. Select the Chooser desk accessory in the Apple menu. Select your printer and close the window.
2. Check to see that your printer is on and ready to print.
3. Select the Print command in the File menu and make any choices needed in the Print dialog box.
4. Click OK or press Return.

You have learned the basics of producing a document, but there are many more things you can do to change the appearance of your document. You can add tabs, headers and footers, change type styles, and set page breaks to make your documents more attractive and informative. Chapter 3 covers these topics and others.

3

# Formatting Text and Adding Style

A word processor puts some powerful tools in your hands. You can think of your computer as your own personal typesetting machine. You can create documents with indented paragraphs, hanging margins, a variety of type styles and point sizes, and you can insert these formats either as you type or when you are finished with the document.

In this chapter, you learn ways to format your document pages by setting margins, indenting, tabbing, and changing page breaks. You learn to center your text or print it flush right, flush left, or justified. You can print your documents in any installed type font in your choice of roman (normal), bold, italic, outline, shadow, or underline type styles. You can print with superscripts or subscripts. Picture fonts, foreign language fonts, and special character fonts make your choices almost limitless.

Does your document need an interstate highway symbol or a palm tree? These symbols are available, and this chapter shows you how to use them. With the techniques you learn in this chapter, you can produce attractive, professional-quality documents.

## *Formatting Document Pages*

One advantage of Works is the ease with which you can change the appearance of your document pages. With no additional typing, you can change the margins, add or delete indents, or even change the page breaks. Working without a word processor, any of these changes would require retyping the entire document.

A collection of tabs, indent markers, line-space specifications, type styles, and so forth, is called a *format*. The default format for your

Works documents is Geneva font in 12-point size, black, roman-style type, with left justification, single spacing, and no tabs.

When you first create your document, any formatting that you set is applied to your entire document. You also can format paragraphs individually. You can have one format for a whole document or as many different formats as the document has paragraphs. Works indicates a paragraph's formatting with icons displayed in the ruler. If you format paragraphs individually, you can see the different formatting markers for each paragraph as you move the cursor.

Works stores the formatting information about each paragraph in an invisible paragraph marker that occurs at the end of each paragraph (you create the marker by pressing Return). Even a single line can be a paragraph. The script in figure 3.1, for example, contains varied paragraph formats.

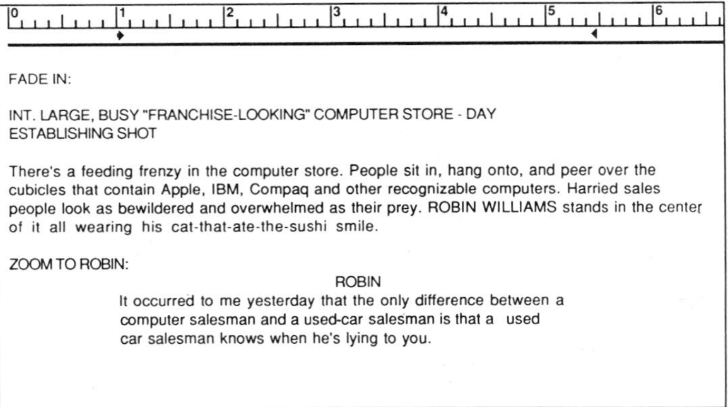


**Fig. 3.1**

*Varied paragraph formats in a script.*

If you have formatted several paragraphs differently, you can make all the formatting the same by using the Select All command in the Edit menu and adjusting the formatting markers. You can make changes to just a few paragraphs at a time by selecting those paragraphs, and then changing the formatting.

To locate the boundaries of your paragraphs, use the Find command in the Search menu and click the paragraph icon to begin your search. Click the Find Next button to highlight the next paragraph marker (paragraphs extend from one paragraph marker to the next).

When you save your document, every character on-screen, including invisible characters such as tabs, spaces, and carriage returns, are saved.

Advanced word processors like Microsoft Word allow you to display all these invisible characters.

To avoid having to reenter formats over and over, you can copy formats within the same document and modify or eliminate the old text but keep the format. Follow these steps to copy formats:

1. Click anywhere in a paragraph that has the format you want to copy.
2. Choose Copy Format on the Format menu, or use ⌘-K.
3. Click inside the destination paragraph.
4. Choose Paste Format on the Format menu, or use ⌘-Y.

You can repeat this Pasting process for multiple paragraphs scattered throughout your document. To paste a format to several *adjacent* paragraphs, select all the destination paragraphs before you paste.

To copy formats from one document to another, follow these steps:

1. Select the paragraph to be copied.
2. Choose the Copy command (or press ⌘-C) on the File menu.
3. Activate the destination document and click the desired insertion point.
4. Select the Paste command (or press ⌘-V) on the File menu.

# *Setting Margins*

New Works users frequently confuse margins and indents. Margins are the white spaces at the left, right, top, and bottom of the page, surrounding the text and graphics. This white space doesn't appear onscreen when you enter and edit text. Indents are the amount by which text is indented inside the margin. Every page has margins, but text can be without indents.

You select the page margins in the Page Setup dialog box by choosing the Page Setup command on the File menu. You can accept the default choices, or you can choose your own margins. To set a margin, go to the Page Setup dialog box (see fig. 3.2) and enter in the appropriate boxes the amount of margin you want (in inches). For example, type *1.5* for a 1 1/2-inch margin, *2.25* for 2 1/4 inches, and so on.

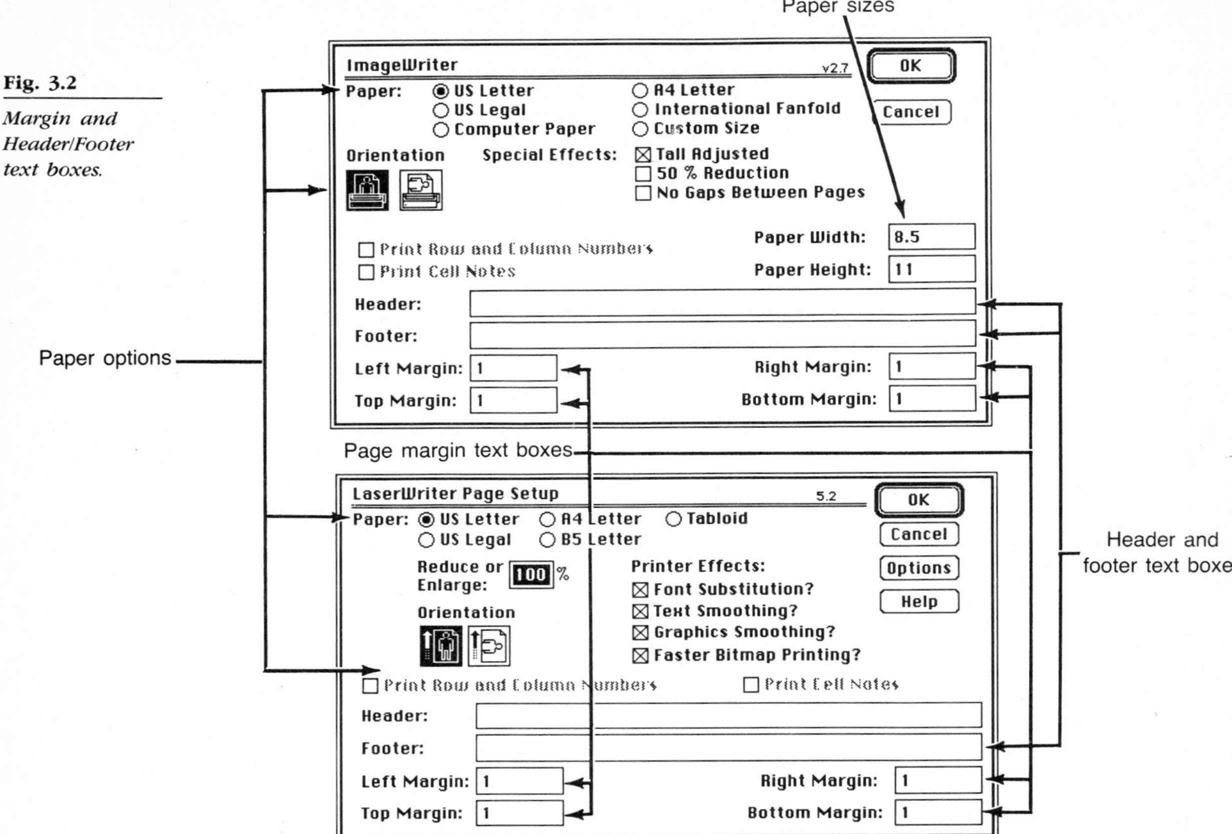


**Fig. 3.2**

*Margin and Header/Footer text boxes.*

When you are deciding on your margins, remember that the left and right margins, when added to the length of the longest text line or graphic in a document, cannot exceed the width of the paper. For example, if you're using 8 1/2-inch wide paper and want a 1-inch left margin and a 1-inch right margin, your text lines or graphics must fit in a 6 1/2-inch line. If you select combinations that break this rule, Works warns you with the dialog box shown in figure 3.3 and *truncates* (does not print) the text or graphics that fall outside the available print area.

Not all printers can print at the outer edges of paper. Many laser printers, including the Apple LaserWriter family of printers, require a minimum of 1/2-inch margins all around the document. Be sure that

The width of your document is greater than the print width you have chosen in page setup. Text or pictures which extend past the right margin will be truncated during printing.

OK

**Fig. 3.3**

*Warning about margin problems.*

you take this requirement into consideration when you set your margins. The margin settings you define in the Page Setup dialog box are used for the entire document. Works uses indent markers to set "temporary margins" within a document (see the following section, "Using the Indent Markers").

Use the Show Ruler command on the Format menu to display a ruler at the top of your word processing window. This ruler shows (in inches) the position of text and graphics relative to the left margin. Zero on the ruler is not the edge of the paper, but is the left edge of the image area. You can remove the ruler from the screen by using the Hide Ruler command on the Format menu (see fig. 3.4).

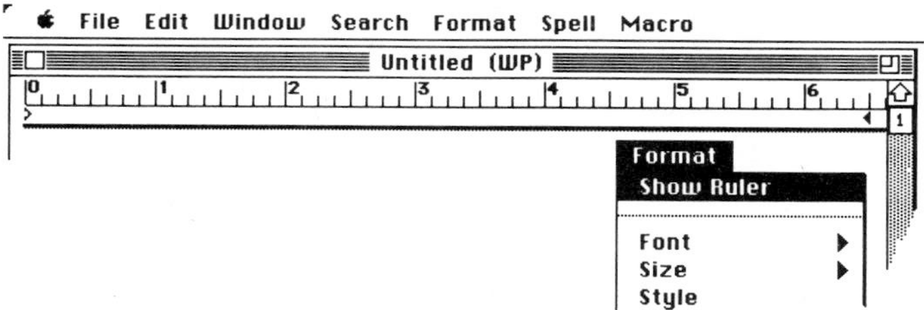


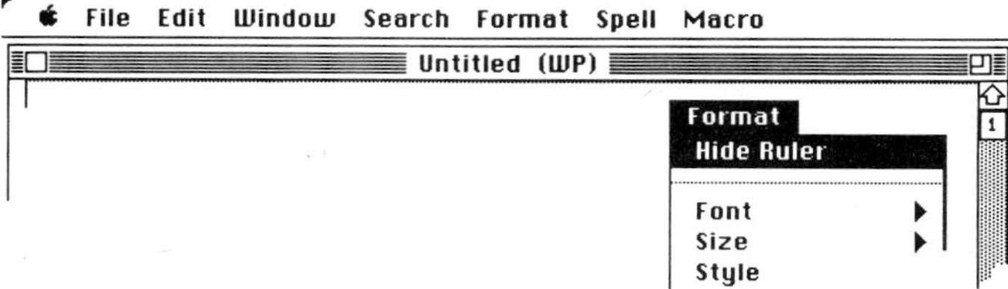


**Fig. 3.4**

*Show/Hide ruler command.*

This screen ruler is the key to setting your document's indents. You also use the screen ruler to set various kinds of tab settings.

# Using the Indent Markers

As you can see in figure 3.5, the ruler area contains markers to help you adjust the paragraph formatting choices you have made. When you open a new document, Works assumes you don't want indents. You can, however, specify indents for any paragraph you choose—for each paragraph, if you want.

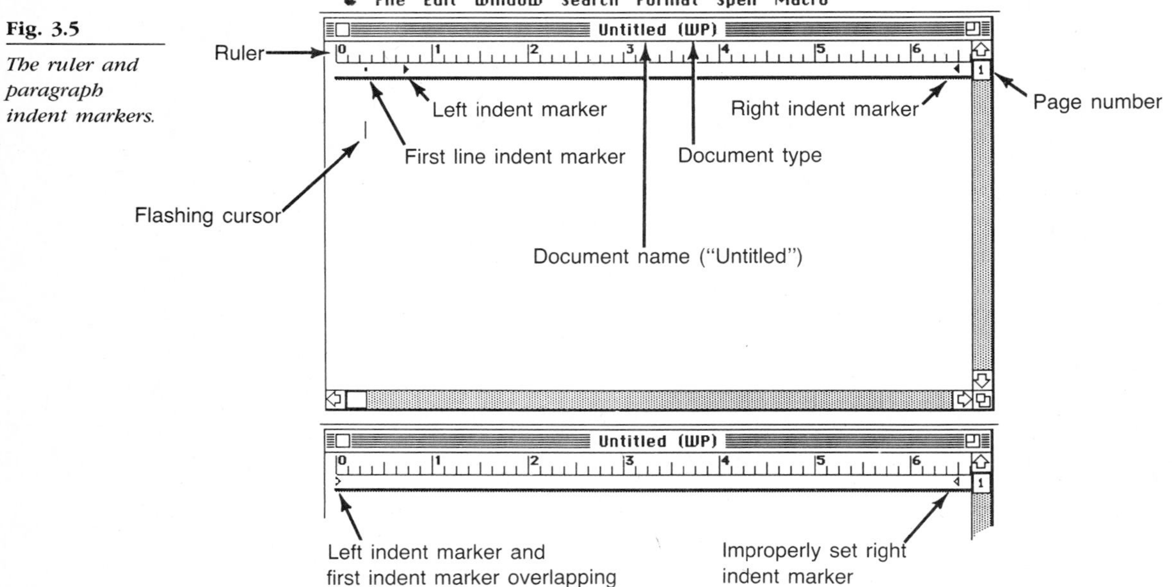


**Fig. 3.5**
*The ruler and paragraph indent markers.*

# Right Indents

The right indent marker is the solid black triangle located along the bottom of the ruler near the right edge of the screen. The long side of the triangle marks the point on the ruler where wordwrap will occur.

When you open a new document, the default position for the right indent marker is 6 1/2 inches from the left margin. You can move the marker before you begin typing; this change affects all the text you type thereafter. If you want to make global changes to your document or changes to selected paragraphs later on, you must select those portions individually to make your changes. Works alters only the selected text.

Moving the right indent marker requires a little practice. When you move the indent marker, it snaps to small gradations on the ruler. To move the right indent marker, use the following steps:

1. Select an entire paragraph.
2. Point to the right indent marker and drag it to the left to its new position.
3. Release the mouse button and watch Works reformat the text.

**NOTE:** If you click outside of the right indent marker, you create a tab marker, which looks like a sideways capital T. In this case, simply drag the tab marker down off the ruler to remove it, and try again. You learn about tabs in the section "Using Tabs."

You can move the right indent marker to the right to make the lines of text longer. The screen scrolls when necessary.

**NOTE:** If you move the left indent marker too far to the right (causing a conflict with the right margin) or if your text does not fit on the page size you have chosen, the marker changes from solid black to a hollow triangle, as a warning. If you don't correct the problem, Works truncates any text outside the print area when you print your document.

## *First-Line Indent*

Works provides a first-line indent marker that makes indenting the first lines of paragraphs easy (see fig. 3.6). The marker is a small black box that appears on top of the left indent marker when you open a new document.

To indent the first line of a paragraph, drag the little square marker (not the left margin triangle) along the ruler to the position you choose. The first line in the current paragraph moves a corresponding amount. Each paragraph you type thereafter begins with an indented line. To indent only certain paragraphs, you must select those paragraphs before you move the first-line indent marker.

## *Left Indents*

You can force entire paragraphs to move to the right of the left margin. Some people call these left indents "temporary left margins" but they

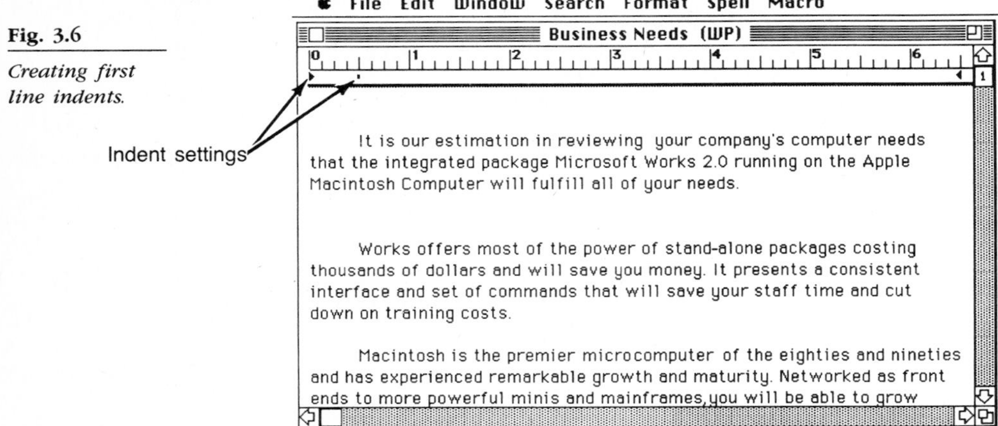


**Fig. 3.6**

*Creating first line indents.*

really are a form of indent. The left indent marker is a solid black triangle. If you have not moved the first line indent marker (the small black box), Works reminds you of that by changing the left indent marker to a hollow triangle. You may need to move the first line indent marker slightly to the right temporarily in order to point properly at the left indent marker.

The long edge of the triangle marks the point on the ruler where the left edge of indented paragraphs will be (see fig. 3.7). To move the left marker, just drag it as you did the right indent marker. The selected text follows the marker's movements. Any paragraphs that you type after you set up indent markers are indented. You also can select previously typed paragraphs and indent them by moving the marker while the paragraphs are selected.

## *Hanging Left Indents*

You can use hanging left indents to add emphasis to a paragraph. To produce hanging indents like the ones in figure 3.8, you use the first-line indent and left indent markers together, as follows:

1. Place the left indent marker to the right of the left margin.
2. Move the first-line indent marker to the left of the left indent.

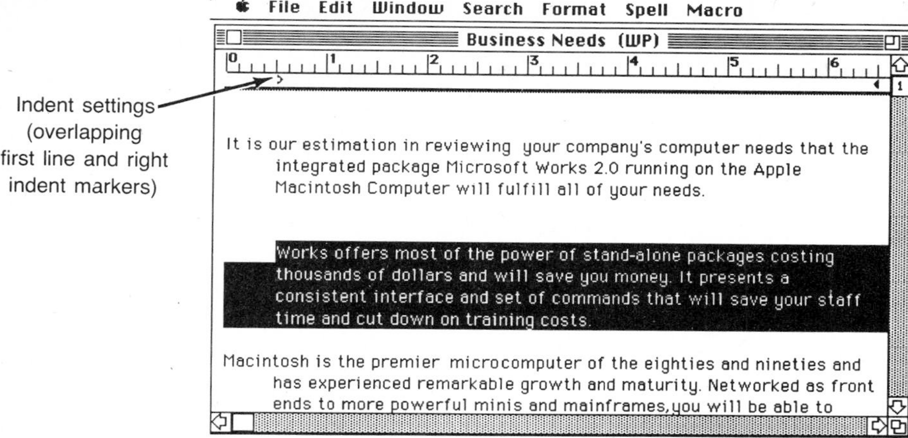


**Fig. 3.7**

*Creating left indents.*

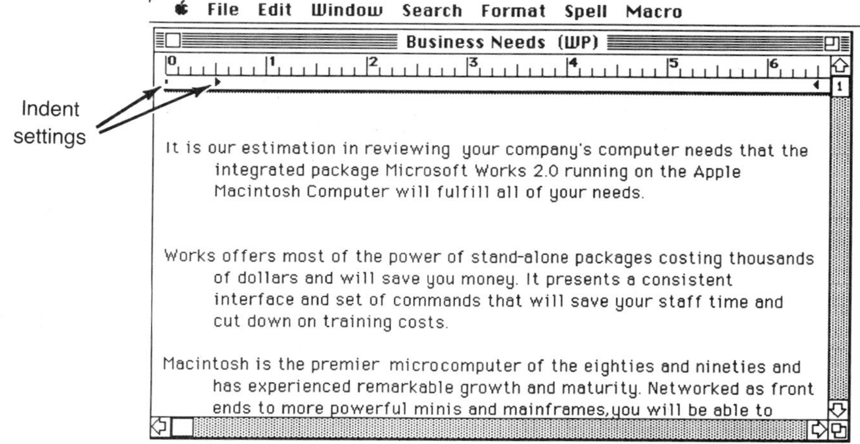


**Fig. 3.8**

*Hanging left indentations.*

As a result, the first line of the paragraph is flush with the left margin and all following lines are indented. This technique is a great way to insert numbers or bullets to the left of indented paragraphs.

## Using Tabs

Tabs enable you to move the cursor a specific distance without using the space bar. When you open a new document, Works provides preset left tabs every half-inch. Because they enable you to move the cursor without repeatedly pressing the space bar, left tabs frequently are used for typing text in tables, and you can use them for indentations.

You press the tab key to move the cursor across the screen to the right to the next available tab. Pressing the Backspace key tells Works to move the cursor back one tab.

You can create custom tab stops. Works offers four types of custom tabs: left, right, centered, and decimal alignment.

Left tabs are identical to those found on your typewriter. A right tab justifies text to the right, against the tab you set, and a center tab produces centered text. When you use the decimal tab for numbers, decimal points are aligned to your tab setting.

## Creating Custom Tabs

Using the ruler, you set tabs by clicking the mouse (see fig. 3.9). When you decide where you want to set a tab, click once to set a left tab, double-click to set a right tab, triple-click to set a decimal tab, and click four times to set a center tab. You can toggle from one kind of tab stop to the next by clicking a tab one more time. (Work's standard tabs don't show on the ruler; only your custom tabs do.)

To set a left tab, for example, make sure that the ruler is visible, and then click once at the desired position on the bottom half of the ruler area. A left tab marker appears. In figure 3.9, two left tabs are set—the first one created with one mouse click and the second one created with five mouse clicks.

**NOTE:** When you set your own tabs, all preset tabs to the left of the new tab disappear.

You can use tab stops to create custom tables of data or information. In figure 3.10, you can see a table with columns created by using different tab stops. Tables enable you to present information in a logical manner. For example, a decimal-centered column enables your readers to compare dollars (or other numbers) at a glance. You may want to use right

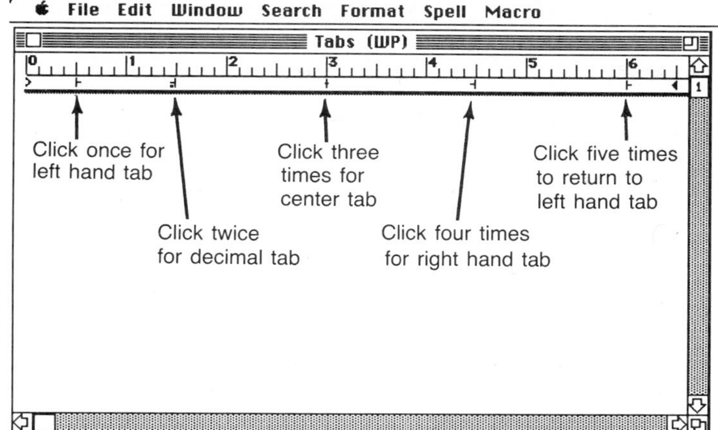


**Fig. 3.9**

*Creating custom tabs.*

tab settings to create columns that will balance out left-justified columns. Centered columns work well when they are between left and right justified columns, or they if they are set by themselves.

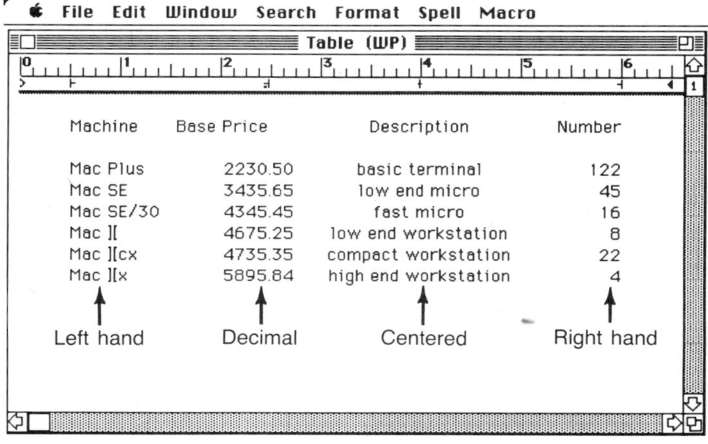


**Fig. 3.10**

*Creating a table by using custom tab stops.*

To move a tab, drag the marker along the ruler to where you want it between the left margin and the right indent marker. When you drag a tab marker, the tab text moves along with it. To delete tabs, drag them off the ruler and release the mouse button.

# Working with Page Formats

Although Works automatically inserts page breaks based on your paper size and margin selections, you can set page breaks manually to suit your document. Often, you don't want a paragraph broken so that only the first line is at the bottom of the page (an *orphan*), or the last line of the paragraph continues to the top of the next page (a *widow*). Widows and orphans distract the reader.

Many times you want to place information at the top of your pages (*headers*) or at the bottom of your pages (*footers*). You can put page numbers, document titles, dates, or anything else you want in your headers and footers, and you can format this information.

## Using Page Breaks

Works calculates page breaks based on the paper size and margins that you set in the Page Setup dialog box. These page breaks are indicated by a dotted line that crosses your document horizontally. If you find that you need a little extra space while typing a document, you may want to change the margin settings to enable you to squeeze that last line on the page.

You can force a page break with the new Version 2.0 manual page break feature. Forced page breaks help you keep together similar portions of text, such as tables. When you create a manual page break, it is indicated by a dashed line across your document. This dashed line lets you know that it is a manual page break, not a "normal" one. To create a manual page break, use the following procedure:

1. Click the first line of text that belongs on the new page.
2. Select Insert Page Break from the Format menu or press Shift-Enter.

A dashed line appears above the line you clicked. The line you clicked becomes the first line on a new page when you print.

Sometimes a forced page break becomes unnecessary. For example, if you insert text above the forced page break, it may no longer be needed. When a change such as this occurs, you often will see two page breaks on-screen: the automatic page break and the forced page break (see fig. 3.11). When you print the text, Works prints a blank page between the two page breaks.

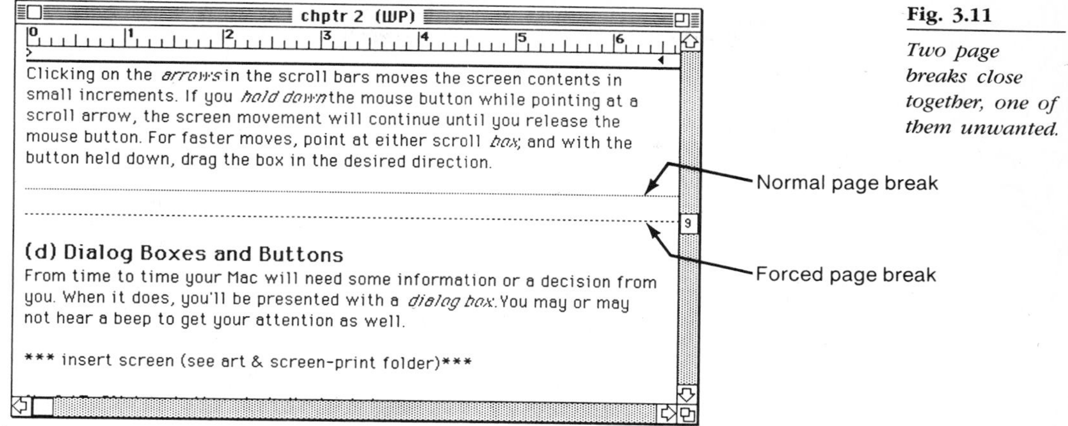


**Fig. 3.11**

*Two page breaks close together, one of them unwanted.*

You cannot remove an automatic page break, but if you use manual page breaks to repaginate, you can remove the manual breaks. To remove an unwanted manual page break, follow these steps:

1. Click anywhere on the line below the forced page break.
2. Choose Remove Page Break from the Format menu, and the forced page break disappears.

## Eliminating Extra Spaces and Blank Pages

Spaces sometimes occur at the end of Works documents (see fig. 3.12). Choose Select All to see the extra spacing. To remove these additional spaces, drag the mouse down from the last character, and delete the spaces by using the Backspace (or delete) key.

Sometimes, the appearance of a dashed line (representing a page break) indicates unwanted spaces. This problem occurs frequently when you are printing labels. Again, simply delete the unwanted spaces.

## Headers and Footers

You use headers, lines at the top of pages, to identify documents or to number and date pages automatically. Footers do the same thing at the bottom of printed pages.

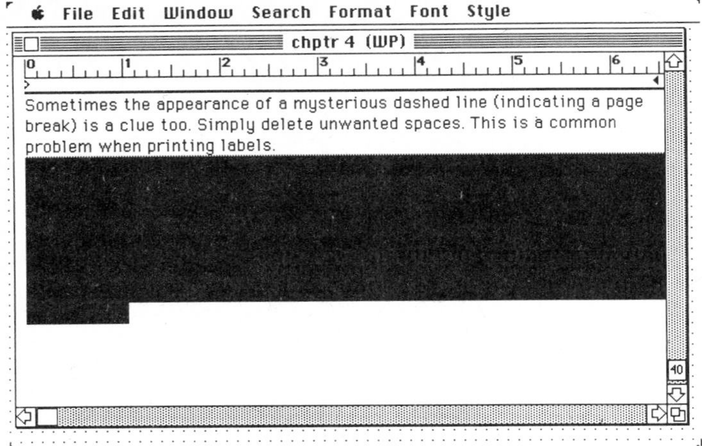


**Fig. 3.12**

*Invisible spaces sometimes pile up at the end of a document, causing Works to print a blank page.*

Headers and footers don't appear on-screen, but you can view them in the Page Preview mode, or when you print your document. You have control over justification and type style, and you also can place the time and date on your document, number the pages, or print a title or the author's name. All these options are controlled through the entries you make in the Header and Footer text boxes in the Page Setup dialog box.

In the simplest case, you enter your text in the Header and Footer boxes, and that text appears on each printed page in your document. In these simple instances, follow these steps:

1. Choose the Page Setup command on the File menu.
2. Type text in either the Header or Footer boxes, whichever you are creating.
3. Click the OK button.
4. Print your document.

You can change the type style, size, and color of your headers and footers. While the Page Setup dialog box is on-screen, choose a new type style, size, or color before you begin typing. To pick a font, pull down the Font submenu; to pick a style, choose the Style submenu; to pick a color, use the Color command on the Format menu. The color options are explained in Chapter 5, "Graphics and Design."

If you want to change the type size or style after typing headers and footers, select the desired header or footer text and then choose a new style. (Font and style options are discussed in the "Adding Style to Your Documents" section of this chapter.) The default type settings are Boston 10-point black for the word processor, and Geneva 9-point black for the spreadsheet and database. To see what type style options Works will use for your headers and footers, select the text and check Font and Style in the Works menu. This habit is a good one to develop.

Works has several shorthand commands for use in headers and footers. The commands begin with the ampersand (&) and are followed by a letter formatting command, which can be either upper- or lowercase. Table 3.1 shows the shorthand commands that you can use in headers and footers.

**Table 3.1**
**Shorthand Commands for Headers and Footers**

| *Command* | *Effect* |
|---|---|
| &l | Aligns following characters to the left margin |
| &c | Centers following characters |
| &r | Aligns following characters to the right margin |
| &p | Prints the page number |
| &d | Prints the date |
| &t | Prints the time |
| &f | Prints the name of the document (file name) |
| &b | Prints the following characters in bold style |
| &i | Prints the following characters in italic style |
| && | Prints an ampersand symbol |

You use combinations of these formatting commands to create headers and footers. For example, &l&d &r&t prints the date on the left and the time on the right. You don't need to separate these commands with spaces, but inserting spaces may make your screen easier to read.

To place a page number in a header or footer automatically, you type &p in the text box. This command makes Works print consecutive page numbers, starting with the number 1. To place the page number where you want, combine &p with other commands such as &c. Add justification to your page numbers by adding the justification command to the front of the command string. The command &rPage &p causes Works to print right-justified page numbers preceded by the word *Page* and a space (see fig. 3.13).

If you don't want headers and footers to appear on your title page, choose the Title Page command on the Format menu. This option prevents Works from printing headers and footers on the first page.

To begin automatic page numbering with a number other than 1, define the starting number by using the Set Page # command on the

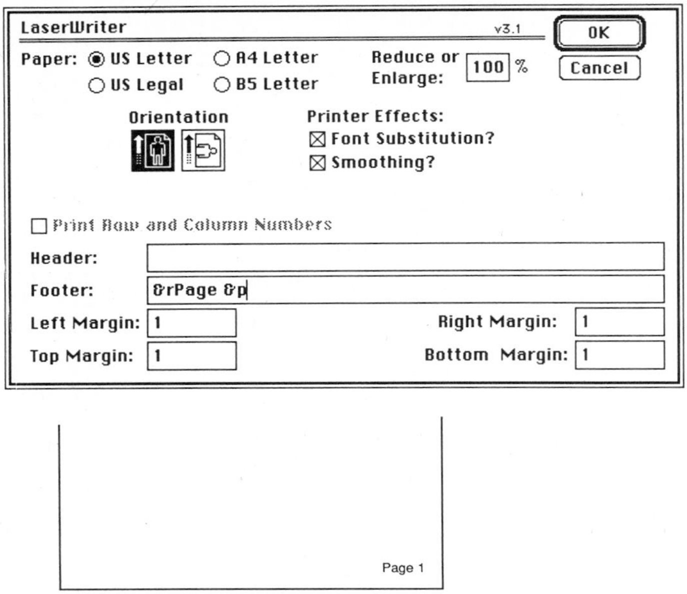

**Fig. 3.13**

*Combining text and a justification command with the page number.*

Format menu. This method is useful for consecutively numbering pages in large documents that you have broken into chapters and stored in separate files.

Suppose, for example, that you are working on a project so big that you cannot fit it all in memory at one time. You enter, edit, and save the first 30 pages in a file. Then you close that document. Your computer's memory is cleared, so you can start a new file to continue the project. Because your first chapter (file) has 30 pages, you set the starting page number at 31 for the second chapter (file).

**TIP:** If you don't want your title page or table of contents page to have a page number but you want the page following to be page number 1, enter a 0 in the Set Starting Page # box. This trick works only if you choose All Pages in the Print dialog box. You cannot specify page 0 as the first page number to print when you are using the From and To boxes.

# Adding Style to Your Documents

Your Macintosh is more than a simple typewriter. Your computer contains graphics routines that allow you to alter all typefaces in logical ways. You can make typefaces bold or italic, and underline them, in addition to creating both shadow and outline effects. Works also enables you to use superscripts and subscripts.

All these features are available throughout your document by using simple menu selection. These features allow you to add emphasis to your document and to create reader interest in your work. Font style commands are available throughout the Works modules. (Changes made to the word processor can be local or global, changes to the database or spreadsheet are global—they change the entire document.)

In figure 3.14, you can see examples of all these formats, which usually are available for any font. You can mix and match type styles, point sizes, color, and other formatting attributes. You can make these choices either before or after you type something.

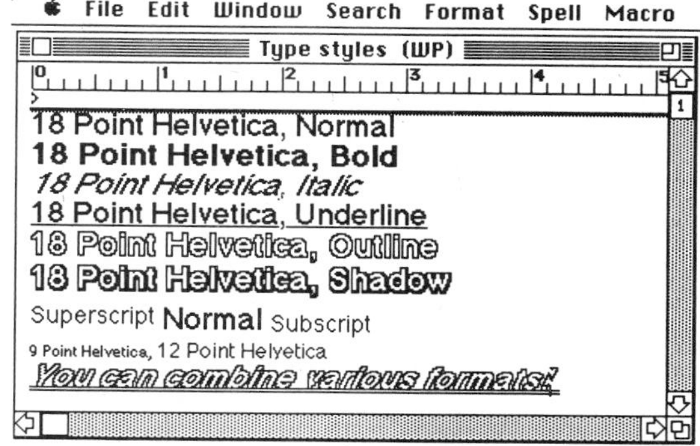


**Fig. 3.14**

*Examples of styles and point sizes.*

Your system contains several basic fonts supplied by Apple. You can use Font/DA Mover to add fonts to your system, add fonts to Works (or any other application), or create suitcase files. You can access suitcase files with the Suitcase II and Font/DA Juggler utilities. You can use these utilities to add fonts to your Works Font submenu. Many fonts are in the public domain, and you can find many proprietary commercial fonts.

The default fonts for Works are 10-point Boston and 9-point Geneva; if you don't load Boston into your system from your Works disk by using Font/DA Mover, Geneva becomes the default.

The appearance of your printed text is different from that on-screen because of the difference in resolution (dots per inch). Line endings and page breaks don't change, but overall sharpness, smoothness, character spacing, and other design elements do. The kind of printer you use and its physical condition also affect the quality of the printed piece. Also important to your final output is whether the font is a bit-mapped font or a PostScript font.

PostScript fonts print to the resolution of the printer (see Chapter 1). All Adobe and Apple LaserWriter fonts are PostScript; all fonts intended for use on the ImageWriter are bit-mapped. Examples of bit-mapped fonts are Chicago, Geneva, Monaco, and New York; examples of PostScript fonts are Helvetica, Times, Bookman, and Palatino. Some fonts can be one or the other (like Courier), depending on the source. Figure 3.15 shows various styles of Helvetica output on a laser printer. Compare that output to the screen shown in figure 3.14.

**Fig. 3.15**

*Examples of Macintosh type styles and attributes on a laser printer.*

24 Point Helvetica
9 Point Helvetica

12 Point Normal
**Bold**
*Italic*
Underline
Outline
Shadow
SuperscriptNormalSubscript

*Attributes can be combined!*

The commands that you use to change type font style, size, and color are shown in figure 3.16. Type is available in a number of sizes, which is measured in points (see fig. 3.14). The lower the number, the smaller the type—10-point Geneva is smaller than 24-point Geneva. However, because designs vary, one 10-point typeface may be slightly larger or smaller than another 10-point typeface. There are 72 points in an inch, which allows 6 lines of 12-point type. Another size scale often used is *picas*. There are 12 picas in an inch (6 points to a pica).

Not all point sizes in every font look good when displayed, especially sizes that have not been installed. Installed sizes for each font are outlined in the Size submenu. You can use uninstalled point sizes, but they appear jagged on-screen and print poorly.

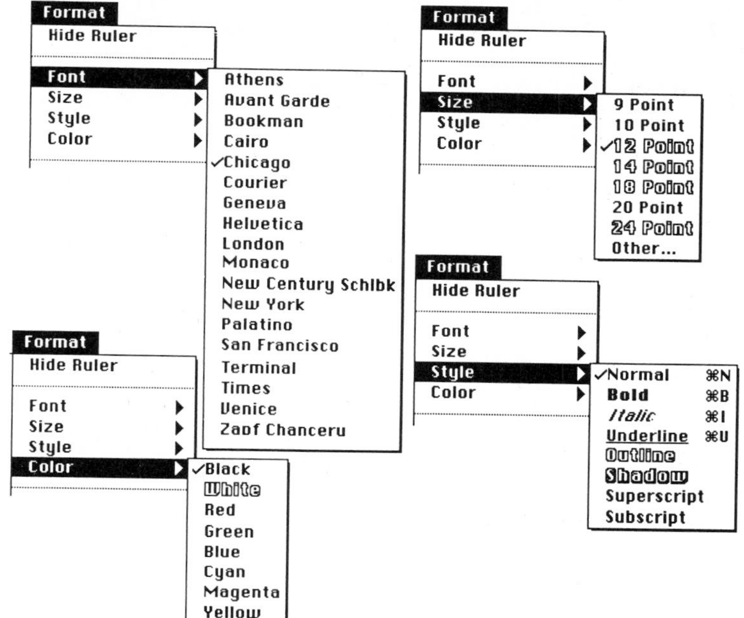


**Fig. 3.16**

*Type font, size, color, and style commands.*

Sometimes you may want to use an uninstalled point size. When you do this, your ImageWriter printer uses a point size twice as large as the uninstalled size you have chosen in the document, and scales the larger type accordingly when printing. Keep this in mind and try to select an uninstalled type size that has a corresponding installed size that is twice as large. (An ImageWriter LQ uses this procedure with font sizes three times that chosen.)

## *Changing Type Sizes and Styles*

To change type size or style, select the text that you want to change. You can select single words, paragraphs, or an entire document (use the Select All command). Pull down the Font or Style submenu from the Format menu (see fig. 3.17). After you make your choices, the results appear on-screen. In figure 3.17, the heading has been selected. It will be printed in 24-point bold outline type. Compare this to the original screen, shown in figure 2.4.

If you select some text and then choose the Normal Text option on the Style submenu, Works eliminates all formatting such as bold, italic,

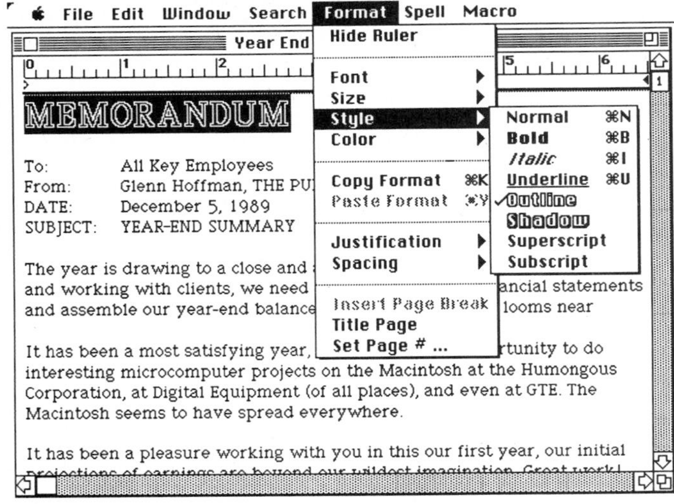


**Fig. 3.17**

*Selecting text, changing point size and style.*

underline, and so forth. Works does not change the point size or type style, however. To change these features, you must select the text and choose a new point size from the Style submenu or change the font from the Font submenu.

Works has keyboard shortcuts for style choices, such as ⌘-B for bold, ⌘-I for italic, ⌘-U for underline, and ⌘-N for normal type.

To remove bold, italic, or underlining, press ⌘-N; anything you type will be in normal text until you apply formatting again. No shortcuts are available for outline, shadow, superscript, or subscript attributes.

**NOTE:** Different typefaces take up different amounts of space on a page, so you may need to adjust margins and page endings after changing fonts.

## *Special Characters*

Many special fonts have been developed for the Macintosh, including foreign language, symbol, and even picture fonts. Standard Macintosh fonts have other symbols that may be accessed using the modifier keys (Shift, Control, and Option). You can locate these symbols using the Key Caps desk accessory.

In figure 3.18, you can see a selection of some special characters and some picture fonts. Remember: Different fonts offer different special characters. If a word contains special characters and you change its font, Works may display or print the wrong special character.

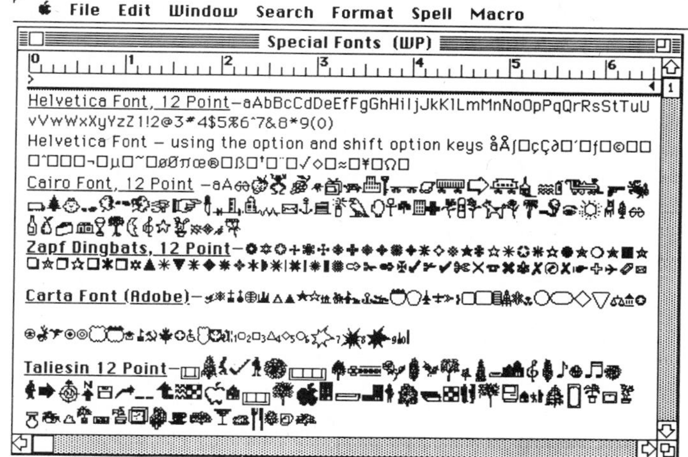


**Fig. 3.18**

*Special characters and picture fonts.*

Many people prefer the appearance of dashes created by holding the Shift or Option key while pressing the hyphen key. These dashes are called *em* and *en* dashes. The em dash is the same width as the selected font's letter m. An en dash is the same size as the width of the selected font's letter n (about half the size of an m).

Both dashes are wider and more pronounced than a hyphen. The em- and en-dash sizes are commonly used as references for the size of a particular typeface and point size.

To create an em dash, press Shift-Option and the hyphen key. To create an en dash, press the Option and hyphen keys together. On-screen, em dashes look larger than normal dashes, and en dashes look smaller. When you search for en and em dashes with the search features, enter your search criteria in the same way you entered the dashes originally.

The regular Works quotation marks look like typewriter quotation marks. For a typeset look, try creating single or double "curly" quotation marks by pressing Shift, Option, and either bracket key together. The Key Caps desk accessory will help you find fonts and keystrokes in which you can use these kinds of quotation marks.

To generate the three dots that make up an ellipsis, hold down the Option key while pressing the semicolon to generate the . . . character.

Ellipses are used in the Macintosh menu for any command that requires additional action (like filling in a dialog box). If you type an ellipsis in text this way, enter the search request the same way.

The Macintosh and Works both support ligatures such as œ and æ. Just press the option key and the appropriate letter key (consult the Key Caps window to see where the ligatures are located and what they look like when displayed). Press the Shift key if you need uppercase ligatures, such as Œ and Æ.

## *Line Spacing and Font Sizes*

Line spacing is a paragraph formatting attribute. To change the line spacing in your document, follow these steps (see fig. 3.19):

1. Position the insertion point in the paragraph you want to change, or select multiple paragraphs or the whole document.
2. Choose the Spacing command on the Format menu.
3. Select your choice of spacing in the Spacing submenu.

You can select spacing before you begin typing or after you have entered the text. Works has four spacing options: single, 1 1/2 spaces, double, and six lines per inch. The first three options are identical to typewriter spacing options; six lines per inch is a standard spacing found on many preprinted forms.

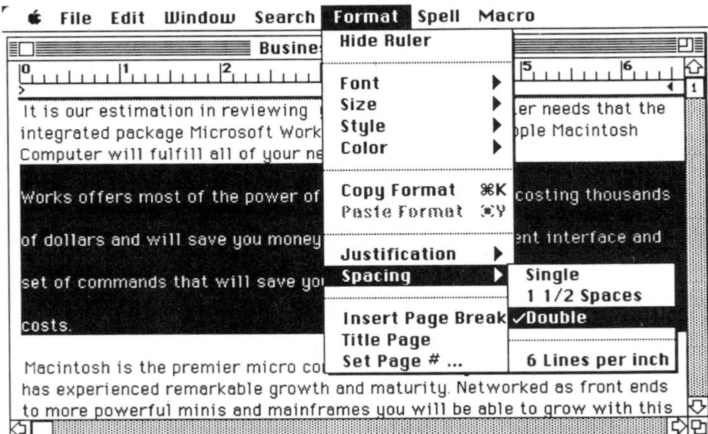


**Fig. 3.19**

*Changing line spacing.*

Blank lines vary in height, just as lines containing text vary in height. Typographers use the term *leading* (pronounced ledding) to describe the size of blank lines. Leading is the space between lines of type, and it is measured in points. A line of 10-point type is commonly set as 10 on 12, which means that the line contains 10 points of type and 2 points of leading.

In a 10-point font, for example, if you measure from the top of the tallest character (h or t) to the bottom of a descender (p or y), that will be 10 points. If you measure from the top of the tallest character of one line to the top of the tallest character of the next line, it will be 12 points—there are 2 points of leading between the lines. It is this leading that prevents the lines of type within a paragraph from touching. In a document using 10 on 12 leading, a blank line is also set as 10 on 12—10 points of blank line and 2 points of leading.

You can change the paragraph spacing by first selecting a blank line and then changing the selected font or type size in order to create the desired effect. For example, to create a larger-than-normal space between paragraphs, choose a bigger font size for the blank lines. To squeeze paragraphs, make the blank lines a smaller size than that used for text. Figure 3.20 shows two 12-point paragraphs separated by an 18-point blank line.

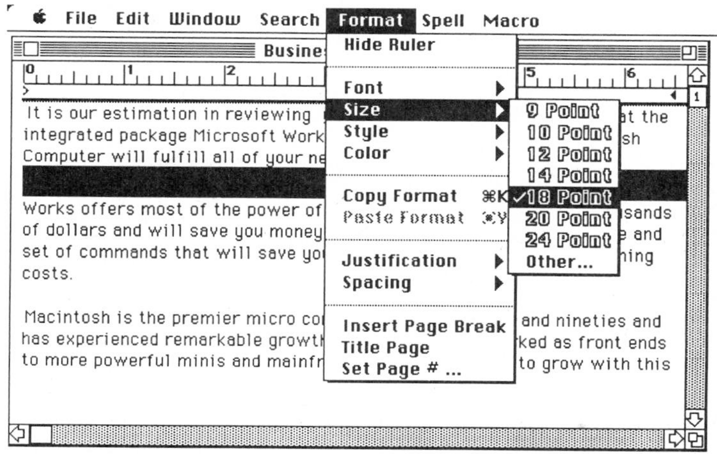


**Fig. 3.20**

*Two 12-point paragraphs separated by an 18-point blank line.*

# *Justification of Text*

Justification is a form of text alignment. Works offers you three choices: left alignment, right alignment, or fully-justified text. Left-aligned text has a ragged right edge, and right-aligned text has a ragged left edge. Sometimes you hear the terms flush left and flush right used for these styles. Fully-justified text is aligned on both edges. This book uses fully-justified text.

Works achieves fully-justified text by inserting spacing between words. Justification is an important overall styling feature and is discussed more fully in Chapter 5, "Graphics and Design." Figure 3.21 shows the various types of justification.

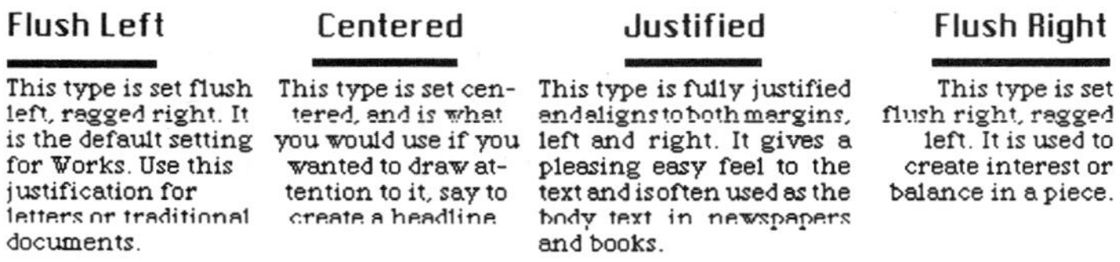

**Fig. 3.21.**

*The various types of justification.*

Flush Left
This type is set flush left, ragged right. It is the default setting for Works. Use this justification for letters or traditional documents.
Centered
This type is set centered, and is what you would use if you wanted to draw attention to it, say to create a headline.
Justified
This type is fully justified and aligns to both margins, left and right. It gives a pleasing easy feel to the text and is often used as the body text in newspapers and books.
Flush Right
This type is set flush right, ragged left. It is used to create interest or balance in a piece.



To align text between margins, select the text and then choose the Left, Center, Right, or Justified command on the Justify submenu of the Format menu. You can center single lines, paragraphs, or entire documents this way. Remember that if you select leading or trailing spaces, Works includes them in the centering process. The default text justification is flush left; that is, Works places the first word of every line at the left margin. Changing justification as you go changes all subsequent text. To change previously typed paragraphs, select them and make your changes.

Because Works does not automatically hyphenate words, the program occasionally must insert quite a bit of space on a particular line to create flush-left and flush-right margins. If you find this process annoying, either hyphenate words manually or purchase additional software, such as WorksPlus Spell, which performs automatic hyphenation.

## *Summary of Keyboard Shortcuts*

In these word processing chapters, you have learned the keyboard shortcuts for the commands. Table 3.2 lists the Works ⌘-key shortcuts. You may find the shortcuts so useful that you will want to keep table

3.2 near your Macintosh until the commands become second nature. These shortcuts will save you many "trips to the mouse," a real plus for fast typists.

**Table 3.2**
**Word Processing ⌘-Key Shortcuts**

| *Keystroke* | *Action* |
|---|---|
| ⌘-B | Turns bold on/off |
| ⌘-C | Copies selected item to Clipboard |
| ⌘-F | Finds (invokes Find menu) |
| ⌘-G | Go to Page # menu |
| ⌘-I | Turns italic on/off |
| ⌘-J | Draw on/Draw off |
| ⌘-K | Copies paragraph format |
| ⌘-M | Prepares to merge (see Chapter 13) |
| ⌘-N | Turns on normal text (turns off bold, italic, superscript, subscript, and so on) |
| ⌘-O | Opens file (invokes Open File dialog box) |
| ⌘-P | Prints (invokes Print menu) |
| ⌘-Q | Quits (asks about saving and exits Works) |
| ⌘-R | Invokes Replace menu |
| ⌘-S | Saves (using last-used file name unless untitled) |
| ⌘-U | Turns underline on/off |
| ⌘-V | Pastes from Clipboard |
| ⌘-W | Closes window |
| ⌘-X | Cuts selected item to Clipboard |
| ⌘-Y | Pastes paragraph format |
| ⌘-Z | Undoes (attempts to undo last action) |
| ⌘-, (comma) | Activates window shown at bottom of Window menu |
| ⌘-. (period) | Stops printing and macro execution |

# Part III

# Graphics and Design

## Includes

Drawing

Graphics and Design

# 4

# Drawing

Works contains a full-featured draw module, which is accessible to both the word processor and spreadsheet modules. You can use it to enhance word processing documents, and you also can use it in spreadsheets and graphs, as described in Chapter 7, "Graphs." In this chapter you learn about all the draw tools; grouping, sizing, and moving objects; working with text objects; and manipulating graphics between the different Works modules by means of the Clipboard. Draw provides all the features necessary to create high-quality desktop publishing projects. Works contains features (for example, spreading text along a line) that are otherwise only available in graphics programs that cost many hundreds of dollars.

The Works draw module creates object-oriented graphics. Sometimes this type of program is referred to as vector graphics because each point created has a position and a directional quality to it. As a result, a collection of points can be described by mathematical equations that allow the points to be grouped as an object. Objects can be squares, ovals, and lines. Even lines created by hand (freehand) are objects. Works has tools (contained in a Toolbox) to create these objects and can fill them with a pattern. This pattern can even be in color (onscreen) and will print in color to a color output device. These features are described in Chapter 5, "Graphics and Design." Objects are bounded by lines that can have various line weights (thicknesses) and patterns. Perhaps the best feature of the Works draw module is the capability to create fully-formatted text objects and to link these objects, a feature that makes multicolumn documents possible.

Objects also can be manipulated; you can change size, location, shape, and pattern, but you must work with the whole object. A circle cannot be broken apart to make a pie slice or half circle, for example. Objects, both text and graphics, can be cut, copied, or pasted from one word processor document to another, and from a word processor to a spreadsheet (with some restrictions, which are discussed in this chapter).

When the draw module is activated, pictures are drawn on a layer "above" your word processing text. This separate layer means that changes you make to the draw layer do not affect your text (see fig. 4.1), and you can flow text around a graphic object if you want. Note that the rectangular object has a transparent and an opaque (black part) pattern or color, called a *fill*. Transparent objects show the underlying objects or text, but opaque objects do not. You can use the draw layer to block out underlying text if you want. Transparent draw objects show the text beneath it.

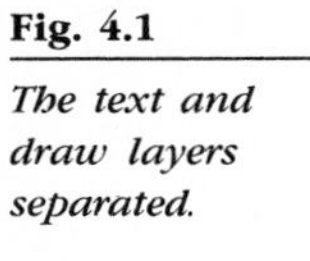

**Fig. 4.1**

*The text and draw layers separated.*

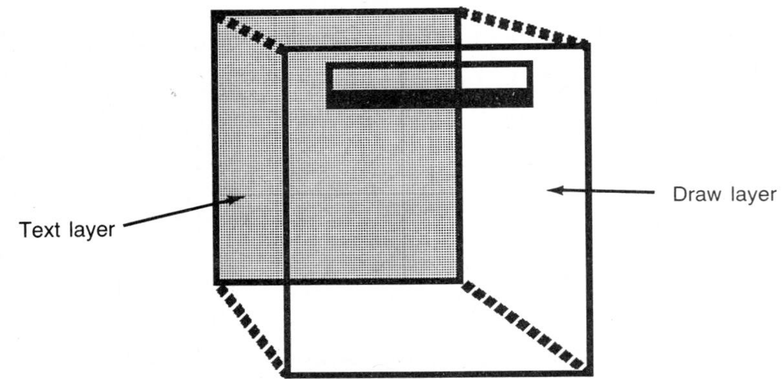


When you draw a group of objects, Works remembers the order in which they were drawn. This order structures a layering of objects so that each object drawn is considered to be in front of the preceding object. The first object drawn is at the back; the last object drawn is at the front. You may find it necessary to change the order of objects that overlap so that you can work with them or view them. The section titled "Moving and Selecting," elsewhere in this chapter, tells you how to work with these objects.

## *Starting the Drawing Process*

The Works word processor has two modes: the text editing mode and the drawing mode. You use only one mode at a time. To toggle between the two modes, select the Draw On command or the Draw Off command on the Edit menu, or use the ⌘-J keyboard equivalent. When you select the Draw On command, the word processing menu changes as shown in figure 4.2, and a Toolbox (or palette) appears on-screen. New menus are provided, including the Fill Pattern and Line Pattern menus, and a number of new commands are activated on the Format menu. In the Line Pattern menu you can select any pattern indicated, white (or opaque), or a transparent fill, as indicated by the slashed zero box. The Line Pattern and Fill Pattern menus have identical menu choices, but separate functions.

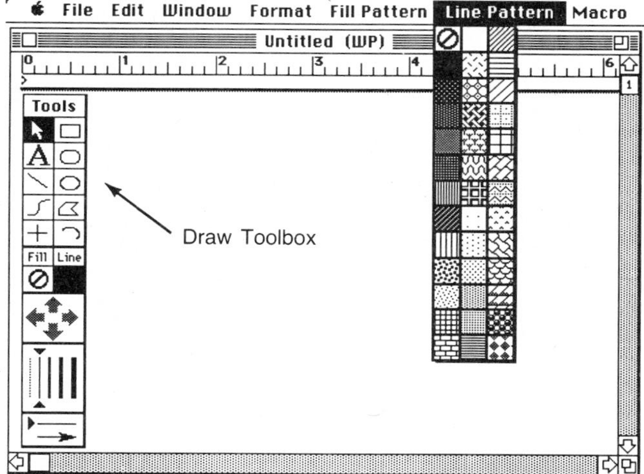


**Fig. 4.2**

*Selecting the Draw command and associated menu changes.*

## *The Drawing Tools*

The Works draw Toolbox contains a number of features that you can use to create objects. These features are identified in figure 4.3. Typically, using a modifier key changes the type of shape or the action of the tool selected. The Shift key enables you to draw perfect shapes, such as straight lines, squares, and circles. At the top of the Toolbox is a title bar with the word "Tools" on it. You drag this bar to reposition the Toolbox on the screen.

The first step in drawing an object is to decide what line weight and line (or fill) pattern you want. You can select a black, white, patterned, or transparent line weight or pattern. The transparent symbol, the

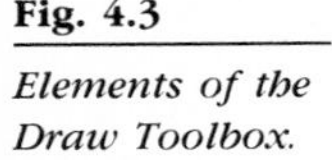

**Fig. 4.3**

*Elements of the Draw Toolbox.*

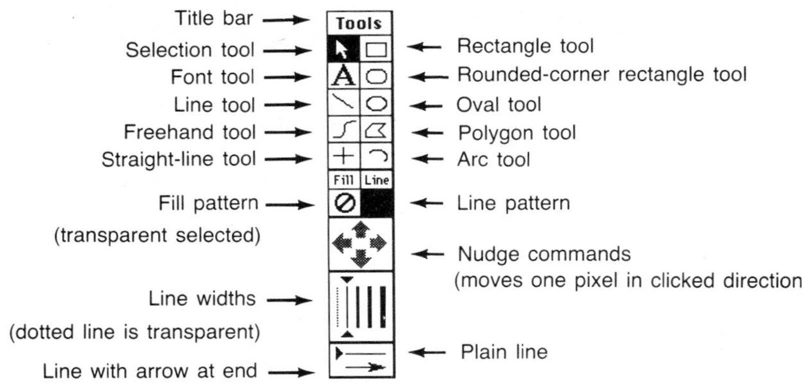


slashed zero, is the default fill and is used when you have not selected a fill. The shape of an object is determined by the tool you click in the Toolbox. In figure 4.3 the Selection tool is selected. Text objects are somewhat different from drawn objects and are discussed in this chapter in a subsequent section called "Working with Text Objects." To draw an object, follow these steps:

1. Choose Draw On in the Edit menu, or press ⌘-J.
2. Select first the line pattern and then the fill pattern from the Line Pattern and Fill Pattern menus. Selections will be shown in the Toolbox in the two boxes below the words `Line` and `Fill`.
3. In the Toolbox, select the tool with which you want to work. Your cursor turns into a cross on the screen.
4. Place the cursor where you want your object to begin.
5. Hold down the mouse button and drag the mouse down and to the right until the object is the correct size, then release the button.

You can change a line weight, line or fill pattern, or color at any time. You do this by clicking the object to select it and then making your new choices in the Line Pattern and Fill Pattern menus or the Line Weight selector in the Toolbox.

You can change the color of the dots, or *pixels*, that make up the image, and thereby change the color of an object. A pixel, or picture element, contains a number of bits of data assigned to each dot on your screen. A pixel is the dot in the *dots per inch* measurement that defines resolution. Most current Macintosh computers that use color use a 4-bit or an 8-bit video board to define a pixel, which yields a color palette of either 16 or 256 colors. System 7.0 supports 32-bit QuickDraw with 24 bits of color, yielding a palette of 16.8 million colors.

To change the color of an object, select the Color-Black Dots or the Color-White Dots command. The new color appears on your screen. You have a choice of eight colors, and a total palette of 64 colors when you have equal numbers of white and black dots (gray pattern). Using the other patterns yields a much wider range of colors.

**NOTE:** If you have a black-and-white monitor, shading the white dots may result in blackening your screen. The color may not print properly (as a shade of gray) to a QuickDraw printer, but will print correctly to a PostScript printer. See the section titled "Working with Color" in Chapter 5.

Figure 4.4 shows a rounded rectangle that has been drawn, and the starting and ending point for the drag. After you draw an object, Draw changes back to the Selection tool; your object is selected; and you can move, resize, or edit the object. A selected object has small black squares around it called *handles*, which define the limits of the object. These handles are used to resize or reshape the object. If you intend to use a tool again to create the same kind of object, you can bypass the Selection tool by holding down the ⌘ key while drawing your object.

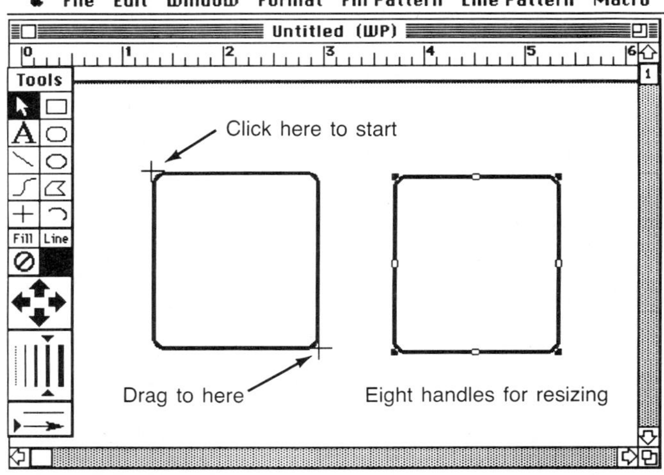


**Fig. 4.4**

*Drawing a rounded rectangle.*

To move an object, drag a section of the object other than its handles. For a transparent-filled object, you must click a side (or line) defining the object. To resize or reshape an object, drag its handle.

If you want to move an object below the page break at the end of a document, you need to create a workspace at the end of your text. You create this workspace by adding blank space. Press the Return key until you have enough space to work in. You then can scroll to see the entire object.

To draw simple lines, select the Line tool from the Toolbox. You also can choose line weight (width), choose to have a plain line, or choose a line with an arrow at the end. Lines can be drawn to any length or angle you desire, and you can resize and alter the lines after drawing them. If you want to draw a line with an arrow at the end, click the arrow icon at the bottom of the Toolbox (see fig. 4.3). Use the plain line icon to draw plain lines.

Draw vertical and horizontal lines by following these instructions:

1. Click the Straight-line tool.
2. Hold down the Shift key.
3. Click a starting point.
4. Drag in the desired direction.

To constrain a line, press and hold down the Shift key (the modifier key) while drawing the line. Holding the Shift key enables you to create horizontal and vertical lines as well as lines at 45- or 90-degree angles. To move a line, click the line, then drag it where you want it. You can resize or change the slope of a line by clicking either selection handle and dragging it to the new location.

Arcs are created with the Arc tool in the Toolbox. Arcs are 90 degrees when drawn, and the direction of the draw determines its curvature. After you have finished drawing the arc, you can extend it by dragging a selection handle up to 360 degrees. In this way, you can complete the entire oval or circle (the arc is a section of this shape) as shown in figure 4.5. Use the Shift modifier key to draw arcs. The arc is drawn to a quarter circle.

The Freehand tool creates lines that follow your hand motion and are unconstrained. Curves are described by mathematical equations for each piece of the line that can best be described as an arc. Arcs are connected to form the curve, and a handle is placed at the point of inflection (where the slope changes direction). After you complete a curve you can move it by dragging a piece of the line. You can reshape pieces of the line by dragging a handle. Figure 4.5 illustrates features of curves.

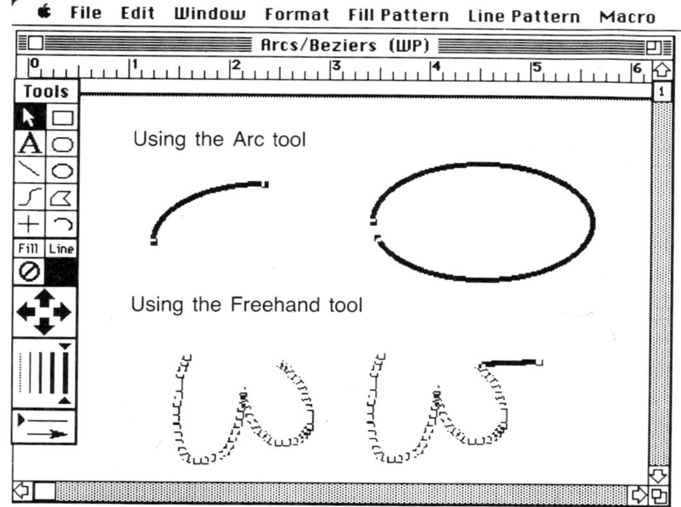


**Fig. 4.5**

*Using the Arc tool to create arcs, and the Freehand tool to create curves.*

You can draw rectangles, rectangles with rounded corners (*rounded rectangles*), and ovals by using the tools that correspond to these shapes: the Rectangle, Rounded-corner Rectangle, and Oval tools. They all work similarly. After you choose the line thickness, fill, and line pattern, shapes are drawn as shown in figure 4.4. It is also possible to draw the perfect shapes of squares, rounded corner squares, and circles by pressing the Shift modifier key while drawing these objects.

*Polygons* are irregular objects with any number of straight sides (no curves), and are drawn differently from other objects. To draw a polygon, follow these steps:

1. Select the Polygon tool in the Toolbox.
2. Click the cross cursor where you want the polygon to begin.
3. Move the cross cursor to the location of the first corner of the polygon and click. Your cursor remains in the cross shape. A line is drawn between this point and the point you created in Step 2.
4. Click the next corner of the polygon to form the second line.
5. Continue to click for each corner.

6. To close the polygon, click the starting point again, or double-click anywhere else to create an open polygon.

The process for creating a polygon is illustrated in figure 4.6. When you select a polygon, handles appear at each corner. The polygon in the lower right corner of fig. 4.6 was selected and its line weight and fill pattern subsequently changed.

**Fig. 4.6**

*Creating a polygon.*

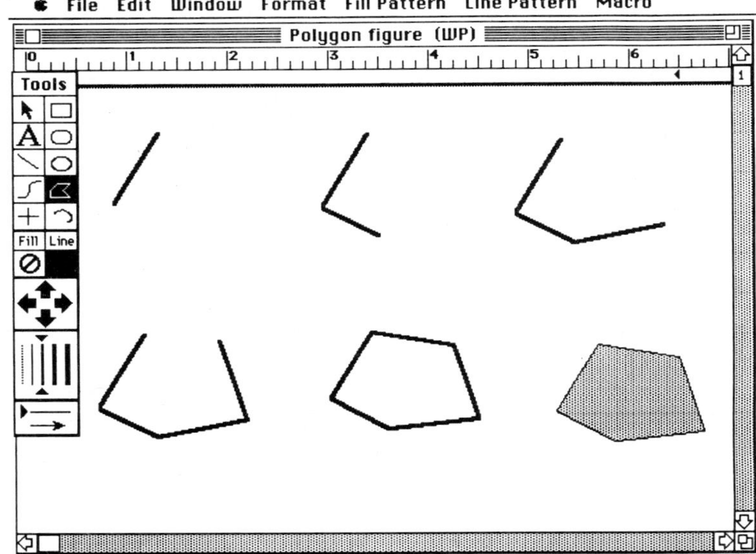


If you make a mistake while creating the polygon, use the Undo command to undo your last action. If you have a complex drawing and want to remove it, you can "cover" it with an opaque (white) shape. You need to position this replacement shape above the shape you want to cover by using the Bring to Front command, discussed in the following section, "Manipulating Objects."

If you want to resize a polygon as a whole unit, you first need to group the polygon by selecting the polygon and choosing the Group Picture command. Then, when you drag a handle, the entire polygon is resized.

## Manipulating Objects

Works enables you to manipulate objects in a variety of ways. You can move, duplicate, resize, align, and group objects. These features are described in the following sections.

You can edit any object after it is drawn. To change the object's line width, line or fill pattern, or color, make your choices in the Toolbox or in the Line Pattern and Fill Pattern menus. Previously drawn objects must be selected to be edited, and you can edit as many objects at once as are selected. You can change colors with the Colors-Black Dots and Colors-White Dots commands in the Format menu, as will be described in the section titled "Working with Color" in Chapter 5.

# *Moving and Selecting*

Objects are selected automatically when you finish drawing them. Works deactivates the Drawing tool and selects the Selection tool. When selecting an object, you place the Selection tool anywhere on the object's border, except the handles. If the object contains a fill pattern, you also can place the Selection tool inside the object. If you deselect an object by choosing another tool or by clicking the window elsewhere, you can reselect that object by choosing the Selection tool in the Toolbox (see fig. 4.3) and clicking the desired object again.

You can select multiple objects by pressing the Shift key and clicking each object. If you select an object that you do not want to be included in the group, you can deselect that object by pressing the Shift key and clicking the object once again. Using the Shift key is a general Macintosh convention to add or subtract an item from a range. An alternate method for selecting a group of objects in the same general location is to use the Selection tool. This technique also is a general Macintosh convention, which means that you can use it in most other similar programs. In summary, select an object by following these steps:

1. Choose the Selection tool on the Toolbox.
2. Click the desired object, and Shift-click any additional objects you want, or encompass the desired object with the Selection tool.

If objects overlap, it may be difficult to select the object you want. You can, however, freeze an object so that it cannot be selected. To freeze an object, select it, press the F key, and click the object. To freeze a group of objects, select all the objects you want to freeze, press the F key, and click any one of the objects. To unfreeze objects, press and hold down the F key while clicking the selected objects again.

To move an object or group of selected objects, drag that object either with a part of the line or in the filled section of the object. If the object is not filled, or transparent, you must click a line to move it. Do not try to drag an object by using one of its handles because this will resize or transform the object, not move it. Selected multiple items move as a group; you can drag any part of any one of them to move all of the items. If you create an object with many handles and little free line space, be particularly careful when you move it. In summary, to move an object, follow these steps:

1. Select the object or group of objects to be moved.
2. Place the Selection tool on the object's border, but not on a handle. If the object has a fill, you can place the Selection tool anywhere inside the object.
3. Drag the selected object to the desired location.

An alternative method for moving an object is to cut it from your document and then paste it back to your document. An object is pasted into your document at the site of your last mouse click.

The order in which each object is drawn determines the object's priority in its own layer. As discussed at the beginning of this chapter, your first object is located at the back, and your last object is at the front.

If objects overlap you may not be able to select the object you want unless you force the overlapping objects to the back by using the Send to Back command in the Format menu. Another method is to select the object you want to bring to the front by choosing the Bring to the Front command in the Format menu. Works adjusts the order of all intervening layers accordingly. This process is illustrated in figure 4.7.

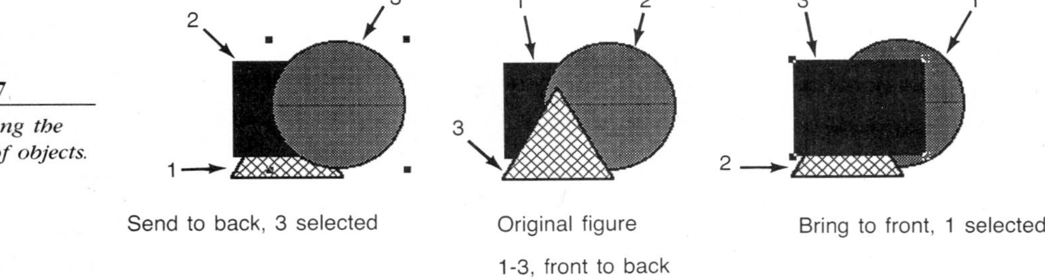


**Fig. 4.7**

*Changing the order of objects.*

## *Copying and Pasting*

The Clipboard enables you to move objects within a document or from document to document. To copy an object, you choose the Copy command in the Edit menu. You then can paste the object at any location in the word processing document or spreadsheet of your choice. The Paste command puts a duplicate object where you click. To perform a simple duplication of an object, use the Copy command followed by the Paste command to place a duplicate object slightly to the right and down, and in front of the initial object. You then can move it to the location of your choice.

Cutting an object removes the selected object from your document and places it in the Clipboard. Deleting (press the Return or Delete key) removes the selection(s) from your document without changing the contents of the Clipboard. You also can remove objects by using the Clear command in the Edit menu. (Note that Clear does not change the contents of the Clipboard.) Remember, if you remove or place an object incorrectly, you can use the Undo command to return the document to its previous state, if you have not performed any additional operations.

Works can paste an object so that it is centered exactly in front of the object of your choice. Select the object on which you want to center the copied object and choose the Paste command. The use of the Clipboard and Scrapbook are discussed further in the section titled "Importing and Exporting Graphics" at the end of this chapter.

## *Grouping and Ungrouping*

When making a complex drawing, manipulate a set of objects as a group rather than go through the process of multiple selections. Selecting a group of objects and choosing the Group Picture command transforms them into a single object with one set of boundary handles. Grouped objects do not have to be connected; once grouped, all movement and formatting changes occur to all objects in the group. You also can create groups of objects within a group by using the Group Picture command again. Figure 4.8 shows different selection conditions.

If you want to break the group apart, choose the Ungroup Picture command to separate the objects. Subsequent operations to each object changes them individually. If you have groups within a group you must apply successive Ungroup Picture commands to each group in order to separate them.

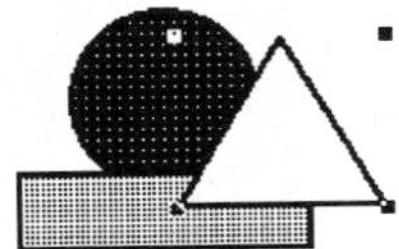

3 separate objects, one selected

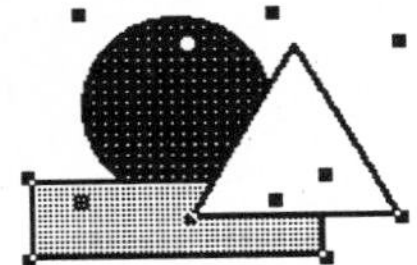

3 separate objects, all selected sequentially

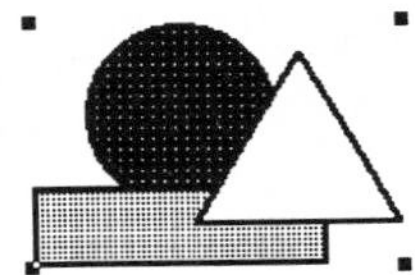

1 group of objects, selected (note the new boundary handles)

**Fig. 4.8**

*Grouping and ungrouping a set of objects.*

# *Sizing an Object*

You use an object's handles to resize it, either making it larger or smaller. This method works for all objects except arcs and polygons. A handle at the midpoint of a side resizes an object in one dimension, and a handle on a corner of an object resizes it in two dimensions. Both handles are illustrated in figure 4.9.

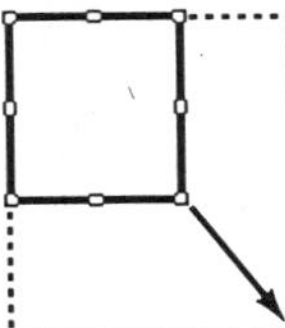

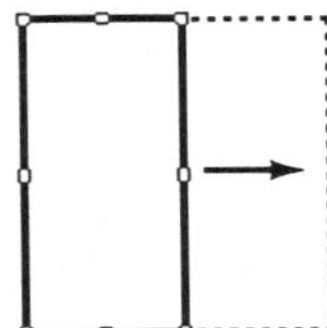

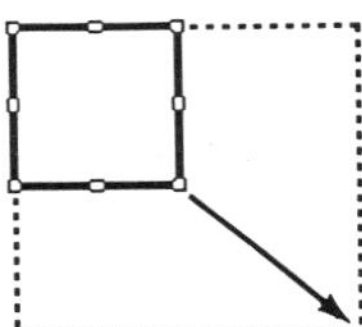

**Fig. 4.9**

*Resizing an object.*

To change the size of a perfect shape such as an equilateral triangle, a square, or a circle, select the object and press the Shift key while dragging one of the handles.

Because arcs and polygons do not contain midpoint handles, dragging the endpoints changes their shape in one dimension. You need to select and group these shapes before you can resize them in two dimensions. To resize an arc or polygon, follow these instructions:

1. Select the object.
2. Issue the Group Picture command. Works places boundary handles on the object.
3. To resize the object in two dimensions, drag a corner handle. To resize the object in one dimension, drag a midpoint handle.
4. Issue the Ungroup Picture from the Format command.

When you resize an object that contains text, the font size does not change. To change the font size, use the Size command in the Format menu.

# Aligning an Object

Works provides two methods for aligning objects on-screen. You can use the Nudge tools in the Toolbox to align objects pixel-by-pixel, or you can set an invisible grid to align objects on a larger scale.

To align objects precisely in any of the four directions, use the Nudge tools in the Toolbox. Clicking any of the four arrows moves a selected object one pixel per click. The arrow cursor keys on your keyboard have the same effect, but you can move selected objects any distance by continuing to hold down the arrow key until the object has reached the desired position.

You can use the invisible Snap To grid, which consists of vertical and horizontal lines, to help align your objects. The grid can be configured by using the Grid Setting command in the Format Menu. The resulting dialog box is shown in figure 4.10. The default setting is 1/8 inch. You turn the grid on or off by using the Grid On command in the Format menu. A check mark in front of the Grid On command in the menu indicates that the grid is on. When there is no check mark, the grid is off.

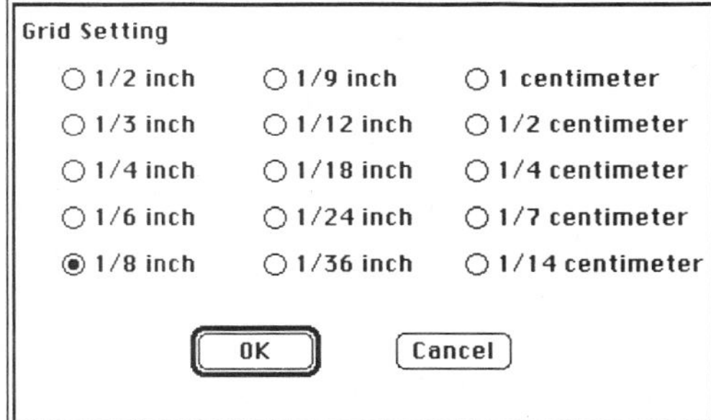


**Fig. 4.10**

*The Grid Setting dialog box.*

All objects drawn before the grid is turned on remain in place, and all objects drawn afterward snap to the nearest invisible grid line. You also can use the grid to align objects with the top, bottom, and center of any other objects, once the Grid Settings dialog box has been set. Works draws a precision grid through the sides and center of objects previously drawn. To use the grid, follow these steps:

1. Select the Grid Setting command in the Format menu.
2. Choose the spacing of your grid in the resulting dialog box, and click OK.
3. Issue the Grid On command in the Format menu.
4. When you have finished drawing and aligning your objects, choose the Grid On command again to turn off the grid.

You can put an object in precise vertical alignment with another object. Follow these steps to achieve this vertical alignment:

1. Select the object to be aligned.
2. While pressing the V key, click the second object along the point or line to which you want the first object aligned.
3. Drag the object to be moved to the desired point and release the mouse button. Works makes any needed fine adjustments.

To align two documents horizontally, use the same procedure, but this time use the H key instead of the V key. To align both horizontally and vertically use the B key. You can resize and align an object by pressing the V, H, or B key while dragging one of the object's handles.

If you want to draw a new object and have it aligned with another, press the V, H or B key, position the pointer at the desired spot and draw the object. Keep pressing the alignment key until you are finished drawing the new object. Works makes the necessary fine adjustments.

## *Working With Text Objects*

Until now, you have been working with text in the text layer of the Works word processor. The Draw layer also supports text, or any character you can type from your keyboard. Text objects (objects in the draw layer that contain text) are separate from the text in the word processing layer and share many common features with other objects previously discussed in this chapter. You can select, move, resize, fill, color, group, align, and send text objects to the back or front. In text objects, Works supports multiple fonts, styles, and sizes, but when text is printed on a printer, it is not printed as a font, but as a graphic.

Text objects allow you to create labels, paragraphs, or columns of text. Multicolumn pages similar to those found in a newspaper or magazine can be created by using text objects you create in Works.

To create a text object, select the Text tool in the Toolbox, represented by the A icon. Your cursor turns into the familiar I-beam you used in the word processing layer. As shown in figure 4.11, click the window to create a three-inch text box, or drag to create a text box of any size. Normally, the borders of a text box are displayed as a box with dashed lines. You can remove these from your display by selecting the Show Column Boxes command in the Format menu. When this command has a check in front of it (its default setting), the text box boundaries show; when there is no check, the boundaries are not visible.

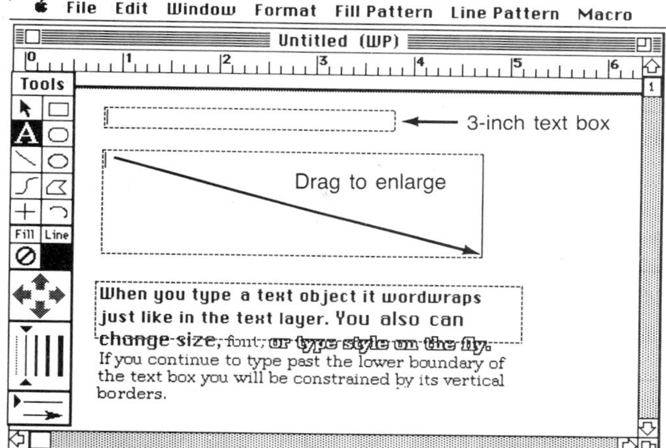


**Fig. 4.11**

*Creating text objects.*

The cursor is inserted into a text box (vertical flashing line) and as you type, Works automatically wordwraps text in a text object. Select a Font, Size, Justification, and Style from their respective submenus in the Format menu. This process is similar to that of using the word processing layer. You can change font, size, or style as you type (see fig. 4.11). Justification applies to the entire text object. Text typed into a text object is constrained by the right and left sides of the object. Additional text flows out beneath the text object, as shown in figure 4.11. When you choose the Selection tool, the text object enlarges to encompass additional text.

To edit a text object, use the Text tool in the Toolbox. Then use the I-beam cursor to select text and change the formatting, or to cut, copy, clear, delete, or paste new text from the Clipboard. The standard Macintosh commands and keystrokes are used to perform all of these functions. You can position the cursor anywhere within the text object to type additional characters or to paste more information.

# Creating Linked Columns of Text

With text objects you can create multicolumn pages by giving each text an order and by flowing text from one object to the next, while staying within the boundaries (indicated by the dashed box) of each text object. Works calls these kinds of text objects *columns* and the process of ordering them *linking*. This feature is your introduction to the world of desktop publishing.

To create a column, choose the Text tool, and press the Option key while dragging a column. You can differentiate a column from a text box by placing a header above it. For example, "Col 1 Link None" indicates that it is the first column with no link established. You can either type in this text box or paste text from another source into the text box. When text is pasted, it is formatted according to the format currently being used by that column.

Unlike the text object shown in figure 4.11, in which excess text flows out the bottom of the box, excess text for linked columns is automatically flowed into subsequent columns. The size of the column does not change as a text object does. You can readjust the size of a column, however, just like any text object. If you insert a sentence into the first column, all the other columns change to accommodate the excess text once you deselect the column. The effect of two linked columns is shown in figure 4.12.

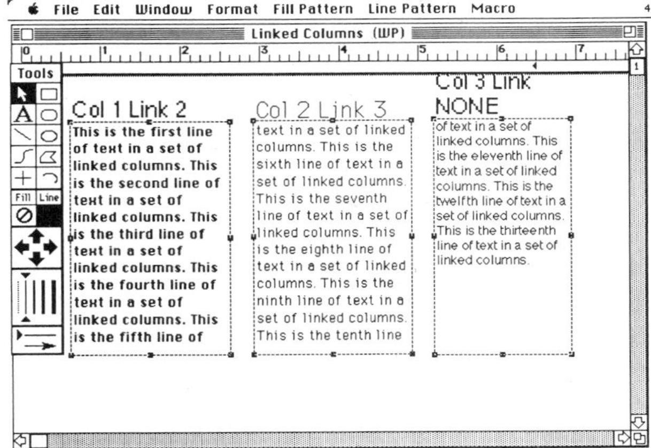


**Fig. 4.12**

*Creating and linking columns of text.*

To create a column, use the following procedure:

1. Select the Text tool in the Toolbox.

2. Move the I-beam cursor to your starting location.
3. Press the Option key while dragging the mouse to create the correct column size.
4. Type or paste your desired text.
5. Choose the Selection tool to move your column into place.

To link columns, follow these steps:

1. Choose the Selection tool.
2. Press the Option key and select each column in the order they are to be linked.

   Use the grid when you position your columns to create balanced, attractively arranged pages.

**NOTE:** You must have enough blank space in the word processing layer of a column placed at the end of a word processing document so that you can scroll the document to see the column. This is true of any object; the scroll bars are associated with the text layer.

You can have up to 32K of text in your linked columns. You will notice that the column headings change to reflect the ordering you have imposed.

Text flows in the column order you have specified, but if there is not enough text to fill a column, the next linked column will remain empty. If there is additional text beyond the last column, that text will extend below the column just as text flows out the bottom of a normal text object (see fig. 4.11). When you add or delete text, you will not see the text flow until you deselect the column. Each column has its own format, and text flowed into it will be formatted similarly.

**TIP:** The column heading contains the information necessary for Works to do the appropriate linkage. You can edit the heading manually without going through the sequence of manually selecting the link order. Use the form "Col column_name Link continuation_name" and press Return to differentiate linked columns in your document. For example, for a set of linked columns pertaining to an interview, use "Col Interview Link Interview_continued" and press Return. Note the column headings in figure 4.12. Use the Text tool to select the column heading and edit it by using the standard procedures. Headings can be any character, upper- or lowercase, but cannot include spaces. If you decide to change a set of linked column headings, start with the last heading linked to and work toward the first. If you change the heading of a column and the heading to which the link should occur does not exist, Works displays an error message. Errors such as linking to a column more than once or linking to a nonexistent column result in an error message. Works will not flow text under these circumstances.

You can turn an existing text object into a column by choosing the Selection tool and clicking the text object while holding down the Option key. When you deselect the object, it becomes a column.

## *Spreading Text*

Works provides an advanced graphics feature for spreading text along a line or an arc. This feature was used to create the text effect shown in figure I.4, and examples of it are shown in figure 4.13. To spread text along a line, place the text in the Clipboard, select a line or arc, and choose the Spread Text command in the Format menu. You do not need to select the entire text from a text object. Any piece of it, or any piece of text in the Clipboard, will do. In the examples shown in figure 4.13, a transparent line was used, but any line pattern or weight will work. All the text is placed on the line and the effect can be to condense the text or to create space between letters.

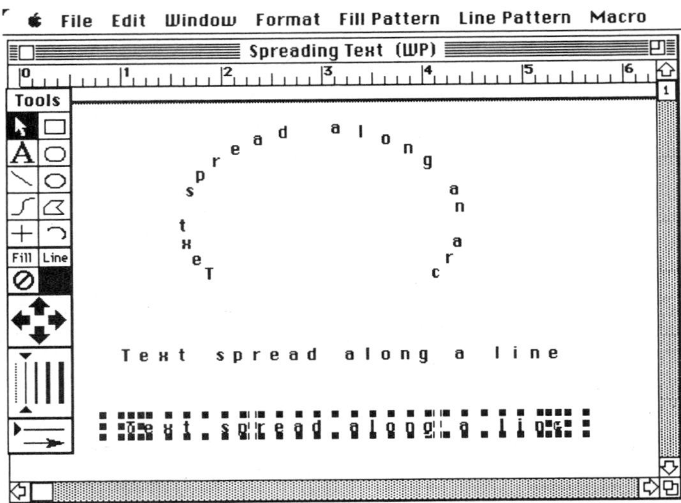


**Fig. 4.13**

*Spreading text along a line or an arc.*

Each character of text is spread out as a separate object, as shown in figure 4.13, where one of the lines of text has all the characters selected. You can select and move individual letters to create very interesting effects, which can be useful in creating logos. To compress or spread out farther the text that is spread along a line or arc, select all the text, choose the Group Picture command in the Format menu, and drag the line or arc handle to the desired position.

# *Importing and Exporting Graphics*

You already have learned about using the Clipboard to import (paste) or export (cut or copy) graphics or text between documents. You also can use Works to import/export combinations of text and graphics together. This section discusses the restrictions Works places on these operations. You may want to refer to the sections in Chapter 1 on "Working with the Clipboard" and "Working with the Scrapbook" for more information. Chapter 1 also includes information about the memory requirements the Clipboard places on certain operations (see the section called "Hardware Requirements").

You can create a single text object with multiple formats. If you paste text containing more than one format, the pasted text retains its format. If you press the Option key, pasted text takes on the format of the target text object.

When you paste a combination of text and objects, your target destination must be able to accept the selection. Whether draw is on or off also affects what can be pasted. Table 4.1 shows the possibilities.

**Table 4.1**
**Pasting Text and Object Combinations**

| *If Draw is* | *In the Clipboard* | *Works pastes* |
|---|---|---|
| Off | text | text, in the form of an object |
| | object(s) | object(s) |
| | text and object(s) | text and object(s) |
| On | text | text |
| | object(s) | object(s) |
| | text and object(s) | object(s) only |

The Clipboard can support several graphics formats, including the *PICT* standard, which is the MacPaint format. PICT (there is a related format—PICT2) draws images using the Apple proprietary graphics program, QuickDraw, at 72 dots per inch. Pasting PICT files into Works results in a graphic object in the Works draw layer. You can resize this object by using its handles in the standard way. The PICT format supports color images through the Clipboard. You can import color images into Works, but you cannot alter the colors of the resulting object through the Color-Black Dots or Color-White Dots command.

A higher resolution bit-mapped standard called *TIFF* (Tagged Image File Format) is commonly used by digital scanners. TIFF files are similar to PICT files but generally are capable of delivering much higher resolution. Currently, scanners can deliver newsletter- or newspaper-quality (150-300 dpi) resolution but cannot produce magazine- or typeset-quality (700-2500 dpi) resolution. Future developments are likely to result in higher-quality scanners.

Another class of formats transferable through the Clipboard are those created by PostScript programs. The formats include PostScript files and a form called *encapsulated PostScript (EPS)*, which contains formatting information and can be used with laser printers or typesetters. Works accepts EPS images from the Clipboard. EPS is a format commonly used in page layout programs like PageMaker, Ready, Set, Go!, and Quark XPress.

Currently, these three graphic formats are the major formats used by Macintosh applications. Other less common forms are being used also, however. A number of programs like SuperPaint, which accepts Draw and Paint images, convert between formats.

Enhanced versions of the Clipboard and the Scrapbook are available in a program package called SmartScrap and the Clipper. SmartScrap creates multiple scrapbook files that you can access as a DA from any program. The Clipper is also a DA that allows you to view and manipulate graphics in the Clipboard. You can resize graphics easily within any application by using the Clipper. These programs are recommended to anyone doing desktop publishing work.

If you create graphics and want to exchange them with other graphics, use a program called SuperGlue II. This program saves graphics in any format in a form that allows other users to view the graphics without owning the application. A similar product called OpenIt! does this as well. OpenIt! also contains an enhanced version of the Clipboard and the Scrapbook.

# Quick Reference Summary

To create a text object, follow these steps:

1. With Draw On, choose the Text tool in the Toolbox (see fig. 4.3).
2. Click the I-beam cursor at the desired position, or drag to form a larger text object (see fig. 4.11).
3. Type the text, formatting as you want. Use the Return key to form new paragraphs, and the Delete key to remove undesired keystrokes.
4. Select another drawing tool. By selecting another tool you stop creating the text object.

To insert text into a text object, do the following:

1. Choose the Text tool.
2. Click an insertion point at the desired location.
3. Type the additional text.
4. Finish by selecting another drawing tool.

To copy and paste text contained in a text object, use the following procedure:

1. Choose the Text tool.
2. Drag to select the desired text.
3. Choose the Copy command from the Edit menu to place a copy of the selected text in the Clipboard.
4. Click the insertion point of where you want to move the text.
5. Select the Paste command from the Edit menu.
6. Finish by selecting another drawing tool.

To move text contained in a text object, follow these instructions:

1. Choose the Text tool.
2. Drag to select the desired text.
3. Choose the Cut command from the Edit menu to move your selection to the Clipboard.

4. Click the insertion point of where you want to move the text.
5. Issue the Paste command from the Edit menu.
6. Finish by selecting another drawing tool.

To cut text from a text object, do the following:

1. Choose the Text tool.
2. Drag to select the desired text.
3. Choose the Clear command on the Edit menu, or use the Delete key. These actions bypass the Clipboard, leaving it unchanged. Alternatively, you can choose the Cut command from the Edit menu to place the selection on the Clipboard.
4. Finish by selecting another text tool.

5

# Graphics and Design

This chapter explores the kinds of projects that are possible by using the word processor with the draw module. Works enables you to create newsletters, advertising samples (see fig. I.4), brochures, and reports. You can also construct forms, labels (see fig. I.8), letterheads, invoices, purchase orders, and other business forms. Either use Works to draw your art, or import clip art or scanned images through the Clipboard to enliven your copy.

This chapter begins by describing some modern graphic design guidelines, which can enhance your work. You learn the procedure for creating a letterhead or logo, and how to define a grid, which you can then use to construct multicolumn designs and sample templates (saved as Stationery) to use later. Works offers some advanced techniques for making your work attractive. You can use spot color, fills and shading, text in runners, and reverses (see "The Drawing Tools" section of Chapter 4).

When in the draw module, fills and shadows are accessed from the Fills menu or by coloring objects with the color commands. Text in runners (angled headlines) are made by using the Spread Text (along a line) command. Reverses are white or light text set on top of a darker background.

Although Works is not a page layout program, you will be surprised at what it is capable of doing. Working through the examples in this chapter should give you some idea of how to use the Works draw module to create attractive projects. By now you have learned all the techniques; it's time to put all your knowledge in perspective.

# *Following Some Basic Design Guidelines*

A successfully designed project accomplishes the purpose for which it was intended. A business form gathers from or imparts to the reader the information required, an ad attracts attention in the crowded marketplace, and a newsletter gets read. Good graphic design contributes to this process by making the message logical and accessible.

What is good graphic design? In general this question has no correct answer. But your work should have an order and a balance to it; experimentation is the key. Because publishers and designers go to considerable cost and trouble to structure their products, you cannot go wrong by collecting the most attractive examples of projects similar to yours. If you have received in the mail a newsletter that you found appealing, or have filled out a form that you found easy to understand, study those designs and use some of their elements in your own work. Then test your results on others, get feedback, and make refinements. This is the design process.

Graphic elements should guide the eye toward the important points you want your work to make. Elements should be balanced, in proportion, and have contrast. Contrast, the balance of text and graphics with white space, is crucial. Perhaps the most common mistake in design is to present too much detail and overwhelm the reader. Your Macintosh gives you the power to use as many typefaces and styles as you care to install. Experience reveals, however, that judicious use of one or two fonts per page is all that is needed. More variety tends only to confuse the eye. Restraint and brevity are goals to be sought.

Conventional wisdom suggests that you use a *sans serif* font for headings, and *serif* fonts for your body copy. Serifs are the small cross strokes at the characters' ascenders and descenders. Some examples of the different font types are shown in figure 5.1. Note that sans serif fonts have a block-like or display-type quality that gives them a boldness consistent with headlines. Three commonly used header/body combinations are Helvetica/Times, Avant Garde/Bookman, and Optima/Souvenir.

A modern approach is to use certain specially designed single-font families (such as Adobe's Stone font) for both display and copy. Stone has a similar serif and sans serif font family. When in doubt, collect the full representation of a single font (like Helvetica, Helvetica Narrow, Helvetica Black, and so on) and use that font by itself. Most important

**SANS SERIF FONTS**

HELVETICA — classic, traditional header, laser font.

Avant Garde — modern display face, laser font.

Stone Sans Serif — Adobe's new display face, laser font.

**Chicago – modern display font, Apple's system font, bit mapped.**

Geneva — modern Helvetica copy, Apple's system font, bit mapped.

**SERIF FONTS**

Times Roman — classic body font, normally a laser font.

Palatino — transitional body font, laser font.

Bookman — modern body font, laser font.

Stone Serif — Adobe's new body font, laser font.

Courier – modern typewriter font, laser or bit mapped.

New York — modern body font, Apple's system font, bit mapped.

**Fig. 5.1**

*Examples of serif and sans serif fonts.*

is to consider the output device and to choose bit-mapped or PostScript fonts as appropriate.

When doing layout work for material like manuals, reports, or any multipage document, creating a consistent format is a good idea. Standard margins and a sense of how your right and left pages look together are the elements of design. Have you ever noticed that books, such as the one you are reading now, usually maintain a standard layout throughout? This layout gives the reader a sense of continuity, and design elements can attract attention to important details like warnings or chapter titles. Being consistent without being boring involves bringing contrast and the element of surprise into your work.

## *Creating Letterheads and Logos*

You may want to create a letterhead for your personal or professional use. Generally, this project requires only a one-column text arrangement. You can use the design layer for your letterhead, and the text layer for your letter.

To set up this type of design, follow these instructions:

1. Insert enough carriage-return characters to enable you to scroll your graphic.

   The number of carriage returns necessary is a judgment you must make based on the size of the graphic you want to insert.

You always can go to the text layer (by choosing Draw Off from the Edit menu) and add or delete carriage returns as necessary.

2. Switch to the draw layer by choosing the Draw On command from the Edit menu.
3. Create your letterhead graphic, or insert your logo.
4. Switch back to the text layer (choose Draw Off), and position the insertion point at the appropriate place. For a letterhead, this spot might be where you would insert the date.
5. Save your work as Stationery (both the draw and text layers are saved). When you reopen the file, Works presents an untitled copy on-screen, leaving your original on disk.
6. Type your letter.

You can use logos or add borders to your finished letter in the draw layer, but you cannot implement a multicolumn layout or wraparound graphics when typing in the text layer. These features require the use of columns in the draw layer and are described in this chapter's section on "Creating a Multicolumn Layout."

## Working with a Grid

A *grid* allows you to place and align headlines, body copy, artwork, margins, and borders so that your work looks balanced. Because you use grids to define column sizes and spacings, defining a grid structure is logically the first decision you need to make when designing a multi-column project. With most of the major desktop publishing programs, such as PageMaker, Ready,Set,Go!, and Quark Xpress, you begin the design process by defining a grid structure. A dialog box that allows you to set a grid is the first one you see when you're using one of these programs. Once you define margin sizes, the number of columns, and spacing, you see on-screen a page marked with dotted lines that indicate your choices.

Because you can define grids in Works (see fig. 4.10 in Chapter 4) that have spacings as small as 1/14 of a centimeter, or 1/36 of an inch, you have no real limitation on the number of columns you can define or the spacings you can set. The real problem is visualizing where each column is. Unlike layout programs, Works doesn't make its grid visible to you on the screen. The program doesn't display your columns with intervening spacing or even show you the margins of your choice until you mark your page boundaries and view the page with the Print Preview feature (see "Fonts, Printers, and Networks" in Chapter 1). But you can get around this problem.

The solution lies in creating temporary markers, which produce a visible grid that you create at the beginning of your layout. Figure 5.2 shows an example of a grid structure viewed in the Page Preview mode.

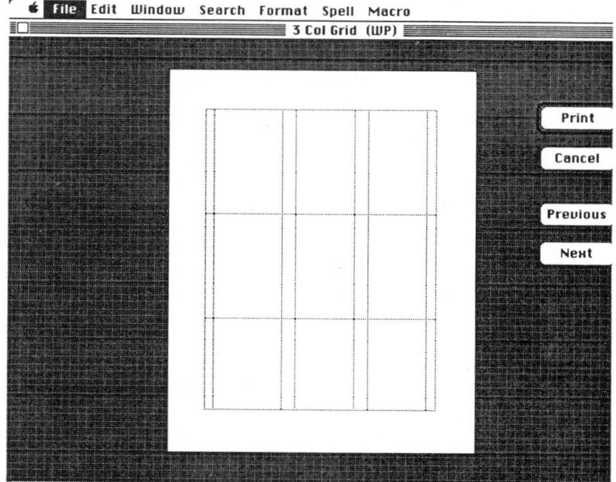


**Fig. 5.2**

*Setting a visible layout grid in the draw module.*

To set up your grid structure, use the following procedure:

1. Begin by defining your page size and margins in the Page Setup dialog box. In the example shown in figure 5.2, the page is letter size (8.5 inches by 11 inches) with 1-inch margins all around.

2. In the text layer, insert enough carriage returns to bring you to the first line of page 2. You then see the dashed line of the automatic page break. This step allows you to scroll the draw layer and see all your graphics. (Remember that the size of the scroll bars is associated with the text layer.)

3. All the remaining work for multicolumn layout is done in the draw layer. Choose the Draw On command from the Edit menu (press ⌘-J).

4. Use the Format menu's Grid Setting command to pick a grid size. In figure 5.2, the grid size is 1/8 inch.

5. Turn on the grid by choosing the Grid On command, also found on the Format menu.

6. To create a multicolumn array, begin by choosing the rectangle tool, and pick a line fill pattern (from the Line Pattern menu) that displays a dotted line all around and encloses your work space on the screen. Some patterns show either only horizontal or only vertical lines, so you may want to experiment. The lines shown in figure 5.2 used the solid gray pattern located three boxes below the transparent pattern box. Leave a 1/8-inch margin all around so that you can see your boundary box on all sides.

7. Next, add your column boxes, by using the Rectangle tool and leaving the correct column spacings. You can draw the first column and then duplicate it by selecting it, copying it, and pasting it. (For more information on drawing columns, see the next section, "Creating a Multicolumn Layout.")

   Normally you will want to subdivide the grid further, with horizontal lines isolating the header or title section from elements of the body copy. For this task, you can use the Line tool constrained to the horizontal grid with the Shift key (or use the Straight-line tool), and use the same line fill pattern as you did before. To measure distances in the vertical direction, use a shareware desk accessory like Super Ruler.

8. To complete the grid, select all the elements you have added to the screen, and choose the Group Picture command from the Format menu.

You can view your work in the Page Preview mode (see "Printing Your Work," in Chapter 2). Because the grid was the first element added to your document, everything else will appear in front of the grid. You may want to save your layout grid so that you can use it over and over. For more information, see this chapter's section on "Using Stationery for Templates."

## *Creating a Multicolumn Layout*

As mentioned in the previous section, incorporating multicolumn text into your design requires that you build columns in the draw layer. (At this point, you may want to go back and refer to "Creating Linked Columns of Text" in Chapter 4.) Creating columns requires some planning but is not difficult to do. Consider first your headline and your major graphic features. You probably should place any photos or art on the page to guide you in laying out your text.

A good way to balance out your multicolumn layout is to use borders and rules, which are horizontal or vertical lines that separate various elements of your page. Rules can be thin or thick. Rules are created by using the Line or Rectangle tool. For thin rules, use the line tool (or straight-line tool) and select the appropriate line width from the Toolbox. For thicker rules, use the Rectangle tool and select both an appropriate line thickness and a fill from the Fill Pattern menu. Use thin rules when working with dense copy; thick rules work best with sparsely used copy areas like headlines. In figure 5.3, a header, borders, and a graphic have been added to the three-column grid shown in figure 5.2. Notice that you do not have to use the grid as drawn. It is just a visual aid.

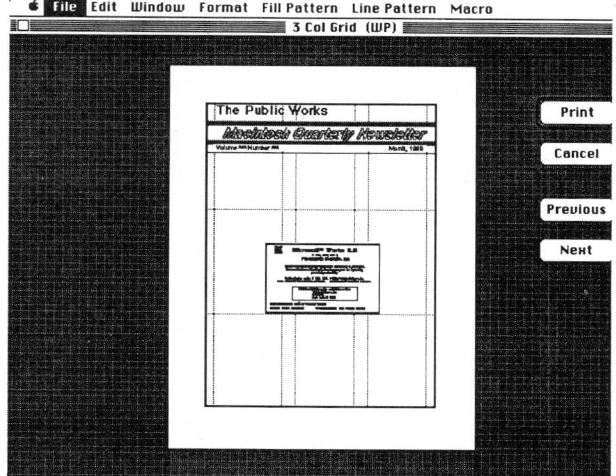


**Fig. 5.3**

*A newsletter template.*

Most layout programs implement a feature called *wraparound*, in which text is made to flow around a graphic so that it becomes an integral element of the design. Although wraparound of an irregular graphic is not possible in Works, careful placement of columns around a graphic generally leads to satisfactory results. Works has a linked-columns feature specifically for the purpose of "autoflowing" your text from one column to the next (see "Creating Linked Columns of Text" in Chapter 4). In figure 5.4, for example, columns are placed around the graphic that was shown in figure 5.3. You can see all the column headings because all objects on the screen have been selected.

You will find that dividing your text into separate files for each story is a convenient approach. You can then easily check spelling and do sim-

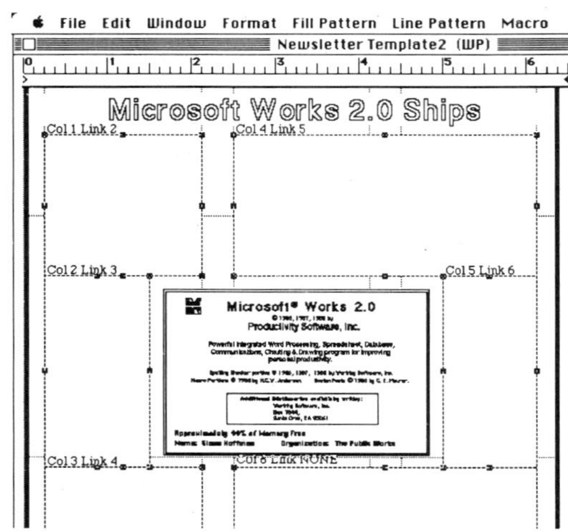


**Fig. 5.4**

*Implementing wraparound with linked columns.*

ple formatting. Consider creating sets of linked columns as a layout template onto which you can place your various stories. You place your text by copying it into the Clipboard, clicking an insertion point at the start of your first column, and pasting in the text. When you paste text into a column (or text object), the text retains its original formatting. If you press the Option key and paste, your text acquires the formatting you defined for the column.

Don't forget that if you make a mistake you can undo it. The Clipboard remains unchanged, and your original story is still in the text file. You can use TXT as the file extension for your text files, and LAY for your layout grid, and store them in the same folder.

After examining your work, if you find it satisfactory, you may want to remove the markers defining the visible grid you created. Simply select the grid and delete it. The result, after text is placed and the grid is removed, is shown in figure 5.5.

# Using Stationery for Templates

When saving your work, you should think about whether you want to use it again in a different form. For example, when you reach the stage shown in figure 5.4 with your headers, graphics, and columns placed, you can use it as a template for any other publication of this type you might want to produce. A *template* is a master design copy, an outline, or a kind of skeleton of your publication.

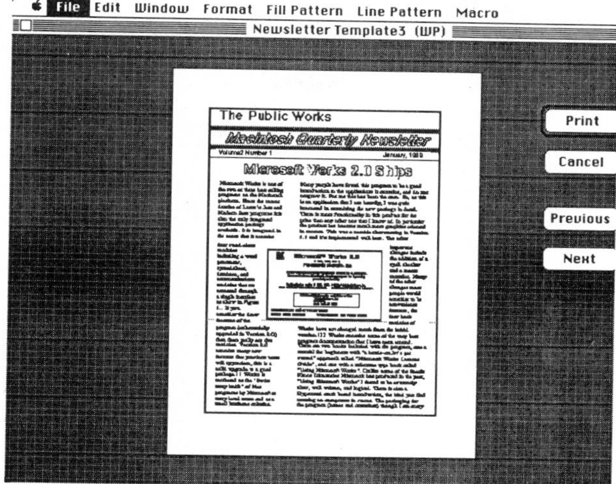


**Fig. 5.5**

*Final newsletter cover page with placed text.*

At the template stage, save your work with the Stationery format. Then when you want to reuse the template for another project, opening the file places an untitled copy on your desktop. This approach prevents you from making unwanted changes to the original template. If you use Works often for producing layouts, you may want to consider creating a template library.

Figure 5.5 shows an example of a newsletter cover page. Generally, you will also need a template for inner pages. Keep in mind that your newsletter, in fact any multipage publication, opens to display two pages side-by-side, a right and a left page. You thus need at least two kinds of templates: a cover master and a page master. And to do a truly bang-up job, you can define three kinds of templates—a cover and both a left- and a right-page master—so that the elements of an open page are consistently balanced and attractive.

Making master pages is a significant feature of advanced layout programs. Although you can use Works to create simple templates, if you find yourself doing a lot of this kind of work, you should invest in one of the three programs mentioned previously (PageMaker, Ready,Set,Go!, and Quark XPress). They offer a number of advanced features, such as easily defined columns, different page views (zoom in/zoom out), and kerning (the space between letters) and leading (the space between lines) control. Some programs are even offering advanced color implementation.

# Producing a Statement Form

You are likely to find that simple graphics, such as business statement forms, are the projects you need to tackle most often. The best way to work with business forms is to create the graphics in the draw layer and use the text layer whenever you want to fill in the boxes. With this method, you never alter the position of the graphic elements.

## Drawing the Form

To start your statement form, set an invisible grid (see "Aligning an Object" in Chapter 4) for doing multicolumn layout. You may or may not choose to go through the procedure of making a marker set to display your grid on-screen, depending on how complex your form is going to be. For a basic statement form, you do not need fine grid spacing.

As you begin drawing the graphic elements of your statement, remember that Works has features that allow you to center objects over other objects, align objects to one side or in the center, and freeze objects. (These features are covered in Chapter 4.) When you have finished creating the statement form, save it as Stationery. You can then use it as a business form template (see fig. 5.6).

**Fig. 5.6**

*A statement form used as a template.*

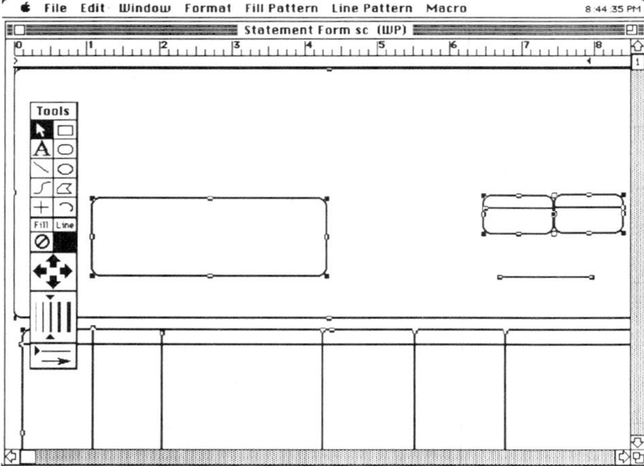


Don't forget to insert enough carriage-return characters to enable you to scroll the draw layer. You can always return to the text layer later and remove these returns to bring the insertion point to the first line in which you need it. This procedure is recommended for all business forms.

## *Using the Form*

Using your statement form is easy. Open your template (Stationery statement form), type the data, and use a Save command to name your document and write it to a file. With Works you can even automate your data entry to forms, using a database and a mail-merge technique. This capability is discussed in the section called "Merging" in Chapter 13, "Tying It All Together." A statement form with data is shown in figure 5.7. Once you have saved it, you are ready to print it, mail it, and wait for your money to arrive.

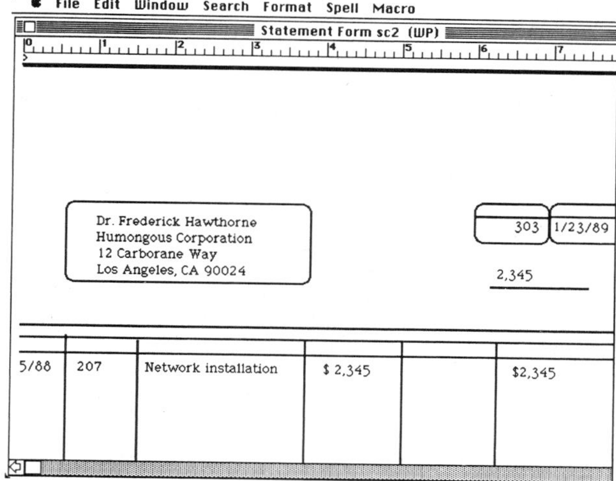


**Fig. 5.7**

*The completed statement, ready to mail.*

## *Working with Imported Forms*

If you find that you prefer to work with pre-existing forms manufactured on special paper, Works can accommodate you. A simple method is to measure the form with a ruler and determine where each piece of text should go. You can then use a grid and markers to set up the form on your screen. Another option is to use the trial-and-error method. Place your text, print the document, and make adjustments as necessary. Works has nudge commands in the Toolbox, and the cursor-movement keys allow larger movements of text.

A more elegant method involves using scanned images as templates. Most Apple-compatible scanners allow the files to be saved in PICT format, the MacPaint-compatible format. You can import PICT files through the Clipboard and place PICT images as a single object in your draw layer. You have the choice of copying the features of the form by using the tools in your toolbox or by switching to the text layer and placing your text directly, with the scanned image guiding your work. This technique is an extremely convenient, fast, and powerful method for forms generation. Shown in figure 5.8 is a commercial statement form imported into Works, touched up in SuperPaint, copied to the Clipboard, and pasted in the draw layer. Figure 5.9 illustrates how you can use the scanned statement form as a template. Note that the new objects almost overlay.

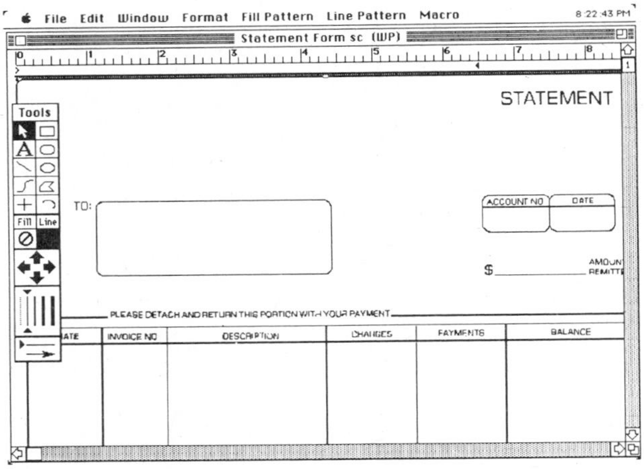

**Fig. 5.8**

*Using an imported scanned statement as a template.*

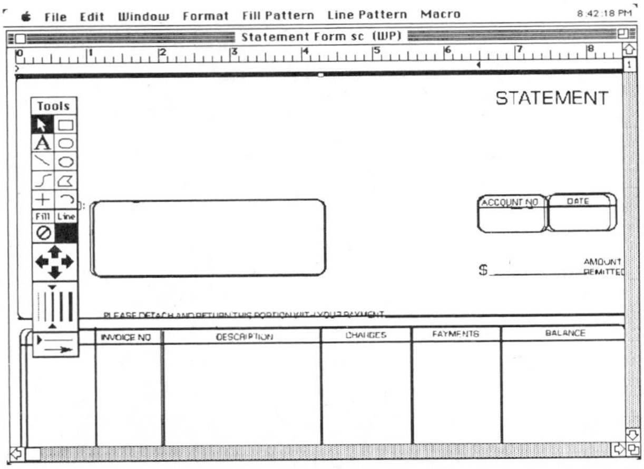

**Fig. 5.9**

*Drawn form placed over the scanned template.*

The Clipboard as supplied by Apple is a powerful tool for importing text and graphics, but you cannot manipulate the contents. If you are going to use the vast library of clip art that is available out there, and you create and want to use the Scrapbook heavily, you should consider the third-party desk accessory SmartScrap and the Clipper. This product was discussed in Chapter 4's section on "Importing and Exporting Graphics." Remember that when scaling graphic elements in the draw module, fonts do not resize. You must resize them from the Size submenu, which is accessed from the Format menu.

# Working with Color

Previous sections have alluded briefly to the use of color in Works. In this section, you learn what colors you have available and how you can use them in Works.

## What Colors Are Available?

Works has some color support, but it is not extensive. The objects in the draw layer offer the most color options of any module contained in Works. Using the two color commands—Color-Black Dots and Color-White Dots—you can mix two sets of 8 colors to produce a palette of colors. Because the pixels on your screen (those tiny dots that are the active picture elements) are too small to be differentiated, they appear blended on-screen. The human eye thus sees a solid color.

The Macintosh II series is capable of displaying 16.8 million colors, and the 8-bit board makes a set of 256 of those colors available on-screen. You can find those colors in the Apple system software Color CDEV in your control panel. At the time of this writing, most of the Macintosh computers that display color, such as the Macintosh II, Macintosh IIcx, and Macintosh IIx, use 8-bit color video boards. In figure 5.10, a single bit and an 8-bit pixel are drawn. The derivation of the Color-Black Dots and Color-White Dots is shown.

You can buy from third-party vendors 24-bit color boards that display near photographic-quality images on compatible monitors. A 32-bit QuickDraw system of perfect color is just around the corner in Apple

**Fig. 5.10**

*An 8-bit color pixel.*

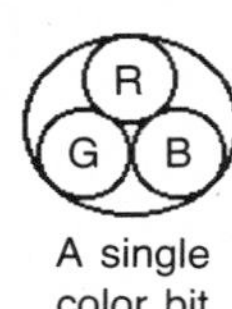


A single color bit

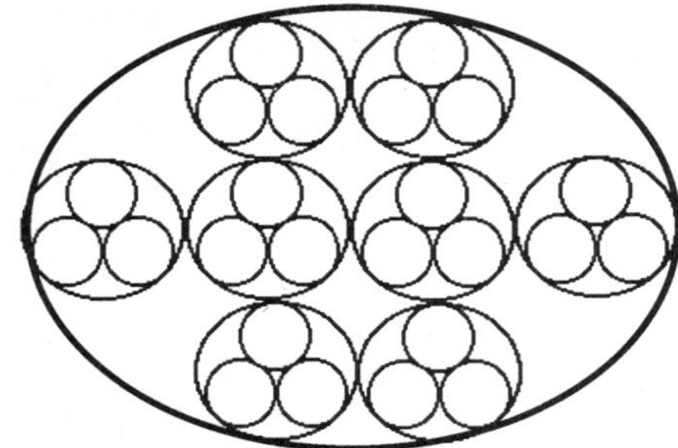

An 8-bit color pixel

System 7.0. This system will produce 24-bit color with an additional 8 bits of information used for other effects.

Several color modeling schemes exist. The Macintosh color wheel, the so-called "color picker," is based on a red/green/blue (RGB) color model. Your color monitor uses RGB phosphors on the screen to display color. The print industry uses the CYMK (cyan, yellow, magenta, black) model. Another approach to modeling color is the print industry's use of the Pantone library of colors, which are blended to match available color inks.

If all these colors are available, why does Works limit you to eight? Color is very memory-intensive, so the limitation probably arises from that consideration. If you create an object in the draw layer (only objects can be colorized), you then must select a fill that sets the density of white and black dots. Your choice of colors for white and black dots results in a wide range of possible colors. With a gray color of equal density black and white dots, you can select only 64 colors. However, other fill patterns expand this range somewhat. The eight colors are the current set of the two four-color ribbons available for the ImageWriter printer, but you certainly can use the color features in Works to print to any printer that supports color. This group includes not only the ImageWriter but also color printers like the Hewlett-Packard InkJet (which can be connected to a Macintosh), and newer, higher end printers just coming into the market. Although these high-end color printers are expensive (some are PostScript, some are QuickDraw), they produce good effects.

# *What Can You Do with Color?*

You should note that a distinct difference exists between the color you might see on your screen (emitted color) and that placed on paper by ink (reflected color). Depending on the color printer you use, expect to see large differences in the way your color output looks.

For those of you working with color screens, colorizing the white dots on your monitor can lead to a darkened, unreadable screen. You should also note that black-and-white QuickDraw printers (like the LaserWriter SC) print colorized white dots as black. Black-and-white PostScript printers (like the LaserWriter NX or NTX) more correctly shade your colorized white dots, if black is not the chosen color.

The best use of color in your design work is probably in what designers call *spot color*—the colored headings or sections of a printed work that gives emphasis to your page. Although full color, commonly called *four-color print work*, requires a full palette, you can use spot color quite effectively with the tools that Works provides. For example, consider how much more effective you can make your statement form if you highlight important text fields with color. When you look at professionally produced publications and forms, notice how much mileage they get from spot color. (At the time of this writing, PageMaker, the major page layout program, supports *only* spot color, although the program will expand to full color support in the near future.)

Color can be added to objects or text only in the draw layer. For example, if you want to create a large colored headline, you create a text object and assign color to it. When you print your work, any color assignment will be sent automatically to an output device that supports color. Your Macintosh system software and your installed printer driver do this for you. For instance, suppose that you want to create the effect of light or white text on top of a darker background (commonly called a *reverse*). Create your background, assign a color to it, and then create a text object above the background. Reverses are effective techniques for emphasizing headlines, quotes, or captions.

To create a color object, follow these steps:

1. Color is a property of a draw layer object. Choose the Draw On command (⌘-J) on the Format menu.
2. Create your object, either a text object or a figure.
3. Choose a line and fill pattern from the Line Pattern and Fill Pattern menus.

**NOTE:** The fill pattern you choose determines the density of black dots (or white dots) you can colorize. Choosing a white or transparent fill pattern may not allow you to see any color. Choosing a gray fill gives a lighter density of color (black dots) than choosing a black fill. Black fill has no white dots.

4. Choose your colors from the Color-White Dots and Color-Black Dots commands in the Format menu. Remember that the order of your objects will affect what you see.
5. When you are finished, issue the Print command on the File menu and your work will be sent in color to any external output device that supports color. You also can photograph the screen with a 35 mm camera and tripod. Use film that is fast enough to allow a 1 second exposure in a darkened room. The ideal lens is a 100-110 mm macro lens. A 55 mm macro lens or a 50 mm normal lens will work, but gives slight distortion at the outer edges of the picture.

# *Chapter Summary*

This chapter covered a lot of ground in its discussion of fonts, color, and design, but only began to touch on the subject of graphic design. Enough information exists to fill an entire book. In fact, many books and magazines are devoted to this subject. It's a fascinating area, one in which you can continually expand your knowledge and expertise.

In this chapter, you learned how to create letterheads and logos, work with a visible grid on-screen, create multicolumn layouts, store your designs as templates, and create statement forms. But Works does much more than just give you the opportunity to create forms and fill them in yourself. With the database module and the forms you create, you can sort, organize, and print the data in your database, automating the whole process of data output. Every time you open your mailbox and look at the letters you receive, you can see this kind of computer power in action. You can read about databases in Chapters 9 and 10, and can find more information about automating database output in Chapter 13's section on "Merging." If you want to learn how to operate this feature more quickly, study the Quick Reference Summary at the end of Chapter 9 and then skip ahead to Chapter 13.

Part IV

# Spreadsheets and Graphs

## Includes

Spreadsheet Concepts

Graphs

Spreadsheet and Database Functions

# 6

# Spreadsheet Concepts

A Works spreadsheet window is like an accountant's pad of ledger paper, except that when you change an entry on a spreadsheet, the effects of the change appear almost instantly. You can test financial calculations with the click of your mouse. Works takes care of all the recalculations and eliminates the need for a pencil, an eraser, or a calculator.

Use your spreadsheet to do your taxes, balance your checkbook, check sales projects, do cash-flow analyses, make personal net worth calculations, or figure your break-even points. The Works spreadsheet is powerful enough to run your business, analyze complex statistics, or do detailed science experiments. Before you can use a spreadsheet, however, you need to design and test it. You learn how in this chapter.

## *Working in the Spreadsheet Window*

Not surprisingly, you work with spreadsheets in a *spreadsheet window*. Each spreadsheet window is called a *worksheet* and is more complex than a word processing window. Figure 6.1 shows a sample spreadsheet window with the various elements marked. In addition to the usual scroll bars, title bar, and zoom, close, and resize boxes, the window contains a worksheet area and an entry bar. Note also that the window contains the characters (SS) in the title bar, identifying the window as a spreadsheet window. The worksheet is a matrix of vertical columns and horizontal rows defining areas called *cells*.

**Fig. 6.1**

*Elements of a spreadsheet.*

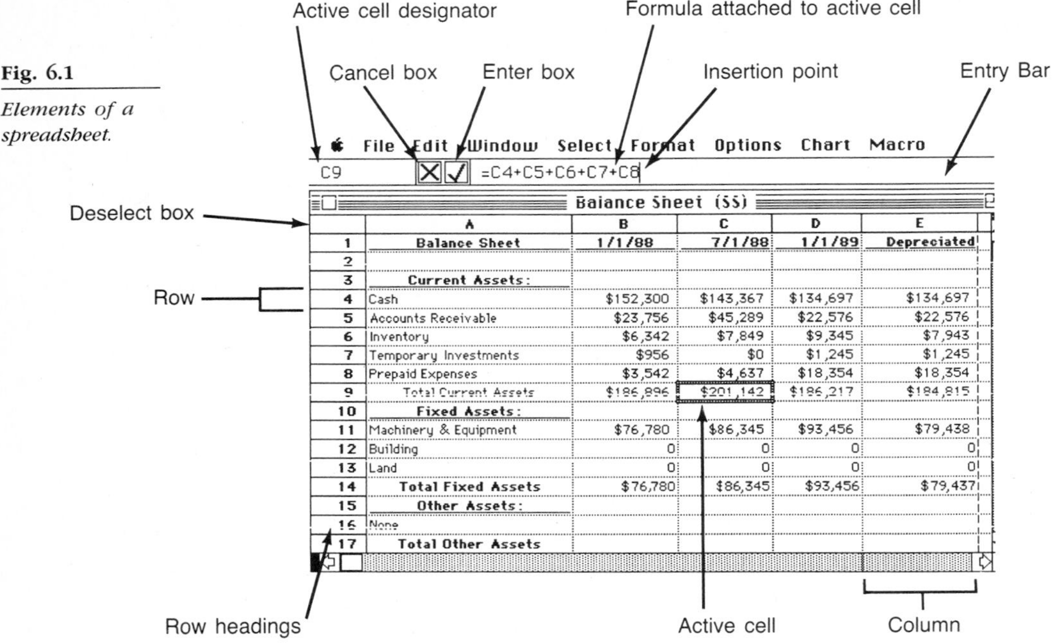


| | A | B | C | D | E |
|---|---|---|---|---|---|
| 1 | Balance Sheet | 1/1/88 | 7/1/88 | 1/1/89 | Depreciated |
| 2 | | | | | |
| 3 | Current Assets: | | | | |
| 4 | Cash | $152,300 | $143,367 | $134,697 | $134,697 |
| 5 | Accounts Receivable | $23,756 | $45,289 | $22,576 | $22,576 |
| 6 | Inventory | $6,342 | $7,849 | $9,345 | $7,943 |
| 7 | Temporary Investments | $956 | $0 | $1,245 | $1,245 |
| 8 | Prepaid Expenses | $3,542 | $4,637 | $18,354 | $18,354 |
| 9 | Total Current Assets | $186,896 | $201,142 | $186,217 | $184,815 |
| 10 | Fixed Assets: | | | | |
| 11 | Machinery & Equipment | $76,780 | $86,345 | $93,456 | $79,438 |
| 12 | Building | 0 | 0 | 0 | 0 |
| 13 | Land | 0 | 0 | 0 | 0 |
| 14 | Total Fixed Assets | $76,780 | $86,345 | $93,456 | $79,437 |
| 15 | Other Assets: | | | | |
| 16 | None | | | | |
| 17 | Total Other Assets | | | | |

## Cells and Addresses

A cell is the basic unit of a spreadsheet and can contain numbers, values, titles, or formulas. Each cell has an *address*, or location, indicated by its column and row headings. For example, the cell in the upper left corner of a spreadsheet, at the intersection of column A and row 1, is A1. The cell to the right of A1 is B1, the cell immediately beneath A1 is A2, and so on. Rows are numbered from top to bottom, 1 through 16,382. Columns are identified with letters from A to Z, then AA to ZZ, and on through IV, from left to right. Works 2.0 spreadsheets have a theoretical limit of 16,382 rows and 256 columns (4,194,000 cells), based on memory available.

You make changes in a cell by selecting it and then using the entry bar at the top of the screen to enter a new value or to change a relationship or formula. Works automatically recalculates all the dependent cells.

## *Using the Entry Bar and the Enter and Cancel Boxes*

Three important elements of the spreadsheet window are the entry bar, the enter box, and the cancel box. The *entry bar* is the area between the title bar and the menu bar. When you type something with a cell selected, it appears in the entry bar. To the left of the entry bar is the *enter box*, which contains a check mark. Clicking this box is like pressing the Enter (or Return) key on the keyboard. If you change your mind about something that you have done to the contents of the entry bar, you can click the *cancel box*, which is to the left of the enter box and contains an X.

To change a cell, you first must make it active by selecting it. The *active cell* is surrounded by a small border, as illustrated in cell C9 in figure 6.1. Works displays the address of the active cell in the entry bar to the left of the cancel box. Only one cell can be active at a time, although any number of cells can be selected. (For more information, see this chapter's section on "Selecting Single Cells and Ranges.") A *selected cell* is highlighted in black on a black-and-white monitor, and in the color you select on a color monitor. If you select a cell, its value appears in the entry bar. If the active cell contains an equation, however, that equation, not the resulting value, appears in the entry bar. The entry bar can show only 238 characters and can handle only 200 characters of any underlying formula you type.

# *Acquiring Basic Spreadsheet Skills*

A good spreadsheet tells a story. Although having all kinds of calculations on a worksheet is possible, keeping distinct computations separate makes more sense. For example, balance your checkbook in one column, and your net worth in another. As you begin to think about how you will use your spreadsheet, try to organize your thoughts and create a good structure. Always look at ways to make your calculations more elegant and compact. As you work with your spreadsheet, you probably will form new ideas for consolidating your work.

## *Opening a Spreadsheet*

Works offers two basic ways to open a new "untitled" worksheet:

- ❑ Double-click the icon labeled `Spread Sheet` in the Open File dialog box (or click the icon once and then click the New button).
- ❑ Choose the New command from the File menu and then either double-click the spreadsheet icon, or select the spreadsheet icon and click OK or press Return (see fig. 6.2). Both methods are analogous to opening a new word processor window.

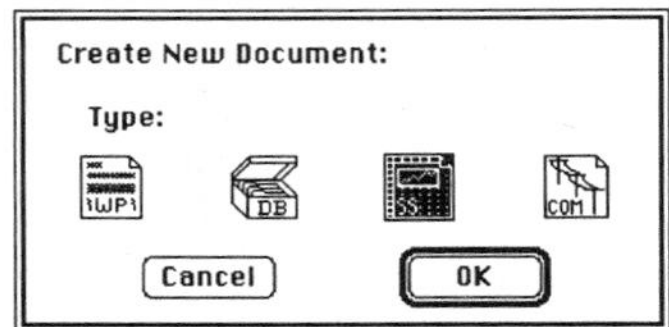


**Fig. 6.2**

*The New dialog box.*

To open an existing spreadsheet file, choose the Open command from the File menu, bringing up the Open File dialog box. With the spreadsheet icon selected, you see only spreadsheets in the scroll box, as shown in figure 6.3.

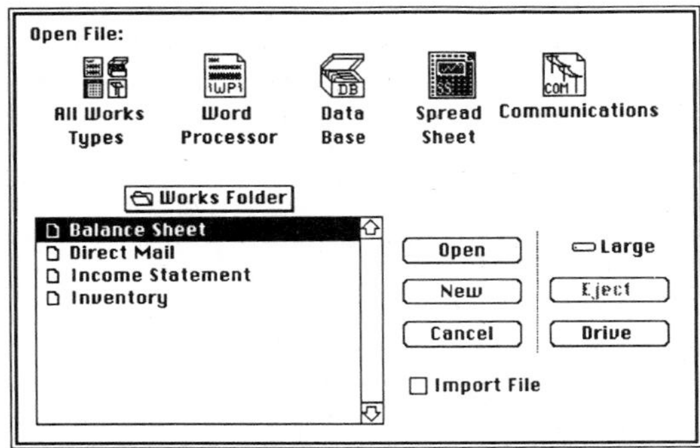


**Fig. 6.3**

*The Open File dialog box with Spreadsheet icon selected.*

## *Making Simple Cell Entries*

You can always enter items into a cell (up to 238 characters) by doing the following:

1. Click the cell to activate it.
2. This step is optional. If you use step 1 without this step, you replace the previous contents of the cell. Click the entry bar to the right of the enter box.

3. Type your label or value. If you are typing an equation, you must type the equal sign ( = ) first.
4. Click the enter box or press Return or Enter.

If you type a label that doesn't fit in a cell, the label overflows to the right until it encounters a nonblank cell. Although the label may be partially obscured on-screen, if you select the cell you can see the entire label in the entry bar. If you don't want the label to extend into the cell to the right, select the cell in which you are working and press the space bar. Then press Return. This action inserts an invisible formatting mark that restrains the label to that cell. You can also widen the column (see "Changing Column Widths" in this chapter).

Works offers you some shortcuts for entering information in the entry bar and then immediately moving to an adjacent cell. Table 6.1 summarizes these movements, and figure 6.4 illustrates them graphically.

**Table 6.1**
**Spreadsheet Data-Entry Shortcuts**

| *To enter value and then activate* | *Press* |
|---|---|
| The cell on the right | Tab or → |
| The cell on the left | Shift-Tab or ← |
| The cell below | Return or ↓ |
| The cell above | Shift-Return or ↑ |
| The same cell | Enter |
| Any other cell | Click that cell |

| | A | B | C |
|---|---|---|---|
| 1 | | Shift-Return or ↑ | |
| 2 | ← or Shift-Tab | Active cell | Tab or → |
| 3 | | Return or ↓ | |

**Fig. 6.4**
*Entering a cell value and moving to another cell at the same time.*

To cancel an entry you make in the entry bar, click the cancel box. If you make an entry in the active cell by clicking the enter box or performing any of the operations in table 6.1, you can return to your previous state by choosing the Undo command from the Edit menu. You can edit your entry in the entry bar by using the standard Macintosh techniques.

# Selecting Single Cells and Ranges

As already mentioned, a simple click both selects and activates a single cell. At times you may want to select a range of cells in order to perform some operation, such as formatting. Works lets you select cells in rows, columns, or blocks (see fig. 6.5). The ranges are highlighted so that they're easy to see.

**Fig. 6.5**

*Selected ranges of a row, a column, and a block.*

| | A | B | C | D | E |
|---|---|---|---|---|---|
| 1 | | | | | |
| 2 | | Q1 Actual | Q2 Actual | Q3 Plan | Q4 Plan |
| 3 | SALES | | | | |
| 4 | WEST | $123,568 | $107,232 | $140,000 | $140,000 |
| 5 | CENTRAL | $113,454 | $110,785 | $140,000 | $140,000 |
| 6 | EAST | $98,876 | $101,867 | $140,000 | $140,000 |

| | A | B | C | D | E |
|---|---|---|---|---|---|
| 1 | | | | | |
| 2 | | Q1 Actual | Q2 Actual | Q3 Plan | Q4 Plan |
| 3 | SALES | | | | |
| 4 | WEST | $123,568 | $107,232 | $140,000 | $140,000 |
| 5 | CENTRAL | $113,454 | $110,785 | $140,000 | $140,000 |
| 6 | EAST | $98,876 | $101,867 | $140,000 | $140,000 |

| | A | B | C | D | E |
|---|---|---|---|---|---|
| 1 | | | | | |
| 2 | | Q1 Actual | Q2 Actual | Q3 Plan | Q4 Plan |
| 3 | SALES | | | | |
| 4 | WEST | $123,568 | $107,232 | $140,000 | $140,000 |
| 5 | CENTRAL | $113,454 | $110,785 | $140,000 | $140,000 |
| 6 | EAST | $98,876 | $101,867 | $140,000 | $140,000 |

By clicking a column heading or a row number, you select the entire corresponding row or column. The first cell in the selected row or column becomes the active cell. To select any block (range) of cells, you drag from the beginning cell (the active cell) to the end of the range. Another way to select a range is to click the first cell and Shift-click the last cell.

The Select menu offers an All Cells command, which highlights everything from the first to the last cell you have used for your spreadsheet. For instance, if you have something in A1 and something in A13, but cells A2 through A12 are empty, the entire range A1 through A13 is selected when you choose All Cells. This choice also activates the first cell in your spreadsheet. You can select all spreadsheet cells on the worksheet, regardless of whether you have made any entries, by choosing Select All which is new in the Edit menu of Works 2.0.

Table 6.2 summarizes the selection options available to you.

**Table 6.2**
**Selecting Spreadsheet Ranges**

| *To select* | *Perform this operation* |
|---|---|
| A block of cells | Click the starting cell and drag diagonally to the last cell<br>*or*<br>Click the starting cell and Shift-click the last |
| A row or column | Click the row or column heading |
| Several rows or columns | Drag from the first row or column heading to the last<br>*or*<br>Click the first heading and Shift-click the last heading |
| All cells to the last used | Choose the All Cells command from the Select menu |
| All spreadsheet cells | Choose Select All from the Edit menu |
| The last cell | Choose Last Cell from the Select menu |

To deselect a range, click anywhere in the spreadsheet. In the process, you also activate the cell in which you click. Another method is to use the deselect box, located above row 1 and to the left of column A (see fig. 6.1). Clicking this box deselects any and all selections without activating any cells.

# *Examining the Types of Spreadsheet Entries*

You can make four types of entries in a Works spreadsheet: labels, values, arithmetic operators, and equations. The sections that follow describe the sort of control that Works gives you in defining these entries, and the shortcuts available to aid in their entry.

As you learn more about Works and its modules, you will find that many of the formatting terms and most of the arithmetic functions are common to both the spreadsheet and database modules. In general the functions that appear in the spreadsheet but not in the database are the ones that do comparison calculations and are locational in nature (that is, these functions examine a spreadsheet cell and seek out a cell in some other direction to do an arithmetic calculation). Chapter 8 gives a full explanation in reference form of all the operators available for building the spreadsheet of your choice.

## Labels

*Labels*, also called titles, are text entries used to describe or explain things in the spreadsheet. In figure 6.1, all entries in column A and in row 1 are labels. If the first keystroke in an entry is a letter or one of most common punctuation marks, Works treats the entry as a label. For example, the following entries are labels:

Sales
%
–1–
"04/10/87"
Q4
"4th Quarter"
"1984"

The third item, –1–, is a label because of the presence of the second minus sign (–). If a minus sign were to the left of the 1 but not to the right (–1), Works would treat the number as a negative number 1.

Although 1984 is a number, the entry "1984" is a label because of the leading double quotation mark, which is the Works method for indicating that a string of characters is a label. The quotation marks are visible in the entry bar but not in the cell. To display quotation marks in a cell, you must enclose them with another pair of double quotation marks. For example, to create a cell displaying the label "4", you enter

""4""

## Values

*Values* are the numbers used in spreadsheet calculations. A value can be positive or negative, with or without decimal points, and in scientific notation if necessary. Works expresses dates and time in a special number format that allows you to do date and time calculations. In figure 6.1, cells in columns B, C, and D (other than row 1) contain values. Through the Format menu's Set Cell Attributes command, Works gives you considerable flexibility in how you display numbers or values. (For more information, see this chapter's section on "Formatting Cells.")

Works treats the following character strings as numbers:

1
−1
12
0.12
12,000
$1200
12%
12E3
12e3

When you enter a percentage amount (12%) or a decimal number with no preceding 0 (.12), Works converts the entry to a decimal value with a preceding 0 (0.12). When you enter a number in scientific notation (12E3 or 12e3), the full number displays in the cell (12000). Works accepts exponential numbers up to E +/− 99. Above this range, Works displays the word `*Error*` in the cell. Whenever Works converts what you have entered into something else, your original entry appears in the entry bar whenever you select the cell.

You can use the number keys and functions on the top row of the keyboard to enter number values. With the Apple extended keyboard, you can use the keypad as an alternative for numeric entry.

**TIP:** Precede negative numbers with a minus sign. Don't enter dollar signs, parentheses, or commas, because Works ignores them in calculations. Later in this chapter, you learn how to display and print these formats ("Formatting Cells"). Don't enter spaces, letters, or any punctuation other than decimal points (periods); otherwise, Works may mistake your value for a label. For example, if you place a space between the 12 and the E3 in 12E3, Works treats the entry as a label. Also, don't enter an equal sign. Works will think you're beginning an equation (see the section on "Equations").

## *Operators*

*Operators* are the mathematical functions used in formulas (equations). Some of these operators are the familiar calculator functions:

| | |
|---|---|
| Addition | + |
| Subtraction | − |
| Multiplication | * |
| Division | / |
| Exponents (number raised to a power) | ^ |
| Negation (makes a number negative) | − |

In addition, Works has 64 built-in functions that you can use in your spreadsheet formulas. These functions include other mathematical operators (such as the random number generator) and statistical, trigonometric, logic, financial, date/time, and some special purpose functions that compare values at other locations. For more information on built-in functions, refer to Chapter 8, "Spreadsheet and Database Functions."

Works give you the choice of typing the operators you want into equations or using a dialog box accessed through the Paste Function command in the Edit menu. Figure 6.6 illustrates this dialog box. To paste a function, you select it in the dialog box and then click OK or press Return. If the entry bar is active, the function is pasted at the insertion point; if the entry bar is inactive, Works pastes an equal sign (=) to start an equation and pastes the function to the right of the =. Typing two operators in sequence leads Works to insert an addition sign (+) between them.

**NOTE:** If you're using ordinary mathematical operators such as +, −, *, and /, you type them as usual.

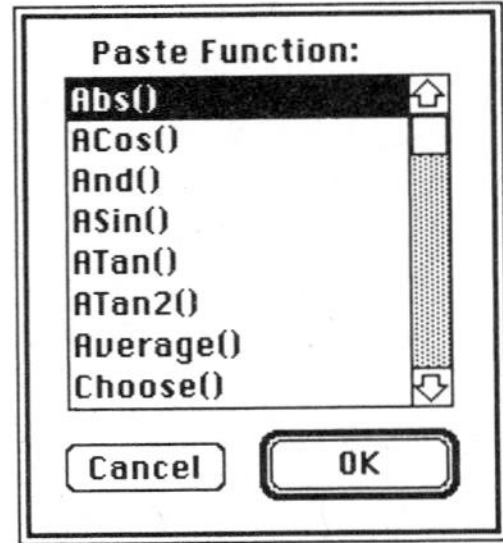


**Fig. 6.6**

*The Paste Function dialog box.*

Works has another set of operators that produce the logical values 1 for TRUE or 0 for FALSE. They are

| | |
|---|---|
| = | Equal |
| < | Less than |

| | |
|---|---|
| <= | Less than or equal to |
| > | Greater than |
| >= | Greater than or equal to |
| <> | Not equal to |

For example, if you write an equation such as C1>D4, and it returns the values 5>3, Works returns a TRUE and places the value 1 in your cell.

In an equation, the order in which you type operators is important. Works performs operations in the following order:

| | |
|---|---|
| ^ | Exponentiation |
| – | Negation |
| * and / | Multiplication and division |
| + and – | Addition and subtraction |
| =, <, <=, >, >=, <> | Comparison operators |

You can force a change in the order in which operations are performed by enclosing operations within parentheses. Works performs the operation within the parentheses first. You can even nest parentheses, and Word handles the operation within the inner ones first and the outer ones last. For example, although 5 + 2 * 3 = 11, the equation (5 + 2) * 3 = 21.

# *Equations*

You create *equations*, or formulas, to tell Works what to do with the values you have entered. An equation consists of a function or set of functions (called *operators*) that operate on defined values, thus producing a new value. To start any equation, you must first type an equal sign (=) in the entry bar. Works tries to treat any entry that starts with an equal sign as an equation. For example, Works views the entry *=04/10/87* as an equation, dividing 4 by 10 and then dividing the results by 87.

Works provides a convenient shortcut for entering cell references into your equations. To enter a cell address, and thus its value, just click it. Works places the address into the equation as a relative cell reference, which is discussed in the next section. Whenever you perform an operation that requires an operator and you don't enter one, Works inserts an addition sign, which is the default choice.

If you click two consecutive cells (after typing the equal sign), Works inserts the default addition symbol between them. You can therefore point and click cell addresses to build any size sum of cells you want. When you want to enter a cell address in an equation, you can either type it or click it. Works offers many shortcuts for entering information by just pointing and clicking; these are covered subsequently in this chapter.

Works enables you either to display the values of the cells in the worksheet by using the Show Values command in the Options menu (the default choice, illustrated in fig. 6.1) or to show the underlying equations by choosing the Show Formulas command in the same menu. Figure 6.7 shows the Options menu with the Show Formulas command chosen. Note that Works displays a check mark beside the selected option in the menu. Figure 6.8 shows the results of choosing Show Formulas. Regardless of how you choose to display the worksheet, any active cell displays its underlying equation in the entry bar.

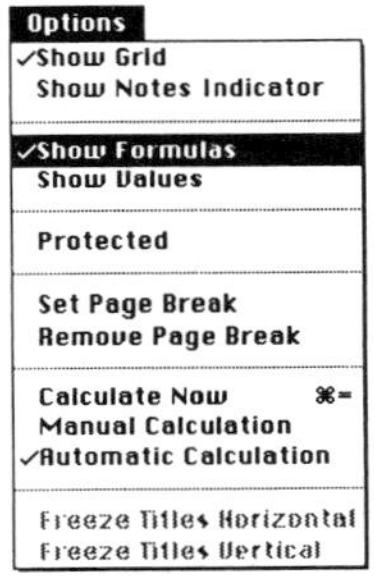


**Fig. 6.7**

*The Options menu with Show Formulas selected.*

File Edit Window Select Format Options Chart Macro

C9 =C4+C5+C6+C7+C8

Balance Sheet (SS)

| | A | B | C | D | E |
|---|---|---|---|---|---|
| 1 | Balance Sheet | 1/1/88 | 7/1/88 | 1/1/89 | Depreciated |
| 2 | | | | | |
| 3 | Current Assets: | | | | |
| 4 | Cash | 152,300 | 143,367 | 134,697 | =D4 |
| 5 | Accounts Receivable | 23,756 | 45,289 | 22,576 | =D5 |
| 6 | Inventory | 6,342 | 7,849 | 9,345 | =D6*.85 |
| 7 | Temporary Investments | 956 | 0 | 1,245 | =D7 |
| 8 | Prepaid Expenses | 3,542 | 4,637 | 18,354 | =D8 |
| 9 | Total Current Assets | =B4+B5+B6+B7 | =C4+C5+C6+C | =D4+D5+D6+ | =E4+E5+E6+E7+E |
| 10 | Fixed Assets: | | | | |
| 11 | Machinery & Equipment | 76,780 | 86,345 | 93456 | =D11*.85/1/1 |
| 12 | Building | 0 | 0 | 0 | =D12 |
| 13 | Land | 0 | 0 | 0 | =D13 |
| 14 | Total Fixed Assets | =B11+B12+B13 | =C11+C12+C1 | =D11+D12+D | =E11+E12+E13 |
| 15 | Other Assets: | | | | |
| 16 | None | | | | |
| 17 | Total Other Assets | | | | |

**Fig. 6.8**

*The results of choosing Show Formulas.*

## *Using Absolute and Relative Cell References*

Works has two different ways of describing the positions of cells in a worksheet, or the cell references. The difference becomes important when you copy and paste equations, because Works makes assumptions about the positions of the cell you copy from and the cell you copy to. An *absolute reference* is defined as a particular cell address and does not change when pasted. A *relative reference*, on the other hand, refers generally to any cell that is located a certain direction and distance away from the cell that contains the equation.

Works differentiates absolute references from relative ones through the use of dollar signs. For example, the cell $A$1 is the absolute reference to cell A1. When pasted—anywhere—it still refers to A1 and in an equation always returns the value of that cell.

When a relative reference is pasted, however, the direction and distance of the reference from the equation don't change, but the actual cell to which the reference points does change. For example, if a relative reference to A1 is located in an equation in cell B1, and the equation is moved to cell C3, the former reference to A1 changes to B3. The address continues to refer to the cell that is in the same row but one cell to the left.

A third type of reference is called a *mixed reference*. Either the row or the column reference is absolute, and the other portion of the reference is relative. Examples of mixed references are A$1 and $A1. When you paste a mixed reference to another cell, either the row remains the same and the column changes, or vice versa. For example, when a reference to $A1 occurs in B1 and is pasted to D4, the column remains as "A" but the row changes to "4."

At any time, you can alter a cell reference by inserting or deleting the dollar sign. Works also provides a set of commands to change the reference type. You can make an absolute cell reference relative by selecting the cell in which it is contained, positioning the insertion point in the entry bar to the right of the cell reference, and choosing the Absolute Cell Ref command (or pressing ⌘-A) after you have opened the Edit menu. The procedure for changing to an absolute cell reference is exactly the same, except that you place the insertion point to the right of a *relative* cell reference before you issue the command. The Absolute Cell Ref command also reverses a mixed cell reference ($A1 changes to A$1, for example).

## *Using Equations*

By default, Works is in the Automatic Calculation mode, as indicated by the check mark in the Options menu next to the Automatic Calculation option. In this mode, Works recalculates your spreadsheet every time you open it. Also, each time you make an entry in a cell, Works recalculates the entire worksheet.

If the worksheet is large, this recalculation may require some time. You can turn off automatic calculation by selecting the Manual Recalculation command in the Options menu. Then, when you want to have Works calculate the spreadsheet, either select the Calculate Now command from the Options menu or press ⌘-=.

> ***Caution:*** When you use the Manual Calculation mode, Works does not update your worksheet unless you tell the program to do so. Therefore, the numbers on your screen will be wrong. If you depend on your worksheet for current information, you must remember to update information when needed.

If you enter an equation that is not logical or that returns an unreasonable result, Works attempts to alert you. Two main types of errors can occur. The first is when you attempt an operation such as dividing a number by zero. Works simply returns `*Error*` in the cell. A second, more subtle error is called a *circular reference*, in which a reference refers to a cell that contains a reference back to the original cell. Because the original cell is not calculated, the second cell cannot have a value. When Works spots this type of error, an alert box appears, and displays a `Circular Reference Found Cells __ to __` message. Click OK or press Return and go back to the spreadsheet to resolve the difficulty. If you do not resolve the problem, Works alerts you by displaying the `Circular Ref Found During SS Recalculation` message. Click OK or press Return, and fix the error.

# *Moving around in a Worksheet*

Frequently, spreadsheets are larger than the screen. To move around in a worksheet, you can use the scroll bars just as you can in any other Works windows. You also can direct Works to go to a specific cell (Go To Cell and Find Cell), to the last cell in a worksheet (Last Cell), or to the active cell (Show Active Cell). All these commands are in the Select menu, shown in figure 6.9. You can use these commands to search for information, titles, equations, and values.

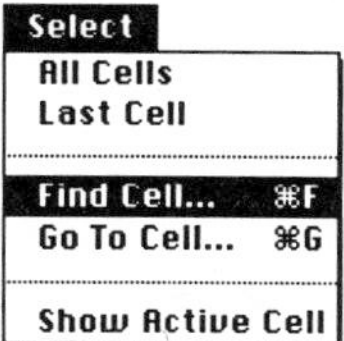


**Fig. 6.9**

*The Select menu.*

# *Moving to a Specific Cell*

To move to a specific cell (without selecting it),

1. Select the Go To Cell command from the Select menu, or press ⌘-G.
2. Type the desired cell address in the resulting dialog box (see fig. 6.10) and either press Return or click OK.

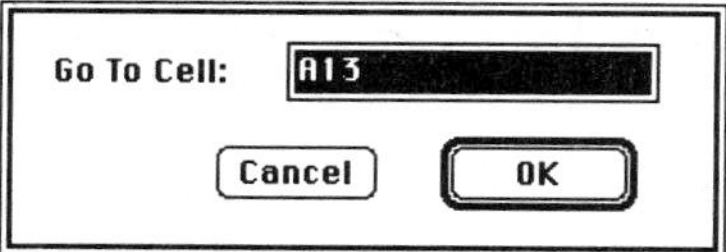


**Fig. 6.10**

*The Go To Cell dialog box.*

Works jumps to the location and shows you the cell and its neighbors without activating it. This command is useful when you are building equations that contain cell references, and you want to have a look around without changing or selecting anything.

The Go To Cell command also can find a cell that contains a particular label or equation. For example, if you want to find the cell that contains the title `Total`, or the equation D4 + F4, or the specific results of an equation (even `*Error*`), you can type this information in the Go To Cell dialog box. Works ignores dollar signs and commas when searching spreadsheets, so you can either type them or omit them. If a cell has been formatted with the Percent option from the Set Cell Attributes dialog box (see "Formatting Cells"), however, you need to type the percent sign when searching. When you click OK or press Return, Works quickly scrolls you to the area containing the cell you have specified.

## Moving to and Activating a Specific Cell

The Find Cell command acts like the Go To Cell command does, except that Find Cell activates the requested cell in addition to scrolling the display. Because Find Cell activates the cell, the cell's contents appear in the entry bar, ready for editing or other use. Find Cell also gives you the option of reissuing a Find command and searching again.

To find a cell and activate it, follow these steps:

1. Press ⌘-F or choose Find Cell from the Select menu. The dialog box then appears (see fig. 6.11).

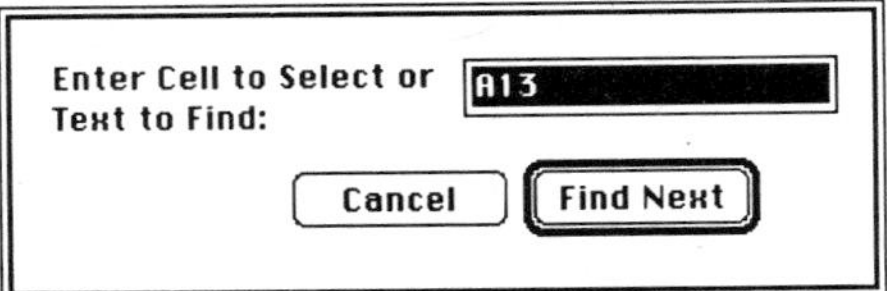


**Fig. 6.11**

*Using the Find Cell command.*

2. Enter a request (a cell address, label, equation, or the results of an equation).
3. Press Return or click the Find Next button. The first matching cell and its neighbors appear, and the first matching cell becomes the active cell.

In cases of multiple occurrences of the item you request (a repeated label or value, for instance), Works takes you first to the occurrence closest to the upper left corner of the spreadsheet (A1). Repeat your request to find the next occurrence. Use ⌘-F to speed up the process.

## Moving to the Active Cell

The Select menu's Show Active Cell command brings the active cell back into view when it has scrolled off the screen. This feature is at the bottom of the Select menu.

## Moving to the Last Cell

The Select menu also contains an option called Last Cell. It takes you to the last cell on a spreadsheet, which is defined as the largest cell, column, and row values containing a value, label, or an equation, and you activate that cell with the Last Cell command. Your worksheet size is defined as the matrix formed by your largest occupied row and your largest occupied column. Often when you choose the Last Cell option, the last cell may be empty. Works still considers it to be part of your worksheet.

# *Editing a Spreadsheet*

You can edit, move, copy, and delete equations and labels by using the standard Macintosh techniques. For instance, you can insert and delete characters in the entry bar just as you do on a line of word processing text. In the entry bar, the pointer changes to the shape of the I-beam cursor, as it does in the word processor module. Cut, copy, paste, and clear operations work as they do in all other Works modules.

With any of the operations discussed in this section, when you try to paste information, values, and formulas into cells that already contain some data, Works alerts you that you are about to overwrite the contents of the cells (see fig. 6.12). Click OK (or press Return) to proceed; click Cancel (or press ⌘-.[period]) to return to your previous worksheet.

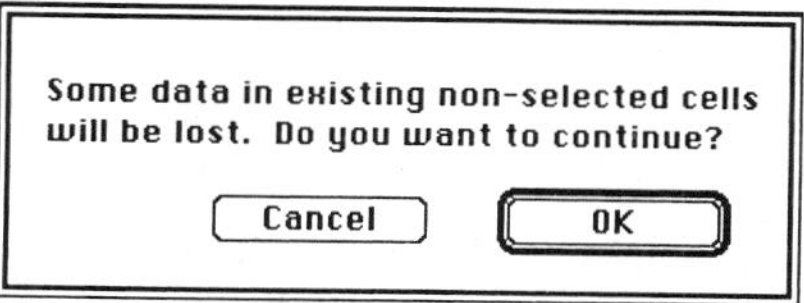
Some data in existing non-selected cells
will be lost. Do you want to continue?
Cancel
OK

**Fig. 6.12**

*The alert dialog box that appears when you try to paste into an occupied cell.*

# *Copying and Pasting Cells*

To copy an equation, follow these steps:

1. Select the source cell.
2. Press ⌘-C or choose Copy from the Edit menu.
3. Select the target cell.
4. Press ⌘-V or choose Paste from the Edit menu.

Works has a special Paste with Options command that enables you to create large spreadsheets without unnecessary retyping. Because each spreadsheet cell has both a value and an attached formula, Works gives you the choice of pasting either just the values or both the values and the formulas. When you choose Paste with Options from the Edit menu, the dialog box shown in figure 6.13 appears. Figure 6.14 shows a worksheet before and after a range is copied with the Values Only option selected in the Paste with Options dialog box.

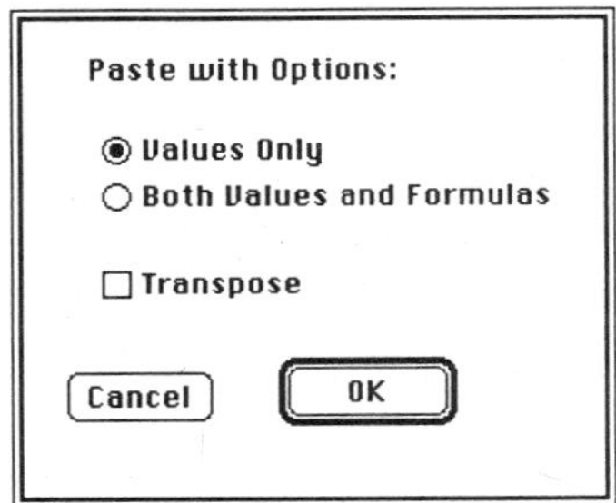


**Fig. 6.13**

*The Paste with Options dialog box.*



**Fig. 6.14**

*The results of pasting Values Only.*

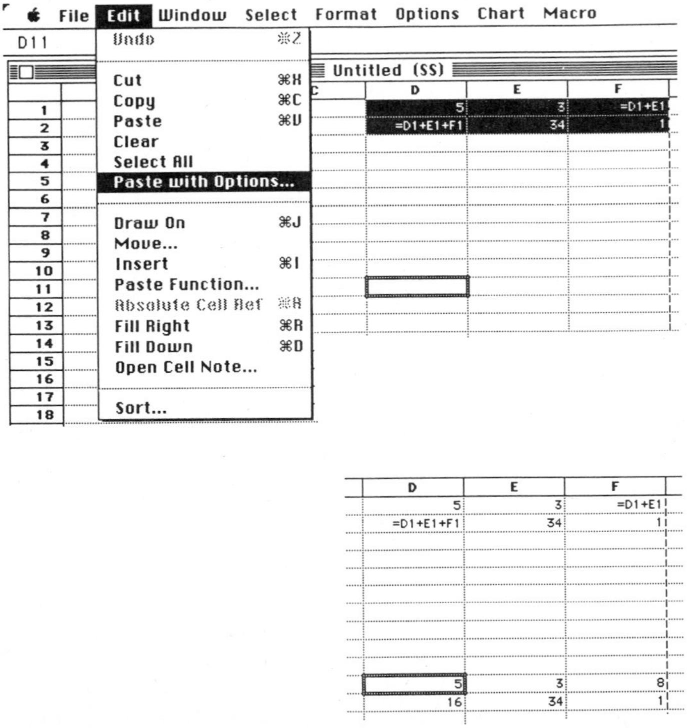

Note in the Paste with Options dialog box a third option labeled Transpose. With this option, you can transpose (paste) a row (or rows) into a column (or columns).

## *Moving Cells*

The Move command in the Edit menu takes a selected range of cells and pastes them into your current document in another location. Choosing this command brings up the dialog box shown in figure 6.15, which queries you regarding the target (destination) cell for the move operation.

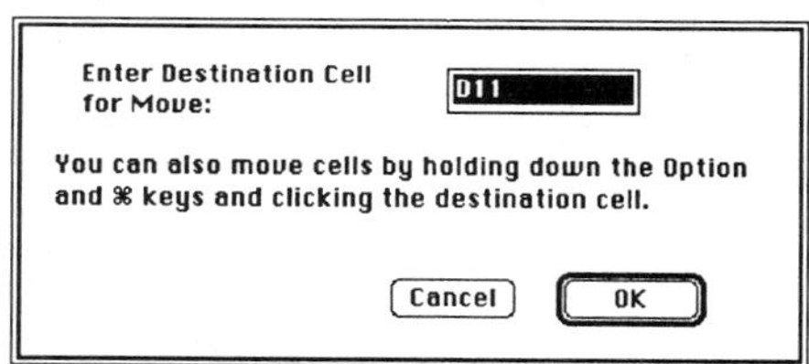


**Fig. 6.15**

*The Move dialog box.*

You can bypass this command and dialog box by pressing the ⌘ and Option keys and clicking the destination cell. Regardless of whether you use the Move command or the shortcut, your selected range moves to the new position with the designated target cell becoming the upper left cell in the range—and the active cell.

**NOTE:** Use Move only when you're moving within a single document. Switching documents requires the Clipboard, so you must use the Cut and Paste commands on the Edit menu for that type of operation. Also, when you move information to new cells, all relative references external to the selected range still point to the same cell values as before. Relative values within the selected range are adjusted to the new range. For information on relative references, read "Using Absolute and Relative Cell References" in this chapter.

## *Copying by Filling Cells*

Another set of commands from the Edit menu that allows you to build spreadsheets quickly is the Fill Down (⌘-D) and Fill Right (⌘-R) commands. These commands copy labels, equations, values, formats, and other elements of the cells you want to duplicate. Before you can use a Fill command, you must have selected both a range of cell(s) that you want to copy and a range that you want to fill. Your initial cell(s), or range to copy, should be the top row for a Fill Down command (see fig. 6.16) or the left column of cell(s) for a Fill Right command (see fig. 6.17). When you use the Fill commands, you paste in all associated cell values, formulas, and formatting. Fill is appropriate for a single cell, a column, or a row of cells.

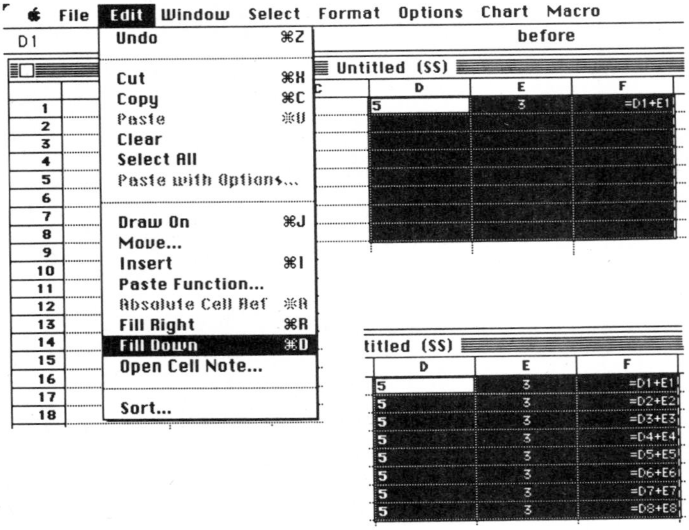

**Fig. 6.16**

*The Fill Down command in operation.*

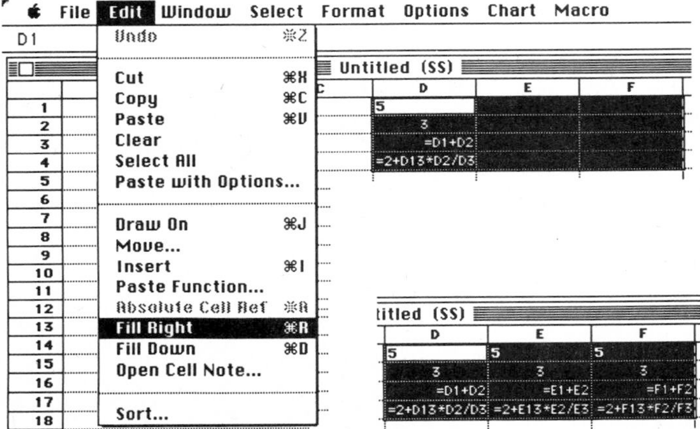


**Fig. 6.17**

*The Fill Right command in operation.*

To fill a range, follow these steps:

1. Select the cells, rows, or columns to be copied.
2. Select the cells, rows, or columns to receive the copies.
3. Choose either Fill Right or Fill Down from the Edit menu, or press ⌘-R or ⌘-D, respectively.

Works copies the contents of the active cells to the selected cells. Equations retain proper relative and absolute references.

> ***Caution:*** Be careful when issuing a Fill command to a row or column. If you do not select a range, Works will attempt to fill the entire limit of a theoretical worksheet. You will find yourself watching the spinning wristwatch for quite some time, eventually undoing the operation.

You need to think carefully when defining ranges with the Fill commands; otherwise, you may unintentionally alter cells. For example, when you fill a cell with new cell references you substantially change and possibly destroy any equation of which the cell was a part. The Fill commands are particularly powerful when used in conjunction with the cell referencing scheme that Works provides. You should be familiar with the material in the section on "Using Absolute and Relative Cell References" so that you understand well the effects of pasting cell references to new locations.

# *Inserting and Deleting Rows and Columns*

Most spreadsheets require the insertion or deletion of rows and columns at various times to add new categories, add new data, organize, or do general housekeeping. Works provides menu entries for easily achieving these tasks, and the program adjusts both relative and absolute references appropriately.

## *Inserting Rows and Columns*

To insert a row, do the following:

1. Select the row heading immediately below the spot at which you want to insert a row.

2. Either press ⌘-I or choose Insert from the Edit menu.

   A new blank row appears, and rows below are pushed down. When you insert a row it has the formatting of the selected initial row.

3. Perform any needed formatting and filling. Works automatically modifies portions of your old equations.

4. Test the worksheet (see this chapter's section on "Testing Spreadsheets").

To insert a column, follow these instructions:

1. Select the column immediately to the right of where you want to insert a column.

2. Either press ⌘-I or choose Insert from the Edit menu. A new blank column appears. Columns to the right of the new one are pushed right.

3. Perform any needed formatting and filling. Works automatically modifies portions of your old equations, renaming columns and many cell references, but you may need to modify some equations.

4. Perform any necessary formatting and filling.

5. Examine equations and test the spreadsheet.

**TIP:** Any cells that were protected in the original column will be protected in the new column.

When you're inserting rows or columns, Works automatically modifies your spreadsheet to rename all the cell addresses affected. For example, if you place a new row above row 6, then the original row 6 becomes row 7. Absolute references are changed to refer to the cell's new address. Relative references still refer to a cell the same direction and distance away. You should always remember to test the spreadsheet after inserting or deleting rows or columns.

> ***Caution:*** Many equations don't automatically include values entered in new lines; other equations do. For example, when you insert a row with additional values in a column that is summed, the sum may not take into account the additional values. Functions like SUM and SSUM minimize these kinds of problems, but even these functions don't eliminate the requirement to test carefully after insertions.

## *Deleting Rows and Columns*

Deleting is as simple as selecting the unwanted row or column and using the Cut feature. You can even select multiple rows or columns at once.

To delete a column or row, follow these steps:

1. Select a row or column (click the row number or column letter).
2. Either press ⌘-X or choose the Cut option from the Edit menu. The selected row or column disappears, and Works renumbers the affected rows, columns, and references.
3. Examine and test your spreadsheet to ensure proper operation.

Remember that the cut column or row replaces the contents of your Clipboard. You can thus undo cuts if you spot your error in time.

**NOTE:** If you remove cells needed for equations, your spreadsheet doesn't work properly. Usually, but not always, Works warns you by presenting a dialog box or by displaying `N/A` or `*Error*` in the affected cells.

# *Formatting Cells*

The key to formatting cells lies in the Format menu (see fig. 6.18), which presents you with options for changing attributes (style, justification, type of value, and so on) and cell borders. The commands for font, size, color, and column width apply to the entire worksheet and are discussed in the section called "Formatting a Worksheet."

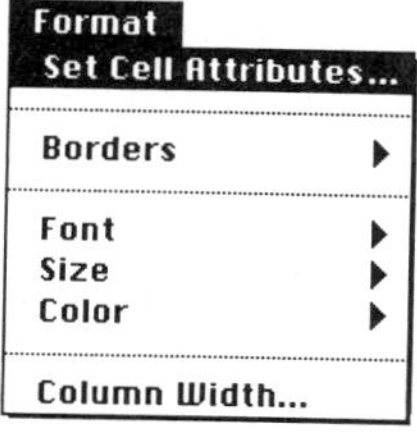


**Fig. 6.18**

*The Format menu.*

## *Setting Cell Attributes*

When you first create a worksheet, all your numeric values are displayed in Geneva 9-point black, treated as normal text, and right-justified. Labels are also treated as normal text but are left-justified. (If you need help remembering the differences between these types of cell entries, review the section on "Examining the Types of Spreadsheet Entries.")

To change the display options in a cell, choose the Set Cell Attributes command in the Format menu. The resulting dialog box, shown in figure 6.19, consolidates a number of commands in Works Version 2.0 that were previously placed directly on the Format menu.

**Fig. 6.19**

*The Set Cell Attributes dialog box.*

Set Cell Attributes:
Display: General, Fixed, Dollar, Percent, Scientific, Date Short, Date Medium, Date Long, Time, Show Day
Align: Left, Center, Right
Style: Bold, Underline, Commas
2 Decimal Places
Cancel OK

**TIP:** Perhaps the handiest shortcut in your spreadsheet is the one that calls up this dialog box when you double-click any cell.

The display options in the left column of the Set Cell Attributes dialog box control the formatting of numbers in a cell:

- *General.* Numbers are displayed precisely, and leading zeros are dropped.
- *Fixed.* Values display a specific number of places to the right of the decimal point. The default setting is 2, and you change it by typing in the Decimal Places text box.
- *Dollar.* Displays dollars-and-cents format to two decimal places (unless you change that setting) and places a dollar sign ($) to the left of your number. When entering a number in a cell formatted with Dollars format, you do not need to type the dollar sign.
- *Percent.* Multiplies an entry by 100 and places a percent sign (%) to the right of your entry. You do not need to type the percent sign in cells formatted with this option.

- *Scientific*. Represents scientific notation. You can use it to express very small and very large numbers. The number 12345 can be expressed as 1.2345E4, and the number 0.12345 as 1.2345E−4. The number 1.2345 is the *mantissa*, E is the *exponentiation letter*, and −4 is the *exponent*. (The exponential letter can be either e or E.)

The second column of display options refers to the date and time formatting.

- *Date Short* displays dates in the form 8/27/52.
- *Date Medium* displays dates in the form Aug 27, 1952.
- *Date Long* displays dates in the form August 27, 1952.
- *Time* format can display time in the 12-hour or 24-hour clock, either in the form 2:04 PM or 14:04. The AM period is the default choice if you don't specify PM in the 12-hour clock. Also, typing *2:4* displays 2:04.
- *Show Day*, when checked, places the day of the week before a medium or long date. With medium dates, the day is abbreviated, as in *Wed*.

**NOTE:** Although you can place the date and time into a cell in several standard formats, Works uses a number representation to do mathematical calculations behind the scenes. Time and date are functions new in Works 2.0 and are described more fully in Chapter 8.

The Align options are entirely analogous to the justification controls offered to you in the word processor module. You can align cell entries to the Left, in the Center, or to the Right.

Three additional formatting commands are contained in this dialog box:

- *Bold* is a type style option. You can also press ⌘-B to change cell contents to boldface type.
- *Underline* is a type style option. You can also press ⌘-I to italicize cell contents.
- *Commas* is another type style. Using it places commas in a numeric cell.

**TIP:** If you want to remove a bold or italicized format, you can use the ⌘-N keyboard shortcut.

## *Bordering the Cell*

You can also format the cell itself rather than its contents. Choosing the Borders command from the Format menu gives you a submenu with six choices. You can border cells Left, Right, Top, Bottom, or any combination of these. You can also choose the Outline command to enclose the cell with borders, and select None to remove all choices. When you select any of these options, a check mark appears next to it.

## *Formatting a Range of Cells*

Frequently, you may want to format a range of rows or columns or a block of cells. To do so, follow this procedure:

1. Select the range.
2. Choose your formatting, including attribute type, type style, alignment, and cell borders.

You can perform these steps either before or after you make your entries. The column or row labels are formatted globally if you select them as a range.

**TIP:** Some cells may appear empty but contain formatting information. To confirm this possibility, you can check the cell by activating it and pulling down the Format menu, or by double-clicking the cell to call up the Set Cell Attributes dialog box.

## *Using Cell Notes*

A new feature in Works 2.0 is the option to attach a cell note to any cell. Cell notes allow you to place information about how the spreadsheet was constructed or about any detail or task you must remember. To attach a cell note to any cell, select the cell and either choose the Open Cell Note command from the Edit menu or press the ⌘ key and double-click. It is not necessary to select the cell first if you use this keystroke. You can open a cell note for viewing by selecting the cell, pressing the ⌘ key, and double-clicking. An insertion point is automatically placed into the cell note; just start typing. Figure 6.20 shows an example of an open cell note. It is a scrolling window, and you can edit it in any of the ways you can edit word processor windows.

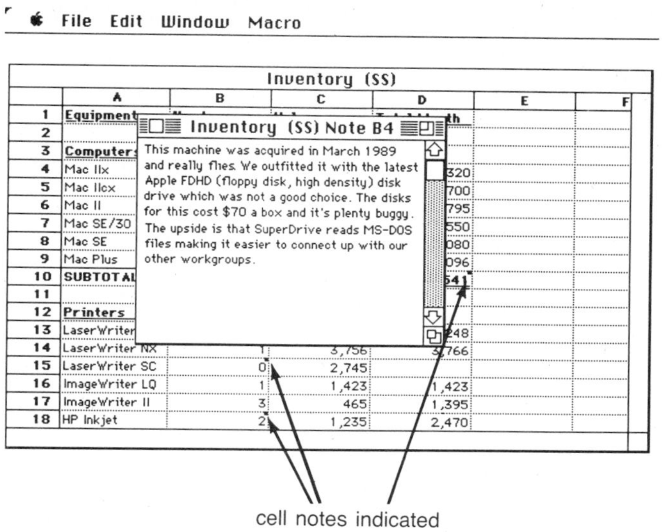
File Edit Window Macro
Inventory (SS)
Inventory (SS) Note B4
This machine was acquired in March 1989 and really flies. We outfitted it with the latest Apple FDHD (floppy disk, high density) disk drive which was not a good choice. The disks for this cost $70 a box and it's plenty buggy. The upside is that SuperDrive reads MS-DOS files making it easier to connect up with our other workgroups.
Equipment
Computers
Mac IIx
Mac IIcx
Mac II
Mac SE/30
Mac SE
Mac Plus
SUBTOTAL
Printers
LaserWriter
LaserWriter NX
LaserWriter SC
ImageWriter LQ
ImageWriter II
HP Inkjet
cell notes indicated

**Fig. 6.20**

*A sample cell note.*

You can tell when a cell note is attached to a cell by choosing the Show Notes Indicator command from the Options menu (see fig. 6.7). Works then displays a small black square in the upper right corner of any cell that has a note. In figure 6.20, cell note markers are displayed in cells B15, B18, and D10.

If you want to move a cell note along with the cell's contents, you should make sure that when using the Paste with Options command, you check the option for pasting Both Values and Formulas. Pasting values alone does not transfer your cell notes.

You can also print your cell notes. Click the Print Cell Notes option in the File menu's Page Setup dialog box. Cell notes are printed after your spreadsheet documents print and can be identified by the cell reference in the title bar.

# *Protecting a Cell*

Spreadsheets are easy to alter, which is both a blessing and a curse. Unless you catch and undo a mistake immediately, you lose the equation forever. The spreadsheet never gives the correct answers again unless you spot the problem and rewrite the equation. To prevent damage to or deletion of a vital equation, you can protect the cell. Protection "locks" the specified cell.

To build a worksheet that includes protected cells, follow these steps:

1. Enter and format your labels.
2. Enter and test your equations; format these cells as needed.
3. Select a range to be protected (usually only labels and equations).
4. Choose the Protected command from the Options menu.
5. Continue selecting ranges and choosing the Protected command until you have protected all important areas.
6. Don't forget to save the protected spreadsheet.

Usually you don't need to protect areas of the spreadsheet that contain values unless you don't want anyone to change the values accidentally.

If you try to modify a protected cell, Works displays a warning in a dialog box (see fig. 6.21). You must acknowledge the warning by clicking OK before Works lets you continue. Then, to modify that cell, you must unprotect it by choosing Protected on the Options menu again. (The Protected command is a toggle). You can turn off protection everywhere in the worksheet by choosing Select All Cells from the Select menu and then specifying Protected on the Options menu twice, removing the check mark.

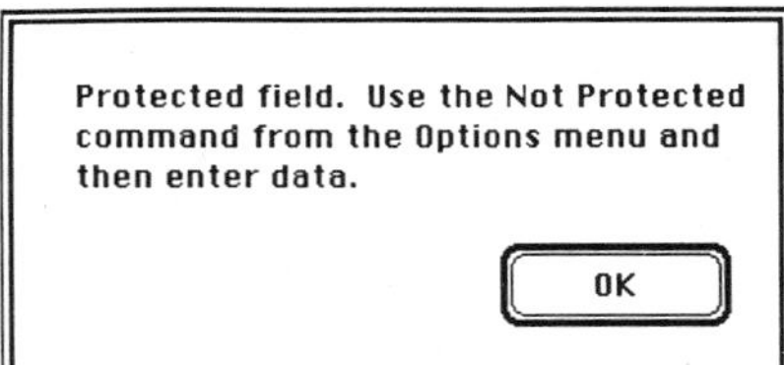

Protected field. Use the Not Protected command from the Options menu and then enter data.
OK


**Fig. 6.21**

*The warning about a protected cell.*

When designing the spreadsheet, you can protect things as you go rather than wait until you finish, but you need to unprotect areas that require changes. Most people find the easier approach to be to wait until a spreadsheet is completed and tested before protecting it.

# *Formatting a Worksheet*

The last four commands on the Format menu—Font, Size, Color, and Column Width—allow you to change the format of your entire worksheet.

## Controlling Font, Size, and Color

You can change the font, size, and color of your spreadsheet. This feature works identically to the word processor module of your spreadsheet. When you choose a color, your grid, heading, labels, and all entries have that color. Select any cell or range of cells, and your highlight appears in the selected color. Your color choice is automatically executed when you print (see "Printing a Spreadsheet").

All these formatting choices work globally throughout your spreadsheet; you can have only one font, font size, and color throughout the spreadsheet. To change any of these formats, select the menu item in the Format menu. Font styles like bold or underline can be individually adjusted. When you open a new spreadsheet the default is Geneva font, 9-point, black.

## Changing Column Widths

Works sets all columns on a new spreadsheet at a width of 12 characters. You may want to widen a column so that it can accept long labels or large numbers. Or you may want to reduce the size of columns that will contain short entries so that you can fit more columns on your screen and paper.

You have two ways to change the width of a column. One way is to point to the top part of the line separating two columns (the part of the line that is in the row of column letters), which is called the *column divider bar*. The pointer then changes to a bar with double arrows (see fig. 6.22). Drag the column to the width you want, and watch the width change as you drag.

The Format menu offers another, more precise way to change column widths. Follow these steps:

1. Activate any cell in the column.
2. Choose Column Width from the Format menu. The dialog box shown in figure 6.23 appears.
3. Enter the number of characters (up to 40) you want for the column width; then either click OK or press Return.

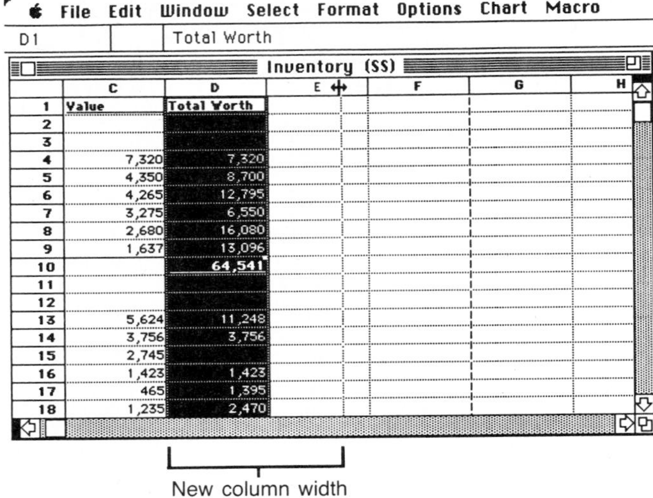


Fig. 6.22

*Dragging to change column widths.*

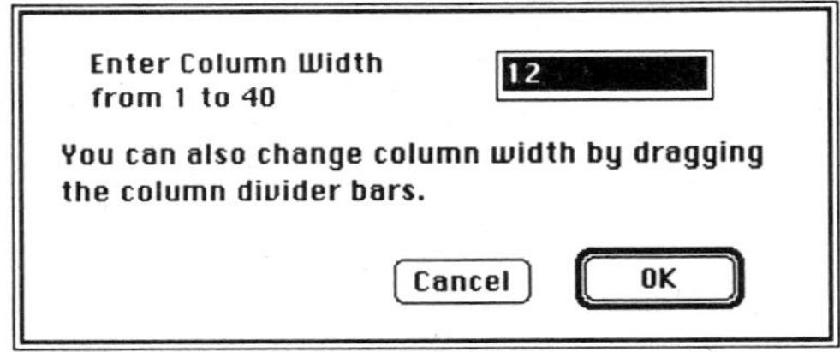


Fig. 6.23

*Using the Column Width dialog box.*

To change the widths of *all* columns, do the following:

1. Select any row by clicking the row number, or select the whole spreadsheet with the Select All command.

2. Choose the Column Width option on the Format menu.

3. Enter a new width and then click OK or press Return.

**TIP:** When setting up column widths, be sure to take into account the space occupied by dollar signs, decimal points, and decimal places. Negative numbers displayed and printed in the Dollar format appear in parentheses; make room for these, too.

# *Sorting a Worksheet*

You can quickly rearrange the rows (but not the columns) on your spreadsheet by sorting them. (If you try and sort columns based on row headings, Works issues an alert box.) You can sort rows in either ascending or descending order, and you can sort on three columns of your choosing, in any order. If you perform more than one set of sorts, the most recent sort takes precedence.

Works uses ASCII code to sort entries in this order: error values, numbers, text, and blanks. (The ASCII code is a basic machine assembly language in which specific characters are converted to a combination of bits. Database sorts in Works also use the ASCII code.) Figure 6.24 shows a listing of ASCII characters, in descending order.

space ! " # $ % & ' ( ) * + , − . / 0 1 2 3 4 5 6 7 8 9 : ; < = >
? @ A B C D E F G H I J K L M N O P Q R S T U V W X Y Z [ \ ]
^ _ ‘ { | } ~ ° c £ •

**Fig. 6.24**

*The ASCII characters.*

**NOTE:** Some specialty characters are missing in the list in figure 6.24. Most fonts do not contain the full ASCII code.

The numbers in the ASCII order refer to numbers used in text strings. Numerical numbers are sorted separately. An ASCII sort ignores upper- and lowercase differentiation and accent marks.

For example, figure 6.25 shows a random collection of cell entries in column A. Column B shows how they appear after being sorted in ascending order; column C shows the same values sorted in descending order. Notice that the blank always ends up on the bottom. Notice also what happens when a number is the first character in a label.

| BEFORE SORT | AFTER ASCENDING SORT | AFTER DESCENDING SORT |
|---|---|---|
| 9 | -1.26E+11 | 9 |
| | -1 | 6 |
| a label | 0 | 0.5 |
| A LABEL | 0.5 | 0 |
| -1 | 6 | -1 |
| 0 | 9 | -1.26E+11 |
| 1 NUMBER IN A LABEL | 1 NUMBER IN A LABEL | b |
| 0.5 | a label | B |
| -1.26E+11 | A LABEL | a label |
| 6 | b | A LABEL |
| b | B | 1 NUMBER IN A LABEL |
| B | | |

**Fig. 6.25**

*Results of ascending and descending sorts.*

> ***Caution:*** Because sorting selected portions of any spreadsheet can create problems, you may want to back up your spreadsheet before you undertake any sort operation.

To initiate a sort, choose the Sort command at the bottom of the Edit menu. The Sort dialog box shown in figure 6.26 appears. In this dialog box, you specify the key columns on which Works should sort your rows. When you specify more than one column in a sort, you should sort the most important key column first, and the least important set of sorts last.

**Fig. 6.26**

*The Sort dialog box.*

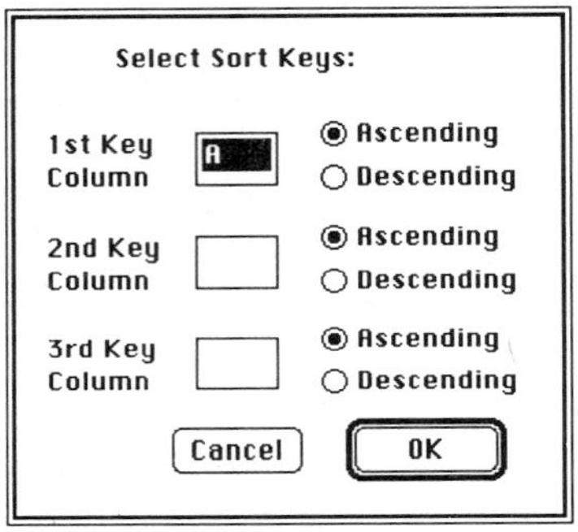

Select Sort Keys:

1st Key Column: A — ◉ Ascending ○ Descending

2nd Key Column: — ◉ Ascending ○ Descending

3rd Key Column: — ◉ Ascending ○ Descending

Cancel OK

For example, figure 6.27 shows a sample three-column spreadsheet of a set of locations. Figure 6.28 shows the results of sorting the spreadsheet in the following order: 1st Key Column, A; 2nd Key Column, C; and 3rd Key Column, B. The locations are thus sorted first by region, next by state, and last by city.

**Fig. 6.27**

*Spreadsheet entries before sorting.*

| | A | B | C |
|---|---|---|---|
| 1 | Region | City | State |
| 2 | WEST | Los Angeles | CA |
| 3 | EAST | Buffalo | NY |
| 4 | CENTRAL | Chicago | IL |
| 5 | EAST | New York | NY |
| 6 | CENTRAL | Indianapolis | IN |
| 7 | EAST | Boston | MA |
| 8 | CENTRAL | St Louis | MO |
| 9 | CENTRAL | Detroit | MI |
| 10 | WEST | Oakland | CA |
| 11 | EAST | Cambridge | MA |
| 12 | EAST | Albany | NY |
| 13 | WEST | San Diego | CA |
| 14 | CENTRAL | Peoria | IL |
| 15 | WEST | San Francisco | CA |
| 16 | WEST | Seattle | WA |
| 17 | | | |

| | A | B | C |
|---|---|---|---|
| 1 | Region | City | State |
| 2 | CENTRAL | Chicago | IL |
| 3 | CENTRAL | Peoria | IL |
| 4 | CENTRAL | Indianapolis | IN |
| 5 | CENTRAL | Detroit | MI |
| 6 | CENTRAL | St Louis | MO |
| 7 | EAST | Boston | MA |
| 8 | EAST | Cambridge | MA |
| 9 | EAST | Albany | NY |
| 10 | EAST | Buffalo | NY |
| 11 | EAST | New York | NY |
| 12 | WEST | Los Angeles | CA |
| 13 | WEST | Oakland | CA |
| 14 | WEST | San Diego | CA |
| 15 | WEST | San Francisco | CA |
| 16 | WEST | Seattle | WA |
| 17 | | | |

**Fig. 6.28**

*Result of a multilevel sort by region, state, and city.*

When selecting the cells to be sorted, you can easily select too many or too few cells. Both errors can create havoc. For example, suppose that you sort a set of rows in a spreadsheet, but you neglect to select the column of labels that refer to the columns of data. The labels remain in their original locations but all the numbers are rearranged. After the sort, then, the numbers are improperly labeled. This problem can occur in most spreadsheet software and is not unique to Works. You can always undo this error if you catch it immediately, but you should always be extra careful when sorting a spreadsheet.

# *Dividing Your Window into Panes*

When dealing with large spreadsheets, you will probably find yourself scrolling back and forth frequently. For example, you will change an income estimate and then scroll down several pages to see the impact on profitability. Or you will change a January number and scroll to the right to inspect the change on the year's total. All this scrolling can be time-consuming and annoying. Works offers a "window pane" feature that lets you look at as many as four different parts of a spreadsheet at once, even if they're widely separated.

In figure 6.29, four panes are visible in the spreadsheet window. Each pane has its own scroll bars and boxes, and each pane can be scrolled independently of the others.

To create a pane, you do the following:

1. Point to the black bar next to the lower left or upper right scroll box. The pointer then changes to a two-headed arrow.

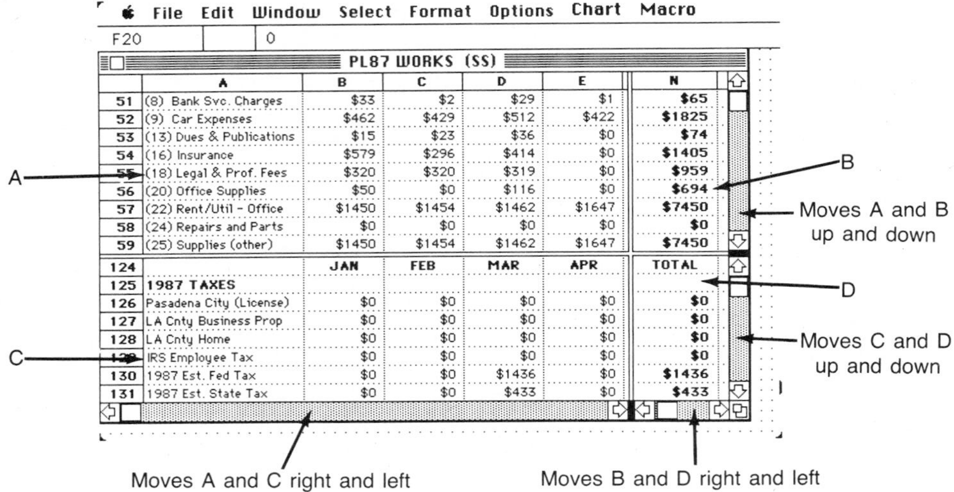


| | A | B | C | D | E | N |
|---|---|---|---|---|---|---|
| 51 | (8) Bank Svc. Charges | $33 | $2 | $29 | $1 | $65 |
| 52 | (9) Car Expenses | $462 | $429 | $512 | $422 | $1825 |
| 53 | (13) Dues & Publications | $15 | $23 | $36 | $0 | $74 |
| 54 | (16) Insurance | $579 | $296 | $414 | $0 | $1405 |
| 55 | (18) Legal & Prof. Fees | $320 | $320 | $319 | $0 | $959 |
| 56 | (20) Office Supplies | $50 | $0 | $116 | $0 | $694 |
| 57 | (22) Rent/Util - Office | $1450 | $1454 | $1462 | $1647 | $7450 |
| 58 | (24) Repairs and Parts | $0 | $0 | $0 | $0 | $0 |
| 59 | (25) Supplies (other) | $1450 | $1454 | $1462 | $1647 | $7450 |
| 124 | | JAN | FEB | MAR | APR | TOTAL |
| 125 | 1987 TAXES | | | | | |
| 126 | Pasadena City (License) | $0 | $0 | $0 | $0 | $0 |
| 127 | LA Cnty Business Prop | $0 | $0 | $0 | $0 | $0 |
| 128 | LA Cnty Home | $0 | $0 | $0 | $0 | $0 |
| 129 | IRS Employee Tax | $0 | $0 | $0 | $0 | $0 |
| 130 | 1987 Est. Fed Tax | $0 | $0 | $1436 | $0 | $1436 |
| 131 | 1987 Est. State Tax | $0 | $0 | $433 | $0 | $433 |

**Fig. 6.29**

*Four panes visible in spreadsheet window.*

2. Drag the black bar until the window pane bar (a solid double line—see fig. 6.29 for a vertical and horizontal set) appears. Keep dragging the window pane bar to the position you want.
3. Scroll the contents of the various panes as needed.

To reposition or eliminate a pane, you point to the black area between the scroll arrows and move the pane off-screen.

# *Freezing Titles*

When you scroll a large spreadsheet or divide your worksheet into panes to have a look around, you may have difficulty knowing exactly what you are looking at. As an aid, Works gives you the ability to freeze titles or labels either as a row (for horizontal freezing) or a column (for vertical freezing). Then as you scroll the spreadsheet, your labels remain in place.

To freeze a row, do the following:

1. Split the window horizontally into panes.

2. Scroll and select the row with the titles to be frozen when it is just above the split bar.
3. Choose the Freeze Titles Horizontal command in the Options menu. This command freezes the row above the split bar so that when you scroll vertically, the row above the pane stays in place.

To freeze a column, follow these steps:

1. Create a vertical pane.
2. Scroll and select the column with the titles to be frozen to the left of the split bar.
3. Issue the Freeze Titles Vertical command from the Options menu. When you scroll horizontally, the title remains stationary to the left of the window pane.

# *Removing the Grid*

By default, Works displays a grid when you open a worksheet. At times you may not want to display this grid on-screen. By choosing the Show Grid command from the Options menu, you can remove the grid. To redisplay the grid, choose the Show Grid command once more. A check mark next to the command indicates that the grid is active, which should be obvious from your screen. Figure 6.30 shows an example of a worksheet without a grid. Note that even without a grid the cell note indicators remain if you have checked that option (Show Notes Indicator). All commands and shortcuts (such as double-clicking a cell to bring up the Set Cell Attributes command) still work.

When you print your spreadsheet with the grid turned off, you can still print the row numbers and column letters, as illustrated in figure 6.31. In order to print row and column headings you must select that option in the Page Setup dialog box. This was discussed in the section titled "Fonts, Printers and Networks" in Chapter 1.

# *Saving a Spreadsheet*

To save a spreadsheet, you use the techniques you learned in the section titled "Saving Your Work" in Chapter 2. Works gives you three options for saving: normal, export, and Stationery. Normal and Stationery do not differ from the manner in which they operated for the word

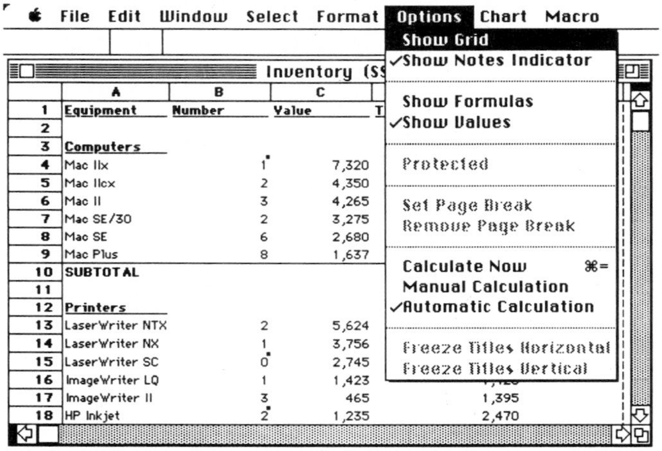

File Edit Window Select Format Options Chart Macro

Inventory (SS

Options menu:
- Show Grid
- ✓Show Notes Indicator
- Show Formulas
- ✓Show Values
- Protected
- Set Page Break
- Remove Page Break
- Calculate Now ⌘=
- Manual Calculation
- ✓Automatic Calculation
- Freeze Titles Horizontal
- Freeze Titles Vertical

| | A | B | C | D |
|---|---|---|---|---|
| 1 | Equipment | Number | Value | T |
| 2 | | | | |
| 3 | Computers | | | |
| 4 | Mac IIx | 1 | 7,320 | |
| 5 | Mac IIcx | 2 | 4,350 | |
| 6 | Mac II | 3 | 4,265 | |
| 7 | Mac SE/30 | 2 | 3,275 | |
| 8 | Mac SE | 6 | 2,680 | |
| 9 | Mac Plus | 8 | 1,637 | |
| 10 | SUBTOTAL | | | |
| 11 | | | | |
| 12 | Printers | | | |
| 13 | LaserWriter NTX | 2 | 5,624 | |
| 14 | LaserWriter NX | 1 | 3,756 | |
| 15 | LaserWriter SC | 0 | 2,745 | |
| 16 | ImageWriter LQ | 1 | 1,423 | |
| 17 | ImageWriter II | 3 | 465 | 1,395 |
| 18 | HP Inkjet | 2 | 1,235 | 2,470 |

**Fig. 6.30**

*A worksheet with the grid turned off.*

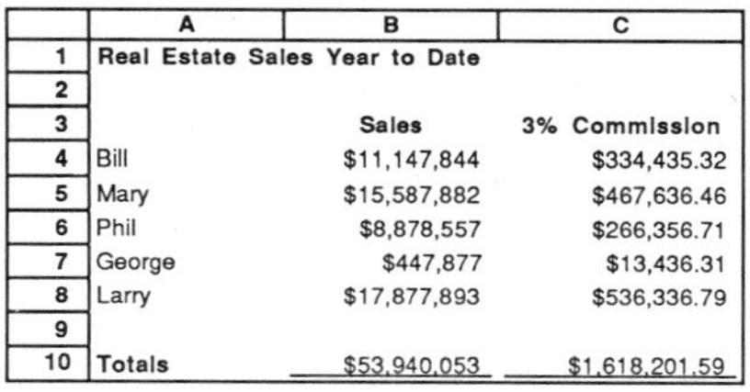

| | A | B | C |
|---|---|---|---|
| 1 | Real Estate Sales Year to Date | | |
| 2 | | | |
| 3 | | Sales | 3% Commission |
| 4 | Bill | $11,147,844 | $334,435.32 |
| 5 | Mary | $15,587,882 | $467,636.46 |
| 6 | Phil | $8,878,557 | $266,356.71 |
| 7 | George | $447,877 | $13,436.31 |
| 8 | Larry | $17,877,893 | $536,336.79 |
| 9 | | | |
| 10 | Totals | $53,940,053 | $1,618,201.59 |

**Fig. 6.31**

*Suppressing the grid but printing the row numbers and column letters.*

processor files discussed previously. Like any other Works file, a spreadsheet contains formatting that allows it to be exported to other Macintosh programs. The formatting is called SYLK. Each cell value is separated from the next by a tab symbol, and a carriage return is placed at the end of each row. Works database files are formatted in the same manner.

When you open a spreadsheet initially it is untitled, so you can use either the Save or Save As command in the File menu; both functions will have identical results in this case. After you have saved your file, use the Save command to save additional changes to the file in which you are working. Save As creates a copy of the file with a file name of your choice. If you select Save As and use the same file name as a file that was saved previously, the contents of the previous file will be replaced by the contents of your new file. Works will give you a warning message that you are about to replace the contents of the file.

Selecting Save or Save As results in an SF Put dialog box. Choose Normal to save a file, Stationery to save a template, or Export to save in SYLK format. Opening a Stationery file puts a copy of your file on the screen with the heading "Untitled."

## Testing Spreadsheets

This warning cannot be issued often enough: *Test your spreadsheets.* Making spreadsheet errors that can go undetected for years is an extremely easy thing to do. These errors can cost companies thousands or even millions of dollars. Spreadsheet errors have even caused bankruptcies.

Before using even the simplest spreadsheet for real work, be sure to examine and test the spreadsheet. Get into the habit of running examples through both your new spreadsheet and a calculator. Test under enough different conditions to check each spreadsheet operation. People have lost their jobs—and lawsuits—because they have failed to test spreadsheets. Don't join their ranks.

## Printing a Spreadsheet

To print spreadsheets, you use the same techniques you use to print word processing documents (see Chapters 1 and 2). Either select Print from the File menu or use the ⌘-P shortcut. To print a spreadsheet, follow these steps:

1. Select Page Setup on the File menu and make your choices (see the following section, "Setting Up the Page"). Click OK or press Return.
2. Give the Print command on the File menu and select the print quality and range you want. Remember that it is always a good idea to use Print Preview to examine your work before you print it.
3. If you have selected color in your spreadsheet, it will print automatically to an output device (printer) that supports color. This is controlled by the printer driver.
4. Prepare your printer and click OK in the Print dialog box, or press Return.

Usually Works prints an entire spreadsheet. You can, however, print parts of a large spreadsheet by selecting them before executing the print request.

By using the Print Window option in the File menu, you can print only the part of the spreadsheet that is displayed in the active window. The row letters and column numbers are always printed, but the entry bar, scroll bars, menu, and so on do not print.

## Setting Up the Page

When printing spreadsheets, you have the same control over Page Setup options that you have with a word processing window. You can request page numbers, headers, footers, special paper sizes, and more. One additional option in the Page Setup dialog box that is not previously available for word processor documents is the Print Row and Column Numbers option (see fig. 6.31), located just below the boxes for the choice of page orientation. (See figs. 1.11 and 1.26 and the section in Chapter 1 on "Fonts, Printers, and Networks.")

Remember that the Page Setup dialog box offers two page orientations: portrait (the icon on the left in the Orientation option) and landscape. The choices are named after the way most people hold a camera to take portraits of people and to take pictures of landscapes. The default orientation, portrait, is great for printing long spreadsheets, but this orientation causes Works to print rows only across the short edge of your paper. Use this choice if you have many rows and only a few columns. Clicking the landscape icon causes Works to print rows along the long edge of the paper. This orientation is helpful for wide spreadsheets. Figure 6.32 shows a spreadsheet printed in both orientations.

You can use the 50% Reduction box on your ImageWriter Page Setup dialog box or the Reduce or Enlarge box on your LaserWriter Page Setup dialog box to change your spreadsheet size. At 50 percent reduction, you can fit twice as much on each sheet of paper. The Reduce or Enlarge box on the LaserWriter dialog box lets you specify the percentage of either reduction or enlargement in your output at any level you choose.

## Setting Page Breaks

Works automatically sets page breaks based on your Page Setup choices. Dashed lines, slightly heavier than the grid lines, appear on the

| | A | B | C |
|---|---|---|---|
| 1 | MILEAGE AND COST | | |
| 2 | | | |
| 3 | Beginning Odometer | 110 | |
| 4 | Ending Odometer | 325 | |
| 5 | **Miles Traveled** | 215 | |
| 6 | | | |
| 7 | Gallons Used | 12.6 | |
| 8 | Cost Per Gallon | $1.25 | |
| 9 | | | |
| 10 | **Total Gas Cost** | $15.75 | |
| 11 | | | |
| 12 | **Miles Per Gallon** | 17.06 | |
| 13 | | | |
| 14 | **Cost Per Mile** | $0.073 | |
| 15 | | | |
| 16 | | | |
| 17 | | | |

| | A | B | C | D | E |
|---|---|---|---|---|---|
| 1 | MILEAGE AND COST | | | | |
| 2 | | | | | |
| 3 | Beginning Odometer | 110 | | | |
| 4 | Ending Odometer | 325 | | | |
| 5 | | | | | |
| 6 | **Miles Traveled** | 215 | | | |
| 7 | | | | | |
| 8 | | | | | |
| 9 | Gallons Used | 12.6 | | | |
| 10 | Cost Per Gallon | $1.25 | | | |
| 11 | | | | | |
| 12 | **Total Gas Cost** | $15.75 | | | |
| 13 | | | | | |
| 14 | **Miles Per Gallon** | 17.06 | | | |
| 15 | | | | | |
| 16 | **Cost Per Mile** | $0.073 | | | |

**Fig. 6.32**

*Spreadsheet printed in portrait and landscape orientations.*

screen, indicating spreadsheet page breaks and the positions of the edges of printed pages. In figure 6.33, Works will print a new page starting at row 15. After that side of the spreadsheet is printed, Works will print the next page starting at column G. At least four sheets of paper are required to print this spreadsheet.

You can force Works to insert page breaks wherever you want them. You cannot, however, choose page breaks that don't fit the paper size you selected during the Page Setup process.

To insert a page break, follow these instructions:

1. Select the cell that should be the upper left corner of the new page.

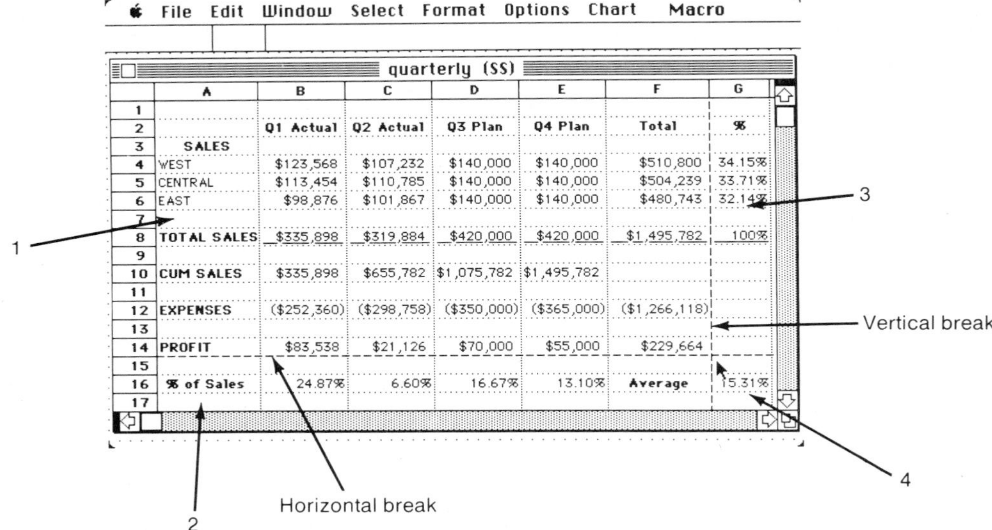


| | A | B | C | D | E | F | G |
|---|---|---|---|---|---|---|---|
| 1 | | | | | | | |
| 2 | | Q1 Actual | Q2 Actual | Q3 Plan | Q4 Plan | Total | % |
| 3 | SALES | | | | | | |
| 4 | WEST | $123,568 | $107,232 | $140,000 | $140,000 | $510,800 | 34.15% |
| 5 | CENTRAL | $113,454 | $110,785 | $140,000 | $140,000 | $504,239 | 33.71% |
| 6 | EAST | $98,876 | $101,867 | $140,000 | $140,000 | $480,743 | 32.14% |
| 7 | | | | | | | |
| 8 | TOTAL SALES | $335,898 | $319,884 | $420,000 | $420,000 | $1,495,782 | 100% |
| 9 | | | | | | | |
| 10 | CUM SALES | $335,898 | $655,782 | $1,075,782 | $1,495,782 | | |
| 11 | | | | | | | |
| 12 | EXPENSES | ($252,360) | ($298,758) | ($350,000) | ($365,000) | ($1,266,118) | |
| 13 | | | | | | | |
| 14 | PROFIT | $83,538 | $21,126 | $70,000 | $55,000 | $229,664 | |
| 15 | | | | | | | |
| 16 | % of Sales | 24.87% | 6.60% | 16.67% | 13.10% | Average | 15.31% |
| 17 | | | | | | | |

**Fig. 6.33**

*Darker dashed lines showing where printer page breaks will occur.*

2. Choose Set Page Break from the Options menu. Works then displays the new vertical and horizontal breaks and repaginates the rest of the spreadsheet.

At times, you may want to remove a manual page break you have previously inserted. At other times, you may decide to move a page break in order to create a more balanced page or to divide the printed spreadsheet more effectively.

To remove a page break, do the following:

1. Select the cell in the upper left corner of the page.
2. Choose Remove Page Break from the Options menu. Works removes both vertical and horizontal page breaks and then repaginates for you.

To remove only a vertical page break, choose any cell to the right of the page break line and then choose the Remove Page Break command. Similarly, to remove only a horizontal page break, choose any cell below the dashed line and then choose Remove Page Break.

# *Chapter Summary*

In this chapter, you learned about a powerful tool for manipulating data: the spreadsheet. With a spreadsheet you can do complex calculations and play "what-if" games to see how changes affect your data. Because Works does all the calculating for you, changes are easy.

This chapter also described how Works provides shortcuts for building your spreadsheet quickly and accurately. You learned how to control fonts and formatting to emphasize your work.

In Chapter 7 you learn how to present your data as graphs to give added meaning to your results. Refer to Chapter 8 for a full listing of the functions available to build your spreadsheet.

# 7

# Graphs

Spreadsheets are valuable sources of data. But without some way of comparing those numbers visually, you may have difficulty knowing what the figures mean. Works gives you the opportunity to define graphs that can help you ascertain trends or demonstrate to others your results. Your graphs are dynamically linked to your spreadsheet; change a number in a cell, and watch your graph change instantly.

With Works Version 2.0, you have the additional tools of both the draw module and color available in your worksheets. You can paste your graphs into your word processor files and then add objects and color to the graphs there.

In this chapter, you learn about the options for graphs, such as the types of graphs, horizontal and vertical titles, legends, scaling, and grids. The discussions also tell you how to plot and print your graphs; how to save graph definitions with your spreadsheets; how to duplicate, modify, rename, and erase graph definitions; and how to work with the draw module and design attractive presentations and output color.

One person's chart is another's graph. Charts are lists of things, like best-selling records; whereas graphs are normally pictures. Microsoft refers to graphs as *charts*, however, not only in the manuals but on your screen as well. The Works menu for creating graphs is called the Chart menu, and the dialog boxes regularly refer to charts. And sometimes Microsoft calls charts (meaning graphs) *plots*. Rather than add to the confusion, this book uses the term graphs, except in commands and names of screens and dialog boxes.

# When To Use What Graph

You have five basic types of graphs available in Works: line graphs (see fig. 7.1), bar graphs (see fig. 7.2), stacked-bar graphs (see fig. 7.3), combination graphs (see fig. 7.4), and pie graphs (see fig. 7.5). Each type of graph is appropriate for a different purpose. With this variety, you can pick the style that presents your data most clearly and effectively.

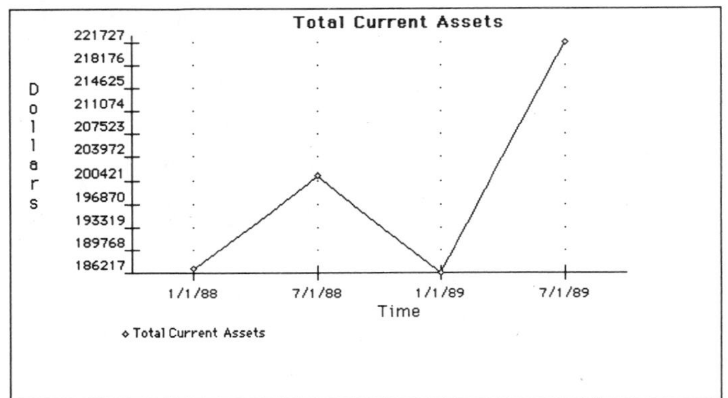


**Fig. 7.1**

*A line graph.*

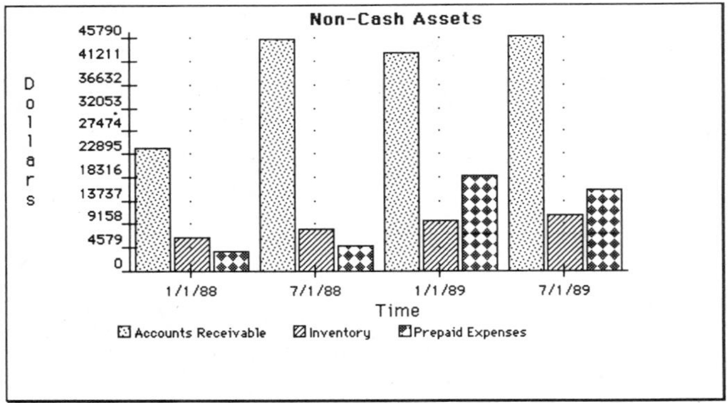


**Fig. 7.2**

*A bar graph.*

Line, bar, stacked-bar, and combination graphs are all variations of a series graph. Series graphs are best for displaying progressive relationships among data. In figure 7.1, for example, the simple line graph shows how the overall cash value of a business changes with time. Other series graphs, such as bar graphs, are more useful for demonstrating one set of variables changing against another set of variables. For

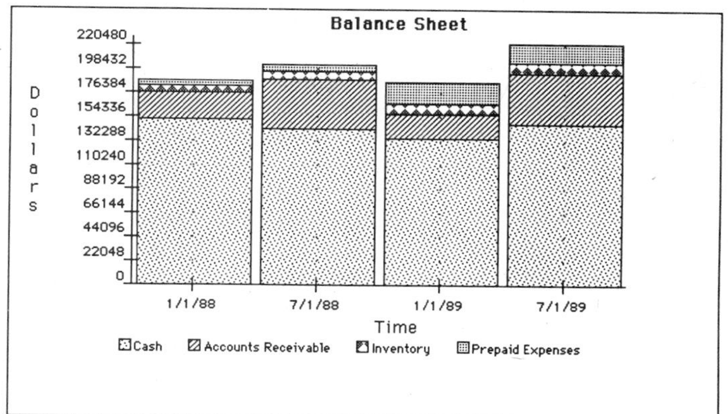


**Fig. 7.3**

*A stacked-bar graph.*

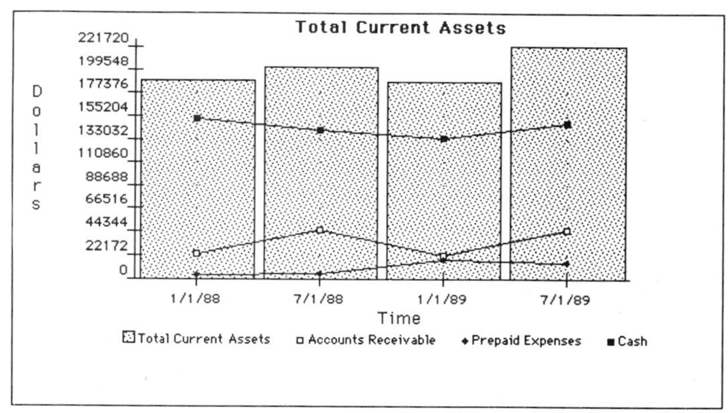


**Fig. 7.4**

*A combination graph.*

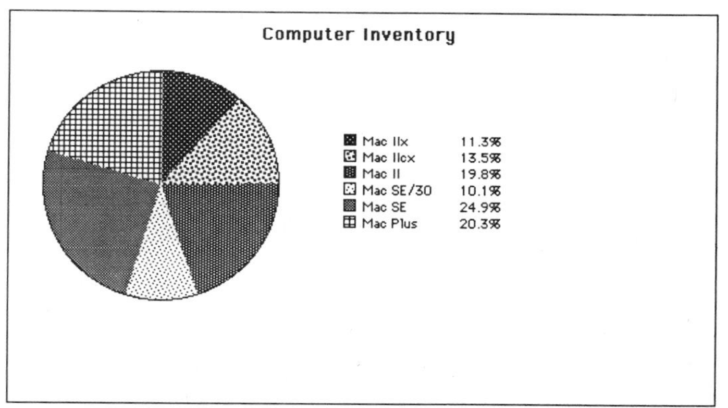


**Fig. 7.5**

*A pie graph.*

example, if you want to look at a set of costs versus each month, you might want to use a bar graph. Stacked-bar graphs are best for showing a set of variables as a component of a whole plotted against another set of variables. This type of graph also gives you a feeling for changes in the total. Figure 7.3 examines the breakdown of the net worth of a business over time. If you were interested only in showing the component pieces of a whole unit, you could use a pie graph. You can use a combination graph to show trends of one set of numbers (with bars) versus another set (with lines) at the same time. This type graph is particularly handy for looking at how small details and the "big picture" change concurrently.

# *Learning Basic Graphing Concepts*

To generate graphs, you use data from your spreadsheets. Your graphs are linked to your data, so you must have the worksheet to which your data is linked open on-screen to view it. You start a graph by choosing a graph type, defining the data to use, and specifying the location of that data. You can specify optional graph titles, scale titles, and the axis scales themselves. You can make other style decisions as well.

Once you have created a *graph definition*, Works saves it automatically. You can save up to eight different definitions per spreadsheet, so you can have as many as eight different graphs for one spreadsheet. Works assigns sequentially numbered definition names. You can easily delete unwanted definitions to make room for new ones (see "Duplicating and Erasing Graph Definitions" in this chapter).

After defining your graph, you can plot it to your screen in the form of a Works window. You print a graph (like any other window) by using the Print Window command on the File menu. And you can include graphs in other documents (as pictures) by using the Clipboard or the Scrapbook with familiar cut-and-paste techniques.

# *Creating Series Graphs*

Here are the basic steps for creating a new series graph:

1. Open a spreadsheet containing the data you want to graph.

2. Open the Chart menu and choose New Series Chart. The dialog box shown in figure 7.6 appears. This dialog box is the key to defining your series graph, setting your parameters, and saving the results.

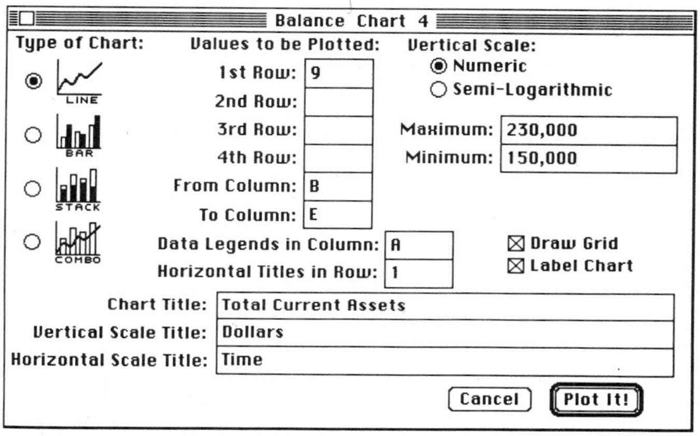

**Fig. 7.6**

*The New Series Chart dialog box.*

3. Select the type of series chart (line, bar, stack, or combo).
4. Define the range(s) to be plotted.
5. Enter titles (optional).
6. Change scale type (optional).
7. Define minimum and maximum scales (optional).
8. Make style decisions (optional).
9. Plot the graph (on-screen).
10. Print the graph.

The following sections describe these steps in detail.

## *Using the Chart Definition Dialog Box*

The Chart Definition dialog box is a standard Macintosh dialog box (see "Using the Boxes and Buttons" in Chapter 1). You can use the Tab key to move from text box to text box and use standard text-editing techniques within each box.

## *Specifying the Type of Graph and the Range of Data*

To specify the type of series graph you want to create, click the button next to the appropriate graph icon in the Type of Chart option. You define one graph at a time. The example in figure 7.6 shows the line graph selected.

A series graph allows you to plot up to four rows of data and any number of columns to represent your data points. To define these ranges, enter spreadsheet location references in the Values to be Plotted text boxes. Works proposes some row and column choices for you when the dialog box opens.

You can plot more than one range on a single graph. For example, suppose that you want to compare cumulative sales to quarterly sales figures. By defining (in the Chart Definition dialog box) the 1st Row as the data of cumulative sales, and the 2nd Row as the data for quarterly sales, you obtain a two-line graph of the type shown in figure 7.7. Works rescales graphs, if necessary, to accommodate the highest value in a multiline plot.

**Fig. 7.7**

*A multiline graph.*

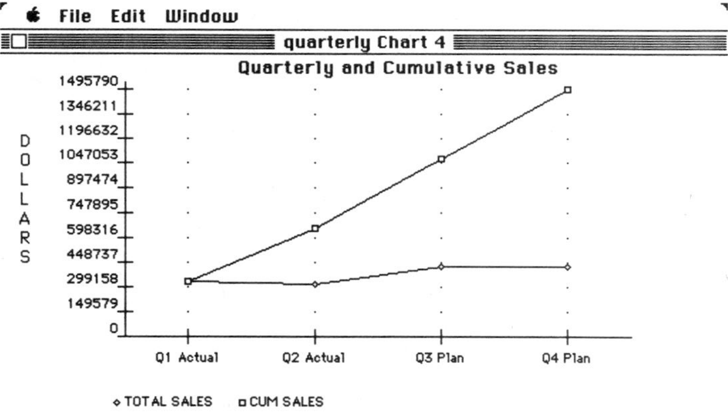


When you click the Combo icon in the Chart Definition dialog box, Works plots the first row as a bar graph and the second, third, and fourth rows as line graphs. When you create a stacked-bar graph, the bottom segment of the stack corresponds to the 1st Row option. The 2nd Row appears above, followed by the 3rd Row and then the 4th Row data at the top of the stack. Simply enter the row number that corresponds to each portion.

You set your horizontal axis points by using the From Column and To Column text boxes. You can label these horizontal axis points with any existing labels in your spreadsheet by specifying in the Horizontal Titles in Row text box the column in which the labels are found. The dialog box in figure 7.6 defines the line graph in figure 7.1. Labels are contained in row 1 of the spreadsheet, and the data is contained in row 9.

## *Improving Readability with Titles and the Grid*

Type the title for your graph in the Chart Title text box. The title then appears inside the graph window underneath the title bar. Defining vertical and horizontal titles with the Vertical Scale Title and Horizontal Scale Title options can greatly help the viewer to understand the purpose of your graph.

With the Draw Grid option in the Chart Definition dialog box, you can place horizontal and vertical reference points on your graph to improve readability. Click to turn the option on or off. The default is on (indicated by an X in the box).

If you don't want Works to display any labels, you can use the Label Chart option to turn off all labels. For example, you may want to cut and paste the graph to your word processor or to another application (such as MacPaint) and add labels later. Click the Label Chart box to toggle labeling on and off. The default is on.

## *Using Vertical Scales*

Another option available to you is the choice of your vertical scale. Usually, Works automatically scales graphs for you, taking into consideration the graph's smallest and largest numbers. When necessary, Works creates scales that include negative numbers, and automatically uses scientific notation. A good practice is to put series data in rows; however, no more than four data series can be used on one graph.

The default vertical scale is ten units per increment, what Microsoft calls *numeric vertical scaling*. If you change the values on your spreadsheet, Works adjusts the graph's scale for you. To determine the top of the scale, Works uses the largest number in the graph. Works then divides that number by ten to create the increments. Therefore, every time you change the largest number in your graph, the scale is likely to change. If this arrangement bothers you, you can define the upper and lower vertical scales yourself.

The Chart Definition dialog box enables you to specify the maximum and minimum numbers that appear on your vertical scale. (You use the Maximum and Minimum text boxes.) Setting your own scale overrides the automatic scaling feature and sometimes improves the graph's appearance, unless your scales are too small to contain the data. For example, if you set the maximum scale at 10,000 and try to plot a value of 15,000, Works overrides your maximum scale. In such a case, Works scales automatically (without warning you).

Sometimes, when displaying a range of numbers that contain very large and very small numbers, you may find a semi-logarithmic scale useful. Choose the Semi-Logarithmic option in the Chart Definition dialog box. Semi-logarithmic scales are used to display extremely large and small numbers on the same plot, as shown in figure 7.8.

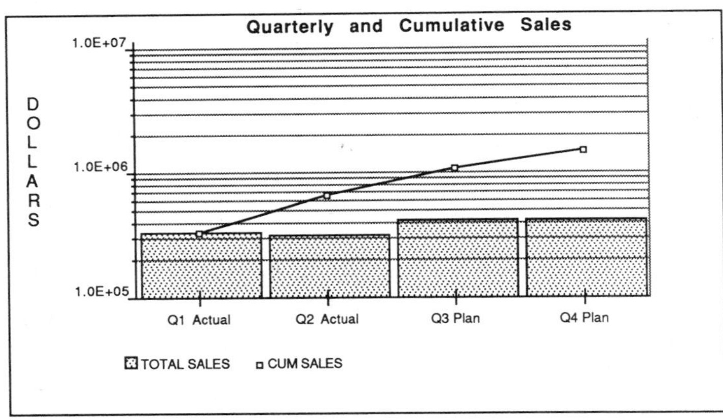


**Fig. 7.8**

*A graph with semi-logarithmic scaling.*

The Semi-Logarithmic option distorts the relative appearance of small and large numbers but allows you to see both types on the same graph. All the data must be greater than zero. You cannot scale stacked-bar graphs with this type of scale, however, because stacked-bar graphs require a linear scale to be drawn.

## *Plotting Your Graph*

After you finish your definition, click the Plot It! button (or press Return) to see the results. Figure 7.9 shows a labeled chart window. You use the resize box in the lower right corner of the window to make the graph smaller. The graph and all associated labels and features scale as you scale the window. As with all Works windows, you click the close box in the upper left corner of the screen to close the window. Move the window to the desired location by using its title bars. Title bars are discussed in Chapter 1.

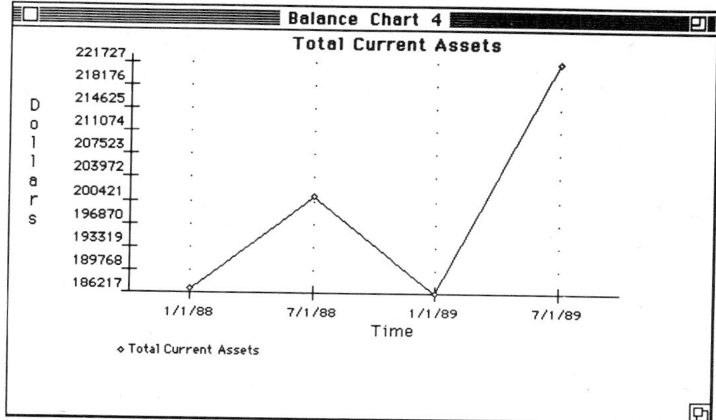


**Fig. 7.9**

*A labeled graph window.*

Remember that Works assigns sequentially numbered names to the definitions for a single spreadsheet, so if you create several graphs for a spreadsheet, their names all look similar. Before you click Plot It!, you should get in the habit of noting the number that Works assigns at the end of your definition name. Then, later, you can find the definition you want without having to view all definitions. If you want to change the chart names, refer to the instructions in the section on "Changing Graph Definition Names" later in this chapter.

## *Viewing or Editing an Existing Graph*

If you have previously defined a graph, you can call it up by choosing the Select Chart Definition command from the Chart menu. This command brings up a window with a list of previously defined graphs, as shown in figure 7.10. Double-click the graph you want to view or edit, or click the graph and then either click OK or press Return. You can then modify the Chart Definition dialog box and replot the graph.

If you want to view a previously defined graph without going through the Chart Definition dialog box, you can choose the Draw Chart command from the Chart menu. Using this command takes you to the same Select Chart Definition dialog box shown in figure 7.10, but Works draws your graph directly.

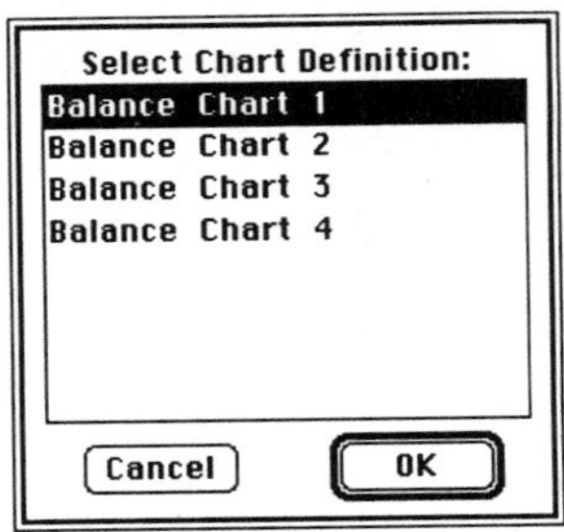


**Fig. 7.10**

*The Select Chart Definition dialog box.*

Here's a shortcut for modifying graph definitions. When a graph is on the screen, you can get to the graph's definition quickly by double-clicking anywhere in the graph. This procedure is a quick way to test new graph design options because you can see the results before making permanent choices.

If you click the graph definition's close box, Works saves your definition and returns you to the spreadsheet. No plot appears.

## Changing Graph Definition Names

In the Chart Definition dialog box and the graph window, the name Works assigns to the graph is displayed in the title bar. And you see a set of generic names when you use the Select Chart Definition dialog box. Works allows you to change the name of any graph and make it more meaningful to you. With the Chart Definition dialog box open, choose Change Chart Name from the Edit menu. Enter the new name in the text box of the resulting dialog box (see fig. 7.11).

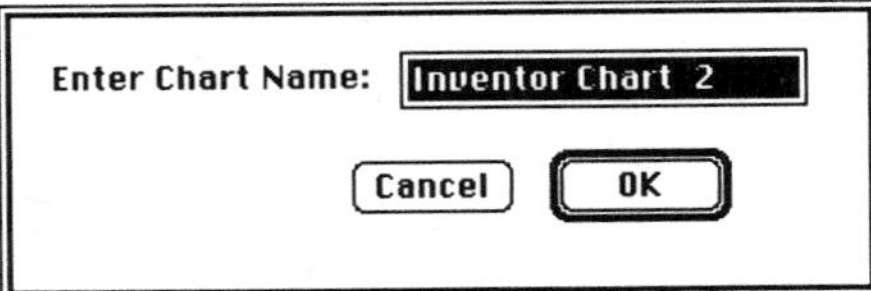


**Fig. 7.11**

*The Change Chart Name dialog box.*

## Printing Your Graph

The process of printing graphs differs slightly from most other Works printing procedures. With the graph on-screen, you simply choose Print Window from the File menu. Because Print Window does not display a dialog box, you cannot make any page setup decisions when printing graph windows. The graph does, however, reflect elements such as window size, grid options, and other characteristics seen on-screen. For example, to print a small copy of a graph, you simply drag the graph window to a smaller on-screen size. If you are using a big screen, you may accidentally make a graph so big that it cannot fit on the printed page. Works truncates your graph without warning.

## *Viewing a Graph and Spreadsheet Together*

To return to your spreadsheet from the graph window, click the close box in the upper left corner of the graph window, or click anywhere in the worksheet to bring it to the top of your screen. When you close a graph window, Works saves the existing definition.

You can see the effect of spreadsheet changes on your graph almost immediately if you display both the spreadsheet and graph windows simultaneously. (The spreadsheet and graph may overlap, however.) Figure 7.12 shows a sample balance sheet spreadsheet and an accompanying line graph. Suppose that when going over the balance sheet you notice that you made a mistake in the accounts receivable figures, which produced the unexpectedly poor results for 1/1/89. When you change the amount in cell D5, the linked graph changes accordingly, as shown in figure 7.13.

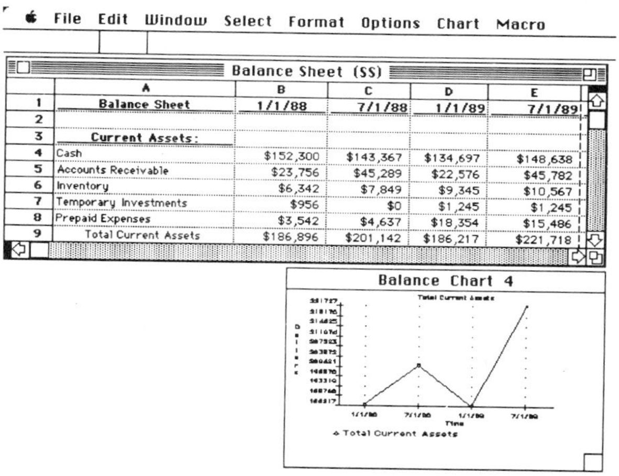

File Edit Window Select Format Options Chart Macro

Balance Sheet (SS)

| | A | B | C | D | E |
|---|---|---|---|---|---|
| 1 | Balance Sheet | 1/1/88 | 7/1/88 | 1/1/89 | 7/1/89 |
| 2 | | | | | |
| 3 | Current Assets: | | | | |
| 4 | Cash | $152,300 | $143,367 | $134,697 | $148,638 |
| 5 | Accounts Receivable | $23,756 | $45,289 | $22,576 | $45,782 |
| 6 | Inventory | $6,342 | $7,849 | $9,345 | $10,567 |
| 7 | Temporary Investments | $956 | $0 | $1,245 | $1,245 |
| 8 | Prepaid Expenses | $3,542 | $4,637 | $18,354 | $15,486 |
| 9 | Total Current Assets | $186,896 | $201,142 | $186,217 | $221,718 |

Balance Chart 4

Total Current Assets

**Fig. 7.12**

*The spreadsheet and its linked graph.*

**Fig. 7.13**

*Viewing changes in the graph after you alter spreadsheet contents.*

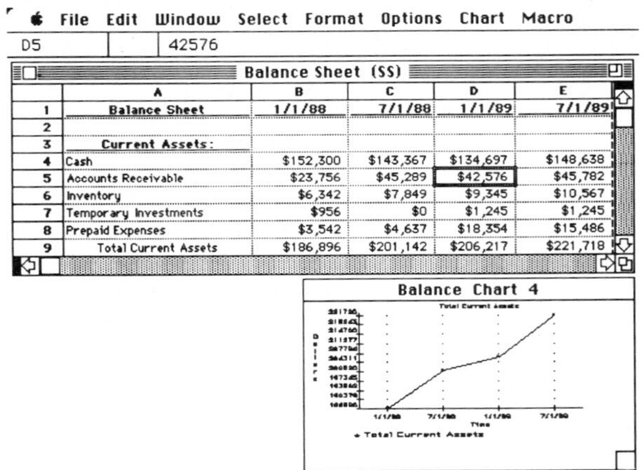


| | A | B | C | D | E |
|---|---|---|---|---|---|
| 1 | Balance Sheet | 1/1/88 | 7/1/88 | 1/1/89 | 7/1/89 |
| 2 | | | | | |
| 3 | Current Assets: | | | | |
| 4 | Cash | $152,300 | $143,367 | $134,697 | $148,638 |
| 5 | Accounts Receivable | $23,756 | $45,289 | $42,576 | $45,782 |
| 6 | Inventory | $6,342 | $7,849 | $9,345 | $10,567 |
| 7 | Temporary Investments | $956 | $0 | $1,245 | $1,245 |
| 8 | Prepaid Expenses | $3,542 | $4,637 | $18,354 | $15,486 |
| 9 | Total Current Assets | $186,896 | $201,142 | $206,217 | $221,718 |

# *Creating Pie Graphs*

Works pie graphs show percentages and are plotted from columns rather than rows. For example, you can use a pie graph to compare the value of the different types of Macintosh computers that your firm owns. This graph was the one shown in figure 7.5.

To create a pie graph, follow these steps:

1. Open the spreadsheet containing the column to be graphed.
2. Choose New Pie Chart from the Chart menu to display a Pie Chart Definition dialog box similar to the one shown in figure 7.14. (This sample dialog box was used to draw fig. 7.5.) Because a pie graph compares only one set of variables in a percentage form, this dialog box is simpler than the one used for series graphs.

**Fig. 7.14**

*The Pie Chart Definition dialog box.*

3. Enter the title of your graph in the Chart Title box.
4. Enter the letter of the column to be graphed in the Plot Values in Column box.
5. Enter the first and last rows to be plotted in the From Row and Through Row boxes.
6. In the Column of Value Titles box, enter the letter of the spreadsheet column containing the slice labels to be used in the graph.
7. Click Plot It! or press Return.

You can have Works compute percentages for you when it draws your pie graph, even if the cells you want to graph don't contain percentages. Because Works rounds to one decimal place when plotting, the spreadsheet percentage and the plot percentage may differ slightly.

# *Transposing Rows and Columns*

Pie graphs require data in columns, not rows. Suppose that you want to create a pie graph, but your data is in rows initially. You can find some empty room on the spreadsheet and retype the numbers and labels by hand, or you can use the Transpose option.

To transpose data means simply to switch columns and rows. When you transpose a row such as A1:D1, for example, it becomes the column A1:A4. To convert a row of cells to a column of cells, perform the following steps:

1. Decide where you want to put the copied data. Make sure that your target column has enough cells to accept the data.
2. Select the cells to copy.
3. Copy the cells to the Clipboard (press ⌘-C).
4. Activate (click) the cell to receive the first number. *Don't forget this essential step!*
5. Choose Paste with Options from the Edit menu.
6. When the Paste with Options dialog box appears, choose Transpose by clicking to place an X in the box. Then click OK or press Return.
7. Works pastes the numbers automatically.
8. Repeat these steps to transpose the labels.

If you attempt to paste into a column containing data, Works alerts you that you are about to overwrite some information. For more information on using the Paste with Options command, see the Chapter 6 section on "Copying and Pasting Cells."

The Transpose option has one major drawback. Because the transposed numbers are not linked to the cells in which the original data was contained, they do not reflect your changes. Neither does the graph, because it's based on the cells you pasted into. For this reason, you may not want to use the Transpose option, or you may want to use it as a test only.

As an alternative to transposing, define a new set of cells: either a column if you are transposing a row (for a pie graph), or a row if you are transposing a column. In each cell, define an equation that makes that cell's contents equal to the original cell. Then when data in your spreadsheet changes, your new cells also change, and the transposed graph is linked to the changes.

# *Duplicating and Erasing Graph Definitions*

To save time when creating similar but not identical graphs, you can duplicate or copy a graph definition and modify it. Here's how:

1. Choose Duplicate Chart from the Chart menu to bring up a dialog box similar to that shown in figure 7.10.
2. Select the definition you want to duplicate. Click the graph name only once.
3. Either click OK or press the Return key. Works then assigns a new sequential graph name.
4. Make the changes you want for this new graph in the Chart Definition dialog box.
5. Plot, save, or cancel as usual.

Remember that Works can store only eight definitions per spreadsheet. If the Duplicate Chart option is dimmed on the Chart menu, you must erase unneeded definitions before copying. Follow these steps to erase a graph:

1. Choose Erase Chart from the Chart menu.

2. Double-click the unwanted graph, or click the title to select it.
3. Either click OK or press the Return key.

The graph definition file is erased from your disk, and you can create a new graph definition for that spreadsheet.

> ***Caution:*** Double-clicking is an erase shortcut. When selecting, be careful that you don't double-click a graph name accidentally. If you do erase the wrong definition this way, you cannot use the Undo feature (⌘-Z).

# *Finding Errors in Graphs*

Works warns you about most graphing errors. For example, Works displays the alert box shown in figure 7.15 if you define a pie graph with too many pie slices. Works displays a different warning if you define a pie graph range with no entries (see fig. 7.16). Before continuing, you must acknowledge these warnings by clicking OK. You are returned to the worksheet to correct your choices.

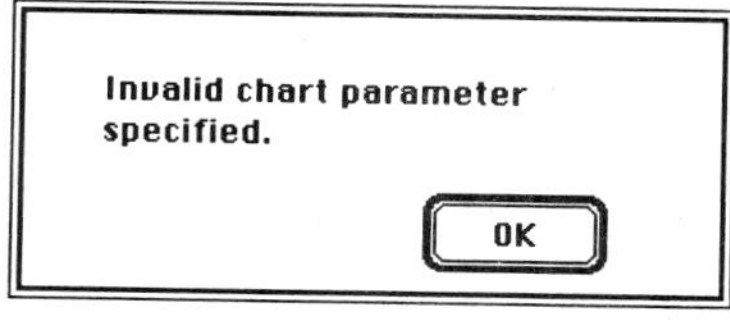
Invalid chart parameter specified.
OK

**Fig. 7.15**

*A warning about having too many pie slices.*

The total of all pie chart entries must be greater than zero.

OK

**Fig. 7.16**

*A warning about having no pie slices.*

# *Using Draw in Spreadsheets and Graphs*

With the Works spreadsheet module, you can use the Draw On command in the Edit menu to put the full-featured draw layer and all its object-oriented graphics and color to work for you in enhancing your work. To highlight a graph you create for your spreadsheet, you copy that graph to the Clipboard (in PICT format) and then paste the graph into the draw layer below the data.

Figure 7.17 shows an example of what is possible in the draw layer within a spreadsheet. This figure contains the spreadsheet used to construct the pie graph in figure 7.5. The company's computer inventory for both the number of different Macintosh types and their assessed values is visible. The grid is turned off and the draw layer activated. You can tell that you are in the draw layer because the toolbox is onscreen.

**Fig. 7.17**

*Using the draw layer in your spreadsheet to create graphics.*

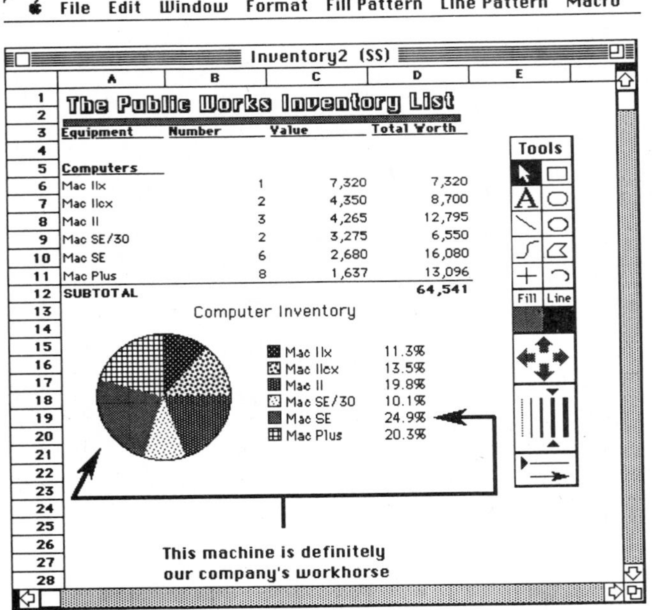


Arrows and lines highlight data supporting the conclusion that the Mac SE is currently the major piece of equipment used by the company. Note that the graph is now an object-oriented graphic and can be placed and scaled just as any other graphic can. In scaling the graph, you also scale the attached text. Note in figure 7.17 that the labels on the graph are not scaled exactly right. The graph and its associated arrows, lines, and text were grouped as a picture so that the graph could be moved around as one object. Titles and the shaded rectangle were added later.

As evidenced in figure 7.17, you can use the draw layer and your spreadsheet to create attractive visual images with your graphs. If you are going to create slides or overheads, you should stick to only the important details. Spreadsheets tend to present more data than the casual user can absorb.

## *Chapter Summary*

In this chapter you learned how to take the data generated bya spreadsheet and turn it into graphic form. Many times a graphic representation of data is more effective and more easily understood than columns and rows of numbers. You learned when to use each of the five graph types that Works offers, how to define and rename graphs, and how to view and print graphs. You also learned how you can combine the Works draw module with graphs and spreadsheets.

In the following chapter, you learn about the dozens of functions that are available for use in Works spreadsheets and databases. Most can be used in both modules; othters are specific to the spreadsheet module. All the functions are very useful.

# 8

# Spreadsheet and Database Functions

Works provides 64 functions to simplify and speed the development of spreadsheets and databases. You can think of functions as built-in equations. All you need to do is provide the variables, and the functions produce the answers. For instance, the Sqrt function finds the square root of a value, and the Sum function sums a specific range of cells. You can, of course, write your own equations in Works, but the built-in functions save you the time and trouble. Works also has functions that help with financial modeling. Some functions allow you to do time/date calculations. Still others perform trigonometric and statistical computations. You can use functions by themselves or include them in complex formulas.

This chapter includes lists of all Works functions, classified by subject (mathematical, financial, and so on), and detailed descriptions of the functions in alphabetical order. The chapter is designed to help you begin using functions for your specific Works applications and to provide you with a handy reference that you can use often.

## *Functions Unavailable in a Database*

All functions mentioned are appropriate to your spreadsheets, and most of them are usable in databases also. In general, because all database records are independent and unrelated to other records, you cannot use functions that provide locational information. Functions that are not appropriate in a database include the following:

- ❑ The IRR and MIRR financial functions

- The HLookup, Index, Lookup, Match, and VLookup location functions

When a function takes a range of cells as its argument, you can use the function in a database only when the range refers to a single field reference, a list of fields separated by commas, or a value. Functions of this type are the following:

- The And, Choose, If, IsBlank, and Or Logical functions
- Any of the statistical functions, including Average, Count, Max, Min, SSum, StDev, Sum, and Var
- The FV, NPV, PMT, PV, and Rate financial functions

All other functions work equally well in both the spreadsheet and the database modules.

# Learning the Parts and Construction of Functions

Functions consist of at least two parts: the *function name* and an *argument* (or arguments). Arguments must be enclosed in parentheses; multiple arguments must be separated by commas. A few functions, such as Error( ), do not use arguments.

## Function Arguments

*Arguments* are the information you provide a function for its calculation. Arguments can be either values or references to cells or ranges containing values. Works displays, or *returns*, the results of its computation in the cell containing the function.

For example, if you use the Sqrt function to find the square root of 9, 9 is the argument. If you want to find the square root of the contents of cell B2, the argument is B2. Figure 8.1 shows how these two Sqrt examples look in a spreadsheet.

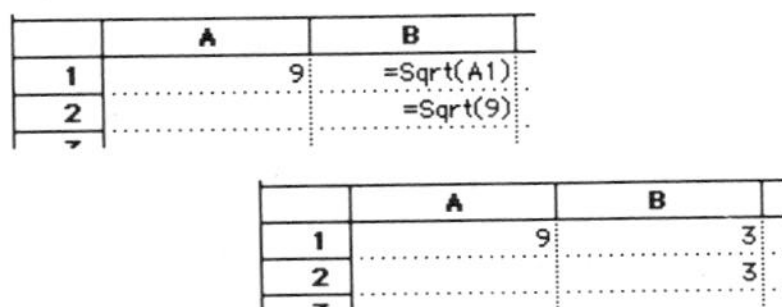


**Fig. 8.1**

*Two ways to find a square root.*

## Function Syntax

When you use functions, certain things must occur in a certain order. This order is called the *syntax* of a function. Syntax is a little like grammar. Some general syntax rules apply to all functions; in addition, each function has its own specific syntax.

Following are some general syntax rules:

- ❑ Precede a function with an equal sign if the function starts a cell entry.
- ❑ Works ignores upper/lowercase differentiation.
- ❑ Spell functions correctly.
- ❑ Don't use spaces between function names and parentheses.
- ❑ Provide all required arguments.
- ❑ Separate multiple arguments with commas.
- ❑ Functions consider cells containing text to be blank.

If Works finds an error, the program warns you by displaying a dialog box that shows the entry and warns that it is incorrect. For example, some format choices are applicable to numbers only, and other choices are for text only. In figure 8.2, Works expected a cell address, like A1, or a number, like 12.5. A label was entered by mistake. No program can find all mistakes, so test your work.

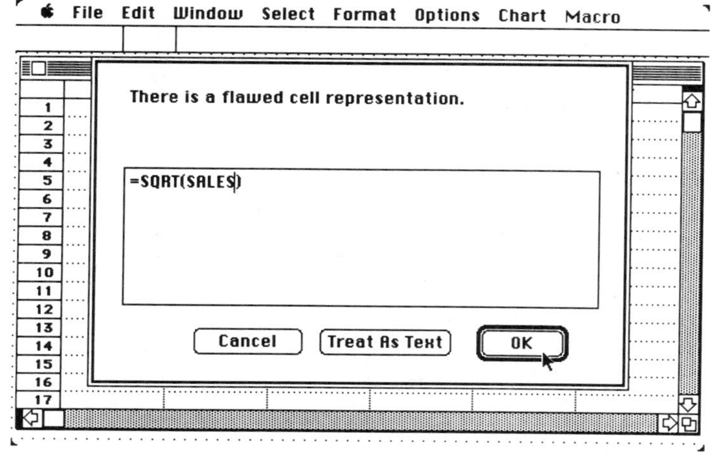


**Fig. 8.2**

*Dialog box containing warning.*

## Using Ranges in Function Arguments

Many functions, such as Sum, use ranges of values for computations. For example, figure 8.3 shows Sum functions in row 8 and column F.

**Fig. 8.3**

*Sum functions in row 8 and column F.*

| | A | B | C | D | E | F |
|---|---|---|---|---|---|---|
| 2 | | Q1 Actual | Q2 Actual | Q3 Plan | Q4 Plan | Total |
| 3 | SALES | | | | | |
| 4 | WEST | 123,568 | 107232 | 140000 | 140000 | =Sum(B4:E4) |
| 5 | CENTRAL | 113454 | 110785 | 140000 | 140000 | =Sum(B5:E5) |
| 6 | EAST | 98876 | 101867 | 140000 | 140000 | =Sum(B6:E6) |
| 7 | | | | | | |
| 8 | TOTAL SALES | =Sum(B4:B6) | =Sum(C4:C6) | =Sum(D4:D6) | =Sum(E4:E6) | =Sum(F4:F6) |

To enter ranges, you either type them or use the pointing, clicking, and dragging techniques you have already learned (see "Selecting Single Cells and Ranges" in Chapter 6). Just as you do with other arguments, you enclose function ranges in parentheses. You use a colon (:) to separate a range's starting and ending locations, and you use commas to separate cell addresses or ranges.

Function ranges can define blocks, parts or all of a row or column, or even noncontiguous cells. You can reference multiple ranges for one function. Here are some examples of ranges used with the Sum function:

| | |
|---|---|
| =Sum(B4:E4) | References cells in a row |
| =Sum(A1:A15) | References cells in a column |
| =Sum(B4:E6) | References a block of cells |
| =Sum(A1,B2,C3) | References noncontiguous cells separated by commas |
| =Sum (B4:E4,G4,A6:E6) | References two ranges and a specific cell |

## Pasting Functions

Remembering the exact spelling of all 64 functions is difficult, and making typos is easy. Therefore, Works provides a Paste Function option on the Edit menu so that you can paste the function and accompanying parentheses without having to type the function name. This option was discussed in the section called "Operators" in Chapter 6. The Paste

Function displays a dialog box containing the names of all Works functions (see fig. 6.6). You choose the one you want, and Works pastes a copy for you.

To use the Paste Function command, follow these steps:

1. Select the cell in which you want to paste the function.
2. Choose Paste Function from the Edit menu.
3. Scroll, if necessary, to find the function you want in the Paste Function dialog box.
4. Either double-click the function's name or click the OK button. The function then appears in the spreadsheet entry bar.
5. Add the necessary arguments.

# *Notes about Some Specific Functions*

Some of Works functions deserve some extra explanation. This section describes the If function, which is one of the logical functions; Version 2.0's new time and date functions; and special traits of the lookup functions.

## *Logical Functions*

Unlike most functions, which return answers based on given arguments, logical functions return only one of two answers: logical TRUE giving the value 1 in a cell, or logical FALSE returning the value 0 in a cell. In figure 8.4, the If function places either a 1 or a 0 in cell B3, depending on whether specified conditions are met. In this case, the contents of cell B1 must be greater than 5 to meet the conditions indicated.

The If function located in B3 is displayed in the entry bar. The first part of the argument (B1) is what the function is to test. Because a cell location has been used, the If function tests any number placed in B1. The >5 portion of the function tells Works to test the value in B1 to see whether it is a number larger than 5. Works is then told to return a 1 if cell B1 is greater than 5, and to return a 0 if B1 is less than or equal to 5. Replacing the 0 in this example with a 9 would cause Works to return a 9 whenever B1 is 5 or less.

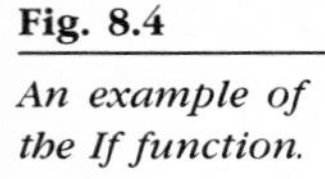

**Fig. 8.4**

*An example of the If function.*

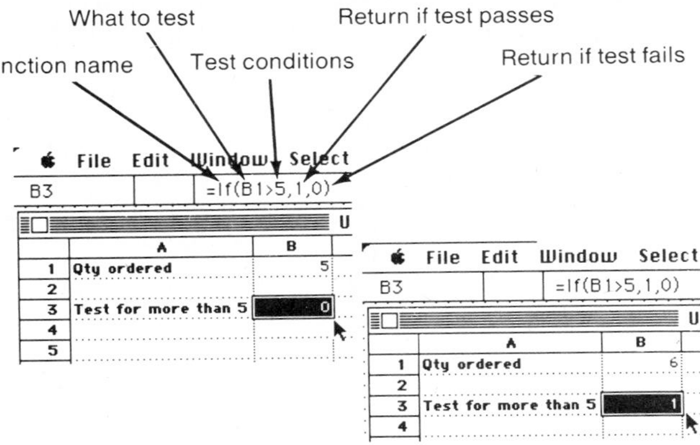

## *Time and Date Functions*

Works 2.0 adds the time and date stamping functions (10 of them) to those available in Versions 1.0 and 1.1. So that it can do numerical calculations on dates and times, Works converts them into a set of internally held values called *serial numbers*. Dates from 0 to 49710 represent January 1, 1904, to February 6, 2040, respectively. Times are stored in a decimal fraction representation of the date's serial number. For example, the date and time 6 AM 8/27/52 would return the serial number 17771.25. This set of conventions is the same one that your Macintosh uses to set the clock time and date internally (using Alarm Clock DA). If you want to check a date's serial representation, open the Set Cell Attributes dialog box and set the Type to General.

You must correctly format the time and dates you enter for the type of format you choose. (These formats are discussed in the section on "Setting Cell Attributes" in Chapter 6.) Works alerts you if you enter an incorrect format. If you use a date or time that is beyond the normal range, you see the value `*Error*` returned in your cell.

## *Lookup Functions*

You can create *lookup tables* and have Works enter data into cells from the tables, based on specific conditions. Lookup tables are simply cell ranges containing reference data that Works uses for computations. In figure 8.5, the range B1 through G2 is a lookup table. The Lookup function in cell B5 checks the quantity-ordered cell, B4. The prices and quantities are listed in the lookup table, and the prices vary according to quantity ordered. In this example, the Lookup function places the appropriate price in cell B5, based on the quantity ordered. Several other Works functions use this lookup approach.

File Edit Window Select Format Options Chart Macro

B5 =Lookup(B4,B1:G1,B2:G2)

Untitled (SS)

| | A | B | C | D | E | F | G | H |
|---|---|---|---|---|---|---|---|---|
| 1 | Qty | 1 | 2 | 3 | 4 | 5 | 6 | |
| 2 | Price | $10.00 | $9.00 | $8.00 | $7.00 | $6.00 | $5.00 | |
| 3 | | | | | | | | |
| 4 | Qty Ordered | 3 | | | | | | |
| 5 | Price at this qty | $8.00 | | | | | | |
| 6 | | | | | | | | |
| 7 | | | | | | | | |
| 8 | | | | | | | | |
| 9 | | | | | | | | |
| 10 | | | | | | | | |
| 11 | | | | | | | | |
| 12 | | | | | | | | |
| 13 | | | | | | | | |
| 14 | | | | | | | | |
| 15 | | | | | | | | |
| 16 | | | | | | | | |
| 17 | | | | | | | | |

**Fig. 8.5**

*An example of the Lookup function.*

# *Categories of Functions*

This section consists of tables that list Works functions by category: special-purpose (table 8.1), mathematical (table 8.2), statistical (table 8.3), trigonometric (table 8.4), logical (table 8.5), financial (table 8.6), and time/date (table 8.7). Use the tables to find the functions you want; then read more about the functions in the alphabetical reference section that follows.

**Table 8.1**
**Special-Purpose Functions**

| *Function Name* | *Action* |
|---|---|
| Error( ) | Returns value `*Error*` |
| HLookup(lookup-value, compare-range,index-number) | Selects value in table, according to *lookup-value* |
| Index(range,row,column) | Selects reference in *range*, according to Index value's *row* and *column* |
| Lookup(lookup-value,compare-range,result-range) | Selects value in table, according to *lookup-value* |
| Match(lookup-value,compare-range,type) | Selects position number of value, according to *lookup-value* |
| NA( ) | Returns value `N/A` |
| Type(value) | Returns type of *value* |
| VLookup(lookup-value, compare-number,index-number) | Selects value in table, according to *lookup-value* |

**Table 8.2**
**Mathematical Functions**

| *Function Name* | *Action* |
|---|---|
| Abs(number) | Returns absolute value of *number* |
| Exp(number) | Raises e to power of *number* |
| Int(number) | Returns integer part of *number* |
| Ln(number) | Returns logarithm, base e, of *number* |
| Log10(number) | Returns logarithm, base 10, of *number* |
| Mod(number,divisor-number) | Returns remainder of *number* divided by *divisor-number* |
| Pi( ) | Returns value of pi |

| | |
|---|---|
| Rand( ) | Returns random number between 0 and 1 |
| Round(number, number-of-digits) | Rounds *number* to *number-of-digits* |
| Sign(number) | Returns sign of *number* |
| Sqrt(number) | Returns square root of *number* |

**Table 8.3**
**Statistical Functions**

| *Function Name* | *Action* |
|---|---|
| Average(values-1,values-2,...) | Returns average of values in *values* |
| Count(values-1,values-2,...) | Returns count of values in *values* |
| Max(values-1,values-2,...) | Returns maximum value in *values* |
| Min(values-1,values-2,...) | Returns minimum value in *values* |
| SSum(values-1,values-2,...) | Returns sum of *values* displayed |
| StDev(values-1,values-2,...) | Returns standard deviation of *values* |
| Sum(values-1,values-2,...) | Returns sum of *values* |
| Var(values-1,values-2,...) | Returns variance of *values* |

**Table 8.4**
**Trigonometric Functions**

| *Function Name* | *Action* |
|---|---|
| ACos(number) | Returns arccosine of *number* |
| ASin(number) | Returns arcsine of *number* |
| ATan(number) | Returns arctangent of *number* |

**Table 8.4**—*continued*

| *Function Name* | *Action* |
|---|---|
| ATan2(x-number,y-number) | Returns arctangent of point (*x-number,y-number*) |
| Cos(number) | Returns cosine of *number* |
| Degrees(number) | Converts *number* from radians to degrees |
| Radians(number) | Converts *number* from degrees to radians |
| Sin(number) | Returns sine of *number* |
| Tan(number) | Returns tangent of *number* |

**Table 8.5**
**Logical Functions**

| *Function Name* | *Action* |
|---|---|
| And(values-1,values-2,...) | Returns 1 (TRUE) if all *values* are not 0; otherwise, returns 0 (FALSE) |
| Choose(index,number-1, number-2,...) | Uses *index* to select value from *numbers* |
| False( ) | Returns value 0 (FALSE) |
| If(number,number-if-TRUE, number-if-FALSE) | Returns *number-if-TRUE* if number is not 0 (TRUE); returns *number-if-FALSE* if number is 0 (FALSE) |
| IsBlank(values-1, values-2,...) | Returns 1 (TRUE) if all *values* are blank or text; otherwise, returns 0 (FALSE) |
| IsError(value) | Returns 1 (TRUE) if *value* is any error value |
| IsNA(value) | Returns 1 (TRUE) if *value* is error value N/A |
| Not(number) | Returns 1 (TRUE) if *number* is 0 (FALSE); returns 0 (FALSE) if *number* is not 0 (TRUE) |

| | |
|---|---|
| Or(values-1,values-2,...) | Returns 1 (TRUE) if any logical value in *values* arguments is not 0 (TRUE); otherwise, returns 0 (FALSE) |
| True( ) | Returns value 1 (TRUE) |

**Table 8.6**
**Financial Functions**

| *Function Name* | *Action* |
|---|---|
| FV(rate,nper,pmt,pv,type) | Computes future value of investment |
| IRR(range,guess) | Calculates internal rate of return of *range* |
| MIRR(range,safe,risk) | Returns modified internal rate of return of *range* |
| NPer(rate,pmt,pv,fv,type) | Computes number of payments of investment |
| NPV(rate,values-1,values-2,...) | Determines net present value of *values* |
| Pmt(rate,nper,pv,fv,type) | Calculates periodic payment of investment |
| PV(rate,nper,pmt,fv,type) | Computes present value of investment |
| Rate(nper,pmt,pv,fv,type,guess) | Determines rate returned on investment |

**Table 8.7**
**Time and Date Functions**

| *Function Name* | *Action* |
|---|---|
| Date(year,month,day) | Returns the date in the format you set in the Set Attributes dialog box |
| Day(serial-number) | Returns the day as an integer between 1 and 31 |

**Table 8.7**—*continued*

| *Function Name* | *Action* |
|---|---|
| Hour(serial-number) | Returns the hour as an integer between 1 and 23 |
| Minute(serial-number) | Returns the minute as an integer between 0 and 59 |
| Month(serial-number) | Returns the month as an integer between 1 and 12 |
| Now( ) | Returns the serial number of the current date and time at spreadsheet recalculations |
| Second(serial-number) | Returns the second as an integer between 0 and 59 |
| Time(hour,minute,second) | Returns the time in the format you set |
| Weekday(serial-number) | Returns the number of the day of the week as an integer between 1 and 7 |
| Year(serial-number) | Returns the number of the year as an integer between 1904 and 2040 |

# Descriptions of Functions

The rest of this chapter provides explanations and examples of Works functions, which are discussed in alphabetical order.

## Abs(number)

With Abs you can enter or reference a number and find its absolute value, which is the "distance" (positive or negative) between *number* and 0. For example, =Abs( − 4) produces a result of 4. This function is useful if you want to find the difference between two numbers without first knowing which is larger. For example, =Abs(10–12) and =Abs(12–10) both return the answer 2.

One use of this function is to change negative financial-function results to positive numbers for later use.

## *ACos(number)*

The ACos or arccosine function yields the radian measure of the angle whose cosine is presented as the argument. For example, the cosine of 0.785 radians (45 degrees) is 0.707; hence, ACos(0.707) returns the value 0.785. Because the interval for the cosine is from −1 to 1, the argument of the ACos function is restricted to that interval.

## *And(values-1,values-2,...)*

The And function analyzes all the *values* in arguments you reference. If all the values are TRUE (not 0), the And function returns a logical 1 (TRUE). If any argument is FALSE (0), And returns a logical 0 (FALSE). For example, cell A2 in figure 8.6 contains an And function that checks the range B1 through E1. Notice how the results change (in A2) when even one of the cells in the tested range changes (C1). Note that the function ignores cells containing text and blank cells.

## *ASin(number)*

The ASin function returns the radian measure of a sine. For example, the sine of 1.570 ($\pi/2$ radians, or 90 degrees) is 1; the function ASin(1) returns the value 1.570.

| | A | B | C | D | E |
|---|---|---|---|---|---|
| 1 | | 1 | 1 | 1 | 1 |
| 2 | 1 | | | | |
| 3 | | | | | |

| | A | B | C | D | E |
|---|---|---|---|---|---|
| 1 | | 1 | 0 | 1 | 1 |
| 2 | 0 | | | | |
| 3 | | | | | |

| | A | B | C | D | E |
|---|---|---|---|---|---|
| 1 | | 1 | -1 | 1 | 1 |
| 2 | 1 | | | | |
| 3 | | | | | |

| | A | B | C | D | E |
|---|---|---|---|---|---|
| 1 | | 1 | text | 1 | 1 |
| 2 | 1 | | | | |
| 3 | | | | | |

File Edit Window Select

A2 =And(B1:E1)

**Fig. 8.6**

*Using the And function.*

## *ATan(number)*

The ATan function returns the measure of the angle whose tangent is supplied as an argument. The tangent of 0.785 ($\pi/4$, or 45 degrees) is 1; the equation =ATan(1) returns the value 0.785.

## *ATan2(x-number,y-number)*

The ATan2 function returns the radian measure of the angle defined by *x-number* and *y-number*; those numbers represent coordinates in two dimensions. For instance, the point (3,4) lies on the terminal side of an angle whose measure is 0.927 radians, or 53.13 degrees. The equation =ATan2(3,4) consequently returns the value 0.927.

## *Average(values-1,values-2,...)*

The Average function sums the *values* listed in the argument of the function and divides that number by the number of values. If the range(s) contain text or blanks, the function ignores them. As an example, the Average function of a range A1:D1 with cell contents of 4, 8, 2, and 10 returns the value of 6.

## *Choose(index,number-1,number-2,...)*

The Choose function returns a number based on the *index* argument. The index, the first part of the argument, tells Works where to look in the rest of the arguments to find the result. For example, the following function yields 30:

```
=Choose(3,10,20,30,40)
```

In this example, Works uses the third entry (30) because the index is 3.

You can substitute cell locations for numbers, so you can use the contents of a cell as the index or for any of the numbers in the argument. Here's an example:

```
=Choose(A1,10,30,A5)
```

In this case, Works inspects the content of cell A1 to determine which of the following arguments to use. If an index value is less than 1 or exceeds the number of available numbers in an argument, the Choose function returns *Error*.

## *Cos(number)*

The Cos function returns the cosine of an angle measured in radians. If you remember your trigonometry, you know that the cosine of an angle is the ratio between the x-coordinate of a point on the angle's terminal side and the length of a line from the origin to the point. Radian measure assumes that the length of the radial line is 1. Consequently, the cosine of a 90-degree angle is 0. Ninety degrees is equal to 1.570 (or $\pi/2$) radians, so the equation =Cos(1.570) returns the value 0.

## *Count(values-1,values-2,...)*

Count counts the numbers in your argument. You can use numbers or references, but you cannot count cells containing text or blanks.

The range can be any group of cells. In figure 8.7, for example, the Count function counts the number of values in cells F91 through F102 and displays the count in B106. You could just as easily count B91 through F103, although you would get a different answer. Because Works ignores text and blanks when counting, however, you cannot specify A91 through A102, all of which contain text. The results of that count would be *Error*.

## *Date(year,month,day)*

The Date function returns the serial date within the range of 0 to 49710 (from January 1, 1904, to February 6, 2040). The arguments of year, month, and day need to be within the specified ranges that represent valid numbers: from 1904 to 2040 for year, from 1 to 12 for month, and from 1 to 31 for day. For example, the function Date(1989,Choose(2,4,3,9),1) equals Date(1989,3,1) equals 31106.

## *Day(serial-number)*

The Day function converts the day portion of the *serial-number* to an integer between 1 and 31. For example, Day(Date(1989,5,15)) returns a value of 15. See Date for more information.

File Edit Window Select Format Options Chart Macro

B106 =Count(F91:F102)

PL87 WORKS (SS)

| | A | B | C | D | E | F |
|---|---|---|---|---|---|---|
| 90 | RECEIVABLES | | | | | |
| 91 | Firstours | $0 | $0 | $0 | $0 | $2500 |
| 92 | Robishion | $0 | $0 | $0 | $0 | $318 |
| 93 | Van Pleer & Tissany | $0 | $0 | $0 | $0 | $445 |
| 94 | DISC | $0 | $0 | $0 | $0 | $488 |
| 95 | Revelco (Entrepreneur) | $0 | $0 | $0 | $0 | $800 |
| 96 | BCC | $0 | $0 | $0 | $0 | $8877 |
| 97 | DST (Advani) | $0 | $0 | $0 | $0 | $1000 |
| 98 | Fadem Berger & Norton | $0 | $0 | $0 | $0 | $980 |
| 99 | A. I. R | $0 | $0 | $0 | $0 | $4582 |
| 100 | Fox Television | $0 | $0 | $0 | $0 | $228 |
| 101 | Dogervision | $0 | $0 | $0 | $0 | $2258 |
| 102 | Light Signatures | $0 | $0 | $0 | $0 | $5659 |
| 103 | | | | | | |
| 104 | **Total Expected** | **$0** | **$0** | **$0** | **$0** | **$28135** |
| 105 | | | | | | |
| 106 | **clients that owe** | 12 | | | | |

**Fig. 8.7**

*An example of the Count function.*

# *Degrees(number)*

With the Degrees function, you can convert radians into degrees. A full circle contains 360 degrees, or 2 radians. The equation used to convert radian measure to degree measure is

$$\text{Degrees} = \text{Radians} * 180/\pi$$

Figure 8.8 shows an example. The answer is slightly less than 180 because of the precision limitations in your Macintosh and Works.

B2 =Degrees(B1)

| | A | B |
|---|---|---|
| 1 | Radians | 3.14159 |
| 2 | Degrees | 179.99984796 |

**Fig. 8.8**

*Using Degrees to convert radians to degrees.*

## *Error( )*

The Error function, which has no arguments, enables you to force an error in your spreadsheet while you are testing it. Then you can see which other cells in your spreadsheet are affected by an error at the chosen point. For instance, if you place an error in cell B1 of figure 8.8, `*Error*` is displayed in B2, indicating that an error in B1 affects the results in B2.

## *Exp(number)*

The Exp function returns e (2.7182818) raised to the power of *number*. This function therefore is the inverse of the natural logarithm function, Ln. For example, the equation =Ln(10) returns 2.303, and the equation =Exp(2.303) returns 10.

## *False( )*

The False function takes no arguments, but the parentheses are required. False is primarily a testing tool that forces FALSE in a cell where you want the FALSE value. This function is useful when you are testing spreadsheets that use logical functions, because you can force the logical situation you want [see also TRUE( )].

## *FV(rate,nper,pmt,pv,type)*

The financial function FV, or future value, usually determines the amount that an investment will be worth after a given time. FV can use other Works financial functions in the process. Here's what FV's arguments mean:

| | |
|---|---|
| *rate* | the annual interest rate in percentage points (for example, 8 percent) |
| *nper* | periods, or length of time in years |
| *pmt* | payments, or annual dollar amount (a negative number) |
| *pv* | present value, or optional dollar amount (a negative number) |
| *type* | either 0 for payments made at the end of each period, or 1 for payments made at the beginning (optional) |

Some arguments can be other Works financial functions. If you don't enter the *type* argument, Works substitutes a 0. Payments and present values are negative numbers because Works treats payments as such. Future value is positive because it's money you will receive rather than give.

For example, suppose that you have $20,000 in an account earning 6.5 percent annual interest, and you plan to add an additional $250.00 at the beginning of each month ($3,000 per year) over a 20-year period. Broken down into pieces of the formula, the figures look like this:

6.5%/12 = monthly interest
20*12 = number of months
–250 = monthly payment
–20,000 = present value
1 = payment at the beginning of the period
$195,734.17 if made at end of period

To find out how much you will have in 20 years, you use the following formula:

=FV(6.5%/12,20*12,–250,–20000,1)

The answer is $196,398.28—not a bad 20 years of work. You can compute a 1-point increase in interest rate by changing one parameter, rate. At 7.5 percent, the yield jumps to $228,514.23. In the argument, Works percentages are entered as shown or as 0.065 with no percentage sign.

## *HLookup(lookup-value,compare-range,index-number)*

The HLookup function examines the first row in a range you define (the *compare-range*). Once HLookup finds the largest value that is less than or equal to the *lookup-value* in a column, the function moves up or down the column the number of rows called for in the *index-number*.

For example, in figure 8.9, the equation in cell A9 uses the block of cells A1 through D6. Each cell in row 1 is tested against the lookup-value (2,000). When the function finds the column containing 2,000 (column B), Works goes down the column the number of rows specified in the index-number portion of the argument (4). The value in cell B4 appears in the cell containing the HLookup equation (A9). Remember that you can substitute cell addresses for the lookup-value or index-number in your arguments.

**NOTE:** Values in the compare-range must be in ascending order.

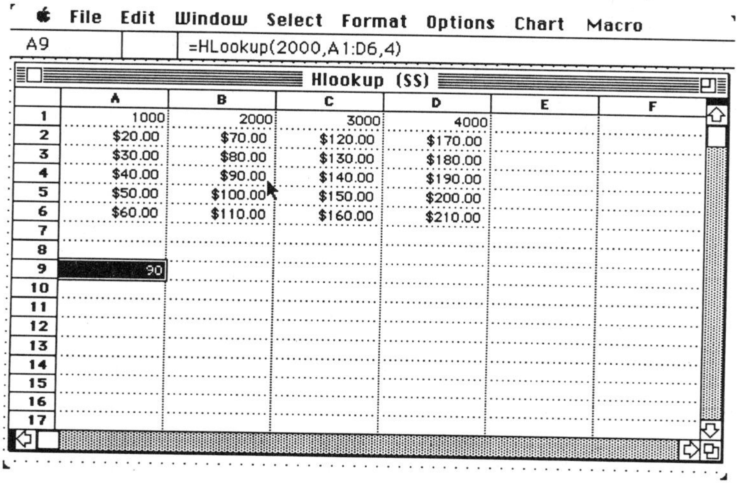

File Edit Window Select Format Options Chart Macro

A9 =HLookup(2000,A1:D6,4)

Hlookup (SS)

| | A | B | C | D | E | F |
|---|---|---|---|---|---|---|
| 1 | 1000 | 2000 | 3000 | 4000 | | |
| 2 | $20.00 | $70.00 | $120.00 | $170.00 | | |
| 3 | $30.00 | $80.00 | $130.00 | $180.00 | | |
| 4 | $40.00 | $90.00 | $140.00 | $190.00 | | |
| 5 | $50.00 | $100.00 | $150.00 | $200.00 | | |
| 6 | $60.00 | $110.00 | $160.00 | $210.00 | | |
| 7 | | | | | | |
| 8 | | | | | | |
| 9 | 90 | | | | | |
| 10 | | | | | | |
| 11 | | | | | | |
| 12 | | | | | | |
| 13 | | | | | | |
| 14 | | | | | | |
| 15 | | | | | | |
| 16 | | | | | | |
| 17 | | | | | | |

**Fig. 8.9**

*Using the HLookup function.*

## *Hour(serial-number)*

The Hour function converts the hour portion of *serial-number* to an integer in the range of 0 to 23. To make the conversion, Works uses only the fractional part of the serial number. For example, Hour(0.5) equals 12.

## *If(number,number-if-TRUE, number-if-FALSE)*

With the If function, you can replace the contents of a cell based on the results of tests. For example, you can specify two different values for a cell based on the results of a test. In figure 8.10, If puts the number 10 in cell B1 if A1 is less than 1, and puts 20 in cell B1 if A1 is 1 or more.

The If function can also perform calculations based on test results. The equation in figures 8.11 and 8.12 tests to see whether the beginning odometer reading in a mileage spreadsheet is larger than the ending reading. If the beginning reading is larger, then Works is asked to divide by 0, which causes `*Error*` to appear in B5 and affected cells (see fig. 8.12). If the beginning reading is smaller, as it should be,

Works is told to subtract the beginning reading from the ending reading, and the miles traveled appear in cell B5 (see fig. 8.11). You can accomplish the same thing in other ways—for example, =If(B4<B3,1/0,B4–B3) and =If(B3<B4, B4–B3,1/0). Another alternative is using the Error function instead of dividing by 0, as in

=If(B4<B3, Error(),B4–B3)

## *Index(range,row,column)*

Index returns the value contained in a specific cell of a range of cells. The first part of the argument is the *range*. Regardless of where the range is in the spreadsheet, Works counts down and then across the number of cells specified in the *row* and *column* arguments, starting in the upper left corner of the specified range.

Indexing can be based on computations or other cell contents or can be specific numbers, as is the case in figure 8.13. Here, Works begins at cell B1 and counts down three rows and over two columns to locate the contents of cell C3. This value is displayed in cell A1.

## *Int(number)*

The Int function rounds numbers down. For example, Int(3.4) rounds down to 3, but a negative number such as –3.4 rounds to –4.

**NOTE:** Some spreadsheets truncate numbers (cut off numbers to the right of the decimal point) with their Int functions. Works rounds. This difference is definitely worth noting if you are used to other spreadsheets, such as 1-2-3.

## *IRR(range,guess)*

IRR takes a series of cash flows (the *range*) and makes 20 attempts at computing the internal rate of return (the interest rate that gives the range a zero net present value). This procedure is called the *iterative technique* because the function makes 20 attempts (iterations) before giving up.

You specify the starting range for the iterations by entering a *guess*; try 0 or 1 to start. If IRR fails after 20 tries, the message `*Error*` appears. The function ignores blanks and labels.

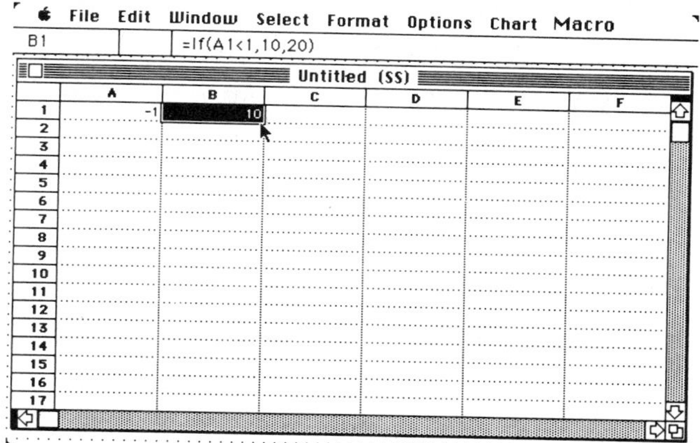






**Fig. 8.10**

*Using If to replace a cell's contents based on test results.*

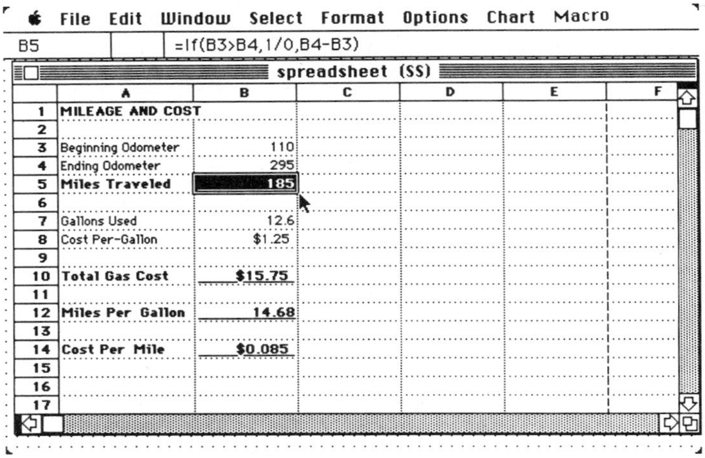

File Edit Window Select Format Options Chart Macro

B5 =If(B3>B4,1/0,B4-B3)

spreadsheet (SS)

| | A | B | C | D | E | F |
|---|---|---|---|---|---|---|
| 1 | MILEAGE AND COST | | | | | |
| 2 | | | | | | |
| 3 | Beginning Odometer | 110 | | | | |
| 4 | Ending Odometer | 295 | | | | |
| 5 | Miles Traveled | 185 | | | | |
| 6 | | | | | | |
| 7 | Gallons Used | 12.6 | | | | |
| 8 | Cost Per-Gallon | $1.25 | | | | |
| 9 | | | | | | |
| 10 | Total Gas Cost | $15.75 | | | | |
| 11 | | | | | | |
| 12 | Miles Per Gallon | 14.68 | | | | |
| 13 | | | | | | |
| 14 | Cost Per Mile | $0.085 | | | | |
| 15 | | | | | | |
| 16 | | | | | | |
| 17 | | | | | | |

**Fig. 8.11**

*Using If to perform calculations based on test results.*

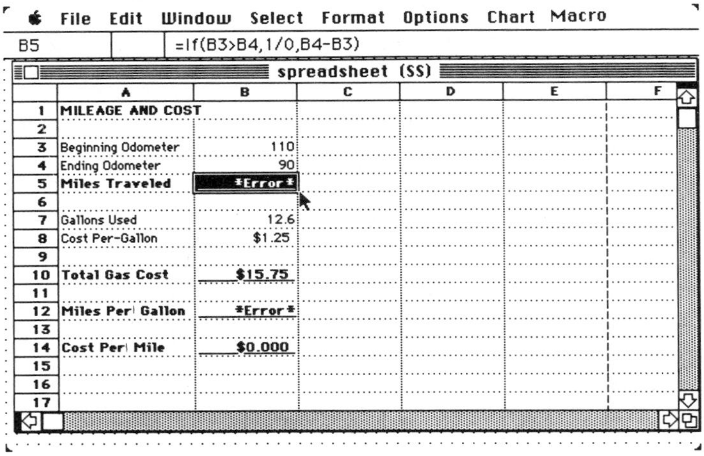

File Edit Window Select Format Options Chart Macro

B5 =If(B3>B4,1/0,B4-B3)

spreadsheet (SS)

| | A | B | C | D | E | F |
|---|---|---|---|---|---|---|
| 1 | MILEAGE AND COST | | | | | |
| 2 | | | | | | |
| 3 | Beginning Odometer | 110 | | | | |
| 4 | Ending Odometer | 90 | | | | |
| 5 | Miles Traveled | *Error* | | | | |
| 6 | | | | | | |
| 7 | Gallons Used | 12.6 | | | | |
| 8 | Cost Per-Gallon | $1.25 | | | | |
| 9 | | | | | | |
| 10 | Total Gas Cost | $15.75 | | | | |
| 11 | | | | | | |
| 12 | Miles Per Gallon | *Error* | | | | |
| 13 | | | | | | |
| 14 | Cost Per Mile | $0.000 | | | | |
| 15 | | | | | | |
| 16 | | | | | | |
| 17 | | | | | | |

**Fig. 8.12**

*Causing Works to display* `*Error*` *if an error condition exists.*

## *IsBlank(values-1,values-2,...)*

IsBlank tests cells or ranges of cells to see whether they're blank. If all tested cells are blank, the function returns a 1; if any cell contains a number, IsBlank returns a 0. IsBlank treats text as blanks.

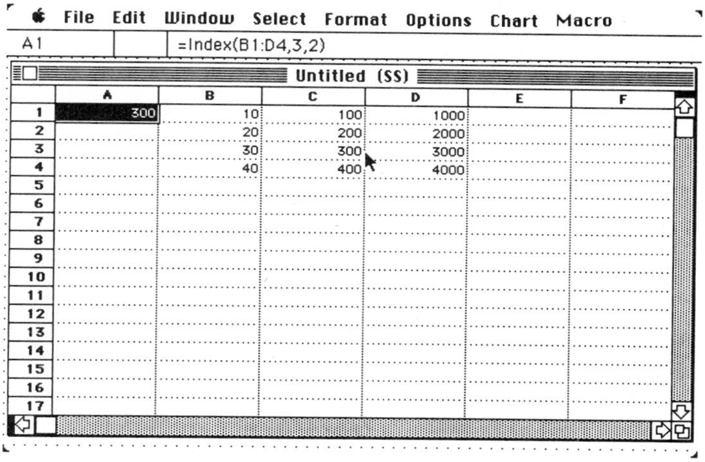

File Edit Window Select Format Options Chart Macro

A1 =Index(B1:D4,3,2)

Untitled (SS)

| | A | B | C | D | E | F |
|---|---|---|---|---|---|---|
| 1 | 300 | 10 | 100 | 1000 | | |
| 2 | | 20 | 200 | 2000 | | |
| 3 | | 30 | 300 | 3000 | | |
| 4 | | 40 | 400 | 4000 | | |

**Fig. 8.13**

*Using the Index function.*

# *IsError(range)*

IsError returns a value of 1 if a cell or any cell in a range of cells contains an `*Error*` warning. If IsError finds no warning, the function returns a 0. You can use this function to prevent `*Error*` messages from appearing on your worksheet, although this practice is generally not recommended because it masks spreadsheet problems.

# *IsNA(range)*

IsNA returns a value of 1 if a cell or any cell in a range of cells contains a not available (N/A) warning. If IsNA finds no N/A warnings, the function returns a 0. You can use this function to prevent `N/A` from appearing on your spreadsheets. Again, this practice is not recommended because it masks problems.

# *Ln(number)*

This function returns the natural logarithm, or the logarithm to base e (2.7182818), of the *number* provided as the function argument. The logarithm is the power to which the base is raised to yield the number.

For example, $e^2$ = 7.389056, so the natural logarithm of 7.389 is 2. Similarly, the Works equation =Ln(7.389056) returns the result approximately equal to 2.

## *Log10(number)*

Log10 yields the base 10 logarithm of a positive *number*. This function is the inverse of base 10 exponentiation. For example, the equation to find the log of 10 is =Log10(10), and the result is 1. As always, you can substitute a cell reference for the number.

## *Lookup(lookup-value,compare-range,result-range)*

The Lookup function examines a range you define (the *compare-range*) and returns the largest value that is less than or equal to the *lookup-value*. Lookup puts the results in *result-range*. See figure 8.5 for an example of the Lookup function.

**NOTE:** Values in the compare-range must be in ascending order. Both result-range and compare-range must be the same length.

## *Match(lookup-value,compare-range,type)*

The Match function compares the *lookup-value* with the numbers in the *compare-range* and returns a number indicating the position in the *compare-range* where the match was found. A match is found only when a number in the compare-range matches the lookup-value in accordance with the *type* of match specified in the third argument of the function.

**NOTE:** The Match function returns the number of the comparison value in the compare range. If it matches the third value, a 3 is returned, if it matches the 8th value, an 8 is returned.

The numbers in the compare-range are scanned from left to right and from top to bottom. If the compare-range is A1:B2, for example, the cells are scanned in this order: A1, A2, B1, B2. If match type is 1, the match is the largest number in the compare-range that is less than or equal to the lookup-value. If the match type argument is 0, the number in the compare-range must be equal to the lookup-value; if no number in the range matches the lookup-value, the function returns an error message. If the match type argument is −1, the match is the smallest number in the compare-range that is greater than or equal to the lookup-value.

**NOTE:** The order of the compare-range values is important when you use match types 1 and −1. For match type 1, the values must be in ascending order. For match type −1, the values must be in descending order.

One possible use of the Match function is shown in figure 8.14. This spreadsheet classifies clients according to the number of orders they have placed in the past year. Those who have placed the fewest orders are assigned customer status 1; those who have placed the most orders are assigned status 5. The matching is done by an equation in column C. Note, for instance, that the equation in C3 is

=Match(B3,$A$12:$A$16,1)

Notice that the specified match type is 1, which specifies that the matching number be the largest value in the compare-range which is less than or equal to the lookup-value. The number meeting that specification in the compare-range (A12:A16) is 100. Because 100 is the last number in the range, the equation returns the value 5.

This function is especially useful with other table-oriented functions, such as HLookup, VLookup, Index, and Lookup. The advantage to Match is that it always returns an integer value, which can be used as an argument for one of the other functions. You might use the status number generated in the preceding example to index into a table of values so that your spreadsheet can automatically determine discounts, set the frequency of sales calls, or provide other handy information.

## *Max(values-1,values-2,...)*

Max yields the highest number in the range specified in the argument. You can use values, cell locations, or ranges as arguments. The function ignores text and blanks. When A1:D1 contains 4, 6, 10, and 5, for example, Max(A1:D1) returns 10.

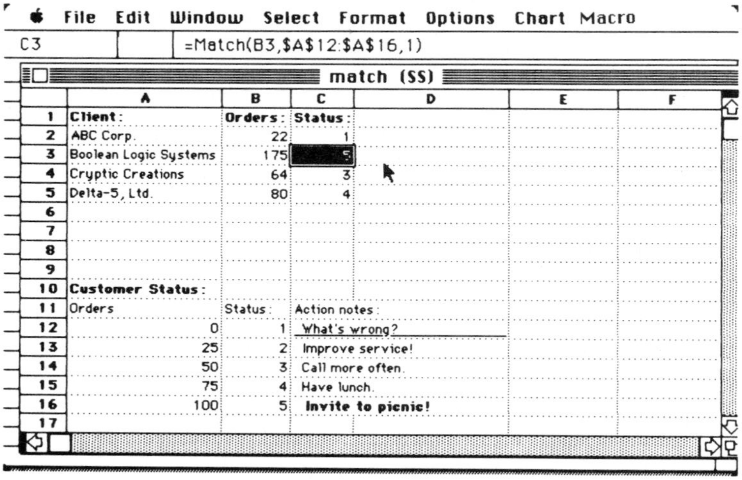

File Edit Window Select Format Options Chart Macro

C3 =Match(B3,$A$12:$A$16,1)

match (SS)

| | A | B | C | D | E | F |
|---|---|---|---|---|---|---|
| 1 | **Client:** | **Orders:** | **Status:** | | | |
| 2 | ABC Corp. | 22 | 1 | | | |
| 3 | Boolean Logic Systems | 175 | 5 | | | |
| 4 | Cryptic Creations | 64 | 3 | | | |
| 5 | Delta-5, Ltd. | 80 | 4 | | | |
| 6 | | | | | | |
| 7 | | | | | | |
| 8 | | | | | | |
| 9 | | | | | | |
| 10 | **Customer Status:** | | | | | |
| 11 | Orders | Status: | Action notes: | | | |
| 12 | 0 | 1 | What's wrong? | | | |
| 13 | 25 | 2 | Improve service! | | | |
| 14 | 50 | 3 | Call more often. | | | |
| 15 | 75 | 4 | Have lunch. | | | |
| 16 | 100 | 5 | **Invite to picnic!** | | | |
| 17 | | | | | | |

**Fig. 8.14**

*Using the Match function.*

# *Min(values-1,values-2,...)*

Min is identical to the Max function, except that Min yields the lowest number in the range specified in the argument. Arguments can contain values, cell locations, or ranges. Mix ignores text and blanks. When A1:D1 contains 4, 6, 10, and 5, for example, Min(A1:D1) returns 4.

# *Minute(serial-number)*

The Minute function converts the minute portion of *serial-number* to a minute as an integer between 0 and 59.

# *MIRR(range,safe,risk)*

MIRR computes modified internal rates of return, taking into consideration the *safe* and *risk* arguments. Safe is the rate returned by an investment that will finance negative cash flows. Risk is the return from reinvestment rate of positive cash flow. For instance, suppose that you have these cash flows in cells A1 through A5:

A1 $-50000$
A2 20000
A3 $-3000$
A4 30000
A5 5000

Suppose also that you borrow money at 18 percent to finance the negative cash flows while reinvesting the positive cash flows at 19 percent. The modified internal rate of return would be 9.29 percent. The equation is =MIRR(A1:A5,18%,19%).

## *Mod(number,divisor-number)*

The Mod function returns the remainder after division. For example, 5 divided by 3 leaves a remainder of 2, so the equation =Mod(5,3) returns the value 2. Similarly, =Mod($-5$,$-3$) returns the value $-2$.

All is well as long as the dividend (*number*) and the divisor (*divisor-number*) have the same sign: the result is positive for a positive dividend and divisor, and negative for negative numbers. But erroneous results occur when the dividend and divisor have different signs. Notice, for example, in figure 8.15 that the equation =Mod(5,$-3$) in cell C4 returns $-1$, and that =Mod($-9$,4) in cell C5 returns 3.

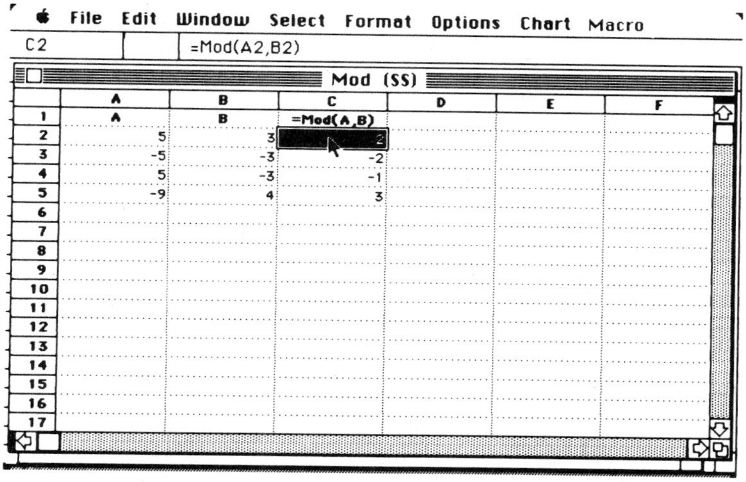

File Edit Window Select Format Options Chart Macro

C2 =Mod(A2,B2)

Mod (SS)

| | A | B | C | D | E | F |
|---|---|---|---|---|---|---|
| 1 | A | B | =Mod(A,B) | | | |
| 2 | 5 | 3 | 2 | | | |
| 3 | -5 | -3 | -2 | | | |
| 4 | 5 | -3 | -1 | | | |
| 5 | -9 | 4 | 3 | | | |

**Fig. 8.15**

*Using the Mod function.*

Apparently, this unusual behavior results from a bug in the Works. If you experiment with the Mod function, you will find that it returns the difference between the divisor and the expected answer. For instance, the answer you would expect from =Mod(5,−3) is either 2 or −2. (Opinion differs on whether the result of modulus division of mixed numbers should reflect the sign of the dividend or of the divisor.) But =Mod(5,−3) returns − 1, which is equal to the difference between the divisor, −3, and the expected result, −2. Similar results are obtained with the equation =Mod(−9,4), which returns 3 rather than the expected result, 1. And 1 is, of course, the difference between 4 and 3. Be careful in using this function!

## *Month(serial-number)*

The Month function converts *serial-number* to a month in the form of an integer within the range of 1 to 12.

## *NA( )*

The NA function takes no arguments, but the parentheses are required. NA is primarily a testing tool that forces N/A to display in a cell where you want the N/A value.

## *Not(argument)*

Not returns a logical 0 (FALSE) if the result of the *argument* is TRUE, that is, a value other than 0. Arguments can be values, equations, or cell locations. Conversely, Not returns a logical 1 (TRUE) if the result of the argument is 0 (FALSE).

Here are two examples of this function:

=Not(1+2=4) yields a 1.
=Not(1+2=3) yields a 0.

## *Now( )*

The Now function returns the serial number of the current date and time when the spreadsheet is recalculated. The integers in the range of 0 to 49710 represent the dates in the range of January 1, 1904, to February 6, 2040. The fractional part from 0 to 0.999 represents times from 0:00:00 or 12:00:00 midnight to 23:59:59 or 11:59:59 PM.

## *NPer(rate,pmt,pv,fv,type)*

NPer computes the number of periods of an investment involving constant cash flows. For instance, you can use NPer to determine how long you need to pay off a loan at a particular monthly payment level.

NPer uses the following arguments:

| | |
|---|---|
| *rate* | the interest rate in percentage points (for example, 1 percent) |
| *pmt* | payments |
| *pv* | present value |
| *fv* | future value (optional) |
| *type* | either 0 for payments made at the end of each period, or 1 for payments made at the beginning (optional) |

Suppose that you want to find out how long you need to pay back an $18,000 car loan at 12 percent by making $400 monthly payments at the beginning of each month (period). You use this formula:

```
=NPer(1%,-400,18000,0,1)
```

The answer is 59.271277992 months. (You could have substituted 0.01 for 1% in the equation; Works accepts both forms.) This simple example uses a monthly interest rate of 1 percent because the payment periods are months. Payments are always negative numbers. Optional arguments such as fv and type default to 0 if you don't specify them.

## *NPV(rate,values-1,values-2,...)*

The NPV function computes the net present value of future cash flows, given a constant rate of interest (*rate*). Cash flows occur at the beginning of constant intervals. Values can be numbers, equations, or cell or range references. NPV ignores text and blanks if they occur in the ranges you specify.

## *Or(values-1,values-2,...)*

The Or function returns either a 1 (TRUE) if any value in the argument is TRUE, or a 0 (FALSE) if all arguments are FALSE. Arguments can be values, equations, or cell references. Here are two examples of Or:

=Or(1+2=4,1+2=3) yields a 1.
=Or(1+2=4,1+2=5) yields a 0.

## *Pi( )*

Pi inserts an approximation of the mathematical constant that is its namesake: 3.14159. No arguments are required, but the parentheses are.

## *Pmt(rate,nper,pv,fv,type)*

Pmt yields an investment's periodic payment, assuming constant cash flows. In other words, if you know the amount, interest rate, and duration of a loan, you can use this function to determine the amount of your regular payments. The arguments include the following:

| | |
|---|---|
| *rate* | interest rate per period |
| *nper* | net present value |
| *pv* | present value |
| *fv* | future value (optional) |
| *type* | either 1 for payments at beginning of period, or 2 for payments at end of period (optional) |

Here's an example. Suppose that you want to buy a house, and you require a $300,000 loan for 30 years. The going rate for fixed mortgages is 10 percent, and you plan to make payments at the first of each period. To calculate your approximate monthly payment, you use the following function:

Pmt(10.0%/12,360,300000,0,1)

The answer is $2,610.96 per month. The annual interest rate (10 percent) is divided by 12 months to get the appropriate interest rate for the rest of the assumptions. (You also can enter 0.10/12 rather than 10.0%/12.) Notice the use of an equation (10.0%/12) in the function.

## *PV(rate,nper,pmt,fv,type)*

You can use PV, or present value, by itself or with the other financial functions. PV's elements are the following:

| | |
|---|---|
| *rate* | interest rate per period |
| *nper* | net present value |
| *pmt* | payment (a negative number) |
| *fv* | future value (optional) |
| *type* | either 0 for payments at beginning of period, or 1 for payments at end of period (optional) |

Imagine that you have $1,200 dollars a month to spend on house payments. With PV, you can calculate how much you can afford to borrow, given current interest rates and the length of the mortgage. Assume that the rate is 10 percent, the mortgage is for 30 years, and you will make a payment at the beginning of each period. You use

=PV(10%/12,30*12,−1200,0,1)

According to this function, you can afford a house that costs roughly $137,880. But if interest rates go back to 18 percent, you had better find a house with an $80,818 mortgage.

Notice the use of two equations in the example; they save you some manual calculations. The first equation (10%/12) makes the interest rate compatible with the periods (months). The second equation (30*12) computes the number of months in 30 years (360). Works substitutes 0s if you omit the optional arguments type and fv.

## *Radians(number)*

With Radians( ), you can convert degrees to radians. You can use values, equations, or cell references as arguments. Radians(180) equals 3.14159 ($\pi$).

## *Rand( )*

The Rand function generates a new positive random number (at recalculation) between 0 and 0.999. No arguments are accepted, but the parentheses are required. To see Rand( ) at work, enter =Rand( ) in a cell. Then hold the ⌘ key and repeatedly press the equal key (=), causing Works to recalculate the spreadsheet. Each recalculation yields a new random number in the cell containing the Rand( ) function.

## *Rate(nper,pmt,pv,fv,type,guess)*

Another financial function, Rate determines the probable rate of growth for an investment, given the initial value of the investment and its probable value at the end of a known time period. This function's arguments are these:

| | |
|---|---|
| *nper* | period |
| *pmt* | payment (an optional negative number) |
| *pv* | present value |
| *fv* | future value (optional) |
| *type* | either 0 for payments at beginning of period, or 1 for payments at end of period (optional) |
| *guess* | a starting point for solving the equation |

Suppose that you purchase a 1964 Mustang convertible for $8,000 and plan to keep it for 10 years, at which point you think it will be worth $13,000. You can estimate the percentage yield of this investment by using

=Rate(10,0,−8000,13000,0,.1)

The investment yields 4.97 percent, ignoring any expenses, such as storage costs or insurance and maintenance if you drive the car. If you have extra predictable expenses—for example, $400 per year for storage—you enter that amount as a payment (pmt):

=Rate(10,−400,−8000,13000,0,.1)

The results of this equation look even worse: Your yield is less than 1 percent.

**NOTE:** Works substitutes 0s if you leave out the optional arguments type and fv. If your guess (starting point) is too high or low, Works gives up trying to find an answer after 20 iterations. Choose another guess, and have Works try again.

## *Round(number,number-of-digits)*

The Round function yields numbers rounded to the precision specified by the *number-of-digits* argument. If you specify 0 digits, Works rounds to the nearest integer. The expression =Round(1.23456,3), then, produces the answer 1.235. Remember that you can use cell locations in place of numbers, so =Round(A1,3) is also acceptable. If you want to round off pi to three digits, you use =Round (Pi(),3), which returns 3.142.

## *Second(serial-number)*

The Second function converts a *serial-number* to a second in the form of an integer within the range of 0 to 59.

## *Sign(number)*

The Sign function tests for positive or negative numbers. Again, you can substitute cell references or equations for numbers in the argument. Positive numbers produce a 1, negative numbers produce a −1, zeros produce a 0. Note the following examples:

=Sign(10) yields 1.
=Sign(−3) yields −1.
=Sign(0) yields 0.
=Sign(3−3) yields 0.
=Sign(3+1) yields 1.

## *Sin(number)*

The Sin function calculates a sine when the number is an angle in radians. Sin(0) equals 0, and Sin((Pi( )/2) equals 1.

## *Sqrt(number)*

Sqrt yields the square root of a positive *number*. If you use a negative number, an `*Error*` warning appears.

## *SSum(values-1,values-2,...)*

The SSum function is designed to return the sum of values in a range exactly as it appears on the screen. For example, in figure 8.16, cells B2 through C3 all contain 0.333, and cells B4 and C5 contain 0.334. Cell B5 contains the equation =Sum(B4:B2). Cell C5, however, uses =SSum(C4:C2). If the cells are displayed in the General format, as shown in figure 8.16, both columns add up to 1, just as they would on pocket calculators. But if all six cells are formatted for dollars and cents with two decimal places, things get sticky. In figure 8.17, cells B4 and C4 still contain 0.334 but display as $0.33 because of rounding done by the Dollar format. The Sum function in cell B5 doesn't produce the results you would get if you added the displayed numbers with your calculator. Instead, the answer in B5 is based on the actual cell contents. Note, however, that the SSum function in cell C5 displays the sum of the *displayed* values.

**NOTE:** The SSum function uses the displayed resolution to determine the answer. Therefore, the number adds up correctly. If Sum( ) is used, the answer may not look correct according to what is displayed on the screen (or printout).

**Fig. 8.16**

*Using Sum and SSum in General format.*

Untitled

| | A | B | C |
|---|---|---|---|
| 1 | | | |
| 2 | | 0.333 | 0.333 |
| 3 | | 0.333 | 0.333 |
| 4 | | 0.334 | 0.334 |
| 5 | Total | 1 | 1 |

Equation is=Sum(B4:B2)

Equation is=SSum(C4:C2)

**Fig. 8.17**

*Using SSum in Dollar format.*

File Edit Window Select Format Options Chart Macro

C5 =SSum(C2:C4)

Untitled (SS)

| | A | B | C | D | E | F |
|---|---|---|---|---|---|---|
| 1 | | | | | | |
| 2 | | $0.33 | $0.33 | | | |
| 3 | | $0.33 | $0.33 | | | |
| 4 | | $0.33 | $0.33 | | | |
| 5 | Total | $1.00 | $0.99 | | | |
| 6 | | | | | | |
| 7 | | | | | | |
| 8 | | | | | | |
| 9 | | | | | | |
| 10 | | | | | | |
| 11 | | | | | | |
| 12 | | | | | | |
| 13 | | | | | | |
| 14 | | | | | | |
| 15 | | | | | | |
| 16 | | | | | | |
| 17 | | | | | | |

When only a single cell is referenced in SSum, the actual value is shown. Text or blank values are ignored.

## *StDev(values-1,values-2,...)*

Given numbers, equations, or appropriate cell references, StDev yields simple standard deviations. The function ignores text and blanks. To calculate StDev, Works uses the formula

Sqrt(Var(values-1,values-2,...))

The Sqrt and Var functions are described in this chapter.

## *Sum(values-1,values-2,...)*

Sum adds the numbers found in the specified range. You can use values, cell references, or ranges. See also SSum().

**NOTE:** Be careful when inserting rows and columns in areas of a spreadsheet containing Sum or SSum functions. For example, in figure 8.18, the NORTHEAST region has been inserted as row 7, but the Sum function does not include row 7 in its computations. As you can see in the entry bar, the Sum function looks only at rows B4 through B6. Also note the problem in the percentage column, G. You may need to redefine the Sum range because rows aren't automatically included in the Sum totals.

## *Tan(number)*

The Tan function returns the tangent of the angle (expressed in radian measure) supplied as an argument to the function. Remember that the tangent is the ratio of the x-coordinate to the y-coordinate on a unit circle. The x-coordinate is 0 for the angles $\pi/2$, $3 * \pi/2$, $5 * \pi/2$, and so on (equivalent to 90 degrees, 270 degrees, 450 degrees, respectively). Consequently, the Tan function returns an `*Error*` message for those values because division by 0 is not defined. Two examples of the Tan function are Tan(0.785), which returns 0.999, and Tan(45*Pi()/180), which returns 1.

File Edit Window Select Format Options Chart Macro

B8 =Sum(B4:B6)

quarterly (SS)

| | A | B | C | D | E | F | G |
|---|---|---|---|---|---|---|---|
| 1 | | | | | | | |
| 2 | | Q1 Actual | Q2 Actual | Q3 Plan | Q4 Plan | Total | % |
| 3 | SALES | | | | | | |
| 4 | WEST | $123,568 | $107,232 | $140,000 | $140,000 | $510,800 | 34.15% |
| 5 | CENTRAL | $113,454 | $110,785 | $140,000 | $140,000 | $504,239 | 33.71% |
| 6 | EAST | $98,876 | $101,867 | $140,000 | $140,000 | $480,743 | 32.14% |
| 7 | NORTH EAST | $120,000 | $78,955 | $48,878 | $44,774 | $292,607 | 19.56% |
| 8 | TOTAL SALES | $335,898 | $319,884 | $420,000 | $420,000 | $1,495,782 | 100% |
| 9 | | | | | | | |
| 10 | CUM SALES | $335,898 | $655,782 | $1,075,782 | $1,495,782 | | |
| 11 | | | | | | | |
| 12 | EXPENSES | ($252,360) | ($298,758) | ($350,000) | ($365,000) | ($1,266,118) | |
| 13 | | | | | | | |
| 14 | PROFIT | $83,538 | $21,126 | $70,000 | $55,000 | $229,664 | |
| 15 | | | | | | | |
| 16 | % of Sales | 24.87% | 6.60% | 16.67% | 13.10% | Average | 15.31% |
| 17 | | | | | | | |

**Fig. 8.18**

*After inserting a row at the bottom of columns containing a Sum function.*

# *Time(hour,minute,second)*

The Time function converts the hour, minute, and second to a serial-number representation. This conversion yields a number in the range of 0 to 0.999, which represents the times of 0:00:00 or 12:00:00 midnight to 23:59:59 PM or 11:59:59 PM. For example, Time(12,0,0) equals 0.5. Other examples are Time(0,12,0), which returns 0.00833, and Time(18,0,0), which returns 0.75.

# *True( )*

The True function takes no arguments, but the parentheses are required. This function is primarily a testing tool for equations containing logical functions. True( ) forces TRUE in a cell where you want the TRUE value. You then can see the effect of TRUE entries on other areas of the spreadsheet.

## *Type(value)*

The Type function checks a cell and returns a number based on the type of cell entry the function finds. This function displays a `1` if the cell contains a number, a `2` if the cell contains text or is blank, a `16` if the cell contains `*Error*`, and an `8` if the cell contains `N/A`. Formulas and cell references are treated as numbers.

## *Var(values-1,values-2,...)*

Var returns the variance of numbers in a range. Adding the population average as the last argument yields the population variance. In figure 8.19, cell A6 illustrates a typical use of the Var function. Cell B6 shows the Var and Average functions used together to get a true population variance by including an average of the entire population. Cells containing text or blanks are ignored.

## *VLookup(lookup-value,compare-range,index-number)*

The VLookup function examines the first column in a range you define (the *compare-range*). Once VLookup finds in a row the largest value that is less than or equal to the *lookup-value*, the function returns the value in the row that is *index-number* columns to the right of the leftmost column in the compare-range.

In figure 8.20, the range used is A1 to D6. Works goes to row 4 (because of the lookup-value of 4). At row 4, Works moves right to the third column because of the index-number of 3 supplied in the entry bar. Remember that the lookup-value and index-number can be cell references or equations rather than values.

**NOTE:** Values in the compare-range must be in ascending order.

**Fig. 8.19**

*Using the Var and Average functions.*

| | A | B | C | D |
|---|---|---|---|---|
| 1 | 12 | 12 | | |
| 2 | 5 | 5 | | |
| 3 | 18 | 18 | | |
| 4 | 20 | 20 | | |
| 5 | 2 | 2 | | |
| 6 | 61.8 | 49.44 | | |
| 7 | | | | |
| 8 | | | | |
| 9 | | | | |
| 10 | | | | |
| 11 | | | | |
| 12 | | | | |
| 13 | | | | |
| 14 | | | | |
| 15 | | | | |
| 16 | | | | |
| 17 | | | | |

| | A | B | C | D |
|---|---|---|---|---|
| 1 | 12 | 12 | | |
| 2 | 5 | 5 | | |
| 3 | 18 | 18 | | |
| 4 | 20 | 20 | | |
| 5 | 2 | 2 | | |
| 6 | =Var(A1:A5) | =Var(B1:B5,Average(B1:B5)) | | |
| 7 | | | | |
| 8 | | | | |
| 9 | | | | |
| 10 | | | | |
| 11 | | | | |
| 12 | | | | |
| 13 | | | | |
| 14 | | | | |
| 15 | | | | |
| 16 | | | | |
| 17 | | | | |

# *Chapter Summary*

In this chapter, you learned about the range of functions you can use in your spreadsheets and databases. These functions include arithmetic, logical, statistical, trigonometric, financial, time/date, and locational (or comparative) functions. All 64 functions are available except those that require locational information. By using these functions you can create sophisticated applications for your work in business or at home.

File Edit Window Select Format Options Chart Macro

A8 =VLookup(4,A1:D6,3)

VLookup (SS)

| | A | B | C | D | E | F |
|---|---|---|---|---|---|---|
| 1 | 1 | 10 | 20 | 30 | | |
| 2 | 2 | 40 | 50 | 60 | | |
| 3 | 3 | 70 | 80 | 90 | | |
| 4 | 4 | 100 | 110 | 120 | | |
| 5 | 5 | 130 | 140 | 150 | | |
| 6 | 6 | 160 | 170 | 180 | | |
| 7 | | | | | | |
| 8 | 110 | | | | | |
| 9 | | | | | | |
| 10 | | | | | | |
| 11 | | | | | | |
| 12 | | | | | | |
| 13 | | | | | | |
| 14 | | | | | | |
| 15 | | | | | | |
| 16 | | | | | | |
| 17 | | | | | | |

**Fig. 8.20**

*Using the VLookup function.*

# Part V

# Databases

## Includes

Databases

Database Reports

# 9

# Databases

With Works, you can organize information in much the same way that you would set up card files. These organized collections of information are called *databases* and are stored in digital form rather than on paper. On an 800K floppy you can store the equivalent of 200 pages of data, which you can then edit, organize, search, sort, and manipulate with the click of a mouse. Moreover, you can produce custom lists and reports from your databases and merge database information with your word processing documents to create personalized form letters, mailing labels, preprinted forms, and more. In this chapter, you learn how to design and use your database to gather information. The chapter also gives you shortcuts and tips for working with databases.

## *Understanding Database Terms and Features*

Databases are similar to spreadsheets in many respects. Often these two types of files are formatted in similar ways. Databases use many of the functions that were examined in Chapter 8 and many of the commands you learned in previous chapters. Indeed, some spreadsheets, such as Microsoft Excel, are used as database engines. Databases, however, are meant to work with independent sets of data, and spreadsheets are more often used to work with interacting sets of data.

A database is any organized collection of data sets called *records*. A record can be anything for which you want to keep an organized list. Your address book is an example of a database, with the address information for each person serving as a database record. Another example of a database is the program your travel agent calls up on the computer to book your plane flight.

In Works, you can display your database information on-screen in a *list* window, reminiscent of a worksheet. You can also view your database records individually in a style Works calls a *form*.

When you need paper copies (so-called "hard copy") of information from a Works database, you print database *reports*. An example of a database report is shown in figure 9.1. You create *report definitions* to specify totals, subtotals, headers, footers, and other features for the printed report. These topics are covered in detail in Chapter 10.

**Fig. 9.1**

*List of names, in the form of a database report.*

| Last Name | First Name | Salut | Company | Address |
|---|---|---|---|---|
| A & F Office Sup | | | A & F Office Supply | 633 Main Street |
| A.B.E. Radiation I | | | A.B.E. Radiation Measurement Lab, Inc. | Box 214 |
| AAA | | | American Automobile Association | 15 Highland Street |
| Alamo Rent-A-C | | | Alamo Rent-A-Car | |
| Albertella | John V. | Mr. | Citizens Against Toxic Waste Foundation | 9 North Third Street |
| Alexander | Mark | Mr. | Newton-Wellesley Answering Serv | 268 Center Street |
| Alten | Dee | | Chipside Green | Chip Avenue |
| American Acader | | | American Academy of Envirn. Medicine | P.O. Box 16106 |
| American Airline | | | American Airlines | |
| American Chemic | | | American Chemical Society | 1155 Sixteenth Stree |
| American Expres | Cust. Serv. | | American Express | 777 American Expres |
| American Public | | | American Public Health Association | 1015 Fifteenth Street |
| Apfel | Bob | Dr. | Yale University, Dept. of Mech. Eng. | P.O. Box 2159 |

## *Viewing Records in a Form*

To display records in the form format, choose the Show Form command from the Format menu. Works enables you to view your database records individually in this manner and to enter and edit records. Figure 9.2 shows an individual record from an address book in the *form* style.

**Fig. 9.2**

*Viewing a record in the form window.*

File Edit Window Organize Format Report Macro

Addresses (DB)

Last Name MacConnection
First Name
Demographics
Address 14 Mill Street
City Marlow ST NH Zip 03456
Interests
Group Type
Date Sent Reply
Company MacConnection
Work Phone (800)622-5472 Phone (800)622-5472
Salut

Database forms may remind you of cards in a card file or of printed paper forms. You fill in the blanks on the forms while entering or editing information in your database.

Records consist of *fields*, which are like the blanks on printed paper forms. Most records contain more than one field. In figure 9.2, for example, all the information contained (15 fields) equals just one individual address (record). The information you place in each field is called an *entry*, and you type it in the entry bar, just as you do in a spreadsheet.

When you design a new database, you create the fields and therefore the form used to organize your data. You can change the sizes of fields, move them around, change their appearance, and add and delete fields, even after you finish designing a form.

## *Using the List Feature*

For many applications, you will find yourself using the *list* window more often than the form window. To display the list window, you choose the Show List option from the Format menu. (After Show List has been selected, the menu option changes to Show Form, and vice versa.) Show List displays all your records in a list or matrix format similar to a worksheet (see fig. 9.3).

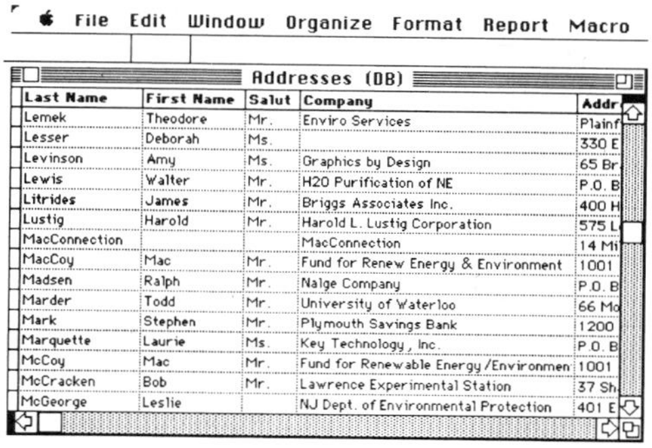
File Edit Window Organize Format Report Macro
Addresses (DB)
Last Name | First Name | Salut | Company | Addr
Lemek | Theodore | Mr. | Enviro Services | Plainf
Lesser | Deborah | Ms. | | 330 E
Levinson | Amy | Ms. | Graphics by Design | 65 Br
Lewis | Walter | Mr. | H20 Purification of NE | P.O. B
Litrides | James | Mr. | Briggs Associates Inc. | 400 H
Lustig | Harold | Mr. | Harold L. Lustig Corporation | 575 L
MacConnection | | | MacConnection | 14 Mi
MacCoy | Mac | Mr. | Fund for Renew Energy & Environment | 1001
Madsen | Ralph | Mr. | Nalge Company | P.O. B
Marder | Todd | Mr. | University of Waterloo | 66 Mo
Mark | Stephen | Mr. | Plymouth Savings Bank | 1200
Marquette | Laurie | Ms. | Key Technology, Inc. | P.O. B
McCoy | Mac | Mr. | Fund for Renewable Energy/Environmen | 1001
McCracken | Bob | Mr. | Lawrence Experimental Station | 37 Sh
McGeorge | Leslie | | NJ Dept. of Environmental Protection | 401 E

**Fig. 9.3**

*After choosing the Show List command.*

You also can use Show List to rearrange records and to copy parts of one record to another, with your records displayed in list format. Show List frequently speeds the entry and editing of records as well. In the list window, records become *rows*, fields become *columns*, and field names become *column headings*. If a record is too long to fit on the screen, you can use the horizontal scroll bar to view the record's entire contents. If all your records don't fit on-screen at once, use the vertical scroll bar to display the records that do not fit. Information that does not fit in the field on the screen display is still retained in your database file and appears in the entry bar when you select that field entry. For example, note in figure 9.3 that the Address column is truncated on-screen.

To select a field in the list window, click its column heading. To select a row, click the corresponding record selector box. The box to the left of the field names is called the deselect box. You click it to deselect whatever you have selected—an entire record, multiple records, or a single field. This box is similar to the deselect box in a spreadsheet window.

**NOTE:** If you double-click rather than click a field, Works gives you the opportunity to change field names or attributes. Click the Cancel button if you activate this feature accidentally.

## *Moving between List and Form Views*

You can return to form view from the list window by clicking Show Form on the Format menu, and return to the list window by clicking Show List. Works provides two shortcut methods, however, for switching between the list and form windows. You can press ⌘-L (for list) to toggle between the two views, or you can double-click. To move from the form to the list window, you double-click any white section of a form that isn't part of a field or field name. To move from the list to the form window, you double-click any record selector box to the left of a record (or blank).

## *Creating a Database*

Creating a database involves the following basic steps:

1. Think about the organization of your new database.
2. Open a new database window.
3. Enter and name fields to create the rough form.
4. Alter field sizes as necessary.
5. Rearrange field locations (optional).
6. Enter your records.
7. Name and save the database.

These steps are explained in more detail in the rest of this chapter.

## *Designing the Database*

Whole books have been written about the art of designing databases. The process of developing those first few databases is always a learning experience. But with Works, you can go back and change your design later if you're not satisfied. During the process of designing and creating a database, you should keep in mind the following basic principles:

**Keep your database simple.**

Designing a fancy database is easier than maintaining one. Updating complex databases can take hours or even days, and large databases consume memory and disk space, too. You should avoid the temptation to collect trivia. Otherwise, you may run out of room for new records because you're tracking too much unneeded information.

**Consider your future requirements.**

If you plan to create a mailing list and search or sort it by ZIP code, you probably need a separate field for the ZIP code. Many people don't create enough separate fields in their first database design. For example, they may create a single field for city, state, and ZIP code. When you use this approach, you can sort the database by the city name only.

If you plan to create personalized form letters, you probably need a salutation field in addition to the usual first and last name fields. For example, you address a letter to a judge *The Honorable John S. Smith*, but you probably want the salutation of the letter to read *Dear Judge Smith*. If the judge were a close friend, however, you might want the salutation to read *Dear John* instead.

If you plan to sort the list by people's last names, you either must have a last name field in your database or always enter names with the last name first in a single name field.

**Establish standards.**

Computers take things more literally than humans do. You may treat Washington, D.C., The District of Columbia, our nation's capital, and even DC as the same place, but Works does not. Write down the rules you plan to use, and make them available to anyone who enters and edits records.

**Test your database by using a representative data sampling.**

You can add fields later, but before entering much data, you should think things through and try out the database. Otherwise, you may later need to update hundreds or even thousands of records manually. Be certain to test your database with enough data to catch potential problems. If you need an additional field for some unanticipated reason, you're better off making that discovery when you have only a few records in the database.

## *Opening a New Database*

The quickest way to open a new database window is to choose either the New command (⌘-N) or the Open command (⌘-O), both of which are on the File menu. If you use the Open command, the Open File (SF Get) dialog box results (see fig. 9.4). (You also can click once to highlight the database icon and then click the Open button.) This dialog box is entirely analogous in operation to other Works modules. With the database icon highlighted, the dialog box only shows database files in the scroll box.

**Fig. 9.4**

*Opening a new database.*

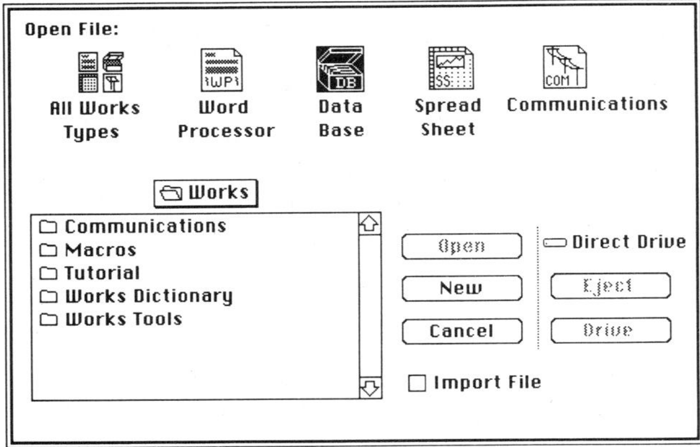


Another way to open a new database file is to choose the New command from the File menu and then either double-click the database icon in the resulting dialog box (see fig. 9.5), click OK, or press the Return key.

**Fig. 9.5**

*The dialog box that appears after you choose the New command.*

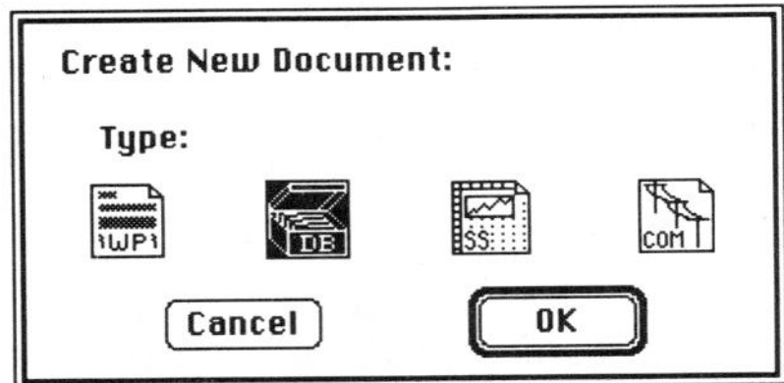

## *Naming Fields*

With either method you use, Works opens a window labeled `Untitled (DB)` and displays a Field Name dialog box in which you must indicate the first field name. Works suggests using the name Untitled1 for the first field name, Untitled2 for the second, and so on (see fig. 9.6). You can either use this name or type a new one of your own.

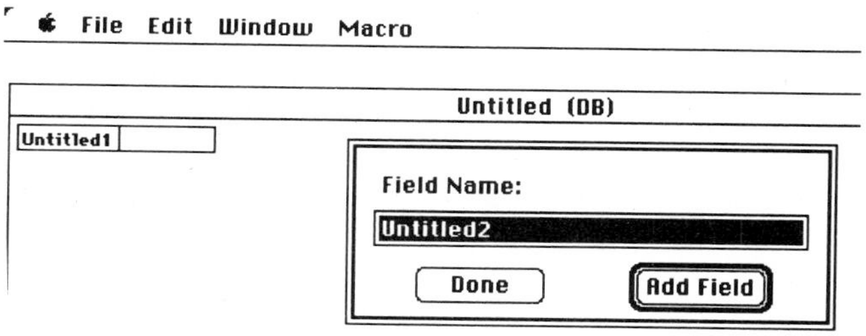

**Fig. 9.6**

*The Field Name dialog box.*

To add the field to the file, either click the Add Field button or press the Return or Enter key. You can rename the field before clicking the Add Field button, or you can place all untitled fields on the screen and rename them later. (See the next section on "Renaming Fields.")

Whenever you click the Add Field button or press Return or Enter, Works adds the new field to the screen in a *field box* and displays another Field Name dialog box (see fig. 9.7). Works keeps adding new fields until you click the Done button.

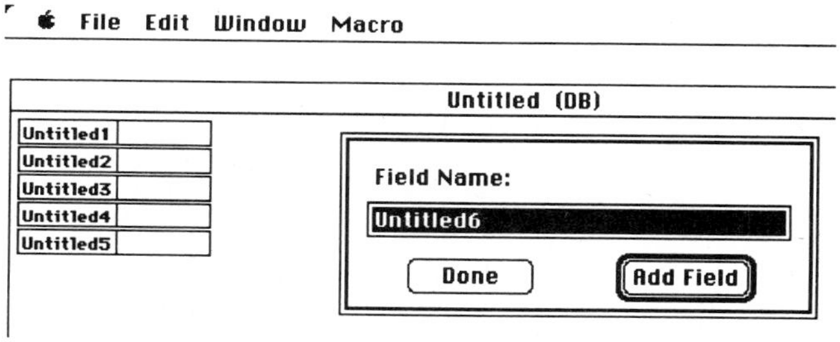

**Fig. 9.7**

*Adding fields to the database.*

Although Works allows you to use up to 64 characters for a field name, try to use short but descriptive names. Especially if others will use the database you create, or if much time will elapse between work sessions, a descriptive, meaningful name can be a great help in identifying the fields. Field names must start with a letter, not a number or a space. Most punctuation marks— hyphens, parentheses, and periods—are not permitted. You can, however, use colons and dollar signs. If you enter an illegal character, Works warns you, as shown in figure 9.8. Then you can click the OK button and enter an acceptable field name.

**Fig. 9.8**

*Warning about an illegal field name.*

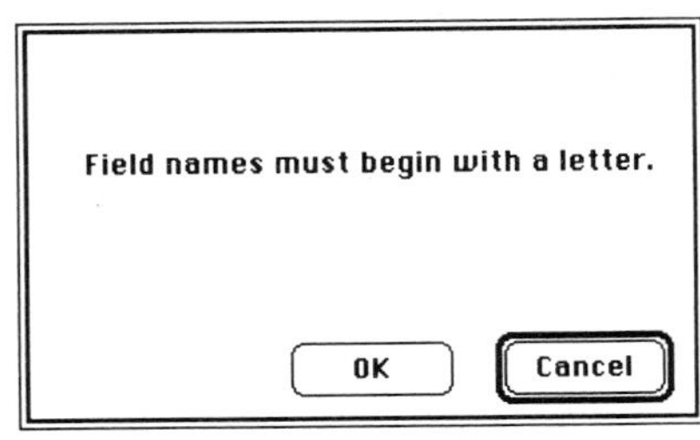
Field names must begin with a letter.
OK
Cancel

## *Renaming Fields*

You can always rename a field by selecting the field name in either the list or form window and issuing the Change Field Name command from the Edit menu. Choosing this command brings up the same Field Name dialog box that appears when you are defining the database. As a short-cut, you can go directly to this dialog box by double-clicking the field name or column header in either the form or the list window.

## *Moving Fields*

While you are designing your form, or even after you have used it for a while, you may want to change the location of a field. Appearance may be an issue. Convenience when moving from entry to entry may be another consideration. Or you may need to move the labels around to make room for bigger fields.

To move a field on a form, you take the following steps:

1. Point to the field name. The cursor becomes a hand, as illustrated in figure 9.9.
2. Press the mouse button and drag the field where you want it (see fig. 9.10). A box outlined in dashes appears, showing you where the field will be placed.
3. Release the mouse button when the dashed box is in the proper location.

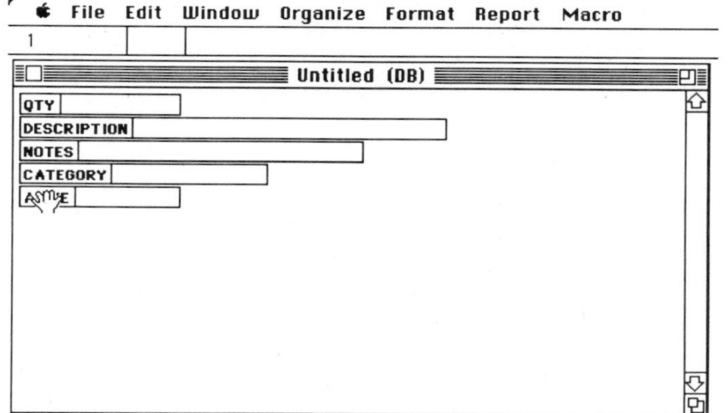


**Fig. 9.9**

*Pointing to the field name.*

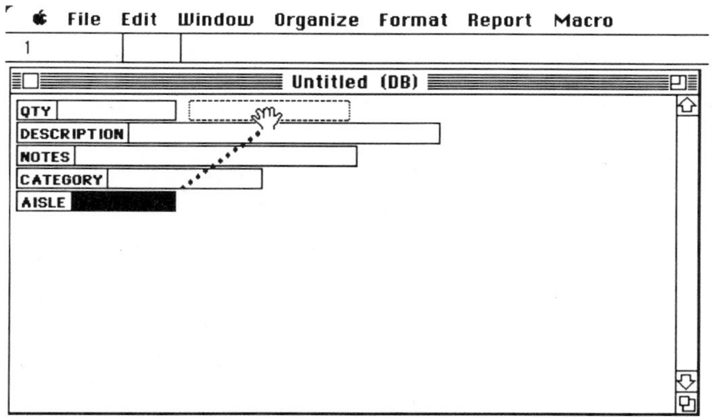

**Fig. 9.10**

*Moving the database field.*

**NOTE:** If you overlap fields, you will not be able to see the field that was positioned first. You can drag a field so that part of it runs off the right edge of the screen; this procedure is OK for temporary "parking" while designing a form. You cannot, however, drag fields off the left side of the screen.

To move a field in a list window, follow these steps:

1. Position the cursor on the column heading you want to move. Just as in the form window, the cursor changes into the shape of a hand.

2. Drag the Salut column to the left of the First Name column, as shown in figure 9.11. The Salut column will then be moved to

the left of the First Name column, or whatever column whose heading is highlighted. This process works identically to moving a column in a spreadsheet.

**Fig. 9.11**

*Moving columns in a list window.*

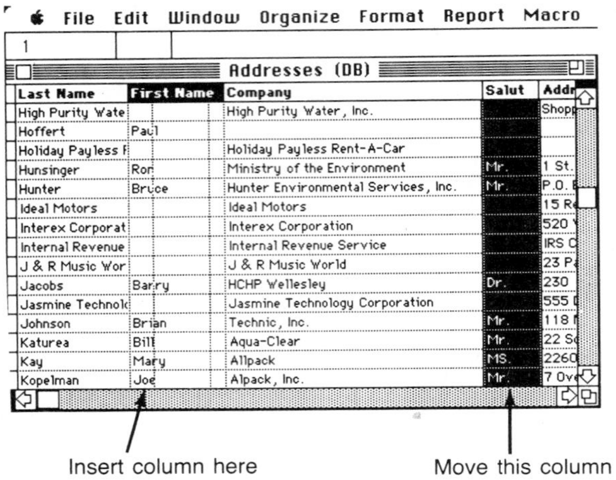

Insert column here

Move this column

## *Changing Field Sizes*

The white part of the field box on the database window is where you enter your database information in the Form layout. Whenever you need to, you can make this white area larger or smaller than the sizes assigned by Works when you create the fields. To adjust a field's size in the form view, follow these steps:

1. Point to the right edge of the field box. The cursor becomes a double-headed arrow, as shown in figure 9.12.
2. Hold down the mouse button and drag the box to the size you want, as illustrated in figure 9.13.
3. Release the mouse button.

**NOTE:** No single field can exceed 250 characters.

You can change the size of a field any time, even after you have entered data. When you change size, you don't affect the field's contents. For example, if you make a field shorter than its contents, the contents remain unchanged; you just can't see everything. To reveal

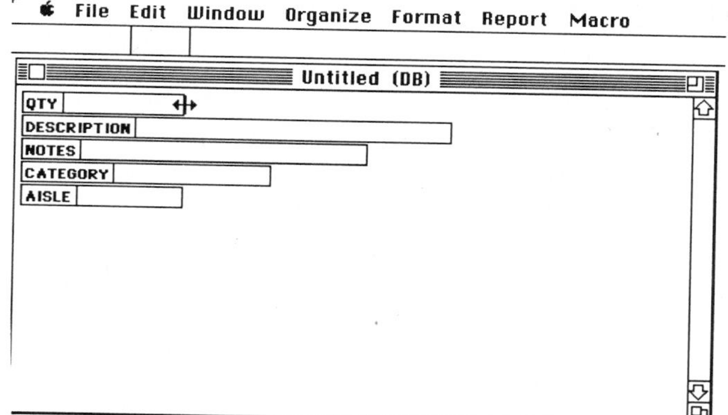


**Fig. 9.12**

*Pointing to the edge of the field box.*

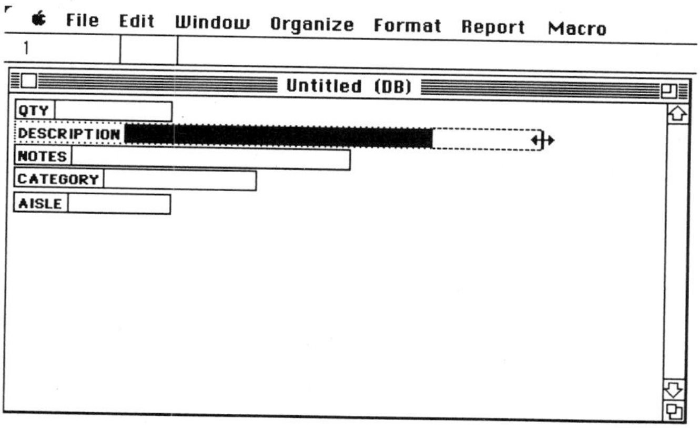

**Fig. 9.13**

*Dragging the field to change its size.*

the entire entry, make the box bigger again. When you change the size of a field box in one record of a list window, you change that field box in the rest of the records in the database.

Changing the size of a field in a list window works similarly. When you position the cursor on the side of the column heading, you get the same double-arrow cursor. Dragging the column heading resizes the column.

## *Adding Fields*

You can add a field any time, using a variety of methods. Works can be in either the form or list window.

One way to add a field in the form window is to choose Add New Field from the Edit menu. Works then displays the Field Name dialog box, which you used when you first defined the database (see figs. 9.6 and 9.7). You name the new field and change its size and location the same way when you are creating your database. If you're adding a field in the form window, Works determines the field's initial location for you by placing the field in the first blank area that is large enough to accommodate the data. You then can move the field to wherever you want.

**TIP:** Here's a shortcut for adding fields in the form window. The method seems like magic, but it works. Point to the position where you want the upper left corner of the field to appear, and then drag a brand new field box to the appropriate length. The New Field dialog box, which is actually called the Field Name dialog box, appears the moment you start dragging. Besides saving you a trip to the Edit menu, this technique puts the field right where you want it.

In the list window, when you select Add New Field, Works adds the field at the end of the record. The field is the rightmost entry on your screen. To move the field to the appropriate position, point to the field name and drag the field to its new location.

## Deleting Fields

You can delete an entire field and its contents at any time—in either the form or list window—by choosing the Delete Field command on the Edit menu. Works then removes the field and its contents from every record in your database. The field disappears, and Works closes up the database as if the field never existed.

If you make a mistake, you can restore the deleted column by choosing the Undo command on the Edit menu. As a precaution, however, you still should back up your database before deleting fields.

Don't confuse the Delete Field option with cutting and pasting or backspacing to delete data in a specific field. Unless you use the Undo option immediately after removing a field with Delete Field, the deletion is irreversible. Deleted fields do not go to the Clipboard.

## Specifying Formats

The Format menu affords you considerable variety for displaying your forms in clear and effective ways. You can alter the appearance of your database by selecting from a variety of formats on this menu. For example:

- You can display field names and field data in boldface text, bordered, or unbordered.
- You can choose the font, size, and color for your database fields.
- You can set specific field attributes, such as display type and alignment.

## *Controlling the Style of Field Names and Data*

Figure 9.14 shows examples of how you can use the Bold Field Name, Bold Field Data, Border Field Name, and Border Field Data options to affect the appearance of your database fields.

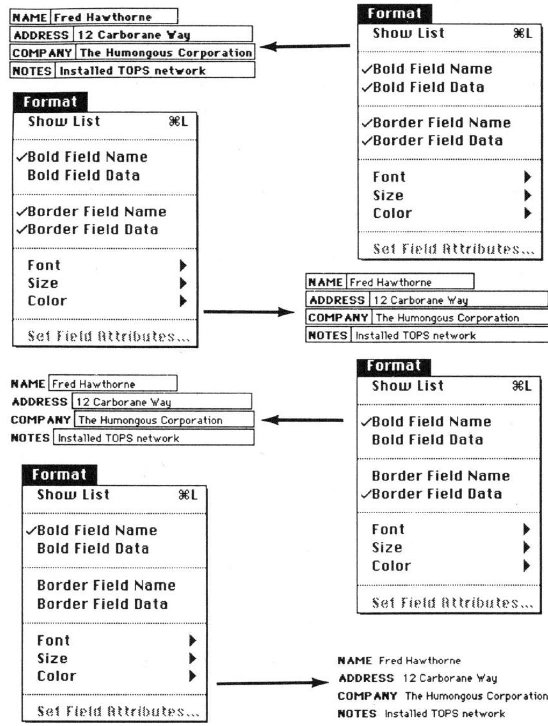


**Fig. 9.14**

*Using the Format menu to boldface and border field names and data.*

Note that you can choose to boldface or border field names and field data. The format defaults are bold field names, roman (not bold) field data, bordered field names, and bordered field data. When an option is active, a check mark appears to the left of the option.

## *Changing Font, Size, and Color*

Works 2.0 allows you to change the font, size, and color of your database fields. The Font, Size, and Color commands, located on the Format menu, work exactly as they do in other Works modules. (See Chapters 1 and 3 for more information on using these three commands.) Any choice you make with these three menu items affects the entire database display. Your database default is 9-point Geneva black, but you can specify any choice and print to any output device that supports color.

## *Specifying Field Attributes*

Just as the spreadsheet portion of Works lets you specify cell formats, the database gives you control over field formats. The controls are called *field attributes* in the database. By specifying field attributes, you tell Works two things: what kind of information will be stored in a field, and how you want the contents to be displayed. Each field can have its own attributes.

To change field attributes, you select the appropriate field (column in the list window, field name in the form window) and then choose the Set Field Attributes command from the Format menu. Selecting this option displays the Set Field Attributes dialog box shown in figure 9.15. (As a shortcut you can double-click the field data portion of a field in either the list or form window. But if you make a mistake and click the field name, Works gives you the Field Name dialog box instead.)

**Fig. 9.15**

*The Set Field Attributes dialog box.*

Set Field Attributes For Address

Type: Text, Numeric, Date, Time
Display: General, Fixed, Dollar, Percent, Scientific
Align: Left, Center, Right
Style: Bold, Underline, Commas
Decimal Places
Computed Show Day
Cancel OK

To make field attribute choices, you click the appropriate buttons in the Set Field Attributes dialog box. Dimmed choices are not available for the selected field type. For example, you cannot select the Commas option for text fields. The default choices are shown in figure 9.15.

## *Specifying Field Type and Display*

The first choice you make in the Set Field Attributes dialog box should be the Type: Text, Numeric, Date, or Time. As already noted, this choice determines what other options are available. For example, numeric field types can be displayed in several different formats, chosen under the Display option.

## *Text Format*

Many entries you make in a database are simple text, such as names, addresses, and notes. Therefore, Works assumes that all fields contain text unless you tell the program otherwise.

Sometimes you may want to let Works believe that a column contains text even if the fields always contain numbers, such as a ZIP code or telephone number. The reason is explained in the following section ("Numeric Format") and in the discussion on searches. For now, you need remember only that you can type anything you want in a text field, and Works displays the text as entered. Unless you make a different alignment choice, Works displays text fields left-aligned.

## *Numeric Format*

The Numeric option tells Works that you intend always to enter numbers—and only numbers—in the selected field. If you choose the Numeric attribute, Works challenges any nonnumeric entries in that field, as illustrated in figure 9.16.

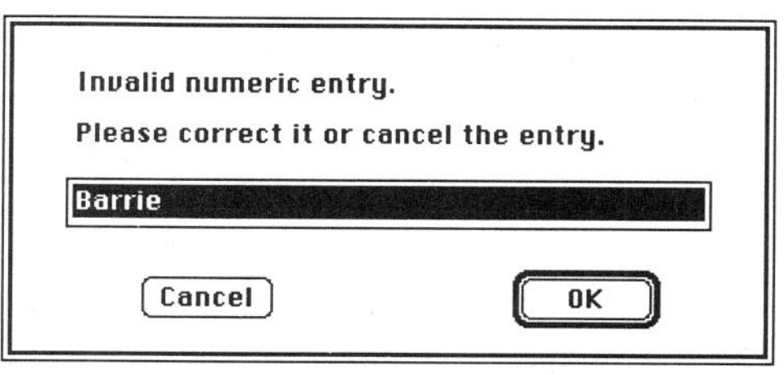


**Fig. 9.16**

*Warning about nonnumeric entries.*

When you define a field as numeric, you have a choice of display formats as well. Spreadsheet users will find them familiar:

- General
- Fixed
- Dollar
- Percent
- Scientific
- Commas

Refer to Chapter 6 for a full discussion of these formats.

**NOTE:** Works drops leading zeros when you enter them in numeric fields. For example, Works stores and displays the numeric version of the ZIP code 02156 as 2156. Besides upsetting the post office, this arrangement produces incorrect results if you sort by ZIP code. If you define telephone number fields as numeric, you will find that Works doesn't like dashes or parentheses either. Define your telephone numbers as text, not numbers, if you want telephone numbers to look like (617)244-9078 or 617/244-9078, or even 617-244-9078.

### *Date Format*

If you tell Works that a field will contain dates, you can enter them in a variety of formats. All the following entries are permissible:

Short Date: 8-27-52
Short Date: 8/27/52
Short Date: 8.27.52
Medium Date: Aug 27, 1952
Long Date: August 27, 1952
Medium and Show Day: Thur, Nov 27, 1952
Long and Show Day: Thursday, November 27, 1952

For storage purposes, Works converts these entries to their shortest form: 8-27-52.

The options for displaying and entering dates appear under the Display heading in the Set Field Attributes dialog box when you select the Date type. For example, you can enter a date in any of the preceding formats and have Works display it in any of the formats you request in the Set Field Attributes dialog box. Note that Works doesn't support European date formats, but Version 2.0 does support date math.

Whenever you want to enter the date into a field, you can do so by pressing the ⌘-D keyboard shortcut. This method does not work, however, when the field is a calculated date field.

**NOTE:** Works calculates date and time by using a serial-number calculation. This topic is discussed in some detail in Chapter 8. You may want to refer to that chapter for more information.

### Time Format

If you tell Works that a field will contain time, you can enter hours and minutes in a variety of formats, including both 12- and 24-hour formats. Works deals with only hours and minutes, not seconds, and assumes AM unless you enter *PM* or the 24-hour equivalent of a time. Table 9.1 shows some examples.

**Table 9.1**
**Examples of Time Formats**

| *What you enter* | *What Works displays* |
|---|---|
| 9:10 | 9:10 AM |
| 9:10 PM | 9:10 PM |
| 21:10 | 9:10 PM |
| 9:1 | 9:01 AM |

You must leave a space between the numbers and the AM or PM when you make entries. You can shorten AM to A or PM to P if you prefer; Works adds the M for you.

> ***Caution:*** You can change a text field to a date, time, or numeric field at any time. If the data is not in an acceptable format, however, Works deletes the data. When you change a date, time, or numeric field to a text field, all data is retained.

### Setting Field Style and Alignment

You can boldface and underline data in fields, and you can display numbers either with or without commas. You also can define the number of decimal places in numbers. See "Specifying Field Attributes," elsewhere in this chapter, for specific instructions.

The Align column in the Set Field Attributes dialog box contains options for setting the alignment of cell contents. Your choices are Left (the default for text, date, and time), Right (the default for numbers), or Center. These alignments are the same as the alignment choices for the Works spreadsheet.

## *Specifying Computed Fields*

You can have Works compute data for a field, based on the contents of other fields in a record. In this respect, the Works database is like the Works spreadsheet. For example, if your form contains an hourly rate field, you can have Works use the arguments you provide, compute annual earnings, and place the results in a computed field. The entry bar in figure 9.17 shows an example of a typical equation. Works calculates the annual salary by multiplying the contents of the RATE field times the number of hours in a week (40) and then the number of weeks in a year (52).

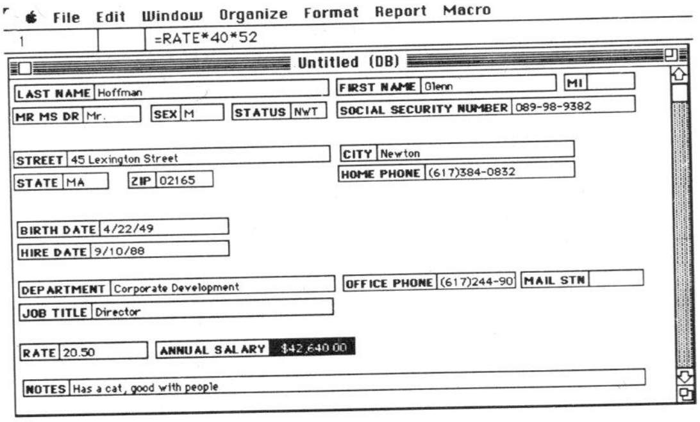

**Fig. 9.17**

*Multiplying the contents of the RATE field by 40 hours and then 52 weeks to produce the annual salary.*

Here are the basic steps for creating a computed field:

1. Create the field or fields that will hold the values, if it does not exist already.
2. Define a separate computed field by choosing the Set Field Attributes command from the Format menu, and then check the Computed choice in the Set Field Attributes dialog box (see fig. 9.15). As a shortcut, you can double-click a field to bring up this dialog box.
3. Click OK. The Set Field Attributes dialog box disappears, and an equal sign (=) appears in the entry bar. Supply the equation for the field.

Now, when you type data in the value field(s), you create results in the computed field. Look at an example: a grocery database shown in figure 9.18. Suppose that you want to add a computed TOTAL COST field, which computes the cost of purchasing the number of items specified in the QTY field. Figure 9.18 shows a computed field that multiplies the quantity purchased times the unit price to provide the total cost. The equation is displayed in the entry bar.

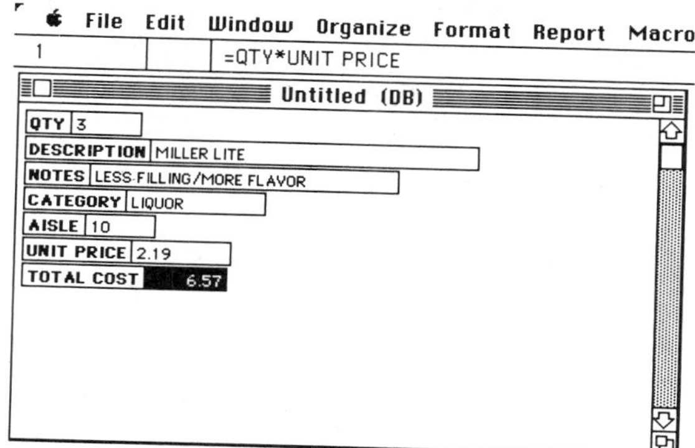


**Fig. 9.18**

*Example of a computed field.*

You build equations in computed fields in much the same way you create spreadsheet equations. Computed database fields always start with an equal sign and contain at least one field name, sometimes many. Click field names to include them in an equation. (You can type field names, but this process is slower and error prone.) Equations can contain up to 250 characters.

In addition, one or more operators are required. Arithmetic operators tell Works what you want done with values. Works supports the following operators in database computed fields:

| | |
|---|---|
| + | Addition |
| – | Subtraction |
| * | Multiplication |
| / | Division |
| ^ | Exponentiation (raises to a power) |
| – | Negation (changes a positive to a negative number) |

See Chapter 8, "Spreadsheet and Database Functions," for more information about the arithmetic operators.

You can create computed fields by using the operators and functions discussed in Chapter 8. In general, however, you cannot use any function that requires some sort of linkage or knowledge of data in another record. This restriction includes any function that takes a range as an argument, because database records are independent of one another. Spreadsheet functions are optional, and if the function is supported in a database it can be imported from the spreadsheet. As mentioned in Chapter 8, functions inappropriate in a database include the MIRR and IRR financial functions and the Index, HLookup, Lookup, Match, and VLookup special-purpose functions.

Some functions that in a spreadsheet take a range as an argument can be used in a database for a single field reference, a list of fields separated by commas, or a value used in place of the range. These functions include

- The And, Choose, If, IsBlank, and Or logical functions
- The FV, NPV, Pmt, PV, and Rate financial functions
- All statistical functions (Average, Count, Max, Min, SSum, StDev, Sum, and Variance)

All other functions discussed in Chapter 8 are supported by the Works database.

# *Entering, Saving, and Editing Data*

You enter, save, and edit data in either the list or form window in the same way. Enter data one field at a time; use the typing techniques you have already learned. When you finish entering data, you need to save it in a disk file. If you try to close a database file with unsaved changes, Works displays an alert box. You can enter more records or change existing information later. In the editing process, you use the word processing techniques you have already learned.

## *The Data-Entry Process*

You begin to enter data either by clicking once in any field data box (see figs. 9.2 and 9.3) or by clicking in the entry bar. An insertion bar cursor appears in the entry bar along with an enter box and a cancel box, just like in the spreadsheet entry bar (see fig. 9.19). Using standard Macintosh editing techniques, you type your field entry. If you click the enter box, your information is entered. Clicking the cancel box returns you to the original field data.

To enter data into fields, follow these steps:

1. Select the record in which you want to make the entry.
2. Select the field in which you want to make an entry.

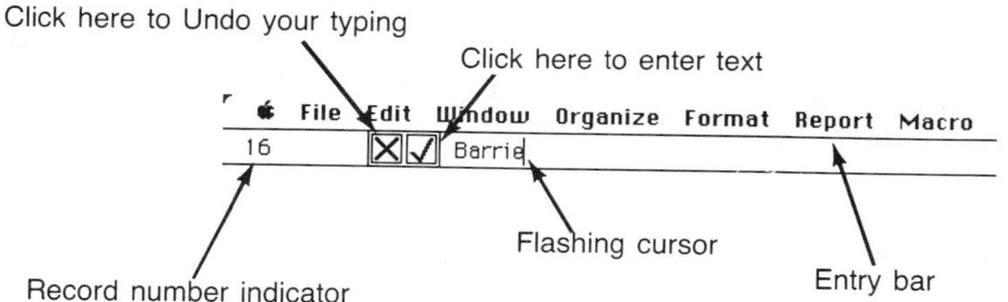


**Fig. 9.19**

*Using the entry bar to enter, inspect, and edit data.*

3. Start typing. Your entry appears in the entry bar at the top of the screen. You both enter and edit text and numbers in this entry bar.

4. After entering and editing the entry, terminate the entry by clicking the enter box or by pressing one of the keys listed in table 9.2.

   Works checks the entry to ensure that it's of the proper type (text, numeric, date, or time) and uses the new data to update your record. (The record is updated in memory only; the disk copy of your database does not change at this point.)

5. Select another field in either the current record or a new record, and make another entry.

6. Continue the process until you have finished all entries.

7. To update the disk copy of your database, you must use one of the Save commands, as described in the next section.

You don't have to click the enter box after each entry. Table 9.2 lists some shortcuts Works gives you for entering data in a database and moving to the next entry field. If you want to enter the data without changing the active field, use the Enter key.

If your system clock is set correctly, you can enter the current date by holding down the ⌘ key and pressing D (⌘-D). You can also enter the current time (again, your system clock must be set properly). Simply select the appropriate field and press ⌘-T.

**TIP:** Here's another data-entry shortcut that helps eliminate repetitive typing. When entering data into a database, press ⌘-" (quotation mark) to reproduce the entry from the same field in the preceding record.

**Table 9.2**
**Methods of Entering Items and Changing Active Fields**

| *Key* | *Result* |
|---|---|
| To enter data into a List window: | |
| Tab | Enter data and move to next field (right) |
| Shift-Tab | Enter data and move to preceding field (left) |
| Return | Enter data and move to next record (down) |
| Shift-Return | Enter data and move to preceding record (up) |
| ← | Enter data and move left |
| → | Enter data and move right |
| ↑ | Enter data and move up |
| ↓ | Enter data and move down |
| To enter data into a Form window: | |
| Tab or → | Enter data and move to the next field of a record list window position |
| Shift-Tab or ← | Enter data and move to the preceding field of a record by list window position |
| Return or ↑ | Enter data and move to the next field by field order number |
| Shift-Return or ↓ | Enter data and move to the preceding field by field order number |

## *Saving Database Entries*

When you make changes in a database (such as adding entries or editing records), Works doesn't automatically save those changes to disk. They exist in memory only. When you try to close a database window, Works asks whether you want to save the changes you have made. If you click the Yes button or press the Return key, Works saves the changes, thus updating the disk copy of your database. If you answer No, or if you leave Works without saving because of a hardware, software, or power problem, Works doesn't save your changes.

You can ask Works to save your changes whenever you like. Get into the habit of saving your work every 15 minutes or so (and whenever you're interrupted). Use the techniques you have already learned: choose the Save option on the File menu, or press ⌘-S.

Databases when saved use the same Standard File Put boxes that all other Works modules use (see "Saving Your Work" in Chapter 2). To save a new database for the first time, use either the Save (⌘-S) or Save As command on the File menu. The Save dialog box appears with the name "Untitled," which you change to the file name of your choice. For a previously saved database, the Save command saves your changes, bypassing the dialog box. The Save As command displays the dialog box and gives you a chance to create a copy with a new file name. You can save as a Normal file, save as Stationery, or save as Export. Stationery allows you to open a copy of the database as an untitled window, and Export allows you to save the text-only portion of the database in the standard SYLK format. SYLK is exportable to the spreadsheet and to other standard Macintosh programs.

You can also use the Save As command to save a copy of your database (what's on the screen, not necessarily what's written to disk). Using the Save As command has only one wrinkle. When you sort your database records to obtain a subset (as explained in the section on "Sorting, Searching, and Matching Capabilities"), using the Save As command leaves you in the original database while creating your newly named copy. If you're not aware of this situation, you can accidentally destroy your original database.

## *Editing Procedures for Records*

You can edit any field in any record either while you are first entering the record or later. Here's how:

1. Select the appropriate record if it's not already on the screen. (To move to the record in back, you use the Return key; and to move to the record in front, use the Tab key.)
2. Click the field you want to edit. The entry then appears in the entry bar.
3. Use the standard selecting, deleting, and inserting techniques to change the entry in the entry bar.
4. Click the enter box or press the Return key.
5. To update the disk copy of your database, use the Save functions.

# Sorting, Searching, and Matching Capabilities

The real importance of a database lies in its capability to be sorted, organized, and queried so that you can extract important information. A database for airline flights would be useless if you couldn't ask which plane goes to Albuquerque on Sunday at 3:00 PM. Although Works stores your records in the order in which you enter them, you can easily rearrange the records. In database terms, reorganizing is called *sorting*. You can also use a Find feature to look for individual entries. Lastly, if you know something about the entries in which you are interested, you can search based on a set of criteria.

## Sorting Your Data

With Works, you can sort a database field in ascending or descending (backward or forward) order, as text or numerics, and in chronological order. You can sort by field in either the form or the list window. To sort a database field, select that field and issue the Sort command from the Organize menu. Works displays the dialog box shown in figure 9.20.

**Fig. 9.20**

*The Sort dialog box.*

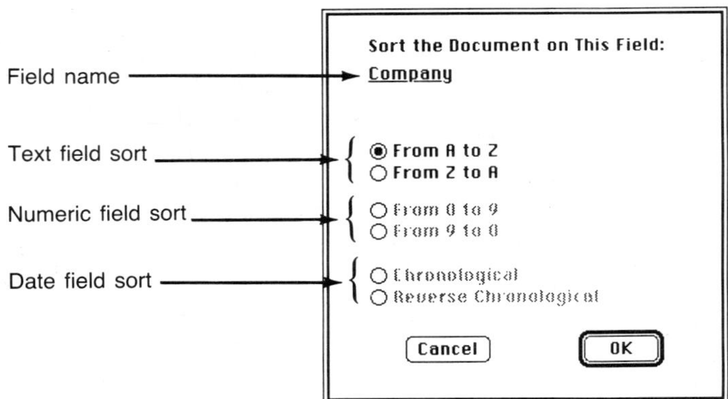


When you sort a field, the Sort dialog box dims any choices that are not appropriate to the sort. Figure 9.20, for example, refers to the sorting of a text field (From A to Z and From Z to A). The middle choices are for a numeric sort (From 0 to 9 and From 9 to 0), and the bottom two choices are for sorting a date field (Chronological and Reverse Chronological).

If you want to do a multilevel sort, you should sort your most important field last. You may want to refer to Chapter 6's section on "Sorting a Worksheet" for more details on sorting.

If you sort a field that contains numbers but is defined as a text field, the results may surprise you. When a field is defined as text, Works treats the digits as characters, and the first digit is the first character in the alphanumeric sort. Therefore, the first character is the most important sorting criterion, and one (1) precedes two (2)—always. For instance, in an ascending text sort, the number *10,200* appears before the number *20* because Works ignores the numeric value of the two entries and arranges them according to rules about sorting text.

Notice how the result of a sort on the MSN field changes in figures 9.21 and 9.22 when the field is defined first as text and then as numeric. When the field is defined as text, 1 always comes before 2, 2 before 3, and so on, regardless of the size of the number (see fig. 9.21). When the field is defined as numeric, the numbers are sorted into correct numerical order (see fig. 9.22).

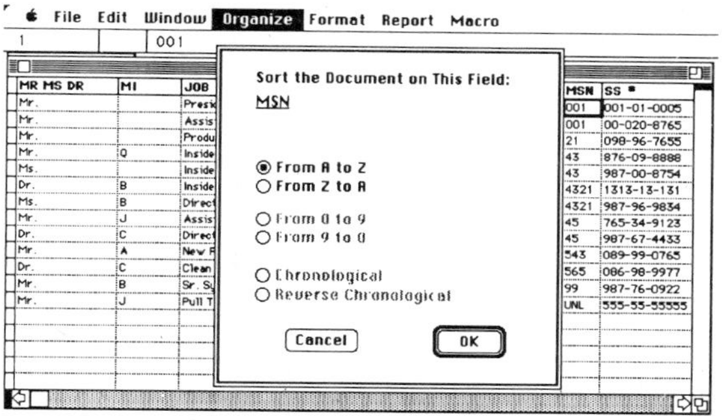

**Fig. 9.21**

*Field containing numbers sorted as text.*

If you make the wrong sort request, you usually can use Undo to put your database in the order in which it was arranged before the sort. You must, however, use Undo immediately. Sorts occur only in memory, so the disk copy of your database stays in the old order until you update the database by using the Save command.

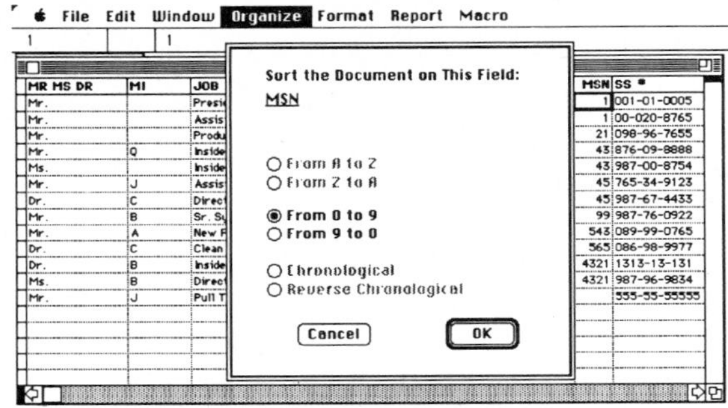


**Fig. 9.22**

*Field containing numbers sorted as numeric.*

# *Searching the Database*

You can use the Works search features to find specific items of interest without scrolling through your entire database to find a particular record. If you want to find items that occur in multiple records, you can use the matching feature to locate all records that meet your search criteria.

With the Find Field command on the Organize menu, you can have Works find a specific record. To find groups of records, you use the Match Records command, also on the Organize menu. Both options have command shortcuts. Pressing ⌘-F is the same as choosing Find Field, and ⌘-M represents the Match Records command.

## *Finding Specific Records*

Use the Organize menu's Find Field option to search for specific single occurrences of information. When you select this option, Works presents a dialog box prompting you to enter what you want to find (see fig. 9.23). This entry can be any set of characters for which you want to search. Click the Find Next button or press the Return key, and your dialog box disappears. Works highlights the first entry that contains your text, selecting the entry and placing its contents in the entry bar.

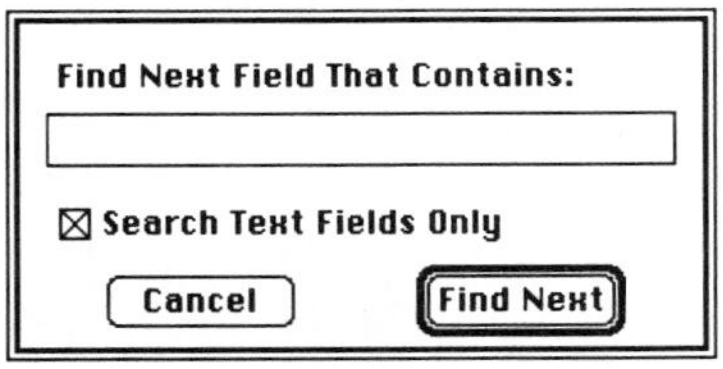

**Fig. 9.23**

*The Find Field dialog box.*

Find Next Field That Contains:

☒ Search Text Fields Only

Cancel    Find Next

If you later want to search for another occurrence of the same word, select the Find Field option again. Works displays your previous search request, which you can use to look for additional occurrences. Either press Return or click the Find Next button to search again. To speed things up, try to get into the habit of using the ⌘-F shortcut. Works tells you when it finds the last occurrence of the word specified. Click OK to make this dialog box disappear.

Usually, Works checks all fields. You can, however, ask Works to check only fields that are defined as text fields (the default). Or you can expand the search to include numeric and date fields. To expand the search, click to remove the X from the Search Text Fields Only box.

## *Finding Groups of Records*

When you specify the Match Records option on the Organize menu, Works displays all the records that meet your search criteria. Although this command works in the form window, Match Records is most useful in the list window. After you choose Match Records, Works displays a dialog box that looks similar to the Find Field dialog box (see fig. 9.24). To enter the search criteria, you use the same techniques you use for Find Field: type the text string and then click OK. For example, in figure 9.24, Works is told to match only records containing the word *park*.

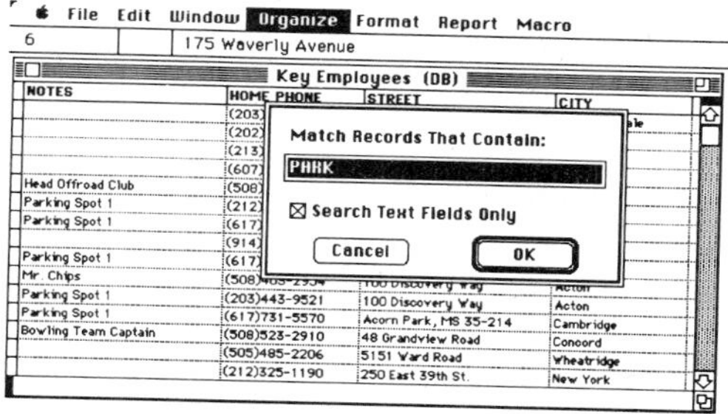


**Fig. 9.24**

*Matching records that contain the word* park.

To find the word(s) for which you're searching, Works looks either in every text field or everywhere in the database. You tell Works to search the entire database by clicking to remove the X in the Search Text Fields Only box, as you do in the Find Field dialog box. For example, Works finds employees with the last name of Park or the first name of Parker. If someone in your database lives on Park Lane, Works finds that occurrence of the word, too. And if the NOTES field contains Parking spot, that also qualifies.

When you use the Match Records feature, Works displays a collection (or subset) consisting of the records that meet your search criteria. For example, figure 9.25 shows records containing the word *park*. You can scroll through the records in either the form or list window, you can print the window, and you can cut or clear the entries. If this list of records is important, you can save it under a different name, using the Save As command. Remember, however, that doing so still leaves you working on the screen in your original database.

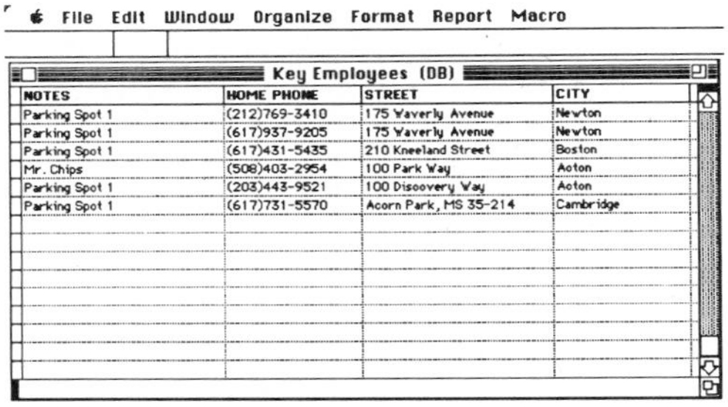

| NOTES | HOME PHONE | STREET | CITY |
|---|---|---|---|
| Parking Spot 1 | (212)769-3410 | 175 Waverly Avenue | Newton |
| Parking Spot 1 | (617)937-9205 | 175 Waverly Avenue | Newton |
| Parking Spot 1 | (617)431-5435 | 210 Kneeland Street | Boston |
| Mr. Chips | (508)403-2954 | 100 Park Way | Acton |
| Parking Spot 1 | (203)443-9521 | 100 Discovery Way | Acton |
| Parking Spot 1 | (617)731-5570 | Acorn Park, MS 35-214 | Cambridge |

**Fig. 9.25**

*The list of matching records.*

To return to the full database, click the Match Records option on the Organize menu a second time, or select the Show All Records command. You also can use the ⌘-M shortcut to return to the full database.

## How Works Handles Search Requests

Remember that any special characters containing accent marks require the exact characters for a search. And if you put a space in front of a search request, Works finds only the occurrences preceded by at least one space. For example, if you search for " *wood*", Works doesn't find *dogwood* but does find *woodwork*. Spaces at the end of search requests are important, too. If you request "*clean* ", Works doesn't find records containing *cleaning* or *cleanliness*. Works doesn't distinguish between upper- and lowercase letters when you use the Find Field and Match Records commands. For example, as far as Works is concerned, the words *Parks, parks, PARKS*, and *pArks* all match.

Works searches for dates and times a little differently than you might expect. The program will not even look at date or time fields unless you remove the Search Text Fields Only restriction. When Works does look at date and time fields, however, the program searches these fields as if they were text. Therefore, if a date field is displayed in the long form, you need to search for the date in the long form. For example, if you search for *4-19-82*, Works does not find *Monday, April 19, 1982*.

## *Using Selection Rules*

When your database grows, looking for all the records containing *park* or everybody in *Marketing* may not be easy or practical. You may need to find more specific groups, such as everybody in Marketing or Sales who earns more than $20,000.00 but less than $50,000.00 and is female. Works enables you to set up *selection rules*, also called *comparison phrases*, to help with this kind of searching.

Selection rules are also an important part of report designing, so you need to understand how they work. Don't be put off by their apparent complexity. All you need to do is tell Works three things:

1. Which field(s) to search
2. What the rules are (comparison phrases)
3. What to look for (comparison information)

You use selection rules all the time in conversation—for example, "Who earns more than I do?" and "Does he live on the same street as you do?" Works answers questions just like these. In Works, you must use specific phrases that the program can interpret. Works accepts 14 comparison phrases:

equals
is not equal to
is greater than
is less than
is greater than or equal to
is less than or equal to
is blank
is not blank
contains
does not contain
begins with
ends with
does not begin with
does not end with

### *Making a Simple Record Selection*

By combining these phrases with field names from your database and your specific requirements, you can make almost limitless comparisons and selections. To make a simple record selection, follow these steps:

1. Choose the Record Selection command from the Organize menu. Works displays a dialog box similar to the one shown in figure 9.26.

**Fig. 9.26**

*The Record Selection dialog box.*

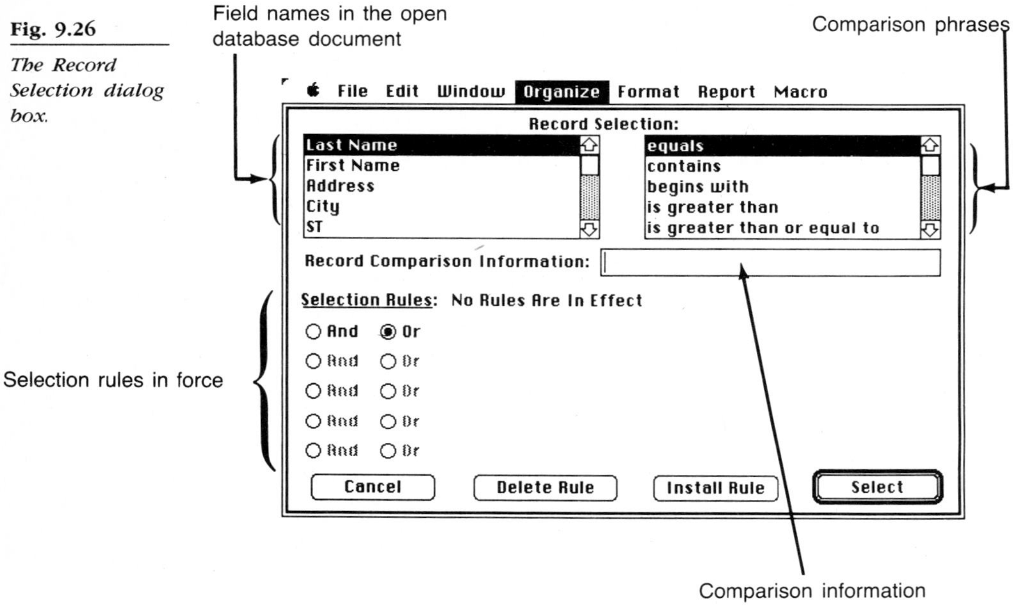

2. From the left scroll box, choose the field you want to use in the comparison.
3. From the right scroll box, select one of the comparison phrases.
4. Enter the comparison information in the text box labeled Record Comparison Information.
5. Click the Install Rule button. Works list your rule in the dialog box.
6. Press the Return key or click OK. Works displays a subset of your database that matches your comparison.

If you make a mistake or want to remove a rule, you can click the Delete Rule button. Note that this button deletes only the last rule you created. You cannot move back through your list of selection rules. If you're unhappy with an earlier selection rule, you will probably have to erase some good ones to reach it.

Clicking Cancel returns you to your database without additional searching. Your search criteria are stored with your saved database and retained with your screen document in case you want to use those criteria again.

**NOTE:** You cannot use all 14 phrases for some types of fields, so only applicable comparisons (based on the type of field you have selected) are shown in the phrase window. For example, if you select a date field, Works doesn't display `contains`, `begins with`, `ends with`, and other text-related comparison phrases.

Works tells you if it cannot find any records. Works also informs you if you made an error in constructing your rule. Common errors include forgetting to enter comparison phrases and trying to enter text when comparing numeric fields. When these situations arise, correct your entry and try again.

## *Specifying Multiple Selection Rules*

You can limit choices further by specifying up to six restrictions. For instance, you can select records for employees hired before January 1, 1987, earning more than $10.00 per hour, and working in California (see fig. 9.27). You can enter multiple rules when you first start the selection process, or you can add to the selection rules after you have tried a selection or two. Works remembers the last rules you used and lets you add to them.

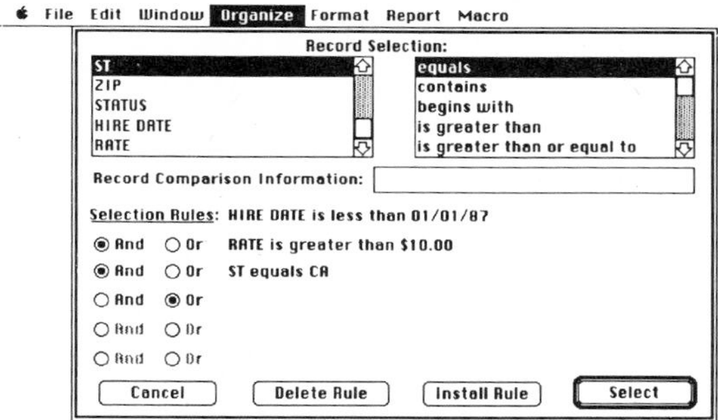


**Fig. 9.27**

*Using multiple selection rules.*

You probably use the two words *and* and *or* in conversation all the time. "I'll take a pound of clams and a pound of the fresh trout." "How many Beatles albums do I have that are on either compact discs or cassette tapes?" "I want something that's both hot and spicy."

With Works, you can make selection requests like these, too. You have seen how And works by itself in figure 9.27. In that example, And restricts the display only to records that meet all three conditions: employees hired before 01/01/87 *and* earning more than $10.00 per hour *and* working in California. You can use And to refine the selection even further, by using multiple And selection criteria:

And RATE is greater than $10.00
And RATE is less than $40.00

And what about the Or feature? By adding Or selection criteria, you can widen your search to include other possibilities. For example, by adding "Or HIRE DATE less than 01/01/70" to the selection rules in figure 9.27, you can have Works also find the names of employees hired before that date, regardless of their sex or location.

Practice will help you perfect these selection skills. The key point to remember is that And restricts while Or expands the number of records that are selected.

## *Saving Copies of Selected Data*

You can save a copy of the records you have selected by using a different file name and the Save As command from the File menu. When you use Save As, Works prompts you for a new file name. As noted previously, you create this file but remain on-screen in your original (superset) database. The database module differs from all other Works modules in this regard.

If you select data and use the Save command or ⌘-S shortcut rather than Save As, you may permanently damage the disk copy of your large database. In effect, you replace the large database with the new smaller subset. Works alerts you to this problem if you attempt to use the Save command. If you do make this blunder, rest assured that the large database is still in memory and can be saved under its old file name. But you need to catch your mistake soon after you have made it; Undo cannot help here.

You need to keep another point in mind. If you copy records from one database into a new database, you have to keep both the original and the new database up-to-date thereafter. For example, suppose that you have both a national personnel database and a California database containing the names of the same employees. When someone moves, you must record that employee's change of address in both databases. Don't make extra work for yourself without a good reason.

# Changing the Database

After you have defined a database, or even after you have worked with it for a while, you may decide that you need to make some modifications. This section discusses what is involved in changing field types; deleting records; inserting records in a list; dividing the list window into panes and grids; cutting, copying, and pasting information; and duplicating fields.

> ***Caution:*** Before modifying a database, make a backup copy, particularly if you have invested a great deal of time and effort in the original design or in editing data. Then, if things go badly, you don't have to redesign the database or reenter many hours worth of work to get back to where you started.

## Changing Field Types—Risky Business

You can change field type (one of the field attributes) after entering data into your database, but a better—and safer— approach is to make this kind of change beforehand. Otherwise, you run the risk of losing all or some of your entries in the changed field. This loss might occur for a variety of reasons. For example, if you change a text field to a date field, you eliminate any entries that don't conform to the program's date formats.

If you must change the definition of a field that contains data, keep in mind the following guidelines:

- ❑ Save a copy (backup) of your database first.
- ❑ You can always change time, date, or number fields to text, but if you try other conversions, you will probably lose data. Works warns you with an alert box indicating that your cell(s) could not be converted to the destination type.
- ❑ You can recover data by using the Undo command if you use it immediately.

## Deleting Records

The best way to delete an entire record is to select it in the list window. Follow these steps:

1. Click the box to the left of the record you want to delete. Works then highlights that record.
2. Use either the ⌘-X shortcut or the Cut option on the Edit menu to cut the record. If you make a mistake, choose Undo from the Edit menu.

To delete multiple, adjacent records, follow the same procedure, but drag rather than click to select the records. Works highlights the records from the point at which you begin to drag to the point at which you release the mouse button.

# Inserting Records in a List

You can always add records at the end of a database and have Works sort them into place. But you also can add new records precisely where you want them without sorting. Just as you can insert rows in a spreadsheet, you can insert records in a list.

To insert a record, use this procedure:

1. Select the record immediately below the spot at which you want to insert the new record.
2. Either choose Insert Record from the Edit menu or press ⌘-I. (Figure 9.28 shows the location specified and command selected.) A blank record appears, as illustrated in figure 9.29 (where row 9 was chosen).
3. Enter the data manually or paste it in.

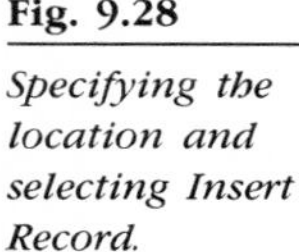

**Fig. 9.28**

*Specifying the location and selecting Insert Record.*

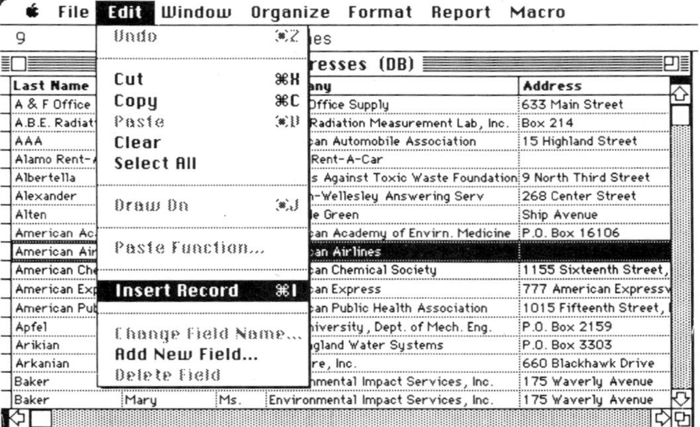

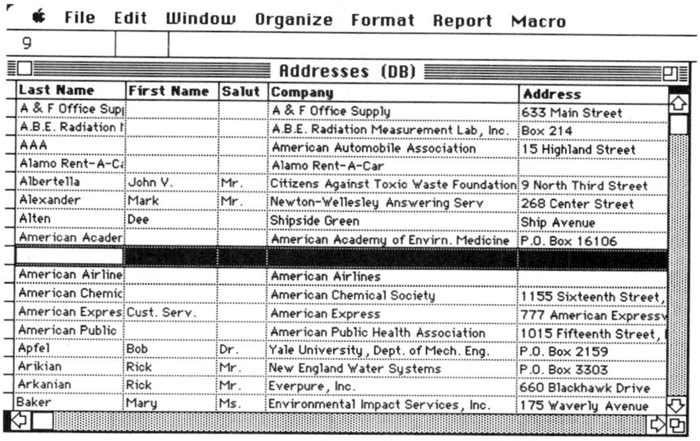

File Edit Window Organize Format Report Macro

9

Addresses (DB)

| Last Name | First Name | Salut | Company | Address |
|---|---|---|---|---|
| A & F Office Sup | | | A & F Office Supply | 633 Main Street |
| A.B.E. Radiation | | | A.B.E. Radiation Measurement Lab, Inc. | Box 214 |
| AAA | | | American Automobile Association | 15 Highland Street |
| Alamo Rent-A-C | | | Alamo Rent-A-Car | |
| Albertella | John V. | Mr. | Citizens Against Toxic Waste Foundation | 9 North Third Street |
| Alexander | Mark | Mr. | Newton-Wellesley Answering Serv | 268 Center Street |
| Alten | Dee | | Shipside Green | Ship Avenue |
| American Acader | | | American Academy of Envirn. Medicine | P.O. Box 16106 |
| | | | | |
| American Airline | | | American Airlines | |
| American Chemic | | | American Chemical Society | 1155 Sixteenth Street, |
| American Expres | Cust. Serv. | | American Express | 777 American Express |
| American Public | | | American Public Health Association | 1015 Fifteenth Street, |
| Apfel | Bob | Dr. | Yale University, Dept. of Mech. Eng. | P.O. Box 2159 |
| Arikian | Rick | Mr. | New England Water Systems | P.O. Box 3303 |
| Arkanian | Rick | Mr. | Everpure, Inc. | 660 Blackhawk Drive |
| Baker | Mary | Ms. | Environmental Impact Services, Inc. | 175 Waverly Avenue |

**Fig. 9.29**

*The results of using Insert Record.*

# *Modifying the View in the List Window*

When Works is displaying the database in the list window, you can create a split screen similar to a split spreadsheet window. You can create horizontal, vertical, and combined *window panes*. Works enables you to create a maximum of four panes. Figure 9.30 shows a sample list window divided into panes. These arrangements enable you to view different parts of long records without rearranging field order. To control the panes, you pull *split bars*, which are small black rectangles at the upper right and lower left corners of the database window.

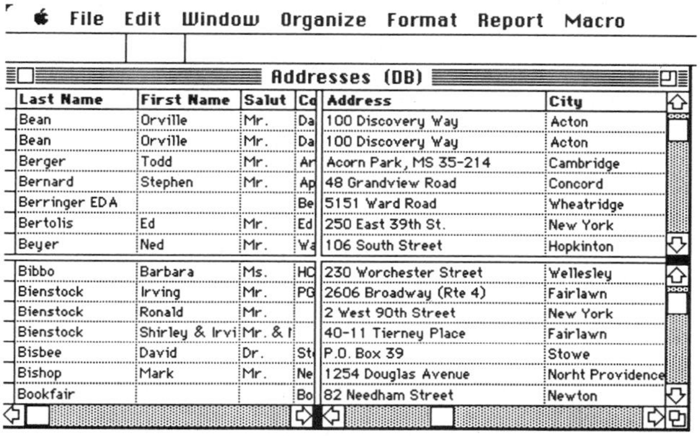

File Edit Window Organize Format Report Macro

Addresses (DB)

| Last Name | First Name | Salut | Co | Address | City |
|---|---|---|---|---|---|
| Bean | Orville | Mr. | Da | 100 Discovery Way | Acton |
| Bean | Orville | Mr. | Da | 100 Discovery Way | Acton |
| Berger | Todd | Mr. | Ar | Acorn Park, MS 35-214 | Cambridge |
| Bernard | Stephen | Mr. | Ap | 48 Grandview Road | Concord |
| Berringer EDA | | | Be | 5151 Ward Road | Wheatridge |
| Bertolis | Ed | Mr. | Ed | 250 East 39th St. | New York |
| Beyer | Ned | Mr. | Wa | 106 South Street | Hopkinton |
| Bibbo | Barbara | Ms. | HC | 230 Worchester Street | Wellesley |
| Bienstock | Irving | Mr. | PG | 2606 Broadway (Rte 4) | Fairlawn |
| Bienstock | Ronald | Mr. | | 2 West 90th Street | New York |
| Bienstock | Shirley & Irvi | Mr. & I | | 40-11 Tierney Place | Fairlawn |
| Bisbee | David | Dr. | St | P.O. Box 39 | Stowe |
| Bishop | Mark | Mr. | Ne | 1254 Douglas Avenue | Norht Providence |
| Bookfair | | | Bo | 82 Needham Street | Newton |

**Fig. 9.30**

*A database window divided into panes.*

To divide a list window into panes, follow these steps:

1. Point at a split bar. The pointer then becomes a two-way arrow.
2. Drag the split bar down in the vertical scroll bar or right in the horizontal scroll bar to create the pane you want.
3. To remove a pane, drag the split bar back to its previous position.

Another way to change the way the list window appears is with the Show Grid/No Grid option, which you access from the Format menu. (The default is Show Grid.) Choosing this option has predictable results. Figure 9.31 shows how the screen looks when the No Grid option is specified.

**Fig. 9.31**

*The list window with the grid turned off.*

| QTY | DESCRIPTION | NOTES | CATEGORY | AISLE |
|---|---|---|---|---|
| 1 | Baby Shampoo | | BABY | 7 |
| | Baby Wipes | | BABY | 7 |
| | Bagels | Water | BAKERY | 3 |
| | Bread - Non-Deli | | BAKERY | 0 |
| | Bread - Wheat | | BAKERY | 0 |
| | Bread, Egg, Sliced | | BAKERY | 0 |
| | Deli/Bakery Other: | | BAKERY | 0 |
| 1 | English Muffins | Raisin | BAKERY | 0 |
| | Hamburger Rolls | | BAKERY | 0 |
| | Hawaiian Rolls | | BAKERY | 0 |
| | Hot Dog Rolls | | BAKERY | 0 |
| | Muffins | Bran | BAKERY | 0 |
| 1 | Drinking Water | | BEVERAGE | 6 |
| | Soda, 7-Up | | BEVERAGE | 6 |
| | Soda, Pepsi Free - No Sugar | Diet drinks | BEVERAGE | 6 |
| | Soda, Regular, Other: | | BEVERAGE | 6 |
| | Water, Sparkling, Large Bottle | | BEVERAGE | 6 |
| | Candy, Other: | | CANDY | 6 |

# *Cutting, Copying, and Pasting Information*

You can highlight database information and copy or cut it to the Clipboard and Scrapbook. This procedure works for single words, entire field contents, complete records, or even an entire database. Remember that if you cut (rather than copy), you delete information from the database. (See Chapter 2 for more information about cutting, copying, and pasting.) The cut procedure removes your selection and places it in the Clipboard in SYLK format, accompanied by the field headings as the first record.

If you just want to remove information from a database, you can select the range and choose the Clear command from the Edit menu. When you use Clear, Works removes the information and clears the contents of the cell(s), but leaves them empty and does not alter the Clipboard.

When you paste in a record or set of records, using the Clipboard, Works inserts the new records above the record currently selected. Be careful that Works is formatted correctly to accept the data. That is, make sure that the field attributes of the target cell(s) are correct. You may also want to check that the field names are in the correct order to accept your data. If you forget the order of the fields in your source database, you can view the Clipboard by using the Window menu. You might also want to have both databases open on your desktop while doing a cut and paste in order to expedite the process.

As with any operation in Works, if you catch a mistake quickly enough, you can give the Undo command to reverse your action.

# Quick Reference Summary

This Quick Reference Summary distills the information you need to set up fields with understandable field names, to vary the length of fields, and to make data entries and corrections. For fuller discussion, refer to the sections mentioned near each operation.

Databases are displayed on-screen in a form or a list window, as shown in figures 9.2 and 9.3, respectively. A form window shows one record of a series of records; a list window shows all records (within the limitations of the screen). To go from form to list, choose the Show List command; to go from list to form, choose the Show Form command. Both commands are on the Format menu.

To open a new database (see "Opening a New Database"), double-click the Data Base icon in the Open File dialog box. Alternatively, click the Data Base icon once and then click the New button. You also can use the New command in the File menu.

The "Untitled" window opens with a Field Name dialog box containing the name Untitled. To label the fields, type the appropriate name in the Untitled box.

When the first Field Name dialog box appears, type the field name, then press Return. If you prefer, use the Caps Lock key to enter the field names in all capitals.

Works prompts you for additional fields and gives you the opportunity to name them as you go. When finished, click Done (see "Naming Fields").

To make each field box larger or smaller (see "Changing Field Sizes"), point to the right edge of the field box. The cursor becomes a double-headed arrow. Then drag the box to its new size while holding down the mouse button.

Most of your fields contain simple text in which you use the general format, but you can change this format to numeric, dollar, percent, scientific (exponential), time, and date formats by using the Set Attributes command on the Format menu (see "Specifying Field Attributes").

A computed field is set by checking the Computed Field box in the Set Attributes command dialog box. You can use the functions described in the section called "Specifying Computed Fields."

To change the field name, follow these steps:

1. Double-click the field name in either the list window or the form window.
2. Enter the new name in the text box of the resulting dialog box. Alternatively, choose the New Field Name command when you have a field (or entry) selected.

As discussed in "Entering, Saving, and Editing Data," you enter data by clicking the field box into which you want to enter data. When you type your new data, it appears in the Entry bar, where you can edit it in standard Macintosh fashion (see fig. 9.19). You enter your new data by pressing the Enter key. Other keystrokes mentioned in table 9.2 enter your data and move you to new locations.

To switch from the form window to the list window, double-click anywhere on the blank portion of your screen, or use the Show List option on the Format menu. A list window is only one record in a set. To go to the next or previous record use the → or ← keys, or use Return or Shift-Return.

To move a field in a list window, follow these steps:

1. Point to the field name with the mouse pointer. The pointer becomes a hand.
2. Press the mouse button and drag the field to the desired location.
3. Release the mouse button.

To change field sizes, do the following:

1. Point the mouse at the right hand field entry box in the list window.

2. When the cursor turns into a two-headed arrow, press the mouse button and drag the field to the desired size.

As described in the section "Sorting, Searching and Matching Capabilities," to sort a field you do the following:

1. Select the field to be sorted ("Sorting Your Data"), or an entry in that field.
2. From the Organize menu, choose Sort; a dialog box appears.
3. Choose the desired Sort order.
4. Click OK or press return.

Use the Find Field command (see "Searching the Database") in the Organize menu to do a character search, one entry at a time. To find all records with entries that match your character string, use the Match Records command.

To select a set of records using search criteria you set, follow these instructions:

1. Choose the Record Selection command on the Organize menu (see "Using Selection Rules"). The resulting dialog box (see fig. 9.26) is configured to correspond to the rules you select.
2. Click the Select button or press Return to select a subset of your database, based on your rules.

To save your database, use the Save command on the File menu. When you sort or select a data subset, the Save As command on the File menu saves your subset under a new name and leaves you in the original database.

# 10

# Database Reports

If you want paper copies of your Works database information to mark up, pass around, or examine, you must print that information. The printing process involves sorting the database and creating report definitions, page setups, and so forth. In Works, you can choose from two printing procedures. You use the Print Window command if you need to print only a few items that fit on a screen. If, on the other hand, you need to print longer reports, you use the report-generation feature, which provides subtotals, totals, and labeling options. In this chapter, you learn how to print both windows and longer reports.

## *Defining and Printing Short Reports*

With the Print Window command, you can quickly produce short reports that fit on one or two screens. This procedure is the same one in the word processor (see Chapter 2):

1. Sort the database into the order in which you want the report printed. You can use the selection features to create a subset of the database if you prefer.

2. Scroll so that the appropriate data appears in the database window.

3. Choose Print Window from the File menu, as shown in figure 10.1.

4. To get the page out of the printer, choose the Eject Page option from the File menu. Laser printers automatically eject the page for you.

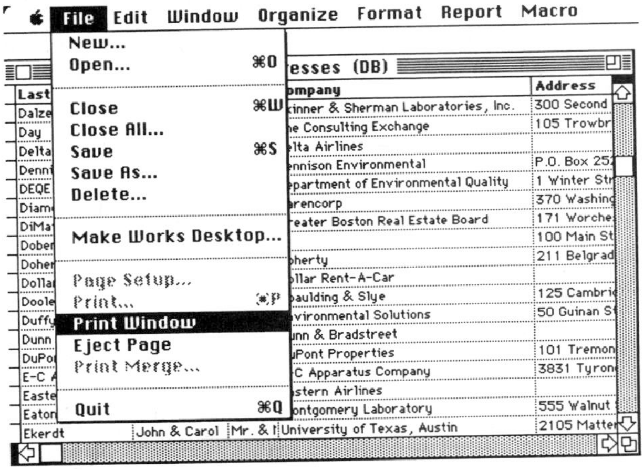

**Fig. 10.1**

*Selecting the Print Window option from the File menu.*

When you use Print Window, you cannot specify page setup information. Nor can you title reports, or total or subtotal data. The Print Window command prints the data exactly as it appears on your screen.

# *Defining and Printing Long Reports*

Works offers some useful database-reporting features. Although the capabilities have some limitations compared to dedicated database programs, you can print lists of items from your database and compute subtotals and totals on numeric fields. You can print all fields or only specific ones, in any order you choose. And you can define paper sizes, set margins, and add page numbers, headers, footers, and so on, by using the page setup features.

To set up reports, you create *report definitions*, in which you designate the fields to include in a report and specify where the fields should appear. You also have some control over when new pages begin. For example, when printing a list of expenses, you can have Works start a new page for each type of expense.

You can store up to eight report definitions in each database file and can define, rename, and delete the definitions at any time. This arrangement enables you to choose and then view or print a variety of reports quickly. Reports are stored with your database in the same way that graphs are stored with the spreadsheets to which they are attached.

**TIP:** Report definitions don't alter the contents or arrangement of your database. If you want records to appear in a particular order in your reports—for example, employees' last names according to state—rearrange your database before you print the report. This sorting process is particularly important if you want your report to contain subtotals or page breaks. If you want to change the horizontal order of a field in the report window, drag the field name to the desired position. Changes of field order made in a report window are not reflected in the original database.

# *Creating a New Report*

The process of creating a new report involves careful preparation. You need to determine the organization of your report and specify the page setup information and printing details. The basic steps are as follows:

1. Open the database window and select the records of interest.
2. Choose the New Report command from the Report menu.
3. Specify page setup information (paper size, margins, headers, and so on).
4. Arrange the fields in the correct order and size (to fit within the left and right margins).
5. Specify subtotals, page breaks, grid or no grid, and so forth.
6. Rename the report definition, if you want.
7. Preview report totals and subtotals by clicking the Print Preview box in the Print Window.
8. Print the report.

The following paragraphs examine some of these steps in more detail.

## *Specifying Record-Selection Criteria*

To restrict the records to be included in your reports, you use the record-selection techniques described in Chapter 9. If you don't use these procedures, your reports will contain all the records in your database. Figure 10.2, for example, shows the report window for printing a report called Addresses Report 1. Two selection rules are in effect. Notice in figure 10.2 that you can use the scroll bars to scroll your selected database subset to view individual records and fields. Figure 10.3 shows a typical report with columns totaled and subtotaled.

**NOTE:** Before creating or using a report, you must first sort your data. Once you are in the Report section, you are only allowed to use the Record Selection option. No sorting is allowed.

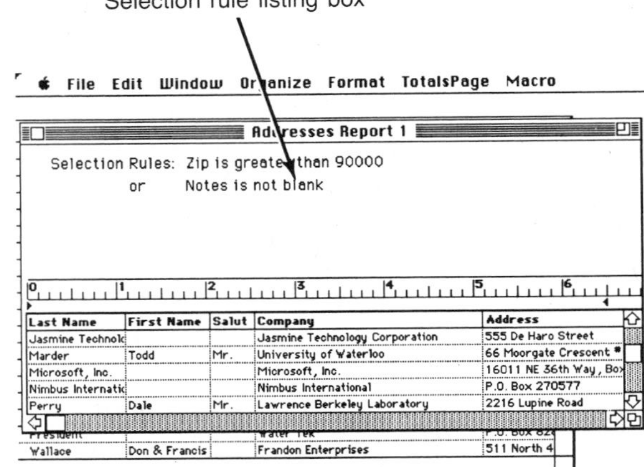


**Fig. 10.2**

*A report window with selection rules displayed.*

BUSINESS AUTOMOBILE EXPENSES June 9, 1987

| Payee | Date | Amount | Notes |
|---|---|---|---|
| Glen Fed Leasing | 1/10/87 | $406.50 | Volvo 760 Lease |
| Glen Fed Leasing | 2/9/87 | $406.50 | Volvo 760 Lease |
| Glen Fed Leasing | 3/25/87 | $426.83 | Volvo 760 Lease |
| Glen Fed Leasing | 4/14/87 | $406.50 | Volvo 760 Lease |
| | | $1,646.33 | |
| Mobil | 4/21/87 | $15.90 | |
| | | $15.90 | |
| Pep Boys | 3/19/87 | $37.72 | company car floormats |
| | | $37.72 | |
| Unocal 76 | 1/9/87 | $14.25 | |
| Unocal 76 | 1/17/87 | $16.93 | |
| Unocal 76 | 1/30/87 | $16.20 | |
| Unocal 76 | 3/11/87 | $15.65 | |
| Unocal 76 | 3/19/87 | $16.10 | |
| Unocal 76 | 3/27/87 | $16.15 | |
| | | $95.28 | |
| | | $1,795.23 | |

Page 1

**Fig. 10.3**

*A typical Works report.*

As you may recall, to begin a record-selection procedure, you open the Organize menu and choose Record Selection. You can create and store one set of selection criteria for each report definition.

In any new report, the record-selection criteria for the report are whatever criteria are in effect in the database window. If you are not satisfied with the selection rules currently in place, you can eliminate them or change them by choosing Record Selection to return to the Record Selection dialog box. (For more information, see Chapter 9's section on "Using Selection Rules.") You can then delete the existing rules and install new ones. Works updates your report window when you click the Select button.

## Using the New Report Option

If you have not previously defined a report, New Report is the only choice available to you on the Report menu; all other options on the menu are dimmed. When you choose New Report, a report window appears, similar to the one shown in figure 10.2. If you have not used any selection rules, the report window displays `Report Rules: No Rules Are in Effect` in the selection rule listing box. If you have defined rules, they are listed in the sequence in which they are applied.

Note that when you have a report window on your screen, your Macintosh contains an additional menu option called TotalsPage. This menu includes options that permit you to define partial and whole column sums and to insert page breaks after sums. These topics are discussed elsewhere in this chapter (see "Computing Totals and Subtotals").

## Defining the Page Setup

You can simplify the report-definition process by setting paper size, margins, reduction ratios, and page orientation before you display the report window. To specify these page characteristics, choose the Page Setup command from the File menu. You may want to review Chapter 1's section on "Fonts, Printers, and Networks," and Chapter 2's discussion of "Printing Your Work," where all the options for the Page Setup command are discussed, including options to produce headers and footers.

Don't worry if you're unsure of how to set up the page for your report. In the report window, Works shows you (on-screen) how much of your proposed report will fit on a printed page between the margin markers. And you can always preview your printed report by checking the Print Preview option in the Print dialog box. This habit is a good one because it saves paper and time.

Figure 10.4 shows the dialog box of the current LaserWriter Page Setup command. The ImageWriter has most of these features as well. Here are some tips to keep in mind as you use this dialog box:

- Use the Header option to create printed report titles.
- Use reduction and landscape orientation for wide reports. (LaserWriters give you fine control over size changes, but ImageWriters allow only 50 percent reduction.)
- Use enlargement for reports having only a few short fields.
- You cannot control fonts, sizes, or color (those settings are global in the database formatting).

**Fig. 10.4**

*Defining the page size, orientation, and margins for a LaserWriter.*

LaserWriter Page Setup 5.2
OK
Paper: US Letter A4 Letter Tabloid
US Legal B5 Letter
Cancel
Options
Help
Reduce or Enlarge: 100 %
Printer Effects:
Font Substitution?
Text Smoothing?
Graphics Smoothing?
Faster Bitmap Printing?
Orientation
Print Row and Column Numbers
Print Cell Notes
Header: MONTHLY REPORT 1 &r&d
Footer: &rPAGE &p
Left Margin: 1
Right Margin: 1
Top Margin: 1
Bottom Margin: 1

## *Designating Which Fields To Print*

When you open a report window, the records in your database—and their field names—appear in the order in which they will be printed. You can use the resize box in the lower right corner of the report window (see fig. 10.2) to resize your report window and thus see more records, but you will always have at least one record and the field names on your screen. To see more fields, you can scroll horizontally; to see more records, scroll vertically.

Note also in figure 10.2 that the left- and right-margin markers delineate the boundaries of your printed report. You use these markers to tell Works exactly which fields to print. You can drag the right-margin marker into different positions on the ruler, but only to the limits of your paper and margin sizes. For example, with letter-size paper and a margin of 1 inch on all sides, you can drag the right-margin marker only between the 1-inch and 7 1/2-inch markers on the ruler.

**TIP:** If you have chosen landscape orientation or have specified reduction in the Page Setup dialog box, the right marker may not be visible. You can find it by scrolling to the right with the horizontal scroll bar.

Works prints any field that is completely to the *left* of the right-margin marker, but fields that are completely to the *right* of the right-margin marker do not print. In other words, if the marker falls anywhere in the middle of a field, Works will truncate the field at the right margin. For example, in figure 10.2, the Address field will be truncated because some of it lies to the right of the right-margin marker. Works prints only the Last Name, First Name, Salut, and Company fields and part of the Address field.

## *Moving and Resizing Fields*

Frequently, after an initial inspection of the screen, you may decide that you want to print fields falling outside the defined printing area. And sometimes you may not want to print items that are currently in the printing area. To change the contents of your printed report in this manner, you can use one of these techniques:

Change the size of the printing area by changing the page setup specifications.

*or*

Drag fields into and out of the printing area.

*or*

Adjust the size of the fields to make them fit.

Moving fields in a report window works exactly the same as it does in a database window. As you know, when you point to a field title, the pointer becomes a hand. You can then use the pointer to drag fields into or out of the printing area or to rearrange the order of fields within the printing area.

**TIP:** When you drag a new field into the printing area, you may push other fields to the right and out of the printing area. By dragging a field out of the area, you create space that will automatically filled by other fields.

Figures 10.5 and 10.6 show an example of moving a column in a report window. The field Last Name is selected, dragged to the right, and placed immediately to the left of the Company field. When the fields are rearranged, the Last Name field will be moved to the *right* of the Company field.

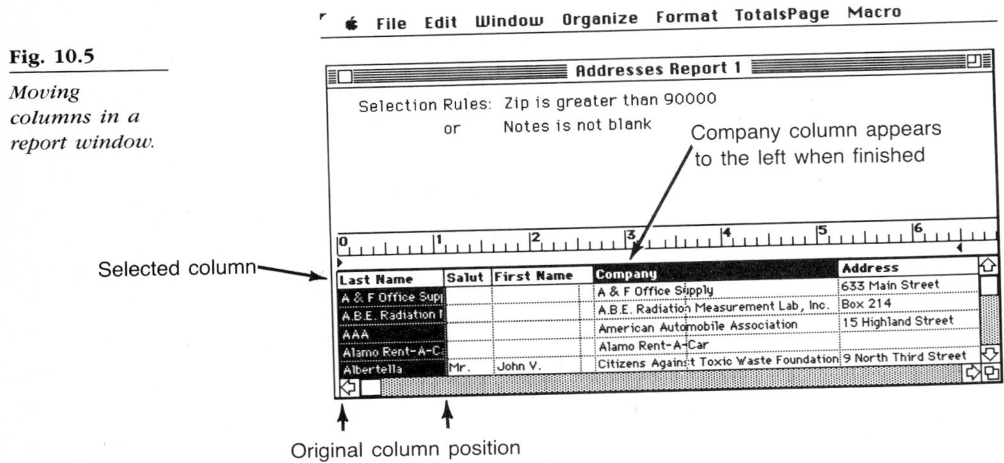


**Fig. 10.5**

*Moving columns in a report window.*

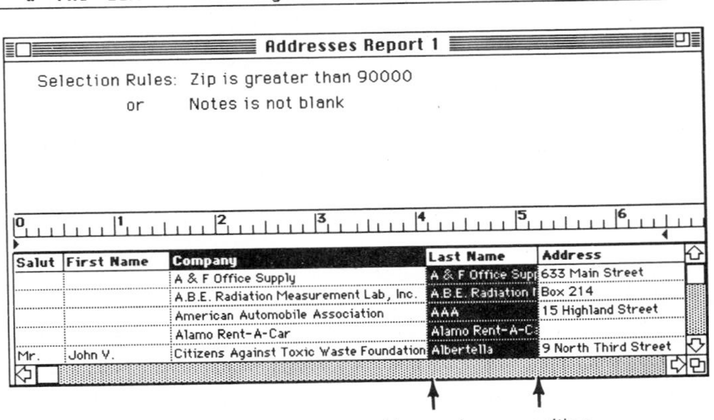


**Fig. 10.6**

*After moving the Last Name column.*

When you move fields in the report window, you don't rearrange them in your database. Each report definition can have its own arrangement.

You already know how to change the size of a field. Point to the right edge of the field title and, when the pointer changes to a double-headed arrow, drag the field to its new size. Then release the mouse button.

When you change a field's size in a report window, you change the field size only for the report definition. The change does not affect the database or the other report definitions. Enlarging a field is a handy way to "push" an unwanted field far enough to the right that Works doesn't print it.

You can squeeze in additional fields by reducing field sizes, thereby fitting more fields in the printing area. When you do so, however, you may truncate some of your records and obscure part of the field titles. By changing a field's size, you also change the length of the line that underscores the column heading.

## Computing Totals and Subtotals

Works can compute totals from your numeric fields. Under certain conditions, you also can create subtotals. To define totals and subtotals, you use the TotalsPage menu, which you access through the report window. A check mark preceding an option indicates that the option has been selected for the highlighted column.

### Computing Totals

To compute totals for a field, follow these steps:

1. Select the numeric field that you want totaled (click the field).
2. Choose Sum This Field from the TotalsPage menu. Works then will print a total for the field in the report. You can sum a text field if it is in the correct format (such as ZIP codes). You cannot sum a date or time field.

In figure 10.7, for example, the Amt field is selected, and the check mark by the Sum This Field option indicates that Works will total the Amount field when printing the report.

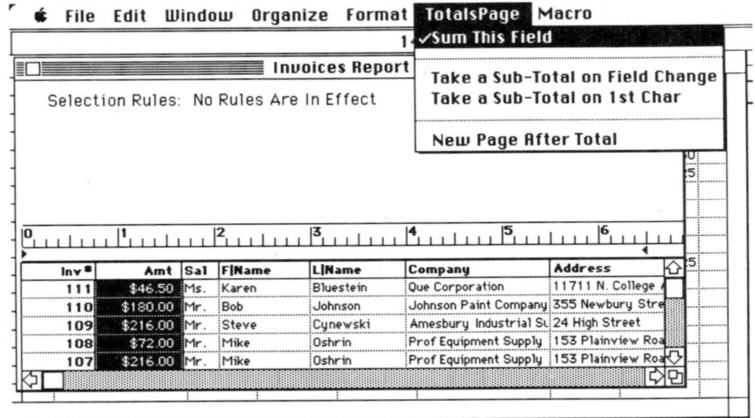


**Fig. 10.7**

*Calculating the total in the Amt field.*

## *Computing Subtotals*

Frequently, you will also want to create subtotals in reports (expense category subtotals, for example). You can use two options on the Totals Page menu for this purpose:

- ❑ Take a Sub-Total on Field Change
- ❑ Take a Sub-Total on 1st Char

**NOTE:** To do partial sums, you must sort your database into the correct order before running the report.

## *Take a Subtotal on Field Change*

When you choose this option from the TotalsPage menu, Works computes a new subtotal whenever the content of a field changes in any way. You can apply both field sums and subtotals field sums together in a report.

To have Works compute subtotals when the field data changes, do the following:

1. Select a numeric field to subtotal by clicking the field name.
2. Select Sum This Field from the TotalsPage menu.
3. Select the key field on which the subtotals should be based.
4. Select Take a Sub-Total on Field Change from the TotalsPage menu.

Works then prints a subtotal in your report whenever the key field's contents change.

For example, suppose that you want a report to list the names of key employees by department and to subtotal their earnings by department. Figure 10.8 shows this report. To set up the report, you would select the EARNINGS 12 MO field and choose the Sum This Field command. Then you would select the DEPARTMENT field (the key field) and choose the Take a Sub-Total on Field Change command. The result is a set of subtotals and a grand total in the EARNINGS 12 MO field.

KEY EMPLOYEE PAY BY DEPARTMENT August 26, 1987

| LAST NAME | FIRST NAME | JOB TITLE | DEPARTMENT | EARNINGS 12 MO |
|---|---|---|---|---|
| Gunlatch | Raymond | President | Corporate | $83,200.00 |
| Gunlatch | Nancy | Assistant to the President | Corporate | $81,120.00 |
| | | | | $164,320.00 |
| Goldberg | Rubin | Director, Engineering | Engineering | $36,400.00 |
| Mi | Sue | New Product Development | Engineering | $58,240.00 |
| | | | | $94,640.00 |
| Flushland | Johnathon | Cleaning Associate | Maintenance | $10,400.00 |
| | | | | $10,400.00 |
| Baxter | James | Director Personnel | Personnel | $41,600.00 |
| Baxter | Tammy | Assistant Director | Personnel | $37,440.00 |
| | | | | $79,040.00 |
| Makit | Willie | Production Supervisor | Production | $26,520.00 |
| Winston | Doc | Sr. Sardine Eye Closer | Production | $16,536.00 |
| | | | | $43,056.00 |
| Norcross | Oliver | Sales | Sales | $62,400.00 |
| Quickcloser | John | Inside Sales | Sales | $52,000.00 |
| So | Mi | Inside Sales | Sales | $52,000.00 |
| | | | | $166,400.00 |
| Berfel | Ferd | Pull Tab Inspector | Test Lab | $18,470.40 |
| | | | | $18,470.40 |
| | | | | $576,326.40 |

Page 1

**Fig. 10.8**

*A report that lists names of key employees by department, with subtotals of their earnings by department.*

If you plan to use a field for subtotals, you should be consistent when making entries in your records. For example, if you enter *Sales* as the department name for some employees and *Sales Dept.* for others, you will get two subtotals rather than the single total you want. Figure 10.9 illustrates a subtotal problem caused by data-entry inconsistency. In this case, a space appears before the *S* in *Sales* for employee Quickcloser's DEPARTMENT field. Because any difference in a field can cause a new subtotal, you should avoid abbreviations, indiscriminate punctuation and spaces, and other discrepancies.

KEY EMPLOYEE PAY BY DEPARTMENT

August 27, 1987

**Fig. 10.9**

*Subtotal problem caused by inconsistency in data entry.*

| LAST NAME | FIRST NAME | JOB TITLE | DEPARTMENT | EARNINGS 12 M |
|---|---|---|---|---|
| Baxter | James | Director Personnel | Personnel | $41,600.00 |
| Baxter | Tammy | Assistant Director | Personnel | $37,440.00 |
| | | | | $79,040.00 |
| Berfel | Ferd | Pull Tab Inspector | Test Lab | $18,470.40 |
| | | | | $18,470.40 |
| Flushland | Johnathon | Cleaning Associate | Maintenance | $10,400.00 |
| | | | | $10,400.00 |
| Goldberg | Rubin | Director, Engineering | Engineering | $36,400.00 |
| | | | | $36,400.00 |
| Gunlatch | Raymond | President | Corporate | $83,200.00 |
| Gunlatch | Nancy | Assistant to the President | Corporate | $81,120.00 |
| | | | | $164,320.00 |
| Makit | Willie | Production Supervisor | Production | $26,520.00 |
| | | | | $26,520.00 |
| Mi | Sue | New Product Development | Engineering | $58,240.00 |
| | | | | $58,240.00 |
| Norcross | Oliver | Sales | Sales | $62,400.00 |
| | | | | $62,400.00 |
| Quickcloser | John | Inside Sales | Sales | $52,000.00 |
| | | | | $52,000.00 |
| So | Mi | Inside Sales | Sales | $52,000.00 |
| | | | | $52,000.00 |
| Winston | Doc | Sr. Sardine Eye Closer | Production | $16,536.00 |
| | | | | $16,536.00 |
| | | | | $576,326.40 |

Unwanted breaks

Space before "S"

Page 1

## *Take a Sub-Total on 1st Char*

When you choose this option, Works creates a new subtotal whenever the first character in the key field of a record differs from the first character of the preceding record. Sometimes the first character in an entry tells you something about the group to which the item belongs. For instance, first numbers in ZIP codes specify National Postal Areas. Some inventory managers use part-numbering schemes that have significant first numbers, too. If you deal with numbers like these and need to compute subtotals by groups based only on the first character in a field, use the Take a Sub-Total on 1st Char option rather than the Take a Sub-Total on Field Change option.

**NOTE:** This feature is not particularly handy. Even Microsoft admits that it has limited appeal. At first glance, you would think that the feature would calculate subtotals by month in date fields; but it can't. If you use Take a Sub-Total on 1st Char on a field containing the dates 10/01/86, 11/15/86, 12/25/86, and 1/01/87, they all appear in the same group. To subtotal on a month change, you create a new calculated date field and use the following formula:

= month (date_field)

### *Inserting Page Breaks after Totals*

Sometimes you may want Works to begin a new page after each subtotal. For example, you may want each region or expense category to appear on a separate page. To accomplish this division, you use the New Page After Total command on the TotalsPage menu. You select New Page After Total immediately after you define a field to be subtotaled and while the field is highlighted.

To subtotal a field, follow these steps:

1. Click the field you want to subtotal.
2. Choose either the Take a Sub-Total on Field Change or the Take a Sub-Total on 1st Char command.
3. With the field still selected, choose New Page After Total.
4. Complete the report definition and print the report.

## *Turning the Grid On and Off*

Chapter 9 introduced you to the Show Grid and No Grid options, located in the Format menu. When defining a report, you may want to turn off the grid so that it doesn't print on the report.

## *Renaming Fields and Field Definitions*

In a Works database, field names are used as the column headings for reports. Unfortunately, you cannot rename field titles in the report window, so if you need different titles, you must change the field names in the database itself. This change affects all other reports for that database as well.

Renaming report definitions, however, is possible. Works assigns each of your report definitions a sequential generic name containing the database name and a number. For example, if your database is called *Billings*, Works names your report definitions *Billings Report 1*, *Billings Report 2*, and so on. You can change the report definition title at any time by choosing the Change Report Title command from the Edit menu and completing the resulting dialog box (see fig. 10.10). The Edit menu changes when a report window is on-screen: only the Copy Totals (⌘-C) and Change Report Titles commands are available.

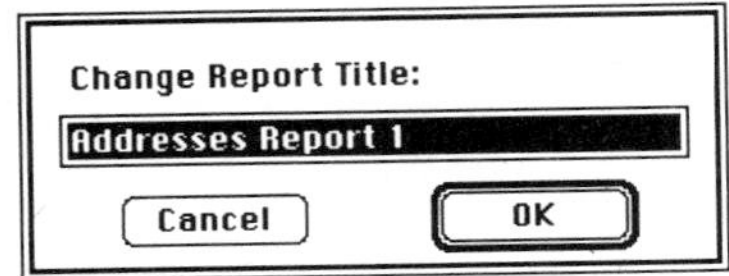


**Fig. 10.10**

*Using Change Report Title to rename a report.*

## Printing the Report

After you create a report definition, you print the report by choosing the Print option from the File menu. The report definition must be on the screen when you request printing. The default choice for printing is Geneva 9-point black. To make changes in the format, you select the appropriate options (Font, Size, or Color submenus) in the Format menu.

Before you begin the printing process, you may want to preview your report subtotals and totals.

### Previewing Report Totals

You can preview your totals and subtotals in two ways. By using the Print Preview option in the Print dialog box, the entire report, including totals and subtotals, is shown. You can use the hand cursor to move the page around. When inside the page, the hand turns into a magnifying glass. Click once to examine full size, and twice to return to the miniature.

The second way to preview your totals and subtotals uses the Copy Totals command in the Edit menu, which copies to the Clipboard the totals and subtotals you have defined with the Take a Sub-Total on Field Change, Take a Sub-Total on 1st Char, and Sum This Field command options. You can use Copy Totals whenever you have defined at least one total or subtotal. You then can view the information in the Clipboard (by selecting Show Clipboard from the Window menu) and copy the totals to another file.

To preview totals and subtotals, do the following:

1. Create a report definition containing at least one summed field.
2. With the report window active, either choose Copy Totals from the Edit menu or press ⌘-C.
3. The resulting subtotals are on the Clipboard.

**NOTE:** Remember that when you use Copy Totals, the copy overwrites whatever was on the Clipboard.

Grids aren't copied even if they're displayed in the report. But Copy Totals does copy field names (column titles) to the Clipboard—and to subsequent windows. In other words, the field names are always copied to the Clipboard in a database regardless of the type of copy operation.

The Print Preview command (chosen in the Print dialog box) also shows you totals and subtotals, as stated above.

## *Choosing Existing Report Definitions*

As mentioned, Works can store up to eight report definitions for each database. To choose one of these report definitions (when you want to print the report or modify the definition), follow these steps:

1. Choose Select Report from the Report menu. Works then displays the list of available report definitions (see fig. 10.11).

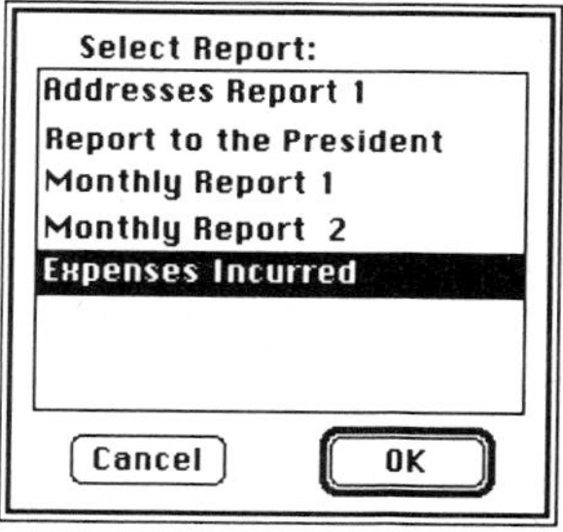


**Fig. 10.11**

*Selecting a report.*

2. Double-click the name of the report you want to use (or highlight the name and click OK).
3. Redefine or print the report. Rename it if you want.

## *Changing, Duplicating, and Erasing Report Definitions*

*Changing* stored report definitions is easy. Use the following procedure:

1. Choose Select Report from the Report menu when a report window is active.
2. In the resulting dialog box, select the report you want by double-clicking the report's name (or highlighting it and clicking OK).
3. Redefine the report (page setup, field locations, totals, and so on).
4. Print the report.

To *duplicate* a report, follow these steps:

1. Choose Duplicate Report from the Report menu.
2. Double-click (or highlight and click OK) to select a report name. Works then displays a copy of the report definition (sequentially numbered).
3. Redefine the report as needed (page setup, field locations, totals, and so on), changing the report name if you want.
4. Run the report.

To *erase* a report, do the following:

1. Choose Erase Report from the Report menu. The screen then displays the list of available report definitions.
2. Select the unwanted report by double-clicking its name (or highlighting it and clicking OK). Works then eliminates the report.

> ***Caution:*** You cannot use Undo to recover erased report definitions, so, when removing them, select with care.

# *Quick Reference Summary*

This section summarizes the steps involved in the procedures discussed in this chapter.

To print a database report, choose the database from the Works Open

File dialog box. To launch Works if Works isn't running, double-click the icon for the database itself. Double-clicking the database icon starts Works and opens the database.

Use the Show List command to display your records in the list window. Use the Sort and Select Records commands in the Organize menu. Move and resize your database fields in the database window so that they are in the correct order and relationship for printing. You are now working on a selected subset of your database.

To open a reports window (see "Creating a New Report"), follow these instructions:

1. Select the New Report command from the Report menu.
2. The Report window that results displays a part of your database along with any selection rules (refer to fig. 10.2).

If you have created reports previously (see "Choosing Existing Report Definitions"), do the following:

1. Choose the Select Reports command in the Report menu.
2. Double-click the report desired.

The triangular margin markers above the field names in the report window are the limits of the printed report. To change printed fields, follow these steps:

1. Move to the left of the right margin marker all fields you want to print by selecting them and dragging the field name. These fields must be entirely to the left of that marker, otherwise the fields will be truncated at the right margin marker.
2. Resize fields to the correct size by dragging the double-arrow cursor on the field name header border.
3. You can move a field in a report window by dragging its field heading to change the order.
4. Make style changes in the Format menu.

**NOTE:** Changes in steps 3 and 4 are not reflected in your database.

To change page setup, add headers and footers, and add a report title (see "Defining the Page Setup" elsewhere in this chapter), use the following procedure:

1. Choose the Page Setup command in the File menu.

2. Fill in all desired text boxes in the Page Setup dialog box for headers and footers, placing your title in the desired place. Use the standard Works nomenclature to format your choices.

3. Select the desired page sizes and margins.

To add totals or subtotals to a field (see "Computing Totals and Subtotals" elsewhere in this chapter), do the following:

1. To sum a field, select a numeric field by clicking the title.

2. Choose the Sum This Field command on the TotalsPage menu.

To subtotal a field, follow these steps:

1. Select a numeric field to subtotal by clicking the field name.

2. Choose the Sum This Field command from the TotalsPage menu.

3. Select a key field (click it) that you want the subtotaled field based on.

4. Choose either the Take A Sub-Total on Field Change or Take A Sub-Total on 1st-Char command, depending on which type of subtotal you want.

To print a report (see "Printing the Report," elsewhere in this chapter), follow these steps:

1. Open the Reports window on your desktop.

2. Select the desired report.

3. Preview any totals or subtotals by using the Copy Totals command in the Edit menu. View the results by using the Show Clipboard command in the Window menu.

4. To preview your report, select the Print command, check the Print Preview option, and click OK. You then can print your work from the Print Preview miniature.

5. Choose the Print command in the File menu, and click OK in the resulting dialog box to print your report.

Reports are saved along with your database. To save a new or changed report when in the database window, choose the Save command (or press ⌘-S).

# Part VI

# Additional Works Capabilities

## Includes

Using Macros

Communications

# 11

# Using Macros

VERSION 2.0

A *macro* is a small program (sometimes called a *script*) that you write for the purpose of accomplishing a certain task. Generally, you can invoke a macro—and thus initiate the program—by issuing a single keystroke or a small series of keystrokes. In your Macintosh system software you were introduced to macros with MacroMaker, the Apple macro program. Macros are a great convenience because they can save you a lot of time by doing repetitive tasks for you.

Two basic types of macro programs exist. MacroMaker is what is called a *keystroke recorder*. The macro program accessed in the Macro menu of all Works modules is also this kind of program. Keystroke recorders are like tape recorders. You turn on the macro recorder to record a series of actions that you initiate with your mouse or keyboard, and you turn off the recorder when you are finished. Additionally, you give your macros names so that you can find them again (especially if they're big hits!), and you save the macros in related files. This type of macro program is graphical (and especially easy to learn and use).

The second type of macro program involves the use of an underlying macro programming language. Macro recorders have this underlying structure also, but it is hidden from you by the graphical interface of the recorder paradigm. In a full-fledged macro program, you can get right in and examine and change the actual language of the macro. This ability makes this type of macro much more powerful but harder to learn. If you want to become a more powerful Works user, you might want to explore a product like WorksPlus Command, a third-party program for use with Microsoft Works. This program, which is described in the last part of this chapter, loads directly into your Works program and replaces the Macro menu with its own menu.

Macro programs have been a particularly fruitful area for third-party development on the Macintosh. You can integrate macro programs that operate over your entire system software for use in Works. When a program writes a macro that can be used in any Macintosh program, the macro is referred to as a *global macro*. Any macro specific to a single program is called a *local macro*. Two products, QuicKeys and Tempo, which write global macros for the Macintosh, also write local macros for Works. These products are described more fully in the last section of this chapter.

## *Using the Works Macro Feature*

You can use macros to perform just about any Works function that you want to accomplish, including inserting text, numbers, or anything you type. Keep in mind, however, that you cannot use any of the following keys when you're defining a macro in Works:

- ❏ Modifier keys: Shift, Option, ⌘, Caps Lock
- ❏ Reserved keys: Delete (Backspace), ’, =, −, +, _
- ❏ Certain accent keys: E, I, N, U, ˜

You can, however, use any of the special function keys F1 through F15 located on your extended keyboard, and you can use the Tab key by typing the word *Tab* in the Key text box (see fig. 11.1) of the Start Recording dialog box.

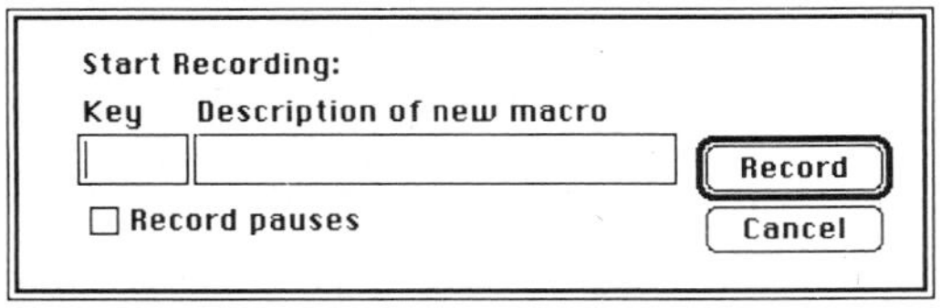

**Fig. 11.1**

*The Start Recording dialog box.*

Start Recording:
Key Description of new macro
Record
Record pauses
Cancel

Macros can also describe any mouse movement, including clicks, drags, pull-down menu selections (which are just drags), and window movements.

You can use macros to perform window operations. Suppose, for example, that you want to zoom or close a window. You can use a macro to define a mouse click at the appropriate location. If you choose to use a macro for a scroll operation, however, you need to understand that scrolls are specific to a particular window or document. Because documents of different lengths have scroll bars scaled to those lengths, using a macro for a scroll requires a specific drag of the scroll box for each document. You can, however, use a macro to bring up the Find dialog box, type in a character string, and go to that string in your document.

Before you begin working with Works macros, make a note of these features and limitations:

*Macros that record mouse movements operate by noting the starting and ending positions of your mouse movements.* Anything that happens in between cannot be represented in a macro. You thus cannot use macros to record curves or freehand drawings.

*Macros are specific to the location in which they are invoked.* For example, you can define a macro to open a word processor document; choose a font type, style, and size; insert your address and the date; and skip some lines to bring you to the recipient's address. If you invoke this macro in the middle of your letter, Works still performs the actions of the macro, but in the position at which you typed the macro's keystroke, not at the beginning of the document.

*Macros are window specific.* That is, they are recorded relative to the upper left position of the window in which they are defined to work. If you move a window, your macro will still work. Any macro that controls a window's condition or the close, zoom, or resize box can be used wherever the window is located.

**NOTE:** If you record a macro that depends on the size of a window, and you subsequently resize the window and play back the macro, the macro may not work. Resizing the window may mean that either your starting point or, more likely, your ending point will fall outside the window's size (if smaller). Drags are recorded relative to the window and not the screen.

## Defining a Macro

When you initially open a Works file (even a new, untitled one), your macro recorder is off, and the Macro menu looks like the one on the left in figure 11.2. To turn on your macro recorder or to access files of previously defined macros, you need to choose the Macros On command from the Macro menu. The menu then looks like the one displayed on the right side of figure 11.2. A check mark appears next to the command that indicates the current state of your macro recorder. With Macros On checked, you can record a new macro, play back one of your existing macros, or work with your previously defined macro files.

**Fig. 11.2**

*The Macro menu.*

To define a macro, use this procedure:

1. Choose the Macros On command on the Macro menu.
2. Select the Start Recording command from the Macro menu to display the Start Recording dialog box (see fig. 11.1).
3. In the Key box, type the letter you want to use to invoke the macro you are recording.
4. Click the Description of New Macro box (or press the Tab key) and give your macro a descriptive name that will help you locate it again.
5. Click the Record button (or press the Return key).
6. Using your keyboard or your mouse, initiate the sequence of actions that you want your macro to represent.
7. End the recording by selecting the Stop Recording command, which is now active in the Macro menu. When you choose this option, Works presents the dialog box shown in figure 11.3.

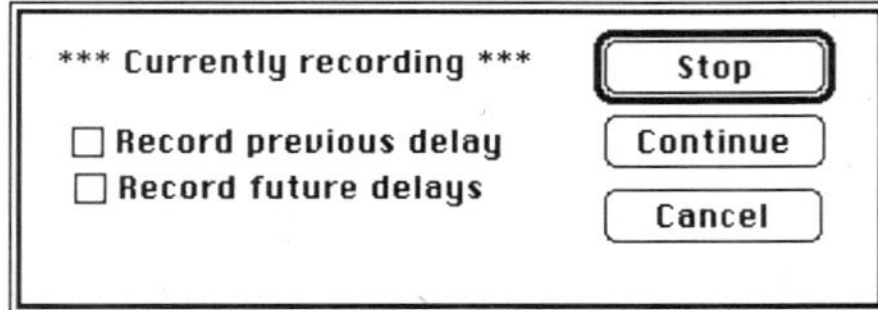


**Fig. 11.3**

*The Stop (Currently) Recording dialog box.*

8. Click the Stop button to terminate and save your macro.
9. When you're finished recording macros, choose the Macros Off command from the Macro menu.

In the Stop (Currently) Recording dialog box shown in figure 11.3, note that you are offered options other than terminating your macro recording session. To continue recording, click the Continue button, which returns you to the Start Recording dialog box. If you discover that you made a mistake while recording, you can cancel the recording process by clicking Cancel or pressing ⌘-. (period), which ends the process and does not save your actions. (You can also cancel recording by clicking the Cancel button in the Start Recording dialog box.) If you check either the Record Previous Delay or Record Future Delays box, you can slow down macro execution by recording your pauses along with your keystroke and mouse actions (see the section on "Using Pauses in a Macro" for more information).

## *Executing a Macro*

You execute your macros by using the Playback And option on the Macro menu. An important thing to remember about macro execution is that you should use a macro *only* in the conditions for which it was defined. For example, executing in a word processor a spreadsheet macro that uses menu commands leads to unexpected results because all the menu items have changed.

To execute a macro, follow these steps:

1. Position the cursor or insertion point at the location where you want the macro to act.

2. With the Macros On option activated, choose the Playback And command from the Macro menu.

   The Playback And command brings up a dialog box similar to the one shown in figure 11.4. In this dialog box, all your defined macros are listed in alphabetical order by descriptions. You also have several choices that allow you to work with macro files. (For more information, see the section on "Working with Macro Files.")

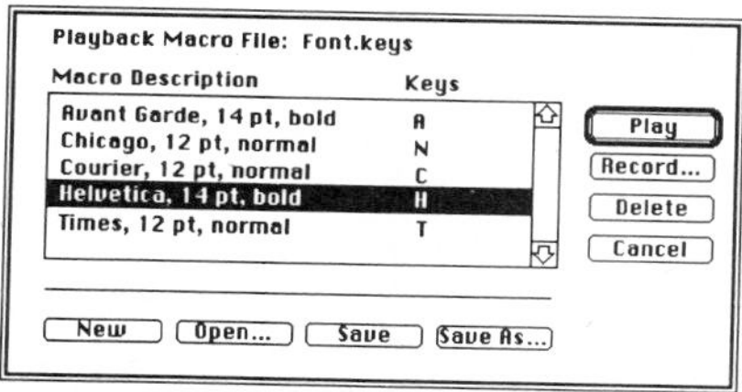


**Fig. 11.4**

*The Playback And (Macro Selection) dialog box.*

3. Double-click the description of the macro you want to execute, type the macro's assigned keystroke (shown beside the description), or click the description once and click the Play button.

If you remember the key you assigned to a macro, you can play back the macro without going through the Macro menu and the Playback And (Macro Selection) dialog box. When you are in the appropriate document, launch the macro by holding down the Option key and pressing the key assigned to your macro. You will find that Works plays back your macro as quickly as possible, sometimes faster than the program can respond by drawing dialog boxes or giving you the time you need to make choices.

If at any time a macro is not performing properly, you can choose the Undo command to restore your document to its condition before using the macro. You also can halt a macro in mid-execution by pressing ⌘-. (period), which returns the document to its state before executing the macro.

## Using Pauses in a Macro

If you need to slow down your macro, you can create *pauses* in the macro. Use one of these techniques:

Choose the Record Pauses option from the Macro menu.

*or*

Click the Record Pauses box in the Start Recording dialog box.

*or*

When in a recording session and in the Currently Recording dialog box, check either the Record Previous Delay box, the Record Future Delays box, or both.

With the Record Pauses command chosen, Works records your macro at the speed at which you execute the action. If you are in the Currently Recording dialog box and choose the Record Previous Delay or Record Future Delays option, Works turns on the Record Pauses command automatically.

## Working with Macro Files

As a convenience, Works allows you to save a set of macros as a file. For example, if you have recorded several style macros for use in a word processor document, you can save them together in a file, as was done in figure 11.4. Then, whenever you want to work on a word processor file, you can call up this set of associated macros. Use macro files for any of your particular Works modules or use defined macro files that will work globally for Works.

You can create new macro files, and rename, save, or open macro files you have previously created, by using commands in the Macro menu or by using the buttons that perform the same functions in the Playback And (Macro Selection) dialog box.

## *Naming Macro Files*

When you begin Works and turn on the macro feature, the program opens a new, untitled macro file automatically. If you click either the Save or Save As button in the Playback And (Macro Selection) dialog box, Works displays the Save As (SF Put) dialog box (see "Navigating the Hierarchical File System" in Chapter 1) in which you can name or rename the macro file and place it in the appropriate folder in your directory (see fig. 11.5). Works proposes the default name Microsoft Works (keys). If you save the file under this name, it will be loaded automatically the next time you select Macros On.

Works comes with a default file called Microsoft Works (keys). You can add to this file (but you have to open it first) or define any number of new files. If you save the Untitled file, it will be stored where you want it (even in the same folder as your file, if you don't move around the HFS). To save it anywhere else, move to the desired location first. (keys) is not a file extension, and it is not required, but it is recommended so that the file is easy to recognize.

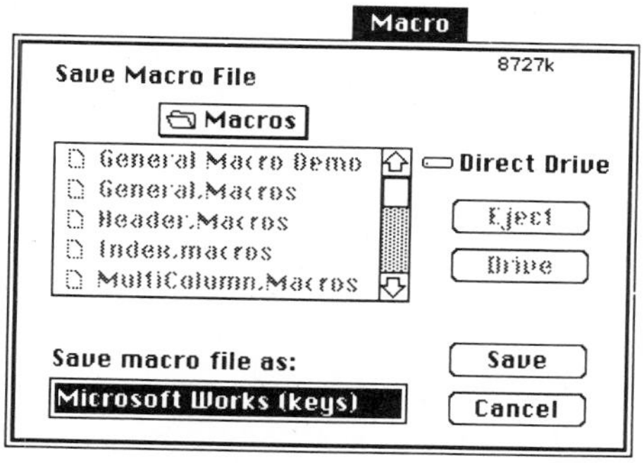

**Fig. 11.5**

*The Save As (SF Put) dialog box for saving the default macro file.*

A file name can include as many as 27 characters, and you can use either upper- or lowercase letters but not the colon character. You should name your macro files in some manner that allows you to differentiate them quickly from your regular files. To help distinguish macro files from other types of files, you may want to use a common file extension for all macros, such as *keys*. For example, you might want to store your style macros under the name *Style.keys*. If you often use a database named Inventory, for which you have defined a set of macros, you may want to define your macro file as *Inventory.keys* and save both the database and the macro file in the same folder.

## Opening Macro Files

Macros are recorded only to an open macro file. To play back a macro, you must have the file in which it is stored open on the desktop. You can bring a macro file to your desktop by choosing the Open Macro File command in the Macro menu. Works then displays an SF Get box, which was described in Chapter 1. You can have as many as 14 macro files open on the desktop at one time, depending on available memory.

**NOTE:** If you use a set of macros to work with a particular Works module, you should consider defining a Works desktop to open the macro file automatically, see "Making Works Desktops" in Chapter 13.

To open a new macro file, follow these instructions:

1. With Macros On selected, choose the Open Macro File command from the Macro menu.
2. In the resulting Open File (SF Get) dialog box, click the New button to create a file.

Alternatively, you can do the following:

1. With Macros On selected, choose the Playback And command from the Macro menu.
2. In the Playback And (Macro Selection) dialog box, click the New button.

To open a previously existing file, do the following:

1. With Macros On selected, choose Open Macro File from the Macro menu.
2. Select the macro file you want; then click the Open button.

Alternatively, follow these steps:

1. With Macros On selected, choose the Playback And command from the Macro menu.
2. In the Playback And (Macro Selection) dialog box, click the Open button and select the appropriate macro file from the SF Get dialog box.

## Saving Macro Files

Like any other file that you open on your Works desktop, you work with your macro file as a document in volatile memory (RAM). Any change you make and any additional macros you record or delete are not retained until you save these changes to disk.

To save a macro file to disk, follow these instructions:

1. If the file is a new one, choose the Save Macro File As command from the Macro menu.
2. Using the Save As (SF Put) dialog box (see fig. 11.5), accept the default name Microsoft Works (keys), or type a new file name in the text box. Then click the Save button.

Alternatively, use the following procedure:

1. Choose the Playback And command from the Macro menu.
2. In the Playback And (Macro Selection) dialog box, click Save As.
3. Accept the default name Microsoft Works (keys), or type a new file name in the text box. Then click the Save button.

If you want to save a previously created file to disk, use the Save Macro File command from the Macro menu, or click the Save button in the Playback And (Macro Selection) dialog box, to replace the file copy of your macros on disk.

## Deleting Macro Files

You can delete a macro file from the disk at any time in the Finder program by using the trash can or by using desk accessories like Disk-Tools II or DiskTop.

To delete a specific macro file, do the following:

1. With Macros On selected, choose the Playback And command from the Macro menu.
2. In the Playback And (Macro Selection) dialog box, select the file to be deleted and either click the Delete button or press the Delete key.

---

**WARNING:** Be careful, because Undo (⌘-Z) does not undo a macro deletion. If you do delete the wrong macro, choose New in the Playback And (Macro Selection) dialog box and click No when Works asks you if you want to `Save changes to current list of macros before closing?` You then can reopen your previous macro file with all the macros intact.

---

## *When You Cannot Use Macros*

You should consider defining a macro for any repetitive task. In some cases, however, you are restricted from using a macro. For example, your macro menu and recorder are disabled by any dialog box that appears on your screen. With a dialog or a message box displayed, you cannot select a Macro menu command, start or stop a recording, or complete any macro command. You must cancel the message or dialog box to continue with your work.

If you are operating under MultiFinder, you cannot define any macro command that switches to another application or program. If you try to do so, you will be launched into that other program without ever completing the definition of your macro. You can define a macro that launches a desk accessory, however, so long as the macro retains the active Macro menu on your screen. Be careful when defining desk accessory keystroke macros. You may encounter some incompatibilities, so test your macro immediately after definition.

## *When You Should Use Macros*

A good candidate for a global macro is a macro that imitates some kind of action which bypasses the menu. For example, if you define a macro that selects one of the choices on the Window menu, you can switch between documents on your desktop with a single keystroke.

To record a set of macros for switching windows, use the following procedure:

1. Open as many windows on your desktop as you want to record macros for.
2. Choose the Start Record command in the Macro menu. Make sure that Macros On is selected.
3. In the Start Record dialog box, fill in a keystroke for the macro. Use 1, for example, for a macro called Window 1, and 2 for Window 2, and so on.
4. Click the Record button (or press Return).
5. Pull down the Window menu and select the appropriate file name. Highest on the list is 1, next lower is 2, and so forth.
6. Choose the Stop Recording command.
7. Save your file. With your macro file open, your keystrokes will now work properly. Select Playback And and double-click the macro name.

Window commands make good global macros, using such keystrokes or mouse movements as Page Up or Page Down (clicking in the vertical scroll bar), Home (moving the scroll box to the top of your document), and End (moving the scroll box to the bottom of your document); and using the close, zoom, and resize boxes.

To record a drag macro, such as the Page Up or Page Down macro, follow these instructions:

1. Choose the Start Recording command on the Macro menu. Make sure that Macros On is selected.
2. Assign a keystroke for the macro, such as < for lower (Page Down) or > for higher (Page Up), and give the macro the name Page Up or Page Down.
3. Click the scroll bar just below the upper scroll arrow for Page Up; or check just above the lower scroll arrow for Page Down.
4. Choose Stop Recording from the Macro menu and click the Stop button (or press Return) in the Stop (Currently) Recording dialog box.
5. Save your file. Click Playback And, then double-click the macro name to activate it.

If you have a certain block of text that you must type repeatedly, such as your address, you may want to define a macro to enter that text. Consider also that if you want to combine macros into sequences, you can define a macro that does several functions in the correct order.

For your word processor, you may want to define macros to choose fonts, styles, and sizes that you use repetitively. A good practice in writing is to define *styles*, sets of formatting commands that you use when typing titles, headers, subheaders, and body copy in a document. A simple keystroke that takes you from one style to another can be quite useful. In general, all formatting choices make good macros.

If you have a document and you want to define formats (or *styles*) for each piece of it (header, body, title, and so on), try a macro. To create such a macro, follow these instructions:

1. Choose Start Recording and assign a key (such as H) and name (header) in the Start Recording dialog box. Then click the Record button (or press Return).

2. If your format includes previous blank lines, type the appropriate number of Returns now.

3. On the Format menu, make choices for *all* the options (Font, Size, Color, Justification, and Spacing). These new choices remove any previous selections.

4. Choose the Style command on the Format menu and on the Style submenu choose Normal (or press ⌘-N). This selection removes all previous style choices. Next, choose all options you want in the Style submenu (bold is ⌘-B, italic is ⌘-I, and so on).

5. Choose the Stop Recording command and click the Stop button (or press Return) in the Stop Recording dialog box.

In addition, you can use a macro to define just about any object that requires a simple click and drag. Note that to draw a column, you need to hold down the Option key *before* you click and drag. Even though the Option key is the modifier that launches the macro keystroke, this key is also part of the procedure for turning text objects into columns.

Databases and spreadsheets contain numerous opportunities to automate repetitive tasks. If you find yourself frequently doing fill-down or fill-right operations in a database, you can define a macro that copies a field entry and pastes it in the direction of your choosing. If you have an area of particular importance in your worksheet, you can define a macro that takes you to that cell immediately.

The list of potential macros is nearly endless. Use your imagination and have fun with them!

# *Examining Other Macro Programs*

As mentioned at the beginning of this chapter, other macro programs are available for you to use in conjunction with Microsoft Works. This section highlights three of these helpful products: WorksPlus Command, QuicKeys, and Tempo II.

## *WorksPlus Command*

WorksPlus Command, created by Lundeen and Associates, is a powerful macro programmer that installs into Microsoft Works. Once you install Command, it launches Works directly and can integrate with another Works accessory, WorksPlus Spell.

WorksPlus Command is a programmable macro recorder that replaces the Macro menu in Works with its own menu. You can define macros by using dialog boxes and recording keystrokes much like the way you can with the macro module in Works.

WorksPlus Command comes with a substantial set of prerecorded macros that you can apply in many Works modules. Some of these macros are very sophisticated and much more powerful than what is possible with the bundled Works macro recorder. As an example, WorksPlus Command includes a set of editing tools that allow you to build a table of contents, create an index, and place automatic headers and footers, totally bypassing the Page Setup dialog box. This feat is possible because WorksPlus Command writes invisible markers (formatting marks) that can later be compiled. To give you an idea of how easily you can use WorksPlus Command to perform what would otherwise be complicated tasks, figure 11.6 shows the Command dialog box you complete to create index parameters.

After you have defined a macro in WorksPlus Command, or if you find that you use one of the predefined macros often, you can create a Works menu called Command. You then can add the macro to that menu by simply checking a box in the Macro Definition dialog box.

A particularly handy WorksPlus Command macro, called GetSelectionInfo, gives information about a selection of a range of cells in a

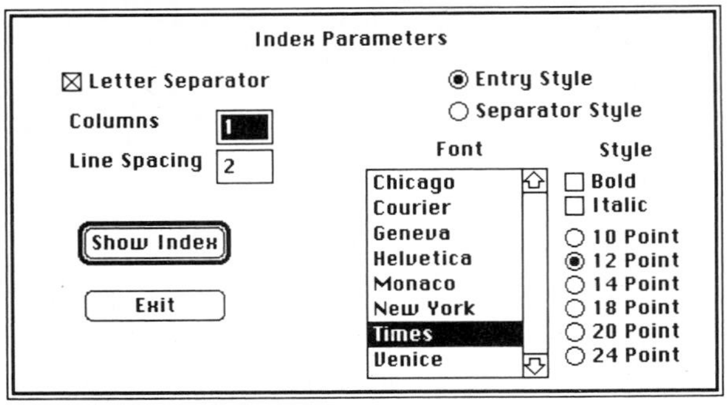

**Fig. 11.6**

*Creating an index with WorksPlus Command.*

worksheet or entries in a database. Figure 11.7 shows a database and the type of information you can obtain when you use this macro.

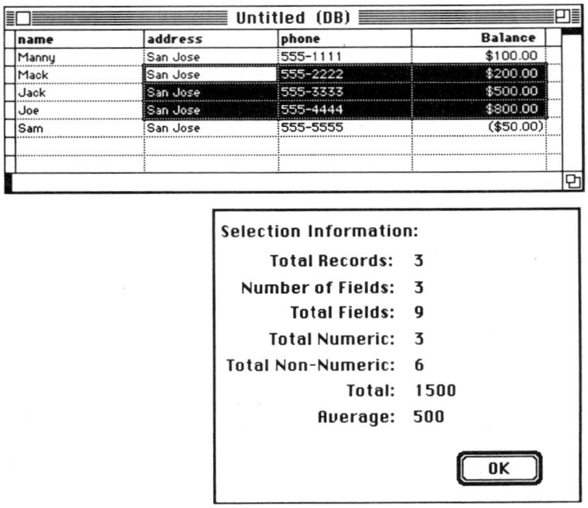

**Fig. 11.7**

*The results of using the GetSelectionInfo macro from WorksPlus Command.*

Among the other functions implemented in this program are macros that perform the following tasks:

- ❑ Resize graphics in percentages of vertical and horizontal
- ❑ Convert letter cases from upper to lower, and vice versa
- ❑ Save all files on the desktop in one keystroke
- ❑ Create various style definitions and markers, and work with many formatting commands

- ❑ Save individual copies of word processing documents used in a database merge
- ❑ Implement the fill-down command in a database
- ❑ Import a database from another program
- ❑ Dial a selected phone number

WorksPlus Command creates a macro file that is attached to the Works document in which the file is created. The real power of this program is that you can open the macro file and use WorksPlus Command's high-level programming language to edit or build macros. WorksPlus Command macros are programmed in a high-level Pascal-style language that can be debugged (using a built-in debugger) and compiled. The compile operation converts the word processor text of the Command macro file into an internal format so that it executes faster.

Using the WorksPlus Command programming language, you can even create your own dialog boxes with buttons, check boxes, text boxes, and the other standard Macintosh features to control your macro while it is running. And you can set a password to prevent other users from altering your macros.

In spite of its extensive capabilities, the program is easy to work with, and simple keystroke macros are easy to define.

## *QuicKeys and Tempo II*

These two other keystroke macro recorders deserve mention. Both are written to be used globally with your Macintosh but can be used to create a set of macros specifically with Works. QuicKeys is a product of CE Software, and Tempo II is offered by Affinity Microsystems.

QuicKeys is a CDEV that allows you to assign menu choices, clicks and drags, file choices, text blocks, and a set of special window and function key choices to any keystroke equivalent of your choice. If you do not like the currently assigned keystroke of a command, such as ⌘-W for Close (with windows), you can reassign the keystroke, and QuicKeys overrides the original assignment. With QuicKeys, any set of keystroke actions is permissible. You can also build sequences with QuicKeys. Figure 11.8 shows how the QuicKeys control panel appears.

Tempo II is another full-featured keyboard macro program that creates macro files. It is especially good for building sequential macros and includes conditional branching and the capability to remember menu

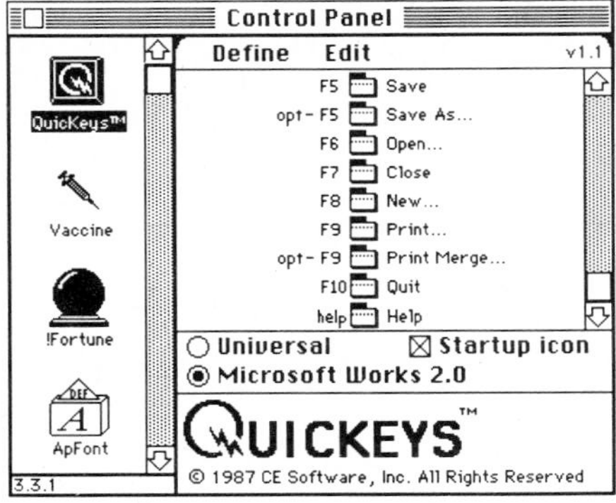


**Fig. 11.8**

*The QuicKeys control panel.*

selections by name. In general, users who are accustomed to some sort of programming tend to favor Tempo II over QuicKeys, but both are slick pieces of work.

## *Chapter Summary*

In this chapter, you learned what macros are and how they can be used to take the drudgery out of repeatitive keystrokes and procedures, and increase your efficiency at the same time. This chapter explained how to create macros with the new Works macro feature. You also learned about separate macro programs that can be used with Microsoft Works.

12

# Communications

With a modem, you can use your Macintosh to exchange information over regular telephone lines with other modem-equipped computers anywhere (see fig. 12.1). The Works communications module makes this feat possible. You can turn your Macintosh into a "terminal" that can be connected by telephone to large time-sharing computers such as those run by CompuServe, GEnie, Delphi, The Source, and hundreds of other information vendors. And you can access smaller low-cost or free services called bulletin board systems, or BBSs. (Appendix B provides references to commercial information services as well as bulletin boards.)

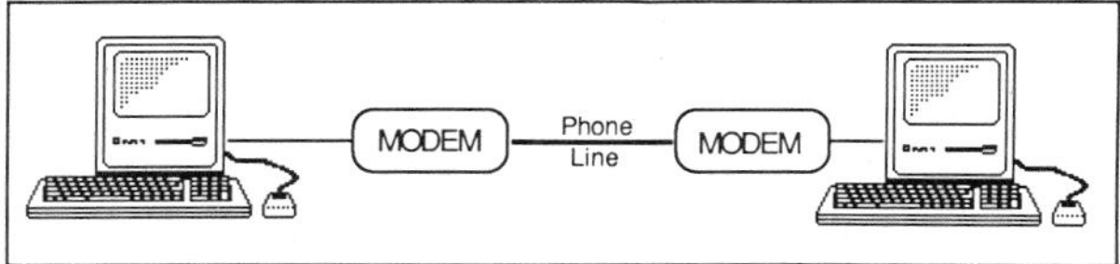


**Fig. 12.1**

*Computers connected by modems, cables, and a telephone line.*

Works also communicates directly with other personal computers; you send and receive information from either your keyboard or your disk. With a process called *background communications*, Works can exchange data this way even while you're busy doing other things —such as working on a spreadsheet or word processing document.

Businesses use these communication procedures to exchange spreadsheets, databases, and interoffice memos with far-flung offices. Hobbyists exchange programs, graphics, and ideas the same way. In this chapter, you learn about the terms and processes involved in these types of data sharing.

# *Understanding Communications Terms*

When computers send and receive information over telephone lines or through cables, the process is called *data communications*. Communications can go in either direction. When you receive information, text, or files from another computer, the process is called *downloading*. If you send information, text, or files to another computer, the process is called *uploading*.

The two computers participating in data communications need certain devices and certain *protocols*, or communications methods. Works' communications feature supports a wide variety of protocols, which make your Macintosh compatible with many different types of computers. These protocols enable you to collect and convert selected information from non-Macintosh computers such as IBM PCs. Chapter 13 offers more insight into this capability.

For practically all communications applications, you need a *modem* to connect your Macintosh across a telephone line to another computer with a modem. A modem is a device that converts digital signals generated or received by your computer into voice frequency signals which your telephone can transmit. A modem (contraction for modulator-demodulator) translates, or *modulates*, the electrical signals into telephone tones. Modems also convert the tones that arrive over telephone lines back into computer signals through a process called *demodulation*.

A large number of vendors, including Apple, Hayes, and U.S. Robotics, offer Macintosh-compatible modems. They range in price from less than $100 to more than $500. When purchasing a modem, you usually should specify that it be fully Hayes AT command set compatible (most are). Features that affect the price include the brand name, information exchange speed, the number of automated features, and the quality of bundled software.

# *Buying the Right Modem*

To take full advantage of Works communications features, your modem should have the following characteristics (in the United States and Canada):

- Hayes-compatibility with the AT command set standard (see the section on "Using Smart Modems")
- The capability to answer the telephone line automatically
- At least a 1200-baud, and preferably a 2400-baud, information exchange rate (most commercial and bulletin board services operate at these speeds)
- A cable compatible with your Macintosh model
- Direct connection to telephone lines (through a modular telephone jack)

Works supports additional modem features, including faster speeds and advanced security systems. A knowledgeable dealer can help you pick the right modem for your application. Users outside of the United States and Canada probably will want appropriate non-Bell compatibility (in addition to or instead of Bell 212A).

## Direct-Connect Modems versus Acoustic Couplers

A *direct-connect* modem plugs into a modular phone jack and sends signals from the computer directly into the phone line. Several commercial networking systems use the phone lines in a building to create networks of microcomputers. PhoneNET by Farallon Computing is one such example. Normally these networks have limitations on the distance between two computers (they must be in the same building) and the number of *nodes* (attached computers) possible.

An *acoustically coupled* modem, on the other hand, requires that you place the phone handset into the modem's rubber cups in order to exchange data. Acoustic couplers are less reliable and offer fewer features than the more popular direct-connect modems, so acoustically coupled modems are not now in common use. With an acoustic coupler, you cannot fully use all the Works communications options. Most users opt for today's more full-featured "smart" direct-connect modems.

## Using Smart Modems

A *smart* modem (originally a Hayes trademark) contains its own microprocessor and helps with the communications process. For instance, this type of modem can dial the outgoing computer phone calls for you and automatically answer incoming computer calls.

Works can simplify things for you by taking advantage of the smart modem's automatic features. Works knows how to carry on "conversations" with the modem itself. That is, Works tells the modem what to do and then waits for its response. Works also keeps you informed of what's going on. For Works to control and monitor the modem, the program must "speak" the modem's control language. Some industry standards have been developed for controlling smart modems. The most popular standard among microcomputer users is the Hayes AT standard, which Works supports. Using this standard, an exchange between Works and the smart modem might look something like this:

| *Works* | *Modem* |
|---|---|
| ATB1 (these are the settings) | OK (settings accomplished) |
| ATDT16172449078 (dial this number) | OK (message received)<br>DIALING (modem emits phone tones)<br>RINGING (receiving phone rings)<br>CARRIER DETECT (computer answers) |

(Data is then exchanged. The process may be interactive or automatic.)

| | |
|---|---|
| + + + (hang up) | OK (message received) |
| ATHO (automatic hang up) | OK (carrier gone) |

When you use Works, command exchanges like this one appear onscreen from time to time. Fortunately, you don't need to learn how to understand them or even how to issue such commands directly to your smart modem. Works takes care of those tasks for you. You control Works by using simple menu commands and screen buttons, as usual.

# *Working with Communications Documents*

A Works *communications document* consists of a collection of stored settings, a list of phone numbers, and a place to view information as it is exchanged. You can save multiple communications documents on disk, but you can have only one communications document open at once. You select and open a communications document as you do other Works documents, by using the Open (SF Get) dialog box, shown in figure 12.2. When you highlight the Communications icon, only communications files show up in the scroll box.

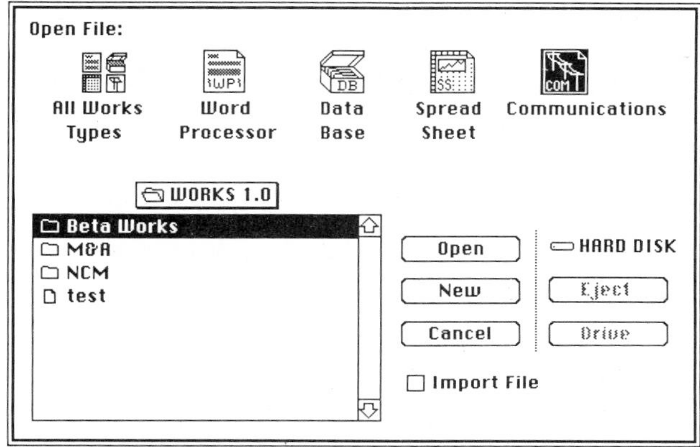


**Fig. 12.2**

*Opening a communications document by using the Open File dialog box.*

**NOTE:** You can have a communications document on your desktop along with other types of documents, such as spreadsheets and databases or word processing projects. While using a communications document, you can create and exchange other types of Works documents (see fig. 12.3).

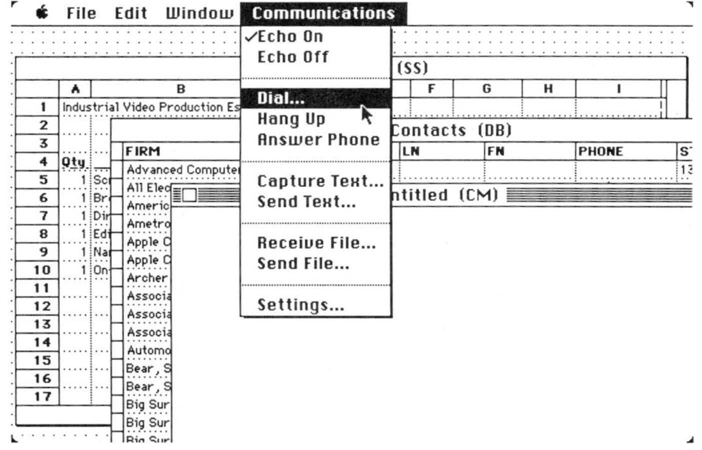


**Fig. 12.3**

*Communications document and other documents on a desk.*

# *Using the Communications Settings Dialog Box*

Perhaps the biggest stumbling block to successful communications is the wide variety of communications settings available. In addition to setting both computers' modems to send and receive information at the same speed, you must make other decisions. You make most of them in the Communications Settings dialog box. The default settings are shown in figure 12.4. These are the normal settings used by most of the big commercial information services. When you open a new communications window, Works asks you to make specifications in the Communications Settings dialog box.

Communications Settings:
Type: TTY VT-100 VT-52 Auto-wrap NewLine
Baud Rate: 300 2400 9600 1200 4800 19200
Delete Key Means: Delete Backspace
Data Size: 8 Bits 7 Bits
Stop Bits: 1 Bit 2 Bits
Number of screens: 4
Parity: None Odd Even
Handshake: None Xon/Xoff Hardware Both
Phone Type: Touch-Tone® Rotary Dial
Line Delay: 0 Character Delay: 0
Capture Text When Document Opens
Connect To:
Cancel OK

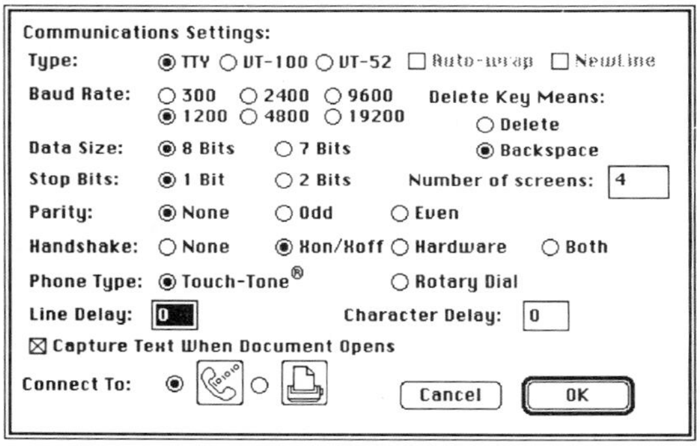

**Fig. 12.4**

*Default settings in the Communications Settings dialog box.*

You can change these settings any time by taking the following steps:

1. Choose the Settings command from the Communications menu.
2. Type the number of screens you want to review during your communications session in the Number of Screens text box.
3. Indicate a line or character delay, if you want one, in the Line Delay and Character Delay text boxes.
4. A number of other options (discussed below) are available to you in this dialog box, including terminal type, baud rate, data size, stop bits, parity, handshake, phone type, and modem port.

   The other options are filled in with defaults. Each option is covered in detail in the following sections.
5. Click the OK button, or press the Return key.

Your choices in this dialog box depend on the computer at the other end. Before using the communications features, you should understand the choices available and gather some information about the computers you intend to call. Normally the commercial services provide this information in their literature, or you can call the systems operator (the *sysop*, or person in charge) of a bulletin board to obtain this information.

The following paragraphs describe the settings you find in the Communications Settings dialog box.

## Terminal Type

You can have your computer *emulate*, or mimic, several different computer terminal types or even behave like a simple "teletype" terminal. Among the choices are the TTY or teletype terminals, the VT-100, or the VT-52 terminals. The VT series are terminals used with Digital Equipment Corporation VAX series computers. In Works, the default terminal type is TTY. This so-called "dumb" terminal sends and receives only ASCII characters. To change terminal types, you click the button next to the alternative you want. The other terminal types offer a few additional features not found in TTY mode, such as special characters for word processing, function keys, escape codes, ringing receiving terminal bells, and so forth. See "Using Control Codes and Special Function Keys" elsewhere in this chapter.

## Auto-wrap

In VT-100 or VT-52 mode, Works provides an auto-wrap feature. Version 1.0 does not have this capability. Auto-wrap automatically reformats lines on the screen, just like your word processor automatically wraps text when you type it. Text is then easier to read, and words aren't divided arbitrarily, as is the case when you don't use the feature. You select or disable auto-wrap by clicking the Auto-wrap option in the Communications Settings dialog box. This option usually is enabled, as indicated by an X in the box.

Notice that if you select the TTY terminal type, the Auto-wrap option appears dimmed in the Communications Settings dialog box. In TTY mode, auto-wrap is not available.

## NewLine

Many telecommunications systems differentiate between a carriage-return character and a line-feed character. Usually, when a carriage-return character is received, the cursor on the receiving computer's screen moves back to the leftmost position on the current line. A separate line-feed character must be sent to move the cursor down one line to a "clean" part of the screen. Therefore, if you are receiving information from a system that sends only carriage returns (as opposed to carriage returns plus line feeds), new lines of text overwrite preceding lines on your screen.

This arrangement isn't a problem if you don't need to read the text and are simply saving it to disk for later use. But if you want to read the text as it comes in, you want Works to display each new line below the preceding one.

The NewLine option in VT-100 or VT-52 mode (not available in Works Version 1.0) enables you to accomplish this task if the sending computer cannot. When you invoke this feature (an X appears in the box), Works executes a "carriage return plus line feed" whenever the program receives a carriage return. That is, Works moves the cursor down one line each time the system receives a carriage-return character. To disable the NewLine option, you click its box (so that the box does not contain an "X").

If you select TTY as the terminal type, the NewLine option appears dimmed in the Communications Settings dialog box. This feature is not available for that type of terminal.

## Baud Rate

*Baud* is an antiquated term used to refer to the speed of information transmission. A more accurate term is *bits per second*, abbreviated BPS. Nonetheless, people have the habit of referring to modems as being 300-baud, 1200-baud, 2400-baud, and so forth. The so-called bits are tones that represent binary digits—logical 1s and 0s that are pieces of letters.

1200 baud is currently considered an average or slow speed. Most bulletin boards support 2400 baud. Advanced communications and some data-like FAX transmissions normally occur at 9600 baud. The higher the baud rate, the faster the information travels. When you send or receive a file of information, a higher baud modem normally translates into a cheaper transmission because you use the service for less time.

When using a high-speed modem (like 19,200 baud), if the line is sufficiently noisy, the baud rate needs to be set to a lower rate to avoid error transmission. Reduce the rate one setting at a time until clean data transfer results. Also, note that when your modem is faster than the receiving modem, data transfer occurs at the slower speed.

Modems on both ends of an exchange must be set for the same speed. Not all modems operate at all speeds, but a modem with a higher rated speed can normally be adjusted to transmit at the lower frequencies. Generally (but not always), faster modems cost more than slower ones. Sometimes users with fast modems purposely slow them to improve the reliability of data transmission over noisy telephone lines. Find out which baud rates are supported by the modem connected to the computer you intend to call. Then tell Works.

**NOTE:** The highest baud rates offered by Works (9600 and 19,200) aren't normally used with modems. These baud rates can be useful when two computers are directly connected to each other through a cable. This procedure is sometimes used for data conversion tasks. See Chapter 13 for more information.

Just because two modems are set at the same speed doesn't mean that they're automatically compatible. Other operating characteristics usually need to be matched. Works is set to start with the most commonly used settings, but you may have to change one or more of them from time to time. Read on.

## Character Settings

*Character settings* are part of the protocols necessary to communicate between computers. Think of these settings as determining the language used to decipher the transmission. Three settings that you must determine are the data size, the stop bits, and the parity of the transmission. Over the years, several data-representation standards have been developed.

Some systems use as their *data size* an eight-bit signal to represent each character; other systems use only seven bits. When computers exchange information, they need to use the same number of bits to represent characters at both ends. If you use the wrong data size option, data may be "scrambled," as shown in figure 12.5.

Another variable is the number of bits used to separate characters when they're exchanged. These extra 0s and 1s are called *stop bits.*

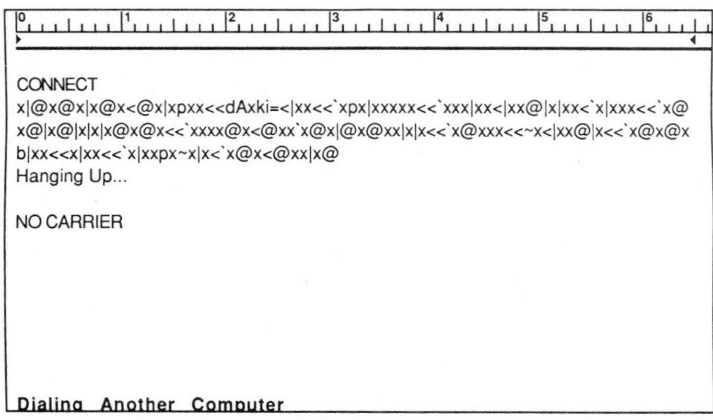


**Fig. 12.5**

*Scrambled data resulting from incompatible settings.*

Works offers a choice of one or two stop bits. You should match the number of stop bits used by the other system.

Many communications devices use a simple kind of error detection called *parity checking*. Parity checking, briefly, is a method of adding extra bits to each transmitted character so that the number of 1s is either even or odd. All you need to know about parity checking is that your computer and the remote computer should both use the same parity setting. Works offers three choices: None, Odd, and Even. You and the other computer user should agree on a parity-checking technique (odd or even). Or you both can choose to exchange data without parity checking by clicking the None option in your Communications Settings dialog boxes.

## *Handshake*

When data is "flying" back and forth at high speeds, both Works itself and the hardware (your Macintosh and modem) may need to pause from time to time to catch up. Therefore, you need to be able to tell the sending computer to stop sending momentarily while your system "catches its breath." And you must notify the sender when your system is ready to begin receiving again. The methods used to accomplish this starting and stopping are numerous—and beyond the scope of this book—but the process is called *handshaking*.

Requests to stop and start data transmission can come from the Works software itself, your Macintosh, or both. Works usually uses a simple handshaking technique called Xon/Xoff, or *asynchronous* handshaking, which is the default setting. In unusual circumstances, you may need to use hardware handshaking in addition to or in place of the Xon/Xoff approach. Even more rarely, technical people may want to defeat handshaking altogether. Works provides all these options.

To select a scheme other than Xon/Xoff, click the appropriate Handshake option in the Communications Settings dialog box. Remember that both your modem and the other system must support the choice you make.

## *Phone Type*

Most telephone lines today support touch-tone dialing, the fastest, most efficient way for your smart modem to dial. If your phone line doesn't work with touch-tone, select Rotary Dial (sometimes called pulse dial) for the Phone Type option in the Communications Settings dialog box by clicking the appropriate button.

If, using the touch-tone method, you hear your modem trying to dial, but you cannot reach the designated computer, try rotary dial. If that procedure doesn't work, contact the phone company, a knowledgeable colleague, or your dealer for help.

## *Line and Character Delays*

Some computers and software packages cannot receive data as quickly as Works can send the data. Moreover, they may not be able to handshake. In these cases, you may find that the receiving software misses characters or even entire lines that you send.

You may be able to correct the problem by having Works pause briefly after each line or character sent. To produce pauses between lines or characters, you change the 0s in the Line Delay and Character Delay boxes to small numbers. Observe the results. Obviously, these pauses slow the whole communications process, so no delay is the best (and the default) choice.

## *Capture Text When Document Opens*

Notice the Capture Text When Document Opens button in the Communications Settings dialog box. If you check this box, Works gives you the option of creating a separate file that will contain the text sent and received during your communications session. For more information, see this chapter's section on "Receiving and Storing Simple Text."

## Connect To

You can connect your modem to either of two outlets on the back of your Macintosh, which are commonly called *ports*. Your printer port has an icon for an printer, and your modem port has a telephone receiver icon. You can use both ports interchangeably. If your printer port is damaged and you need to use your printer on your modem port, select that option in the Chooser DA. If you must connect the modem to the printer port instead, indicate this selection by clicking the button to the left of the printer icon in the Communications Settings dialog box.

## Number of Screens

The Number of Screens text box in the Communications Settings dialog box enables you to scroll back a specified number of screens of previous text. Works Version 1.0 does not offer a scrolling feature. As that program receives text, the system displays the text and then pushes it toward the top of the screen into "alphabet heaven." Once text disappears from the screen in Version 1.0, that text is gone forever. If you don't read quickly or if you want to review something, you need to have the sending computer resend the material (unless you have also saved it to a disk file, in which case you can review the text with Works' word processing feature).

With Works Version 2.0, however, you can review as many as 100 previous screens, and you can specify how far back you want to look. After you set the number of screens in the text box, you can use the scroll bars in the communications window to review your dialog. You can scroll up so that you can review things while new information is still coming in; Works keeps things in order for you. When you finish looking around, you return to the "bottom" of the window to pick up the communications dialog where you left off.

Obviously, the scrolling feature is useful. But why does Works give you a choice of number of screens? The answer is this: to conserve memory. This technique is particularly useful if you have an older 512K Macintosh or if you keep many open documents on your desktop simultaneously. Because you can have many projects going on at once, you may not have enough RAM available for you to be able to scroll through 100 screens of old communications text. With the Number of Screens option, you can specify how much of your computer's memory should be reserved for temporary storage of old text. The more old screens you want to review, the less room you have for other active projects, such as spreadsheets and word processing documents.

To define the number of screens you want to be able to review, click the Number of Screens box and enter a number from 0 to 100. If not enough memory is available to save the requested number of screens, Works warns you with an alert box and saves as many screens as possible. You can sometimes free additional memory for screen scrolling by closing unneeded documents or quitting unneeded programs. The default setting for Number of Screens is 4, which should be plenty for most casual data-communications sessions. You can and should always save entire sessions to disk as word processing documents for later review. For more information, see this chapter's section on "Receiving and Storing Simple Text."

Any text that is visible when you're scrolling can be selected, copied, cut, pasted, and so on with the familiar Macintosh techniques. Because you can have other documents open, you can use the Clipboard to pass text from the communications window to other documents, such as word processing or spreadsheet projects.

## *Changing and Saving Settings*

Changes made in the Communications Settings dialog box are saved as part of the current communications document just like graphs for spreadsheets or reports for worksheets are. To save settings, press ⌘-S or choose the Save option on the File menu to save the file.

To create a new communications document containing the modified settings, you choose Save As from the File menu. Works then preserves the old settings under the old document name and creates a new communications document with the new name you choose. The new document becomes the active one. You also can select the New command from the file menu and double-click the communication icon, or click the communication icon once and then click OK or press Return.

If you need to change communications settings in an active communications document, select Settings from the Communications menu. Make any necessary changes and test the results. Remember that you need to save the communications document if you want the changes to be permanent.

## *Setting Echo On and Echo Off*

Sometimes you will communicate with a computer that sends back to you each character it receives. This process, called an *echo* or a *full-duplex* operation, is often used as a data check. By looking at these echoes, you can be more confident that what you are sending is being received correctly at the other end. If you type a character and see that character written twice on your screen, you have an echo. Both computers are updating your screen. "YYoouurr ssccrreeeenn wwiillll ccoonnttaaiinn ddoouubbllee cchhaarraacctteerrss lliikkee tthheessee." You can remove an echo by choosing the Echo Off command from the Communications menu (see fig. 12.3), and things will look normal thereafter.

A more bizarre problem occurs when the other computer should be echoing and doesn't. You type on your keyboard, and the other computer gets what it needs, but your screen doesn't show anything you have typed. The screen does, however, display the other computer's responses to your typing. This mode of operation is called *echo off* or *half-duplex*. To correct this situation, select the Echo On command from the Communications menu.

Both computers need to be in agreement about echoing. Clicking one option overrides the other. Use Echo Off, the default, if the computer at the other end will send the characters to your screen. Choose Echo On only if the other computer cannot or will not echo. A check mark by the command indicates the current condition.

**NOTE:** Some modems have switches and software commands that can cause additional echoing. If you're seeing three of every character, consult your modem manual, dealer, mentor, or eye doctor.

## *Using the Phone Book*

With each communications document, you can enter and save up to eight telephone numbers and their associated names. Figure 12.6 shows an example of such a list, which you access by choosing Dial from the Communications menu.

You can use the list simply as a reference for manually dialed calls. If you have a compatible smart modem, however, you use the list to choose a number for the modem to dial automatically.

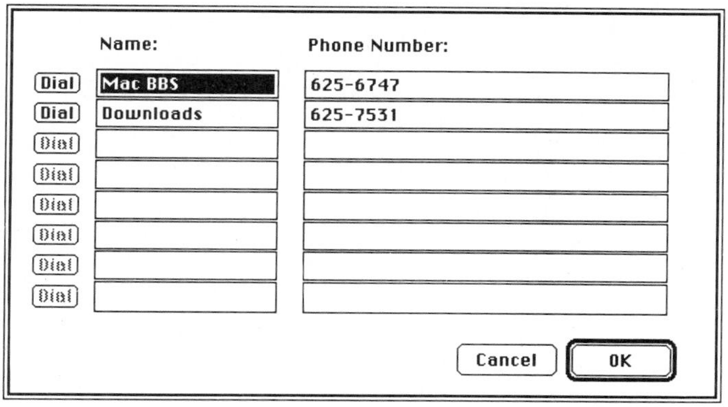

| | Name: | Phone Number: |
|---|---|---|
| Dial | Mac BBS | 625-6747 |
| Dial | Downloads | 625-7531 |
| Dial | | |
| Dial | | |
| Dial | | |
| Dial | | |
| Dial | | |
| Dial | | |

Cancel OK

**Fig. 12.6**

*A typical telephone list.*

## *Entering Numbers in the Phone Book*

Before you can use your modem's automatic-dialing feature, you need to enter at least one telephone number in a communications document phone book. You enter, edit, and delete phone numbers and names in this text box in the standard Macintosh manner. To move from entry box to entry box in the phone list, click or use the Tab key.

Works and most smart modems support the Hayes-compatible convention, which ignores parentheses, slashes, spaces, and dashes, and reads commas as pauses. Therefore, all the following entry styles are usually allowed, and all are equivalent:

1 800 555 1212<br>
1-800-555-1212<br>
1(800)555-1212<br>
1-800/555-1212<br>
18005551212

Works accepts up to 50 characters per phone number. This limit allows you plenty of room, even for complex international numbers that include access codes. Do not type letters—such as 1-800-CARCARE—in the telephone number box. You will not reach the correct party, and you may confuse your modem.

## *Pausing While Dialing*

The autodial feature dials more quickly than you could possibly dial with your own finger. For example, a modem using this feature can dial

> ***Caution:*** Works saves changes in your phone list to disk only when you save an edited communications document. You don't save your changes by clicking OK when in the phone book; Works accepts changes only until you close the communications window. If you have made important changes to your telephone list, be sure to press Y (for yes) in response to the `Save changes?` prompt when you close the communications window.

an entire 11-digit long-distance number in about one second. This feature is great if your system is connected directly to an outside line (like the ones at your home). But what if you're calling from an office phone that requires you to dial 9 (or some other access number) and then pause for connection to an outside line?

By using one or more commas in a telephone number, you cause Works and the modem to pause in the dialing sequence. For example, if you type

9,1 800 555 1212

the modem dials 9 and then pauses briefly before dialing the rest of the telephone number. To extend the length of the pause, use more commas. The exact length of the pause is determined by your modem. Usually, a comma produces a two-second pause. For example, if you type

9,,1-800-5551212

the system dials 9, waits about four seconds for an outside line, and then dials the telephone number. This "art" is an inexact one, and you need to experiment with the number of commas required to produce a delay that works reliably.

You can use commas and extra numbers at the ends of telephone numbers, too. This capability is helpful if your phone service requires accounting codes for long-distance calls.

## *Autodialing from the Phone Book*

Once you have specified or confirmed the communications settings and entered at least one phone number in your phone list, you're ready to dial another computer. To autodial a number, follow these steps:

1. With your modem turned on, choose Dial from the Communications menu (or press ⌘-D). The phone list appears.

2. Click the Dial button to the left of the number you want to dial.

Works sends setup and dialing instructions to the modem and then clears the window so that you can watch the progress. If your modem has a built-in speaker and it's turned on, you can hear the call's progress as well. When the screen displays the word `CONNECT` (or your modem's message for connection), you're ready to exchange information.

## *Dialing with Non-Hayes Compatible Smart Modems*

Some smart modems have command languages that differ from the Hayes AT standard. By reading the modem manual, you can find out which commands to send to instruct the modem to do things Works cannot do. For example, you may need to send the DIAL command rather than the Hayes ATD command. You can send commands to any smart modem from your keyboard. With an open communications window, your keyboard is connected to your modem. If you type the appropriate commands, your modem will execute them. Refer to your modem manual to learn more about entering commands.

## *Dialing Manually*

If you don't have an autodial modem, you must dial phone numbers on a regular telephone and then "trick" Works. To dial manually, follow these steps:

1. To highlight a Dial button, place a comma in a phone number entry box on the telephone list.
2. Use your telephone to dial the number.
3. Click the Dial button next to the comma to get the modem and Works working together.
4. Listen for a ring followed by a high-pitched tone.
5. Either place the phone handset in the coupler cups (if you're using an acoustic coupler) or hang up the telephone (if you're using a manual direct-connect modem).
6. Communicate.

## *What To Do When a Computer Answers*

If you're using a direct-connect modem that has a speaker, you can tell when another computer answers because you hear a high-pitched, continuous tone or whistling on the line. This tone is called the *carrier*.

Shortly, you hear a second, different tone in addition to the first one. Your modem and the other are trying to agree on a communications speed. If all goes well, the speaker soon mutes, and you see the word CONNECT and perhaps other things on your screen. What happens next depends on what type of computer you have dialed and what you want to accomplish.

If you have dialed another Macintosh that is also using the Works communications feature, and if you both have selected compatible settings and echo techniques, you can start typing. Everything you type appears on the other Macintosh user's screen, and vice versa.

Many non-Works communications packages operate the same way. For example, figure 12.7 shows a typical exchange between Works and Hayes Smartcom II software running on an IBM computer. This exchange could just as easily have taken place between two Macintoshes, or a Macintosh and an Apple II. (Notice that boldfaced, underscored, and other special characters are received as plain text.)

**Fig. 12.7**

*A typical exchange between IBM and Macintosh computers.*

```
Setting modem to answer calls...
ATS0=1

OK

RING

CONNECT

Hi Ron! I am typing this from the keyboard of my IBM PC. How does the
connection look at your end?

Hi! 'Looks great. Go ahead and send the text file.

This is a sample of a file sent from an IBM PC
to the Works Communications option over phone lines.
Notice that all text refinements have been lost:

Bold, Italic, Underscore, Superscript, Subscript

Got it. Thanks & bye!
Hanging Up...

NO CARRIER
```

If your system is connected to a different service, such as GEnie, CompuServe, or a local bulletin board, rather than to another personal computer, you must follow the appropriate procedures to identify yourself to the other system. Usually, these procedures, collectively called *logging on*, include typing an account number, password, and possibly some other information. Consult the manuals for the services you intend to use, or get help from their customer service people.

For example, figure 12.8 illustrates a short session between the Macintosh Works program and the U.S. Department of Commerce's Economic Bulletin Board. When the number is used, the Economic BBS answered, as shown in the first few lines of the figure. All typed responses are shown in boldface type.

```
OK

Dialing...

CONNECT
WELCOME TO ECONOMIC BBS

      THE U.S. DEPARTMENT OF COMMERCE'S ECONOMIC BULLETIN BOARD

This bulletin board service provides current economic news and information
produced by the Department of Commerce and other Federal government agencies.

FULL ACCESS TO THIS SERVICE IS LIMITED TO PAID SUBSCRIBERS WHO HAVE A VALID
ACCOUNT NUMBER, BUT "GUEST" USERS MAY VIEW BULLETINS AND DOWNLOAD TWO FILES
THAT DESCRIBE THE EBB AND HOW TO REGISTER FOR THE SERVICE.

IF YOU ARE A GUEST USER, we suggest you download: 1) FILES - a description
of all files available on the system, and  2) REG-FORM - a registration form
that you can complete and mail.

If you have trouble using this service, please call (202) 377-1986 for
assistance.


What is your FIRST Name? RRoonn
What is your LAST Name? Mansfield
RON MANSFIELD
Is your name correct ([Y],N)? y
What is your ACCOUNT # (GUEST if none)? guest
guest, right (Y=[ENTER],N)? yep
Checking Users...
What is your CITY and STATE? Los Angeles, CA

                              WELCOME

                                TO

      THE U.S. DEPARTMENT OF COMMERCE'S ECONOMIC BULLETIN BOARD

If you are new to using computer bulletin boards, the EBB provides you with
three types of services, reading bulletins, downloading files, and sending
messages to us or receiving messages from us.  Functions available on other
computer bulletin board services such as uploading files or sending messages to other
users are not available on this service.

Press [ENTER] to continue? (Return)

BULLETINS will provide you with general economic news, a calendar of release
dates for upcoming economic news, contacts in economic statistical agencies,
and instructions on how to use the bulletin board. (etc.)
                              THANK YOU FOR USING
                           THE ECONOMIC BULLETIN BOARD

RON MANSFIELD from LOS ANGELES, CA
<C>hange name/address, <D>isconnect, <R>egister? d
b'\=E dm2a(#
NO CARRIER
```

**Fig. 12.8**

*Communications with the U.S. government's ECO BBS on-line.*

Note that the BBS requested identification. If the log-on user had been a registered user, the system would have required an account number and possibly a password. Because this user was just a visitor on this friendlier-than-usual system, a name was enough.

Notice also that it was necessary to change the Echo On/Off setting on the Communications menu to eliminate the double characters that appeared when the other computer "echoed back" what was typed. This echo occurred when the first name was typed. Both the government computer and my Macintosh were putting characters on the screen.

After identification, the service explained its features. The explanation fills more than one screen on most computers, so the BBS paused to let the user read the first screen. (Not all services have this capability.) At times like this, the Works scrolling feature comes in handy. When ready to continue, press the Return key to see the next screen.

The BBS then gave the user the chance to register as a regular user. The user declined, and the BBS hung up (disconnected itself from the telephone line). The garbage that followed (`b'\=E` and so on at the bottom of the figure) appeared because the BBS hung up. When the smart modem detected the government computer's disconnection, the modem displayed `NO CARRIER` and also hung up.

## *Hanging Up*

Most smart modems hang up automatically if the connection to the other computer is broken. If, however, you reach a wrong number, make a bad connection, hear a busy signal when you dial a number, or finish exchanging data, *you* may have to hang up. Either choose the Hang Up command from the Communications menu, or press ⌘-= (the equal sign). Works then tells your smart modem to disconnect. You see the message `Hanging Up`, +++ and probably something like `NO CARRIER`.

Closing the communications window may also cause your modem to hang up. If you're quick, however, you can reopen the window and return to your session.

A problem on the phone line can cause one or both systems to hang up without asking you first. If you have call waiting, you lose your session whenever an incoming call signals. Not all phone systems support this procedure, so check with your phone company to see what procedure they use to disable call waiting.

To hang up a dumb modem, choose the Hang Up option on the Communications menu. If you're using an acoustic coupler, simply hang up the telephone.

# Transmitting Data

Now that you have learned the necessary communications terms, the settings you need, and how to use the phone book and your modem, you are ready to transmit data. You can send messages just by typing. You also can send and receive files—both simple and complex.

## Sending Text from Your Keyboard

The process of sending text from a computer keyboard is perhaps the easiest of all data exchanges. Once your system is connected to a compatible computer, you simply type as usual. What you type appears almost simultaneously on both your computer screen and that of the other machine. Likewise, anything typed at the other end appears on your screen. Figure 12.9 illustrates this process. Obviously, you and the user on the other end need to take turns typing. If you both type at once, your screens will be illegible.

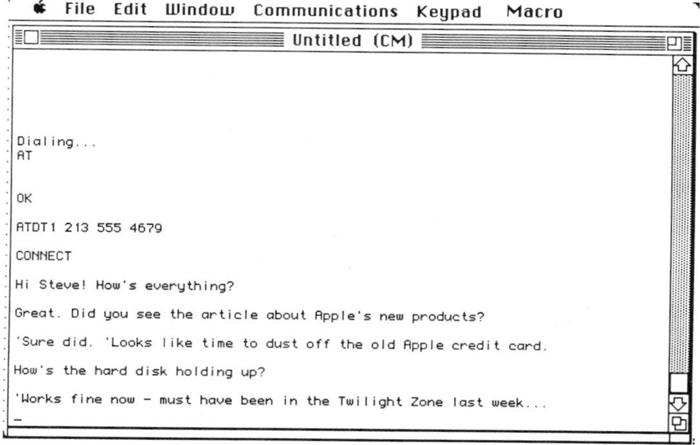


**Fig. 12.9**

*Keyboard data exchange.*

Why type to each other when you can talk over the same telephone line instead? One reason is to let someone know that you're ready to send or receive a file. Typing back and forth this way is easier than picking up the telephone and talking—something that may be impossible if the computers are already connected over your only telephone line.

**TIP:** Typing is also a great communications tool for the deaf. Works should be compatible with most TTY terminals for the deaf. You may want to start with the 300-baud setting when testing compatibility. Your Macintosh also contains features for the physically impaired that enable a person to communicate with just one finger active. This capability is included in the Apple system software as the program Easy Access. In addition, the Apple system software program Close View provides a magnified view of the screen for the visually impaired.

Many bulletin boards and computer services such as CompuServe and The Source have "round tables" in which multiple users log on simultaneously and take turns discussing topics of common interest through their keyboards. These people think typing is more fun than talking.

In summary, to exchange keyboard data, use the following procedure:

1. Open a communications document and dial the other computer. Log on, if necessary.
2. When the computers are connected, take turns typing and reading.
3. Hang up by choosing the Hang Up option on the Communications menu or by pressing ⌘-=.
4. Close the communications window.

## *Sending Simple Text Files*

Before making the telephone connection, you can prepare plain text to be sent. To send a simple text file, follow these steps:

1. Create a word processing file, and save the file to disk.
2. Open a communications document and connect with the other computer.
3. Select the Send Text command from the Communications menu. The Send Text dialog box then appears, with the usual Open (SF Get) dialog box, as shown in figure 12.10.
4. Select the file to send and then click OK, or double-click the file name.

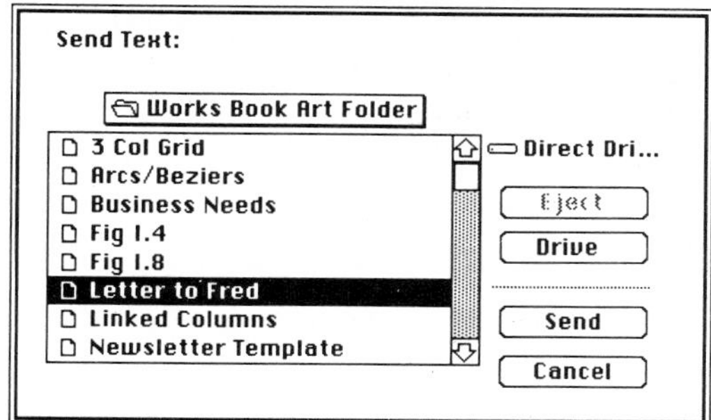


**Fig. 12.10**

*The Send Text dialog box.*

5. Watch the text transfer.
6. Continue with other communications or hang up.

**NOTE:** You cannot send pictures and text attributes with this technique. Some receiving systems ignore or are confused by special Macintosh characters and accent marks. Text is sometimes sent without line feeds (depending on the ASCII format used), which can cause the receiving computer to display lines one on top of the other. If the recipient saves the text to disk and looks at the text with a word processing package, however, everything should be all right.

The program Vantage DA offers such a filtering feature, stripping line feeds (when needed) from ASCII text. Vantage DA offers a host of other utility features. Additionally, a large number of shareware and freeware programs that offer these conversions are available from vendors on BBSs.

## Sending Complex Files

When sending files that contain more complicated text, or programs, or anything with formatting structure, you use the Send File command rather than Send Text. Send File enables you to send almost anything that you can save on a Macintosh disk. Figure 12.11 shows the Send File dialog box.

Before you can take advantage of this capability to send complex files, the communications software on both ends must be compatible. Moreover, the receiving computer must be compatible with the files that you send if they're to be useful at that end. For example, sending a

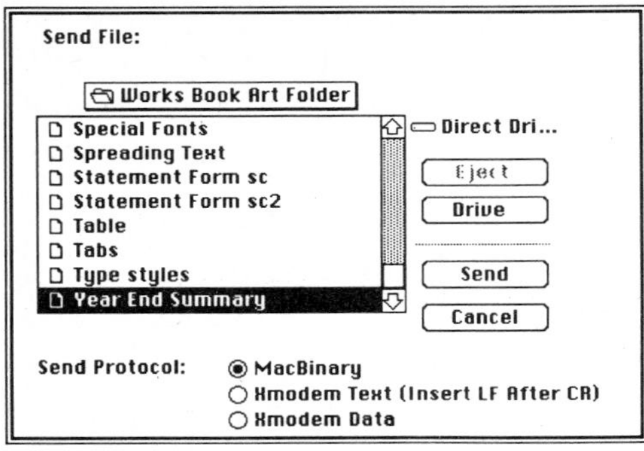


**Fig. 12.11**

*The Send File dialog box.*

Works spreadsheet file to someone who doesn't own a compatible spreadsheet program does little good.

## *Using the Proper Protocol*

These complex exchanges use one of three Xmodem protocols. As mentioned previously, a *protocol* is a set of data-exchange procedures and rules that two computers use together. The computers usually handle this exchange without your intervention, once you get things rolling. Xmodem protocols were designed to facilitate relatively fast and error-free exchanges of complex files containing pictures, control codes, text, and just about anything else found on a disk. The original Xmodem protocol has a number of variations, and Works supports three of them: MacBinary, Xmodem Text (Insert LF After CR), and Xmodem Data.

You make your choice of protocol in the Send File and Receive File dialog boxes, which you access through the Communications menu. Both computers should be using the same protocol. If you try to send or receive data with the wrong protocol, you don't harm your data or your computer. Works simply informs you of problems as it attempts to perform the exchange you have requested.

The *MacBinary* protocol is an Xmodem protocol used by Macintosh computers and others. This protocol is also the one that Works automatically uses to exchange Works files of any kind. In figure 12.12, Works is trying to transmit a file named *Screen 4*, using the MacBinary protocol. Works has checked the size of the disk file and specifies that the file will be sent in 52 chunks, or blocks. MacBinary is the only protocol that transfers the resource fork with the file.

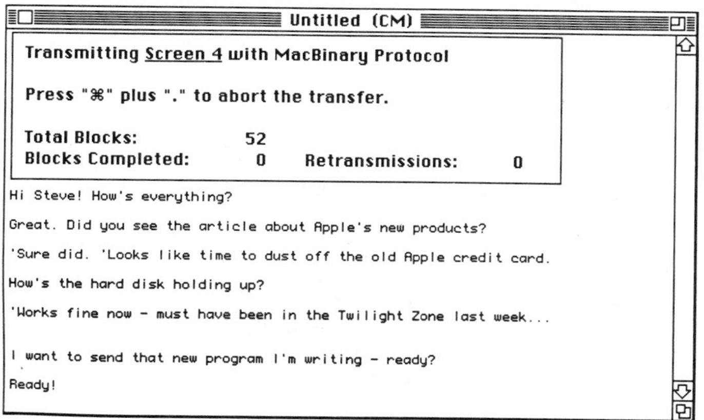


**Fig. 12.12**

*File transmission when using the MacBinary protocol.*

Note that Works tells you how many blocks have been sent successfully (none, in this example) and how many times blocks need to be sent again because of transmission errors. If Works keeps trying to send and resend most blocks, you may have a bad telephone connection or incompatible communications software. To abort an Xmodem file transfer, press ⌘-. (period).

Use the *Xmodem Text* protocol at both ends if you're going to exchange text with a non-Macintosh system. Don't try to exchange formats, pictures, and so on.

Try using the *Xmodem Data* protocol if your Macintosh is connected to non-Macintosh systems and you're sending programs and other files that contain more than just simple text.

## *Following the Step-by-Step Procedure*

To send a complex file or program, with associated formatting or graphics, follow these steps:

1. Locate the files you plan to send.
2. Open a communications window, and connect with the other computer.
3. Select Send File, and pick the correct protocol.
4. Specify the file to send and then click Send, or double-click the file name.
5. Watch the screen as the transfer progresses.
6. Continue with other communications, or hang up.

## *Receiving and Storing Simple Text*

If you check the Capture Text When Document Opens option when you complete the Communications Settings dialog box, Works gives you the opportunity to capture incoming text to disk. After you click OK or press Return in that dialog box, Works asks whether you want to create a text file of your communications session. This feature is only available with Works Version 2.0. Previous versions do not prompt you to capture text. To capture text for an entire session, use the following procedure:

1. Create a new communications document (or open an existing one).
2. If a new document is opened, open the Settings dialog box, make your choices, and be sure to check the Capture Text When Document Opens box.
3. Click OK.
4. When opening a new document, a Capture Text dialog box appears automatically. For a previously saved communications document, you must select the Text Capture command on the Communications menu to bring up this dialog box. The Capture Text dialog box is a Save As (SF Put) dialog box.
5. Works uses *Captured Text* as the default file name for storage. Change this name to something more suitable for your data if you prefer.

3\. Click Capture or double-click the file name.

4\. Choose End Text Capture when you're finished with your session.

You can use the resulting Capture Text dialog box (see fig. 12.13) to place the file of captured text on the appropriate disk and in the appropriate folder in your directory.

A file of captured text is a standard Works word processor document. You do not, however, have to capture text for the entire session. To capture text for only part of a session, follow these steps:

1. Create a new communications document (or open an existing one), specify your settings, and leave the Capture Text When Document Opens box unchecked.

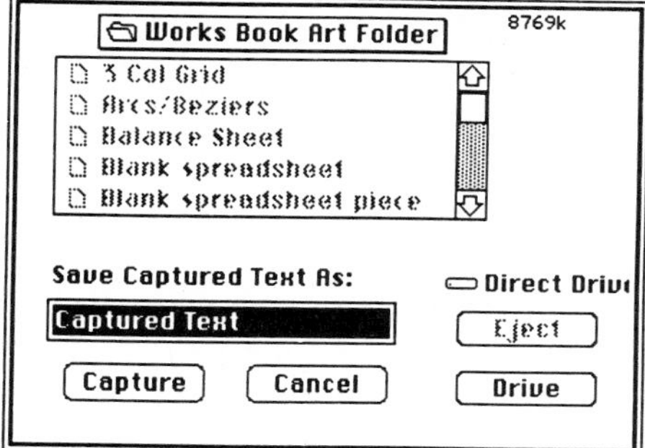


**Fig. 12.13**

*The Capture Text dialog box.*

2. Click the OK button.
3. Start your session and connect with the other computer.
4. To start saving text, choose the Capture Text command from the Communications menu.
5. Type a name for your file in the Capture Text dialog box, and click the Capture button.
6. Select End Text Capture from the Communications menu when you have received all the text in which you are interested.

You can still continue to receive text after you select End Text Capture.

## *Receiving and Storing Complex Files*

Part of the great fun of using information services is discovering new games, utilities, or even updated versions of software you want. After you have established a connection and the sender is prepared to transmit files, select Receive File from the Communications menu. Works then proposes a file name (XModem File), which you can change. Choose the appropriate protocol (see the section on "Sending Complex Files"), keeping in mind that the protocols must be the same for both computers. Then click the Receive button. Works and the other system take it from there, informing you of progress and problems.

## *Compressing Files*

Most computer programs and the files they create are composed of data and an underlying instruction set called *resources*. Programs have been created to strip unneeded resources or information from files on bulletin boards, which condenses or compresses the programs and thus lowers the cost of transmission. This process creates an artificial file that can be reconstituted by a companion program.

The two programs most commonly in use are StuffIt and PackIt, with companion programs called, not surprisingly, UnStuffIt and UnPackIt. The programs are shareware and are normally kept on bulletin boards for you to download. You pay a nominal cost if you decide to keep them and use them. There is no fee for using StuffIt to unstuff a file. You can determine whether a file on a bulletin board is in the compressed form by examining the file's extension. If the extension is .SIT or .PIT, the file has been compressed by StuffIt or PackIt. For example, the file named WORKS.SIT would be Works stuffed by StuffIt.

Although the actions of these file compression programs are beyond the scope of this book, their documentation is generally self-explanatory. StuffIt is among the most useful programs you can own for telecommunications.

## *Printing Incoming Information*

Use the File menu's Print Window option to print the contents of the communications window. You can print only one screenful of word processing communications information. But if you get stuck, you can take MacPaint screen shots (using ⌘-Shift-3, INITs like Capture, or the DA Camera) and later print those.

If, for any reason, you think that you may need to print more than a screenful of incoming information, use the Capture Text feature at the beginning of your session. Then open the resulting text file with the Works word processor to print what was sent and received. If you don't remember to use Capture Text, you can copy and paste text from the communications window to a word processing window. In the communications window, select the text you want to copy and use the Copy command (⌘-C) to copy text to the Clipboard. Go to the desired destination and paste (⌘-V) the text there. This approach, however, is limited and cumbersome compared to the Capture Text feature.

## Using Control Codes and Special Function Keys

Just as you use special key combinations and function keys on your Macintosh for word processing and other tasks, other computer-terminal users do equivalent things with their keyboards. For example, the operator of a teletype can ring the bell on another teletype by pressing Control-G, a keystroke sequence sometimes called the ASCII BEL function.

When you are connected to commercial services like CompuServe, The Source, and Delphi, you may be required to transmit the control characters that activate some of the functions of that service. Some of these are IBM PC (MS-DOS) derived. To transmit a control character (with the Apple extended keyboard) in Works, hold down the ⌘ key and press whatever character is required. For example, to transmit a Control-C character, hold down the ⌘ and Control keys while pressing the C key. Other important combinations you may need to use include ⌘-Option-3 (the Break key), ⌘-Option-Delete (the Delete key), and ⌘-Option-[ (the Escape key).

The control codes and special function keys that you may be asked to send include BEL (rings the bell or beeps the beeper), Backspace (BS), TAB, Form Feed (FF), any of the device control codes (DC1-DC4), Escape (ESC), and BREAK. Table 12.1 lists the popular control codes and special function keys and also shows how to send the codes from Works. For all these codes, you hold down the Option or Control key and press the key indicated in the last column of the table.

**NOTE:** With the exception of sending the ampersand (&), you don't need to press the Shift key when sending control codes. Lowercase letters work just fine.

Many other control codes and special function keys are used on terminals such as the VT-100 and VT-52. You use the Keypad menu when you need to send VT-100 and VT-52 special function key codes. To send a code, pull down the menu and point to the number or code you want to send. The key is then highlighted, as shown in figure 12.14. Releasing the mouse button sends the selected code. The VT-100 and VT-52 functions and keys are listed in table 12.2.

**Table 12.1**
**ASCII Control Codes**

| *ASCII* | *Mnemonic* | *Hex Value* | *Hold down Option or Control key* and press* |
|---|---|---|---|
| NUL | @ | 00 | @ |
| SOH | A | 01 | a |
| STX | B | 02 | b |
| ETX | C | 03 | c |
| EOT | D | 04 | d |
| ENQ | E | 05 | e |
| ACK | F | 06 | f |
| BEL | G | 07 | g |
| BS | H | 08 | h |
| TAB | I | 09 | i |
| LF | J | 0A | j |
| VT | K | 0B | k |
| FF | L | 0C | l |
| CR | M | 0D | m |
| SO | N | 0E | n |
| SI | O | 0F | o |
| DEL | P | 10 | p |
| DC1(Xon) | Q | 11 | q |
| DC2 | R | 12 | r |
| DC3(Xoff) | S | 13 | s |
| DC4 | T | 14 | t |
| NAK | U | 15 | u |
| SYN | V | 16 | v |
| ETB | W | 17 | w |
| CAN | X | 18 | x |
| EM | Y | 19 | y |
| SUB | Z | 1A | z |
| ESC | [ | 1B | [ |
| FS | | 1C | |
| GS | | 1D | |
| BREAK | 3 | | 3 |

*Older Macintoshes don't have a Control key. Use the Option key instead.

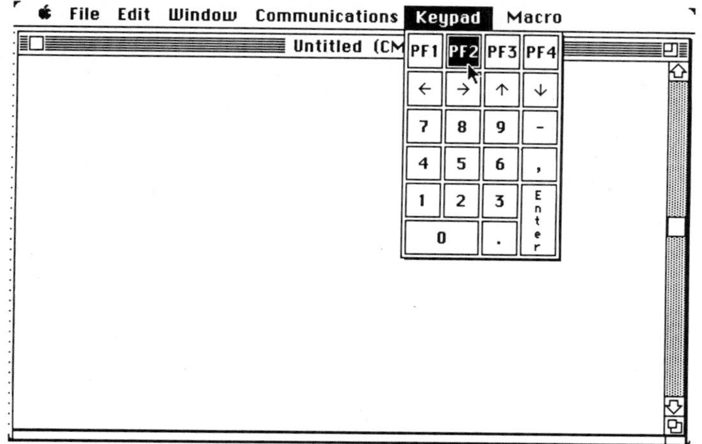


**Fig. 12.14**

*The pull-down communications keypad.*

**Table 12.2**
**VT-100 and VT-52 Functions and Keys**

| *Key or Function* | *To Use from Works* |
|---|---|
| 132-column mode | Not currently available |
| Smooth scrolling | Not currently available |
| Split screen | Not currently available |
| Double-high characters | Not currently available |
| Double-wide characters | Not currently available |
| PF1 | Click PF1 on Keypad menu |
| PF2 | Click PF2 on Keypad menu |
| PF3 | Click PF3 on Keypad menu |
| PF4 | Click PF4 on Keypad menu |
| PRINT ENTER | Click Enter on Keypad menu |
| Up arrow | Click ↑ on Keypad menu |
| Down arrow | Click ↓ on Keypad menu |
| Right arrow | Click → on Keypad menu |
| Left arrow | Click ← on Keypad menu |
| Switch key | Not currently available |

When connected to a host computer while your computer is emulating a VT-52 or VT-100 terminal, any one of the escape codes listed in table 12.3 may be sent to you. The last column in the table explains the function of the escape code.

**Table 12.3**
**VT-100 and VT-52 Escape Codes**

| *Group* | *Sequence* | *Function* |
|---|---|---|
| Cursor | ESC [ Pn Z | Cursor backwards by tab |
| Cursor | ESC [ Pn I | Cursor horizontal tabulation |
| Cursor | Tab | Move to next tab stop |
| Edit | ESC [ Pn M | Delete line |
| Edit | ESC [ Pn L | Insert line |
| Mode | ESC [ > 5 l | Reset Modes-cursor on |
| Mode | ESC [ ? 1 h | Set cursor key application mode |
| Mode | ESC [ ? 1 l | Set cursor key normal mode |
| Report | ESC [ 0 c | Device reports-response ESC [ ? 1;2c |
| Report | ESC [ 6 n | Request cursor position report |
| Report | ESC [ 5 n | Request device status report-ESC [ 0 n |
| Report | ESC Z | VT-100 Who are you—response is ESC [ ? 1;2c |
| Reset | ESC c | Reset to power-up state |
| Reset | ESC [ Ps z | Reset to power-up state |
| Reset | ESC [ ! p | Soft terminal reset |
| Tab | ESC [ 3 g | Clear all tab stops |
| Tab | ESC [ 5 w | Clear all tabs |
| Tab | ESC [ 0 g | Clear tab at current position |
| Tab | ESC [ 2 W | Clear tab at current position |
| Tab | ESC H | Set tab |
| Tab | ESC [ 0 W | Set tab at current position |
| Edit | ESC [ Pn P | Delete char |
| Edit | ESC [ Pn X | Erase char |
| Edit | ESC [ Pn @ | Insert char |
| Erase | ESC [ 2 J | Erase entire display (shift erase); position cursor in home position |
| Erase | ESC [ 2 K | Erase entire line, including cursor position |
| Erase | ESC [ 1 J | Erase from start of display to cursor, including cursor |
| Erase | ESC [ 1 K | Erase from start of line, including cursor position |
| Erase | ESC [ 0 J | Erase to end of page (erase key) |

**Table 12.3—*continued***

| *Group* | *Sequence* | *Function* |
|---|---|---|
| Erase | ESC [ 0 K | Erase from cursor to end of line, including cursor position |
| Erase | ESC [ ? 2 J | Selective erase entire display (shift erase); position cursor in home line |
| Erase | ESC [ ? 2 K | Selective erase entire line, including cursor position |
| Erase | ESC [ ? 0 K | Selective erase from cursor to end of line, including cursor position |
| Erase | ESC [ ? 1 J | Selective erase from start of display to cursor, including cursor |
| Erase | ESC [ ? 1 K | Selective erase from start of line, including cursor position |
| Erase | ESC [ 0 J | Selective erase to end of page (erase key) |
| Mode | ESC [4 l | Disable insert char mode |
| Mode | ESC [ 4 h | Enable insert char mode |
| Cursor | LF | Advance cursor to next line |
| Cursor | ESC [ Pl;PC f | Cursor addressing |
| Cursor | ESC [ Pn B | Cursor down constrain |
| Cursor | ESC [ Pn G | Cursor horizontal absolute |
| Cursor | ESC [ Pn D | Cursor left constrain |
| Cursor | ESC [ Pn E | Cursor next line |
| Cursor | ESC [ Pl;Pc H | Direct cursor positioning |
| Cursor | ESC [ Pn F | Cursor preceding line |
| Cursor | ESC [ Pn C | Cursor right constrain |
| Cursor | ESC [ Pn A | Cursor up constrain |
| Cursor | ESC D | Index—moves cursor down, functions in same manner as LF |
| Cursor | BS | Move back one char and erase |
| Cursor | CR | Move to beginning of line |
| Cursor | ESC E | NewLine function (CR-LF) |
| Cursor | ESC [ u | Restore cursor |
| Cursor | ESC 8 | Restore cursor position and attributes |

**Table 12.3**—*continued*

| *Group* | *Sequence* | *Function* |
|---|---|---|
| Cursor | ESC M | Reverse index—moves cursor to the same position on the preceding line; will not move if at top |
| Cursor | ESC [ s | Save cursor |
| Cursor | ESC 7 | Save cursor position and attributes |
| Mode | ESC = | Alternate keypad mode |
| Mode | ESC [ ? 20 l | Disable auto LF on CR |
| Mode | ESC [ ? 7 l | Disable auto-wrap mode |
| Mode | ESC [ ? 25 h | Disable cursor |
| Mode | ESC > | Disable keypad alternate mode |
| Mode | ESC [ ? 20 h | Enable auto LF on CR |
| Mode | ESC [ ? 7 h | Enable auto-wrap mode |
| Mode | ESC [ 25 l | Enable cursor |
| Mode | ESC [ 20 l | Reset CR on LF |
| Mode | ESC [ > 1 l | Reset modes—disable 25th line |
| Mode | ESC [ > 7 l | Reset modes—exit alternate keypad mode |
| Mode | ESC [ > 9 l | Reset modes—no auto CR on LF |
| Mode | ESC [ > 8 l | Reset modes—no auto LF on CR |
| Mode | ESC [ 20 h | Set CR on LF |
| Mode | ESC [ > 7 h | Set modes—alternate keypad mode |
| Mode | ESC [ > 9 h | Set modes—auto CR on LF |
| Mode | ESC [ > 8 h | Set modes—auto LF on CR |
| Mode | ESC [ > 5 h | Set modes—cursor off |
| Mode | ESC [ > 1 h | Set modes—enable 25th line |
| Erase | FF | Form feed (clear screen) |
| | BELL | Sound Bell |

# *Protecting Your Computer from Viruses*

A *virus* is a computer program that when loaded onto your disk causes your system to fail in some way. The ways in which a virus can corrupt your files, damage your system, or disrupt your resources and work are limited only by the imagination and skill of the programmers who choose to write them. Viruses have been around since the advent of computers, but at the time of this writing they are still rare, and most are benign.

As an example of a virus, imagine a computer program that, once copied to your disk, contains information to reproduce itself continually. After some time your entire disk would be full, and you would no longer be able to continue work. Another virus might simply remove or alter resources that your programs need in order to operate. Many of the common viruses work by attempting to alter the directory (desktop file). Still others are pranks that do no more than place a screen message on your Macintosh or perform similar nondamaging tricks. The Macintosh community has been quite vocal about viruses and their detection and eradication.

A sad fact of life is that if you use a bulletin board and download files, you should check them for known viruses. Screening almost eliminates the possibility that your computer will become infected. The sections that follow discuss the various options for screening and removing any viruses that you might find.

Several commercial, shareware, and freeware products that enable you to check for the presence of known viruses are currently on the market. Some of these programs (the ones that are either freeware or shareware) are distributed on bulletin boards as a public service. Among the recommended shareware or freeware products are

- Virus Detective, Version 2.1.1, a DA
- Vaccine from CE Software, Version 1.0, a CDEV and an INIT
- Interferon, Version 3.01, an application
- Virus RX, Version 1.4a1, an Apple program
- GateKeeper, Version 1.0, a CDEV
- Ferret, Version 1.1, an application

All these products check for one or more known viruses. Additionally, the product Symantec Utilities for the Macintosh (SUM) contains an INIT called Guardian that checks for viruses which try to alter your directory file.

Recently, commercial products have been released that are supposed to counter *all* known viruses. The publishers of these products make the effort of updating the programs as soon as any new virus is brought to their attention. Programs in this category include the following:

- ❏ Virex from HJC Software, Version 1.2, an application
- ❏ AntiToxin from Mainstay, Version 1.1, an INIT and application
- ❏ Anti-Virus Kit from 1st Aid Software, Version 1.0, a CDEV and application set

The best way to avoid catching a virus in your computer is to install one or several of these virus-detection programs, which operate automatically. They tell you if anything you have downloaded is infected, and enable you to purge the virus. You also can download onto a floppy disk and examine the disk by using a detection program *immediately*, but especially before running the downloaded program. Any utility that locks the disks or hard drives you want to protect while you are examining your downloaded files is useful.

**TIP:** The best protection is to BACK UP YOUR FILES (twice if possible), assuming that your backup files have not been infected with the virus. You should also write-protect your original program disks as soon as you get them. (To write-protect a disk, open the plastic tab in the upper right corner of the floppy so that the window shows.)

## *Running Communications in the Background*

While in Works, you can set up and download a communications file and switch into another Works module. When you return to the communications document, your downloading should be either continuing or finished. Operating in the background slows down the transfer process.

If you use MultiFinder, you also can use Works in the background and not tie up your computer. Start capturing the file and then put that session in the background by using another application. When you return, your session should be either complete or continuing. You may want to refer to the Apple Macintosh MultiFinder manual for more information.

## Letting Works Answer the Phone

If your direct-connect modem has a Hayes-compatible autoanswer feature and you enable it, Works and your hardware can answer incoming calls made by other computers. If the other caller has Works or compatible software, the caller can send files to your Macintosh disks, or download files from your disks to the caller's system. This process can take place while you use Works for something else or even when you're away from your computer. Some users use this capability to take advantage of low late-night and early-morning long-distance telephone rates.

To set up Works to answer the phone automatically, do the following:

1. Turn on the modem.
2. Open a communications document.
3. Choose the Answer Phone command from the Communications menu.
4. Watch Works set up your modem for auto-answer.
5. Do other Works projects if you want, but don't close the communications window or quit Works.

As long as you leave the communications window open and the Answer Phone option checked on the Communications menu, Works and your modem answer the telephone and try to establish communications with the caller. They accomplish this task by sending a high-pitched carrier tone, which other modems recognize and respond to.

If you plan to use the autoanswer feature regularly, you need a separate telephone line for this purpose. You don't want your computer to answer calls from humans—unless they're bill collectors or oil lease salespeople.

## Disabling Autoanswer

To disable autoanswer mode, use *any* of the following techniques:

- ❑ Remove the check mark from the Answer Phone command in the Communications menu by selecting the command again
- ❑ Close the communications window

- Turn off the modem
- Quit Works

## Security Considerations

Autoanswer is a powerful and desirable feature, but it presents some obvious security risks. Works offers no password protection, so unauthorized computerists could obtain copies of your important files. Intentional damage, although unlikely, is possible. For obvious reasons, destructive techniques are not described here, but some security precautions are outlined.

The modem itself is your first line of defense. Get in the habit of turning off the modem when you're not using it. If you never intend to use the modem's autoanswer feature, disable it. Read the modem manual. Some manufacturers provide a DIP switch that disables answer mode. Other makers (such as Apple) disable autoanswer with software commands you can send through Works. In fact, Works does this disabling for you.

# Communications Tips and Techniques

This section contains tips and techniques for using Works in certain communications situations, such as when you have call waiting on your phone, or you are using an extension phone. You also learn what happens when you try to use your modem on a phone connected to a central telephone system. Finally, you learn how to simplify and speed up complicated log-on procedures.

## The Case for Multiple Communications Documents

You should remember that if you store multiple computer telephone numbers in a document's phone list, a single group of settings applies to all numbers. Although each communications document can accommodate as many as eight telephone numbers, some computers require settings different from those needed by other computers. You therefore may need to create multiple communications documents even if you regularly call fewer than eight different computers. Then, you can save the telephone numbers of computers that have similar settings in a file containing the appropriate settings. For example, you might create a file for 1200-baud computers and another for 2400-baud numbers. Simply use the Save As choice from the File menu to create separate documents that you can use either with different settings or with different bulletin boards. Use meaningful file names like 1200BPS ECHO or 300BPS VT100 4screens.

## *Disabling Call Waiting*

If your phone line has a call-waiting feature that beeps when someone is trying to reach you while you're using the phone, problems will arise when you're communicating. This problem is a general one and not specific to Works.

When using a modem, you need to disable the call-waiting feature temporarily, or get a separate phone line that does not have call waiting. Otherwise, you must put up with the aggravation of having call waiting garble your transmissions or cause disconnections.

Ask your telephone company how you can disable call waiting temporarily by yourself. In many areas, you can accomplish this task by dialing *70 (asterisk, seven, zero) on touch-tone phones. You can add this string to the telephone numbers in the Works telephone list. You may need to add a comma or two to incorporate a pause. For instance, if you have touch-tone service, a number in your phone list might be

*70,,555 1212

If you have a pulse-dialing (rotary-dial) line, try dialing 1170 (one, one, seven, zero) to defeat call waiting temporarily. Rotary-dial customers might use the following number in the phone list:

1170,,555 1212

When disabling call waiting, don't hang up after entering the disable instructions. Wait until you hear the disable confirmation tone; then dial the computer number immediately. You may need to vary the number of commas, and therefore the length of the pause, to give your phone company's equipment enough time to disable call waiting and send the confirmation tone. Experiment, pioneers, experiment.

When you (or your modem) finish communicating and hang up, the call-waiting feature probably will be re-enabled automatically, so you will have to disable call waiting every time you use the modem. The easy way is to add the disable command to every phone number in your phone lists.

## Using a Modem with Other Telephone Extensions

When you're using your modem and someone picks up an extension phone, information exchange may be garbled or aborted. If asking people to keep their hands off the telephones doesn't help, get a separate modem line or check with a phone store for devices that lock out other extensions when you're using your modem.

## Handling Multiline Installations

Most direct-connect modems require a single-line modular telephone jack, which most telephone companies call an RJ-11. If you have a two-line phone (an RJ-14) or a multiline business phone, you probably need an adapter. Check with Radio Shack or a local telephone store for these items.

## PBX Considerations

If you have an electronic or other central phone system in your office, you may want to get a separate outside line for the modem. If you cannot do so, you may need a special adapter for your modem. Your office phone jack may not be an RJ-11, even if it looks like the one you have at home. Contact the makers or sellers of your telephone equipment for details. Your life will be much simpler if you don't run your modem through the office telephone-switching equipment.

Some PBX systems are pretty "impatient": They expect you to begin dialing promptly after getting an outside line. Certain combinations of modem types or commas in your phone list don't work well with some PBX systems. For example, a smart modem (or comma-laden phone number) that takes a long time to start dialing after requesting an outside line may find that the PBX "got bored" and took back the line for use by someone else.

If you suspect that this problem is happening, try removing unnecessary commas in phone lists. Or try having the phone repair person extend the amount of time that the PBX waits for you to start dialing. Most PBX systems can be modified this way, but you may need to persist to get someone to make the necessary changes. A better approach is to avoid the PBX altogether and get an outside line hooked directly to your modem.

## *Using Automated Log-On Procedures*

Logging on to CompuServe and other services can be fairly time-consuming. You need to remember codes and passwords and account numbers. Some communications programs remember all these procedures for you; you simply replay "scripts" that perform the log-on for you. Perhaps the most useful communications macro you can write is one that will automatically log on for you.

You may also consider the purchase of a program like Navigator, which will automate a session with your commercial service. This program creates a directory of programs and places that you want to visit in your session, and automatically downloads lists of files, thus saving you money.

# *Examining the Most Common Communications Problems*

Thousands of things can go wrong with a data communications setup, but millions of successful data calls are made each day. Once you get the hang of it, data communications are easy. A few problems, however, seem to crop up regularly, particularly for first-time users. These problems are outlined in the following sections, along with some suggested solutions.

## *Modem Doesn't Respond*

Check to see that the modem is on and plugged into a working outlet. Also make sure that the cable connecting the modem to the computer is secure at both ends. And be certain that Works knows which Macintosh connector you're using for the modem (check the Communications Settings dialog box), as shown in figure 12.15. If your modem is connected to the printer port, or if your printer driver is connected to your modem port, you may see an alert box like the one shown in figure 12.15.

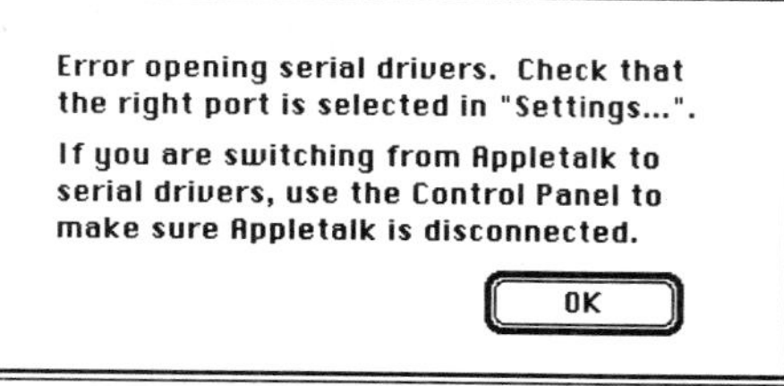

Error opening serial drivers. Check that the right port is selected in "Settings...".
If you are switching from Appletalk to serial drivers, use the Control Panel to make sure Appletalk is disconnected.
OK


**Fig. 12.15**

*An alert box for an incorrectly connected modem.*

Turn off the modem, wait a second, and turn the modem back on again. This sequence of steps is a necessity with smart modems when they get "confused." If you have never used the modem with your computer before, be sure that the modem is truly Hayes-compatible. Suspect the cable. Get dealer help.

## No Dial Tone

Check both ends of the phone cable running between the wall and the modem. If your modem has two jacks, make sure that you have used the right jack on the back of the modem. Also be sure that someone else isn't using the line and has placed a caller on hold.

Check the wall jack (and any phone-line extension cord you're using) with a regular telephone. If you have never used the modem with this particular jack, suspect the jack. Check your modem manual. Most modems need RJ-11, single-line, modular phone jacks. If you have a multiline jack, you may need an inexpensive adapter. Many electronic business phone systems use jacks that look like RJ-11 modular jacks but aren't electrically compatible.

## The Other Computer Does Not Answer

Double-check the telephone list. You may have made a typo.

If a typo is not the problem, call a human who knows the other computer's status. That computer may be down for servicing. Some services have restricted operating hours as well. Moreover, telephone numbers are sometimes changed for security or technical reasons. Privately owned BBS systems disappear frequently. Operators lose interest, their equipment breaks, they move away to college—you name it. Ask around at users' meetings and on other bulletin boards.

## Screen Contents Garbled or Computers Disconnect

For computers to be able to communicate, they both must have compatible settings (communications parameters). If the computers disconnect, try talking to a human at the other end. Match baud rates, type of parity checking, data length (that is, word length), and so on. Write down the settings or create a separate communications document for later use.

Expect minor compatibility problems when exchanging text with dissimilar computers, particularly if your text or the other person's contains foreign characters, accent marks, and so on. So-called standards aren't standard.

If text transmissions appear fine for a while and then start to look garbled, or if the computers hang up for no apparent reason, suspect the telephone connection. This problem is a big one in rural areas—and during electrical storms. Another culprit is extension telephones. If another person in your building picks up an extension on the same line as your modem, your text will be scrambled. Try redialing or waiting for a while.

## Cannot Log On

If the telephone rings and a computer answers but does not let you log on, check for the following potential causes:

- *Incorrect entry of name and password.* Have you entered your name and password properly? Some systems are case-sensitive. That is, they may require passwords in all uppercase or all lowercase letters.

- *Front-end problems.* Sometimes the log-on process requires communication through a money-saving "front-end" computer service such as Telenet. The front-end computer may be working, but the second computer, which is the one you want to communicate with (CompuServe, for instance), may be down for service. Sometimes the important computer is available, but the front-end computer cannot reach the other computer because of problems at the front end. Try a different front end (for example, Tymnet), dial the important computer directly, or call back later.

## *Xmodem File Transfers Don't Work*

Not all Xmodem protocols are compatible. This lack is the "standards" problem again. Try different Xmodem combinations on both ends. Your best bet, when possible, is to communicate from Works to Works, using MacBinary.

## *Works Doesn't Autoanswer*

If Works doesn't autoanswer when the telephone rings, make sure that the modem is connected to the line that is ringing. Some modems have switches and software commands that disable the autoanswer feature. Check your modem manual. Bad cables may make the modem "think" your Macintosh isn't ready to take calls. See your dealer. The modem may be set to answer after a number of rings rather than on the first ring. Have callers let the phone ring longer, or read the modem manual and set the modem to answer sooner.

# *Chapter Summary*

This chapter explained a very useful and interesting feature of Works: the communications module. You learned how, with a modem and Works, you can use your computer to communicate with other computer users by using bulletin board systems. In addition, the chapter told you how to use Works to obtain information from on-line databases.

## Part VII

# Integrating Applications

## Includes

Tying It All Together

Using Works with Other Products

13

# Tying It All Together

Now that you know how to create spreadsheets, graphs, word processing documents, databases, and communication documents, you are ready to learn how to use the different capabilities together. The process is sometimes referred to as *integration* or *information sharing.*

Works offers two ways to share information between windows: copying and merging. Throughout this book, you have learned about using the Clipboard and the Scrapbook to cut, copy, and paste. To prompt your memory of these topics, you may want to review the sections on "Working with the Clipboard" and "Working with the Scrapbook" in Chapter 1, and "Importing and Exporting Graphics" in Chapter 4. In this chapter, you add to your understanding of the use of the Clipboard, Scrapbook, and other information-sharing tools. You also see how to use Works to merge database and word processing documents.

Frequently you will want to move information from module to module. You will most likely find that the word processor contains the most flexibility for formatting, drawing, aligning, and merging and that you will be using it the most heavily of all Works modules. You may want to copy some business projections from a spreadsheet or its associated graph, your best customer list from your database, or some electronic mail sent to you by modem in your communications document.

This chapter assumes that you know how to work with each of the elements described. You must be able to open a file or create a new one, and you need to know how to select information in each module. You should have read the appropriate chapters on working with graphs (Chapter 7) and drawing (Chapters 4 and 5). Also, copying presents certain memory restrictions that were discussed in Chapter 1's section on "Hardware Requirements."

# Copying and Pasting

Works is designed so that you can pass information easily from one window to another through the Clipboard. You can use this feature either by copying the selected information and thus leaving it intact in the source document, or by cutting the selected information and thus removing it from the source. You must have the source document open to cut or copy, and the target document open to paste; both documents can be open at the same time. The windows can be of the same type (such as two word processing windows) or different.

Follow these steps to copy information:

1. Open the source document, or activate it, by choosing its name from the Window menu.
2. Select the information to be transferred through the Clipboard.
3. Open the target document.
4. For a target word processor document, position the insertion point to the left of where the paste should occur. If you want the paste to replace other information, select the information to be removed.
5. For a target spreadsheet or database document, select the cell or entry that will become the upper left corner of the area you will insert. Alternatively, you can select the range of cells or entries into which you are pasting.
6. Choose the Paste command from the Edit menu. Paste leaves the Clipboard unchanged for further paste operations.

# Capabilities and Limitations of Copying

You can copy or move most of your creations from one Works window to another. Table 13.1 lists the types of moves you can accomplish.

Some types of transfers cannot go directly through Works. You cannot copy database reports to word processor windows. You can paste database report totals and subtotals to the Clipboard; but you cannot paste complete reports without using special utilities from other vendors or the public domain (for example, ImageSaver, which is part of the SuperGlue II package, described in Chapter 14).

**Table 13.1**
**Types of Moves Available in Works**

| *From* | *To* | *Results* |
|---|---|---|
| Database | Spreadsheet | Copies records to rows, putting each field in a column. The field names are always copied. |
| Database | Word processor | Copies records to lines, placing a tab between each field and a Return at the end of a record. Field names are always copied as the first line. |
| Database | Database | Copies records to records and fields to fields. Field names are not copied. |
| Report | Word processor | Copies totals and subtotals only |
| Spreadsheet | Word processor | Copies answers only, not equations (unless Show Formulas was selected from the Options menu in the spreadsheet) |
| Spreadsheet | Database | Converts rows to records, values only |
| Spreadsheet | Spreadsheet | Converts cell references, values, and equations |
| Word processor | Spreadsheet | Copies text, values if tab delimited (SYLK format) |
| Word processor | Database | Copies text, values if tab delimited; must be of appropriate format for database to be able to convert. Each field type must be accommodated. |
| Word processor | Word processor | Maintains formatting |

You need to be aware of some other restrictions. Database and spreadsheet windows are limited to a single font, size, style, and color choice, so information from word processing documents destined for databases or spreadsheets automatically conforms to its new environment. On the other hand, when you paste database or spreadsheet information to a word processor document, the information arrives in its original font, size, and style, and all rows and records retain their field or column headings along with the field sizes or column spacings. When you copy a spreadsheet to a word processor window, the equations stay behind, unless Show Formulas is active. Works pastes data from a tab-delimited environment (tabs between fields, a carriage return at the end of each record or row) into a word processor with tabs that retain the original spacings. You can change these elements in the word processing document. Works databases cannot handle pictures, so they are left behind when you copy from a word processing window to a database.

Works copies information to RAM, or random-access memory. When you copy the contents of a big database into a spreadsheet, three copies of the data are in memory: in the database, in the Clipboard, and in the spreadsheet. Sometimes your computer doesn't have enough memory to accomplish the task. When you have this problem, Works displays a warning so that you can cancel the move (see fig. 13.1).

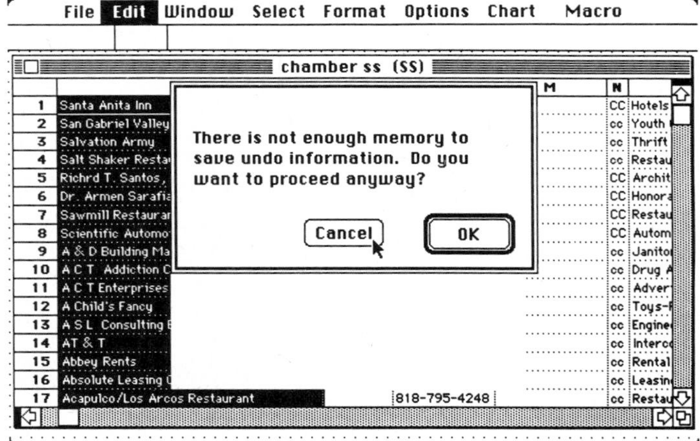


**Fig. 13.1**

*Warning about lack of memory.*

Frequently (but not always), you can avoid this problem by copying small sections of data and repeating the process until you're done. At other times, you have to break up your database, spreadsheet, or word processing document into smaller pieces. Another strategy is to copy only what you need—no unnecessary fields, columns, and so on. Remember that you can flush out the Clipboard by copying a single character or word.

## *Copying from Spreadsheets to Word Processor Windows*

With Works, you can easily copy spreadsheet answers from a spreadsheet window to a word processor window. All the calculations must take place in the spreadsheet window before you move the answers to the word processor window. If you want to make spreadsheet changes and recompute data, you must make those changes in the spreadsheet window and repeat the move.

To move spreadsheet values to a word processor window, follow these steps:

1. Activate the spreadsheet and select the cells to move.
2. Copy the spreadsheet cells to the Clipboard (press ⌘-C).
3. Open the word processor document and make it active.
4. Click an insertion point (where you want to put the spreadsheet results).
5. Paste the Clipboard contents (press ⌘-V).
6. Reformat the word processing document (adjust margins, change fonts, and so on), if needed.

When you paste spreadsheet data, values are separated by tabs that are the same distance apart as the original column widths, and rows are separated by carriage returns. The pasted values always are preceded by the column headings, but you can paste values without column headings by pressing the Option key while pasting. All headings and values are formatted as they were in the spreadsheet. If you paste into a word processor window a selection that is wider than allowed, the selection wraps to the next line. You then need to reformat the selection in the word processor window.

In figure 13.2, a word processor memo has been opened along with a spreadsheet document. Suppose that you want to copy and paste the selected spreadsheet cells into the memo at the position indicated. Notice that in the ruler of the word processor the right margin is set at 6 1/2 inches. The selected range of cells as formatted (column widths), however, is wider.

When you paste the data, Works readjusts the margin of the word processor to include all the material copied to the Clipboard. Figure 13.3 shows the results of the paste. The insertion point is placed at the start

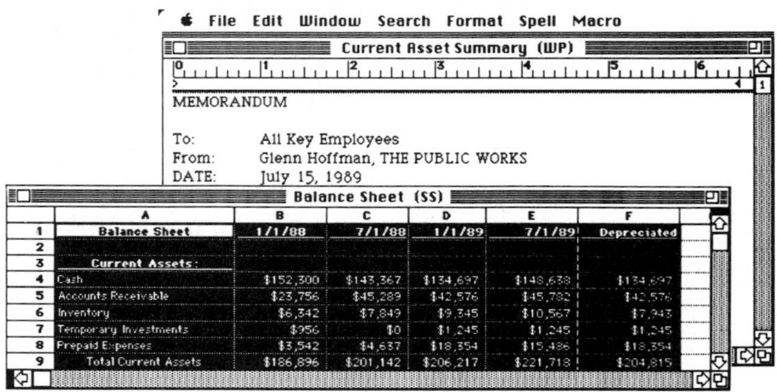


**Fig. 13.2**

*Word processor window and selected data from a spreadsheet before pasting.*

of the paste so that you can see all the tab marks inserted. Notice that the width of the columns indicated by the tab marks is the same as the column width in the original spreadsheet. The formatting from the spreadsheet, 9-point normal Geneva (bold when that was chosen), all transfers with the paste. At this point, you may want to adjust or remove the tab marks and the margins, and change the formatting as you see fit. Note that grids aren't pasted even if they're shown in the spreadsheet window.

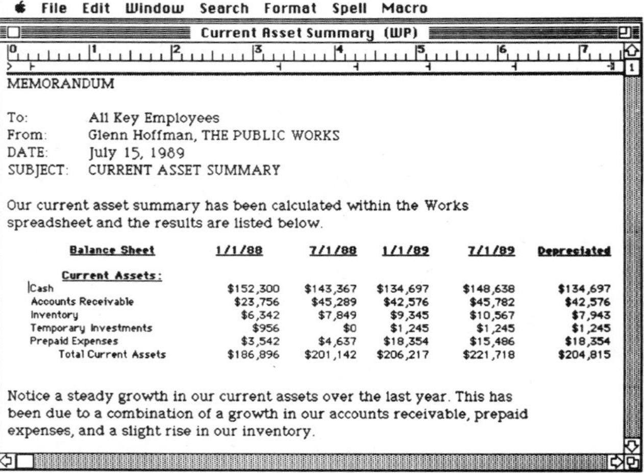


**Fig. 13.3**

*The results of the paste.*

# *Copying Graphs to Word Processors or Spreadsheets*

Works treats a graph like any other drawn object. That is, when you paste a graph from the Clipboard to an open word processor or spreadsheet window, you find yourself in the draw layer with the graph selected as an object to be resized. Works centers the pasted graph, just like any other pasted object. If you want to paste a graph on top of and centered on another object, select that object prior to pasting.

You can paste series graphs with or without grids and labels. You make these choices in the Chart Definition dialog box. You can only *copy* graphs, not *cut* them. (The Cut command is unavailable for graph definitions.) To label graphs, highlight features (with arrows), or colorize graphs, you can use the full power of the draw module.

In figure 13.4, a graph has been pasted into a word processor window. The figure shows the condition of the pasted material immediately after the Paste command is issued. You are in the draw layer (even if you were initially in the text layer), and the object is selected.

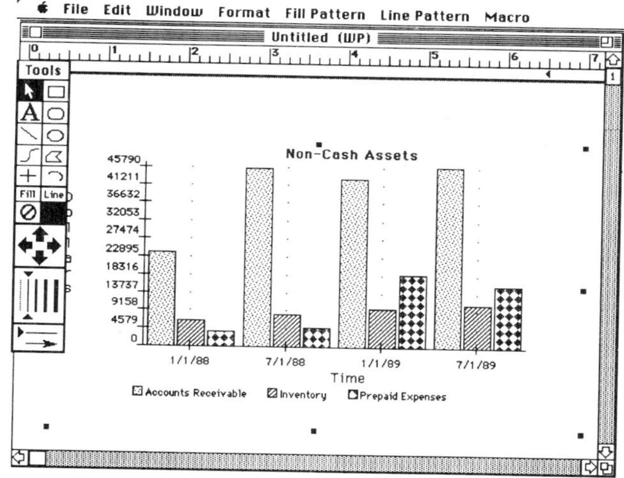


**Fig. 13.4**

*After pasting a graph into a word processor document.*

In figure 13.5, the same graph has been copied to a new word processor window twice. Each of these graphs was moved and resized. Notice that the text attached to the graphs scales with the graphs. Also, to demonstrate the independence of the text layer, the draw layer has been turned off in the figure (with the Draw Off command). Notice that you can then add in the text layer text that will appear under the graphs.

The process of pasting graphs is handled differently in Works 2.0 than it was in previous versions of the program. In Versions 1.1 and 1.0, when you pasted a graph into the word processor window, the graph inserted into your text at the position of your insertion point. Any text occurring after the graph was repaginated automatically. These previous versions of Works did not allow graphs to be pasted into the spreadsheet. In Works 2.0, pasting the graph as an object in the draw layer permits you to add anything you want in the text layer to underlie the graph.

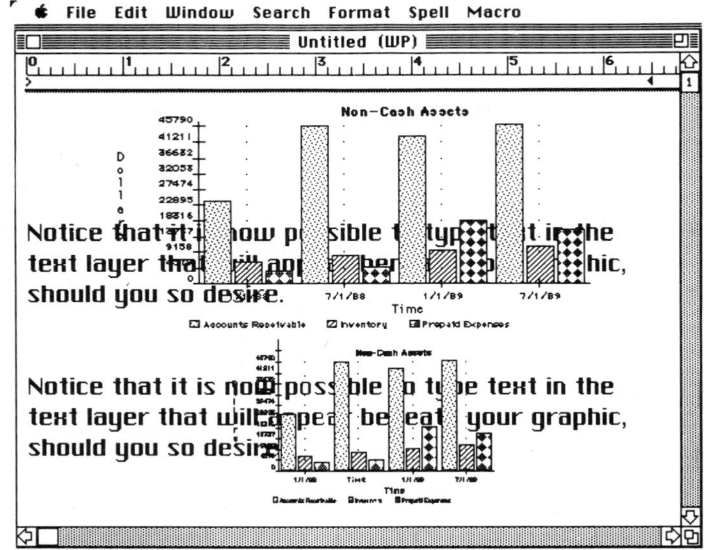


**Fig. 13.5**

*Rescaled graphs and underlying text.*

# *Copying from One Word Processor Window to Another*

Material copied from one word processor document to another can include text only, graphics only, or a combination of the two. When transferring information, you have to adjust your technique according to the nature of what you want to transfer.

To transfer text only, you cut or copy and then paste in the standard manner. Pasting always occurs to the right of the location of the flashing pointer in the target document. Works also copies and pastes attributes (such as size and style of type) and paragraph-formatting information (such as tabs, temporary margins, line spacing, and so on).

When you want to paste graphic objects only, you need to turn on the draw layer (with the Draw On command) in the source word processor document, select the objects, and copy (or cut) them to the Clipboard. When you open the target word processor document, you can paste in the graphics directly, either in the text layer or in the draw layer. You end up in the draw layer after you paste the objects selected.

To paste a combination of text and graphics, you need to return to the text layer. (Use Draw Off or press ⌘-J if you are in the draw layer.)

Select all text and objects you want to copy, and then copy and paste them to the target word processor document.

## *Copying from Spreadsheet to Spreadsheet*

Copying items from one spreadsheet window to another is easy, but one important warning is in order: Because you can copy equations and other cell references to any location in a destination spreadsheet, Works tries to take care of any necessary cell reference changes. This feature usually works properly, but you may inadvertently create situations that Works cannot handle. Therefore, you need to examine and test the destination spreadsheet carefully after any copying. This topic is discussed in detail in the section on "Copying and Pasting Cells" in Chapter 6.

When pasting between spreadsheets, Works copies formulas, values, and attributes (boldface, underscore, commas, dollar signs, and so forth). Because Works automatically modifies copied formulas containing cell references, the formulas usually work in their new (destination) environment. Often Works alerts you to potential errors by displaying `*Error*` in suspect cells (see fig. 13.6.)

File Edit Window Select Format Options Chart Macro

G6 =F6/$F$8

Untitled (SS)

| | B | C | D | E | F | G |
|---|---|---|---|---|---|---|
| 1 | | | | | | |
| 2 | Q1 Actual | Q2 Actual | Q3 Plan | Q4 Plan | Total | % |
| 3 | | | | | | |
| 4 | $123,568 | $107,232 | $140,000 | $140,000 | $510,800 | *Error* |
| 5 | $113,454 | $110,785 | $140,000 | $140,000 | $504,239 | *Error* |
| 6 | $98,876 | $101,867 | $140,000 | $140,000 | $480,743 | *Error* |
| 7 | | | | | | |
| 8 | | | | | | |
| 9 | | | | | | |
| 10 | | | | | | |
| 11 | | | | | | |
| 12 | | | | | | |
| 13 | | | | | | |
| 14 | | | | | | |
| 15 | | | | | | |
| 16 | | | | | | |
| 17 | | | | | | |

**Fig. 13.6**
*Error messages in cells after pasting equations that expect data in cell F6 (see edit bar).*

You also must be certain that you don't accidentally take along cells from the source spreadsheet that reference or replace inappropriate cell locations on the destination spreadsheet. This warning is particularly important if the destination spreadsheet already contains information of any kind.

> ***Caution:*** Above all, be certain to examine and test the destination equations. And test the results carefully, particularly if you have moved an equation to a destination spreadsheet that already includes other cell data of any kind. People have lost fortunes because they haven't taken the time to examine and test after copying things from one spreadsheet to another.

When you want to copy graphics in the draw layer of a spreadsheet, or a combination of graphics and underlying cell values, you use the same procedures used for copying and pasting in word processor documents. See the section on "Copying from One Word Processor Window to Another."

## *Copying from Spreadsheets to Databases*

When you copy a spreadsheet selection to a database, you convert spreadsheet rows into database records. The cells in a row become fields in a record. If you paste cells below a database field, the new data merges to form one combined field. Data from cells pasted to the right of an existing record merges to create a combined record. You can move spreadsheet data to a new database or into an existing database. If the database does not have enough fields to accept the number of columns from the spreadsheet, your data will be truncated.

To copy from a spreadsheet to a database, use the following procedure:

1. Open or create the database in the list window.
2. Be sure that the database contains enough fields to receive the spreadsheet columns.
3. Open the spreadsheet, and highlight the cells you want to copy.
4. Copy spreadsheet cells to the Clipboard (press ⌘-C).
5. Switch to the database window (use the Window menu, or click in the database window).
6. Activate the upper left target cell, or select the desired range of the right size, and paste the cells into the database (press ⌘-V).
7. Modify database field sizes, names, and so on, if necessary.

In figure 13.7, a portion of the spreadsheet shown in the foreground was copied and pasted into the database in the background. Note that row 12 in the spreadsheet has become the first displayed record in the database.

File Edit Window Select Format Options Chart Macro

expenses 87 (DB)

| Date | Payee | CAT | CHK | Amount | Bank | Notes |
|---|---|---|---|---|---|---|
| 4/26/87 | Armstrong Garden | 99.0 | | $178.71 | MC1 | |
| 3/20/87 | Arrowhead | 20.0 | 1511 | $15.51 | SAN1 | |
| 1/30/87 | Arrowhead Water | 20.0 | 1358 | $16.62 | SAN1 | |
| 3/20/87 | Atlantic Financial | 98.0 | 1518 | $15.00 | SAN1 | membership fee - Feedom Line renewa |
| 2/23/87 | | | | | | |
| 1/30/87 | | | | | | |
| 3/16/87 | | | | | | |
| 4/28/87 | | | | | | |
| 3/11/87 | | | | | | |
| 5/8/87 | | | | | | |
| 2/17/87 | | | | | | |
| 1/15/87 | | | | | | |
| 1/15/87 | | | | | | |
| 1/22/87 | | | | | | |
| 1/30/87 | | | | | | |
| 2/5/87 | | | | | | |
| 2/12/87 | | | | | | |

EXPENSE SPREADSHEET (SS)

| | A | B | C | D | E | |
|---|---|---|---|---|---|---|
| 1 | Date | Payee | CAT | CHK | Amount | Bank |
| 2 | 4/2/87 | 20th Century | 16.1 | 1536 | $79.00 | SAN1 |
| 3 | 5/4/87 | 20th Century | 16.1 | 1560 | $296.00 | SAN1 |
| 4 | 4/14/87 | ? | 99.0 | 1544 | $379.70 | SAN1 |
| 5 | 4/23/87 | AAA | 16.1 | 1553 | $500.00 | SAN1 |
| 6 | 1/8/87 | Airport Authori | 9.2 | | $8.00 | CASH |
| 7 | 4/21/87 | Altsys Corp | 25.0 | 1551 | $5.00 | SAN1 |
| 8 | 1/9/87 | American Expre | 98.0 | 1374 | $500.50 | SAN1 |
| 9 | 2/17/87 | American Expre | 98.0 | 1382 | $201.73 | SAN1 |
| 10 | 3/20/87 | American Expre | 98.0 | 1517 | $155.81 | SAN1 |
| 11 | 5/8/87 | American Expre | 98.0 | 1567 | $419.95 | SAN1 |
| 12 | 4/26/87 | Armstrong Gard | 99.0 | | $178.71 | MC1 |
| 13 | 3/20/87 | Arrowhead | 20.0 | 1511 | $15.51 | SAN1 |

**Fig. 13.7**
*Items moved from a spreadsheet to a database.*

If you're moving spreadsheet contents into an existing database, be certain that the order (or formatting) of the database fields matches those of the spreadsheet rows. Otherwise, Works may paste dates from the spreadsheet into fields meant for names in the database, and so on. Remember that when you transfer spreadsheet information to a database, Works moves the answers, not the equations or functions. Moreover, numbers, dollar signs, commas, and decimal points all become text. The best way to transfer numbers is to convert them to General format in the spreadsheet before copying and pasting. After pasting the numbers into the database, you can redefine them as numbers and then add other appropriate attributes (such as dollar signs commas).

When pasting to a database that already contains records, you must take care to avoid overwriting good records in the receiving database. If the location you choose will cause existing data to be overwritten, Works warns you only if that cell or field is not selected. Overwriting selected cells or fields does not result in an alert box. You can, however, use the Undo command (⌘-Z) on the Edit menu to restore your original data.

# Copying from Word Processor Windows to Spreadsheets

Works supports copying and pasting from any module to any other, provided it is in the correct format. To copy text and values from a word processor document to a spreadsheet, you need to format the information in tab or space delimited format. That is, data elements that are to go in cells must be separated by tabs (or by two or more blank spaces). And every pair of rows must be separated by a carriage return. If you leave a blank line in the word processor selection, pasting that selection into a spreadsheet results in a blank row.

Figure 13.8 shows an example of tabular typed material copied into a spreadsheet. Notice that the typed numbers have dollar signs and commas, which Works strips away when pasting from the Clipboard to the spreadsheet. Text is pasted into the spreadsheet left-justified in General format; numbers (any kind) are pasted into the spreadsheet right-justified in the Numeric format. You can use the spreadsheet's formatting options to get back the dollar signs and commas.

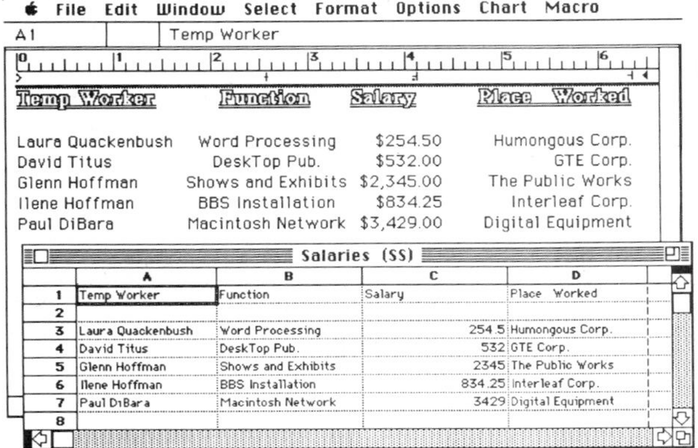


**Fig. 13.8**

*Copying tabular text to a spreadsheet to eliminate retyping.*

When you paste into a spreadsheet, all data assumes the format contained in the spreadsheet. For example, any cells formatted as bold will still be bold. If the paste is to a new spreadsheet, the data assumes the default formatting for spreadsheets, which is 9-point Geneva black.

To paste columns of numbers from a word processor window to a spreadsheet window, follow these steps:

1. Open or create a new spreadsheet.

2. Open (or create) the word processor document containing the tabular material.
3. Highlight the cells you want to copy. Copy the data to the Clipboard (press ⌘-C).
4. Click the upper left destination cell in the spreadsheet.
5. Paste into the spreadsheet (press ⌘-V).
6. Modify the spreadsheet column sizes and add headings, equations, and so forth.

**NOTE:** If you're moving word processing contents into an existing spreadsheet, be sure that the order of the word processing items matches that of the spreadsheet rows. Otherwise, dates from the document may be pasted into fields meant for names in the spreadsheet, and so on.

When you are pasting to a spreadsheet that already contains cell data, be careful not to overwrite good cells in the receiving spreadsheet. If the cell location you choose as the target location will cause data to be overwritten, Works warns you only if you have selected a target range smaller than the source range. The following message appears onscreen:

```
Some data in existing non-selected cells will be lost. Do you
want to continue?
```

You can continue by clicking OK (or pressing Return). If you do not want to continue, you click Cancel (or press ⌘-.).

You can copy graphics from a word processor to a spreadsheet by first turning on the draw layer (choose the Draw On command from the Edit menu), then selecting the objects, copying them (with the Copy command or the ⌘-C shortcut), and pasting them into the spreadsheet. You do not have to be in the draw layer of the spreadsheet; Works automatically turns on the draw layer and leaves the objects selected.

## *Copying from Word Processor Windows to Databases*

Copying from a word processor window to a database is entirely analogous to copying to a spreadsheet window. You format with one tab (or two or more spaces) between each pair of entries, and a carriage return between each pair of records. The database window should be in the list format. A blank line in the word processor selection is interpreted in the paste as a blank record in the database. As an example, the same paste that was done in figure 13.8 is now shown in figure 13.9 for a database window.

File Edit Window Organize Format Report Macro

1 | Temp Worker

| Temp Worker | Function | Salary | Place Worked |
|---|---|---|---|
| | | | |
| Laura Quakenbush | Word Processing | $254.50 | Humongous Corp. |
| David Titus | Desktop Pub. | $532.00 | GTE Corp. |
| Glenn Hoffman | Shows and Exhibits | $2,345.00 | The Public Works |
| Ilene Hoffman | BBS Installation | $834.25 | Interleaf Corp. |
| Paul DiBara | Macintosh Network | $3429.00 | Digital Equipment |

Salaries DB (DB)

| Temp Worker | Function | Salary | Place Worked |
|---|---|---|---|
| Temp Worker | Function | Salary | Place Worked |
| | | | |
| Laura Quakenbush | Word Processing | $254.50 | Humongous Corp. |
| David Titus | Desktop Pub. | $532.00 | GTE Corp. |
| Glenn Hoffman | Shows and Exhibits | $2,345.00 | The Public Works |
| Ilene Hoffman | BBS Installation | $834.25 | Interleaf Corp. |
| Paul DiBara | Macintosh Network | $3429.00 | Digital Equipment |

**Fig. 13.9**

*Tabular information from a word processor copied into a database.*

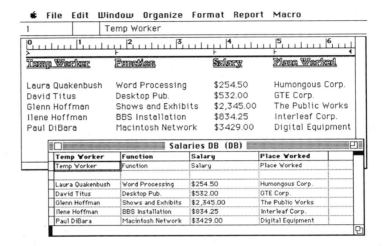

To copy from a word processor to a database, follow these steps:

1. Open (or create) the word processor document containing tabular information to be transferred.

2. Select what you want to copy, and choose the Copy command from the Edit menu (or press ⌘-C).

3. Open or create a database, and activate the entry that should become the upper left cell of the new entry (or select the destination range).

**NOTE:** The best practice is to create a target file before you copy the selection from the source file. Any copy or cut command will replace copy buffer clipboard contents.

4. Paste the cells into the database by choosing the Paste command (press ⌘-V).

5. Modify database field sizes, field types, and so on.

If you're moving a word processor selection into an existing database, be certain that the order of the material in the selection matches that of the database fields. Otherwise, Works may paste dates into fields meant for names in the database, and so on. The format of each item from the word processor must correspond to the format of the database field into which it is being pasted. If you match field attributes in the database (Date or Numeric format, for instance), Works treats the data properly. Otherwise, everything is imported as text.

> ***Caution:*** Unless you set up the database field attributes otherwise, Works transfers numbers as text. Therefore, you should paste numbers from the word processor without commas, dollar signs, parentheses, and so forth. After pasting the numbers into the database, you can define fields as numeric and choose appropriate attributes. You also can define database fields properly before pasting. See "Specifying Field Attributes" in Chapter 9 for more information.

When pasting to a database that already contains records, take care to avoid overwriting good records in the receiving database. If the chosen location will cause existing data to be overwritten, Works warns you with an alert box.

## *Copying from Databases to Spreadsheets*

You may often want to copy data from your database to a spreadsheet so that you can graph database entries. Database records become spreadsheet rows, and fields in database list rows become rows in a spreadsheet. You can move database data to a new spreadsheet or to an existing spreadsheet. Here are the general steps:

1. Open the database (in list view), select the fields to be copied, and choose the Copy command (press ⌘-C).
2. Open or create a spreadsheet and select the range you are pasting to (the upper left cell of the appropriate range).
3. Paste the fields into the spreadsheet (press ⌘-V).
4. Modify spreadsheet column sizes and so on.
5. Add equations, graph definitions, and so forth.

When moving database contents into an existing spreadsheet, be sure that the order of the database fields matches that of the spreadsheet columns. Otherwise, dates from the database may be pasted into cells meant for names in the spreadsheet, and so on. If you use a new spreadsheet with the correct number of columns (step 2), your paste will be absolutely correct. Works recognizes most formats or attributes in the transfer. An example is shown in figure 13.10.

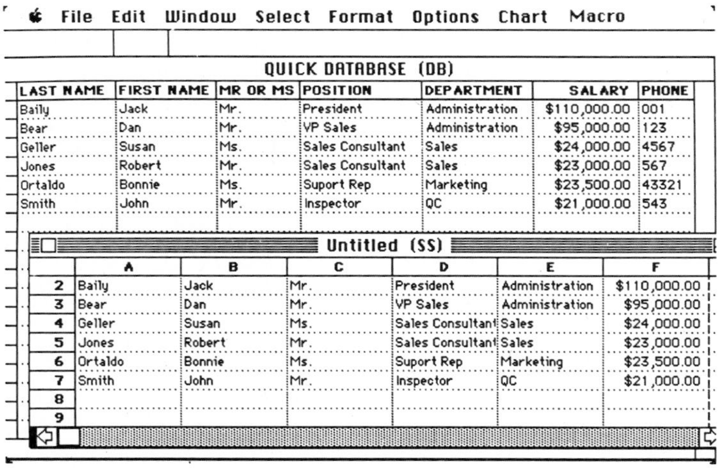

File Edit Window Select Format Options Chart Macro

QUICK DATABASE (DB)

| LAST NAME | FIRST NAME | MR OR MS | POSITION | DEPARTMENT | SALARY | PHONE |
|---|---|---|---|---|---|---|
| Baily | Jack | Mr. | President | Administration | $110,000.00 | 001 |
| Bear | Dan | Mr. | VP Sales | Administration | $95,000.00 | 123 |
| Geller | Susan | Ms. | Sales Consultant | Sales | $24,000.00 | 4567 |
| Jones | Robert | Mr. | Sales Consultant | Sales | $23,000.00 | 567 |
| Ortaldo | Bonnie | Ms. | Suport Rep | Marketing | $23,500.00 | 43321 |
| Smith | John | Mr. | Inspector | QC | $21,000.00 | 543 |

Untitled (SS)

| | A | B | C | D | E | F |
|---|---|---|---|---|---|---|
| 2 | Baily | Jack | Mr. | President | Administration | $110,000.00 |
| 3 | Bear | Dan | Mr. | VP Sales | Administration | $95,000.00 |
| 4 | Geller | Susan | Ms. | Sales Consultant | Sales | $24,000.00 |
| 5 | Jones | Robert | Mr. | Sales Consultant | Sales | $23,000.00 |
| 6 | Ortaldo | Bonnie | Ms. | Suport Rep | Marketing | $23,500.00 |
| 7 | Smith | John | Mr. | Inspector | QC | $21,000.00 |
| 8 | | | | | | |
| 9 | | | | | | |

**Fig. 13.10**

*Records copied from a database to rows in a spreadsheet.*

**NOTE:** Works spreadsheets recognize numbers from Works databases. Most attributes are transferred as well. If dollar signs appear in the database, they also show up in the spreadsheet after transferring occurs.

When pasting to a spreadsheet that already contains cell data, be careful not to overwrite good cells in the receiving spreadsheet. A good practice is to select the range you want to paste to, because if you are about to overwrite data, an alert box appears. You then can check to see if you want to overwrite it.

## *Copying from Database to Database*

If you need to copy the contents of selected database records to a new database, you can use the record-selection and Save As techniques described in Chapter 9. Using these procedures is the best way to create a similar database because Works copies field names, attributes, and other important elements.

If you need to copy records from one existing database to another existing but differently structured database, a few more steps are required. You need to organize the source and target databases so that the field orders are compatible. You don't need the same number of fields, and they don't need the same field names. At a minimum, however, the necessary fields in the destination database must be in the correct order, in anticipation of the transfer. The destination database can have additional fields for data not in the source database. In figure 13.11, the first three columns of entries from the database in the background are copied into the database in the foreground.

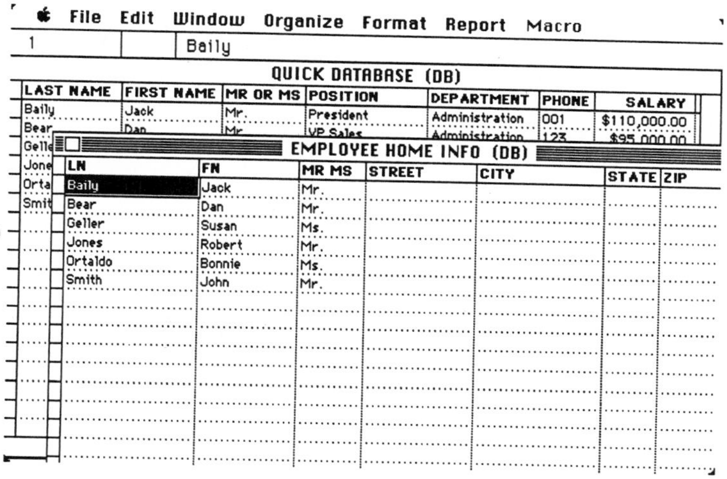

**Fig. 13.11**

*Selected items copied from Quick Database to the Employee Home Info database.*

To copy from database to database, follow these steps:

1. Open the source and target databases in the list window.
2. Arrange the source fields and target fields to coincide with each other (see fig. 13.11). Field names need not match, but their order must be the same.
3. Activate the source database, and select the source items you want to copy (in the example, LAST NAME, FIRST NAME, and MR OR MS).
4. Copy the source items to the Clipboard (press ⌘-C).
5. In the target database window, click the upper left destination field entry (or select the correct range).
6. Choose the Paste command from the Edit menu (press ⌘-V).
7. Modify database field sizes, names, and so on, if necessary.

When pasting to a database that already contains records, you must take care not to overwrite good records in the destination database. If the location specified will cause Works to overwrite existing data, the program warns you with an alert box.

## *Copying from Databases to Word Processor Windows*

Copying entries from a database into a word processor window is entirely analogous to the process of copying cells from a spreadsheet into a word processor window. When you select and paste entries, or records, they are pasted into the word processor with their database formatting intact, and with the field headings listed as the first line. If you want to paste the selection without the field names, press the Option key while pasting. Refer to figures 13.2 and 13.3 for illustration.

When pasted into the word processor document, database fields are automatically separated by tabs. The distance between tab marks is set by the width of the fields in the database. Records are separated by carriage return characters. You may need to modify the word processor document's page setup (margins, reduction, and so forth) to make room for large records; you can do so after pasting.

Database contents usually arrive in the word processor window in a single font, type style, and size. Once the contents have been moved, you can change the font. Grids aren't pasted even if they're shown in the database window.

## *Copying Database Report Totals to Word Processor Windows*

In Chapter 10's section on "Computing Totals and Subtotals," you learned how to copy totals to the Clipboard by using the Copy Totals command, which is on the Edit menu. This command copies any totals and subtotals you have defined with the Take a Sub-Total on Field Change, Take a Sub-Total on 1st Char, and Sum This Field commands. Remember that you can view the Clipboard's contents or copy the information into a different Works window.

In the database report in figure 13.12, the data has been sorted by department. The report definition instructed Works to total on field changes (in the DEPARTMENT field) and to sum on the SALARY field.

The Copy Totals option from the Edit menu was used to create the Clipboard contents shown in figure 13.13. Remember that the first record from each category (each department, in the example) is cop-

| LAST NAME | FIRST NAME | POSITION | MR OR MS | DEPARTMENT | SALARY |
|---|---|---|---|---|---|
| Baily | Jack | President | Mr. | Administration | $110,000.00 |
| Bear | Dan | VP Sales | Mr. | Administration | $95,000.00 |
| | | | | | $205,000.00 |
| | | | | | |
| Ortaldo | Bonnie | Suport Rep | Ms. | Marketing | $23,500.00 |
| | | | | | $23,500.00 |
| | | | | | |
| Smith | John | Inspector | Mr. | QC | $21,000.00 |
| | | | | | $21,000.00 |
| | | | | | |
| Geller | Susan | Sales Consultant | Ms. | Sales | $24,000.00 |
| Jones | Robert | Sales Consultant | Mr. | Sales | $23,000.00 |
| | | | | | $47,000.00 |
| | | | | | |
| | | | | | $296,500.00 |

**Fig. 13.12**

*Database report with totals ready to be copied.*

ied to the Clipboard but that the summed field contains the total for the category rather than the field value for the record displayed.

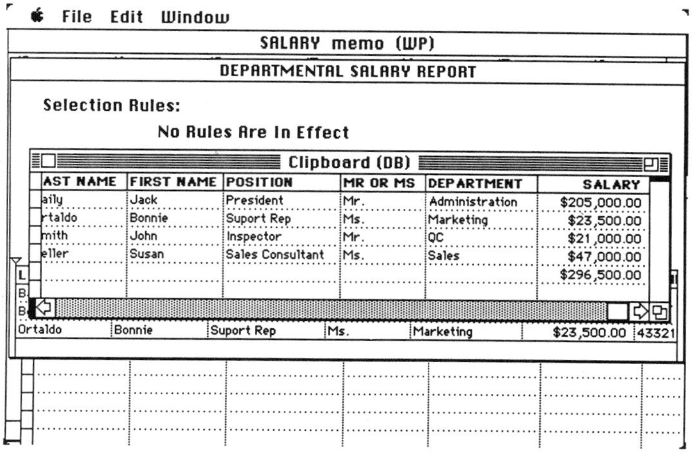

File Edit Window

SALARY memo (WP)

DEPARTMENTAL SALARY REPORT

Selection Rules:

No Rules Are In Effect

Clipboard (DB)

| AST NAME | FIRST NAME | POSITION | MR OR MS | DEPARTMENT | SALARY |
|---|---|---|---|---|---|
| aily | Jack | President | Mr. | Administration | $205,000.00 |
| rtaldo | Bonnie | Suport Rep | Ms. | Marketing | $23,500.00 |
| mith | John | Inspector | Mr. | QC | $21,000.00 |
| eller | Susan | Sales Consultant | Ms. | Sales | $47,000.00 |
| | | | | | $296,500.00 |

Ortaldo Bonnie Suport Rep Ms. Marketing $23,500.00 43321

**Fig. 13.13**

*The Clipboard after the Copy Totals option is used.*

After the salary totals have been copied to the Clipboard, they can be pasted to a word processing document (see fig. 13.14). You can use word processing techniques to delete unwanted text after pasting.

Even if you have turned off the report's grid option, Works displays the Clipboard copies of your totals with a grid. If you transfer the contents of the Clipboard to another window (spreadsheet, word processor, and so on), the grid isn't transferred.

**Fig. 13.14**

*Database report totals pasted into a word processor document.*

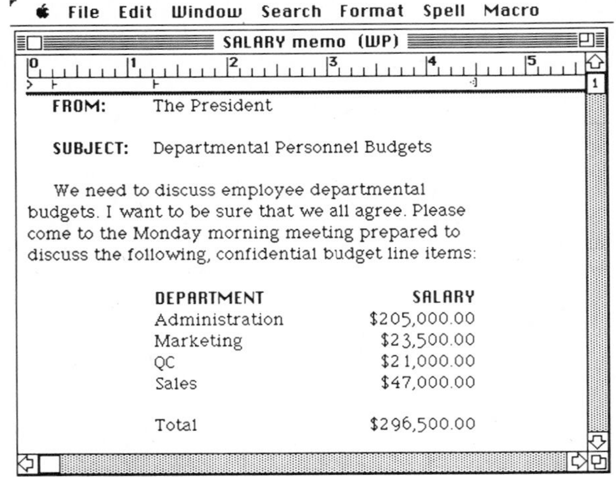


# Copying from a Communications Document

When you capture text during communications, the text becomes a word processor file. Once you quit your session and close your communications document, you can use the information contained in that file in all the ways previously discussed.

If you have executed the Receive File command in the Communications menu to download a file, you can find it saved to disk in the location on the hierarchical file system where you were when you issued the command. Received files can be either stripped text files or text files in any of the popular word processor formats: Microsoft Word, Claris MacWrite, Apple's Teach Text, or Take A Letter. You may want to view stripped text files by using utilities such as MockWrite from CE Software or miniWriter by Maitreya Designs. Works can open some of these kinds of files; you need to experiment.

Many times, downloaded files are compressed. If so, you have to use the appropriate utility before you can view the contained information (see "Compressing Files" in Chapter 12).

When you have text and graphics in the Clipboard, Works normally pastes only the text portion into a communications window to be sent out with a modem. With graphics only, the Paste command is normally disabled.

# Merging

*Merging* is a special form of paste operation that places information contained in a database record into a word processor document to create an individual copy when printed. For example, you can use a Works database to create a mailing list and send personalized mailings to as many people as you specify. Works enables you to merge names, addresses, and other items from your databases with word processor documents to create personalized form letters, to fill in forms automatically, and so forth. During this process, you don't use the Clipboard.

Using the draw module, you can design attractive forms to receive merged data. This process is at the heart of automating a business. Merging also gives you another way to create database reports. The sections that follow discuss some of the potentials of this helpful feature.

## Creating Merge Documents

A merge document is like a normal word processor document except that the merge document contains *placeholders* where you would otherwise type variable information such as names and addresses. These placeholders tell Works to get specific information from one of your databases when printing. When you print a merge document, Works fills in the blanks with information from the records in your database.

Each placeholder contains the name of the database and the database field name containing the appropriate information. The two items are separated by a colon (see fig. 13.15). Theoretically, a merge document can pull information from more than one database, but this procedure is tricky and seldom done.

To create a merge document containing placeholders, do the following:

1. Place both the database and the word processor document on the desktop.
2. Type, edit, and proof the portion of the word processor text that will always print.
3. Position the cursor in the word processor window where you want to add a placeholder.
4. Choose Prepare to Merge from the File menu (see fig. 13.16). The dialog box shown in figure 13.17 appears.

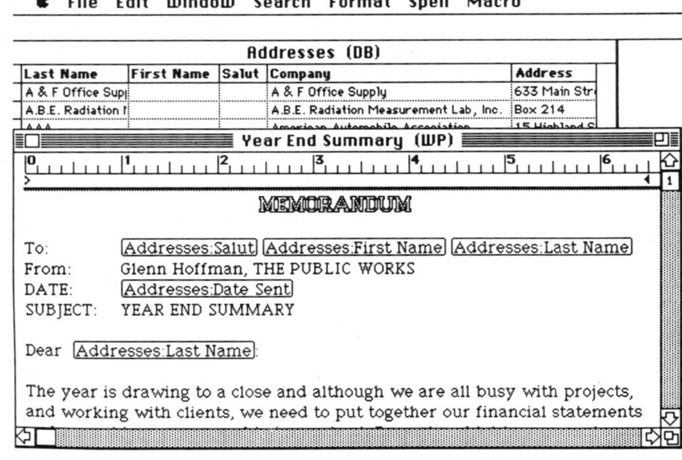


**Fig. 13.15**

*Placeholders showing the name of the database and the fields to be used.*

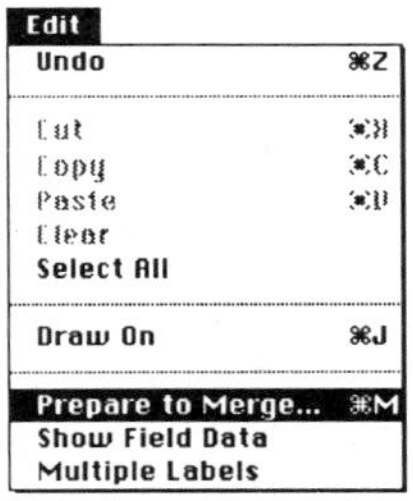

Edit
Undo ⌘Z
Cut ⌘X
Copy ⌘C
Paste ⌘V
Clear
Select All
Draw On ⌘J
Prepare to Merge... ⌘M
Show Field Data
Multiple Labels

**Fig. 13.16**

*The Edit menu with Prepare to Merge selected.*

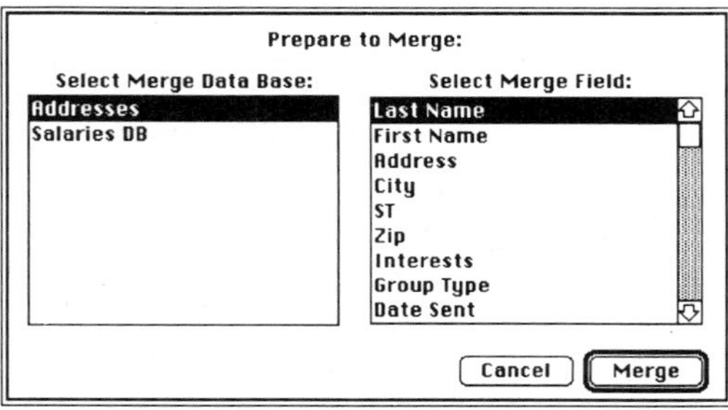


**Fig. 13.17**

*The Prepare to Merge dialog box.*

5. In the scroll box on the left, select the database you want to use (click the name). In the scroll box on the right, select the field. Then click the Merge button (or press Return).

6. Works puts the placeholder containing the name of the database and field into your document at the location specified.
7. Insert necessary spaces, commas, and so forth.
8. Repeat the process until you have installed all the placeholders you need.

To switch from displaying field name placeholders to displaying the field data, you choose the Show Field Data command from the Edit menu. Using this command enables you to preview your work. Figure 13.18 shows the results of displaying field data for the merge document shown in figure 13.15. When you are showing the field data, the Show Field Data command changes to Show Field Names; when you are showing the field labels, the command name changes back to Show Field Data.

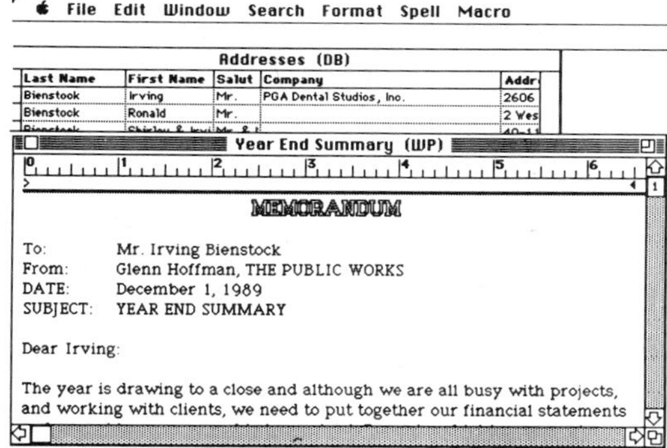


**Fig. 13.18**

*Previewing merge design by selecting Show Field Data from the Edit menu.*

# *Formatting Merged Information*

You can print the information from your database in merge documents, using any available word processor font attribute, size, color, and so on. Simply select the placeholder by double-clicking it and change its type as you would any word processor text. Figure 13.19 shows an example of a printed and formatted merge document. In this example, text was centered and printed in a variety of type sizes and in boldface and italic. The Draw feature and clip art from the Scrapbook also were used.

You can add or delete placeholders at any time by using the inserting, cutting, and backspacing techniques you have already learned. Remember, however, that if you plan to add placeholders, the database must be on your desktop.

**Fig. 13.19**

*An example of a formatted merge document.*

# *Dealing with Placeholder Wrap*

If your placeholders are very long, you may not have an accurate idea of field placement. Works moves the placeholder to the next line on the screen if it does not fit on the previous line. When you print the document, however, the information begins at the original insertion point. If the data is still too large to fit entirely on the second line, Works prints as much information as possible but does not include the information that doesn't fit. For example, in figure 13.20, you can see the effects of word wrap on the badge shown in figure 13.19.

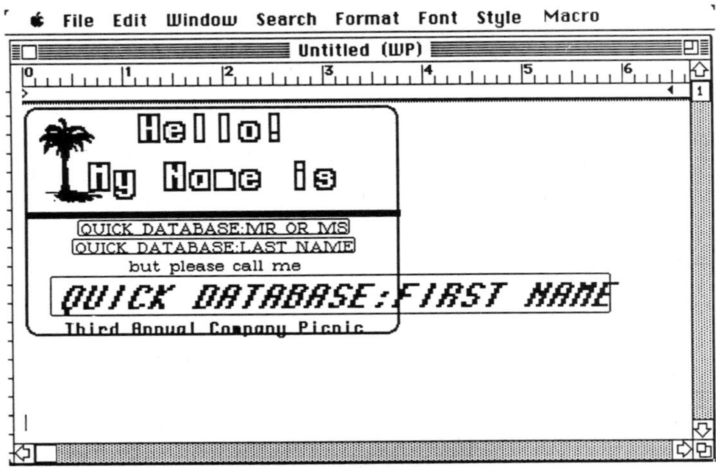


**Fig. 13.20**

*Narrow document margins and long placeholder names, which cause placeholder wrap.*

**TIP:** Works gives you the option of replacing the field name placeholders in the merge document with the first entries from the first record in the merged database. You can then see what an actual record would look like when merged into your document, without having to worry about placeholder wrap.

If you know that you will be using a database for merging, give the database and fields short names, and the placeholders will be shorter.

> ***Caution:*** You cannot edit the contents of a placeholder in the word processor. If you change the database name, you must redo the placeholder selection, that is, delete old placeholders then add new ones.

In addition to wrapping placeholders, Works wraps merged field data to make it fit. The results usually look just fine. In extreme cases, however, a large insertion can turn a one-page document into a multipage document. When designing the fixed text that is repeated in every merge document, be certain to allow enough white space so that all the merge data fits where you want it.

If you plan to use merge documents to fill out printed forms with six-lines-per-inch spacing and boxes in fixed locations, pick a font that is not proportionally spaced and has typewriter line spacing.

## *Changing Database and Field Names: Cautions*

Don't change database or database field names that are referenced in placeholders. If you do, you have to update the merge documents manually to reflect the changes. If you do not have the correct database document on the desktop, the placeholders in the word processor window give the message `NOT ON DESKTOP`, as shown in figure 13.21. You need to have the database open in order to view or print the information in the records. If you delete a field that was used for a merge, you see the message `FIELD NOT IN DB` in the placeholder. In the example shown in figure 13.21, the database called Addresses is not open on the desktop. (Note the effects of placeholder wrap in the first two lines of the document.)

## *Printing Merged Documents*

After you have set up a merge document, you're almost ready to print. First, you must be certain that your database is in the order you want (sort it) and that you have selected only the records you want to print. If you don't restrict the records, Works prints them all. (See Chapter 9's section on "Sorting, Searching, and Matching Capabilities.")

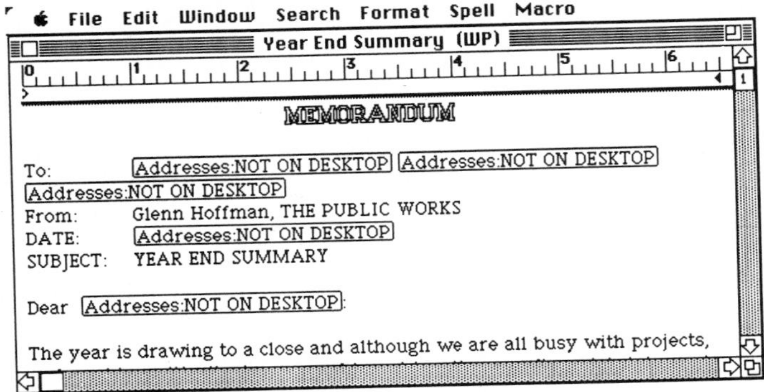


**Fig. 13.21**

*Error messages that appear if you forget to open your database.*

To print a custom merged document, use the following method:

1. Sort or select the records you want to print in the specified database, and arrange them in the appropriate order.
2. Use the Record Selection or Match Record commands in the Organize menu to select the records to print.
3. Activate the word processor document, make any needed changes, and adjust the page setup if necessary.
4. Prepare your printer.
5. Select the Print Merge command from the File menu. A dialog box results.
6. Select the print options (see Chapter 1, "Getting Started," and Chapter 2, "Entering, Editing, Saving, and Printing Text"), and then click the OK button (or press Return).

You can preview your merge by selecting the Print Preview option in the Print dialog box. After viewing one or more records, you can proceed to print. When you give the Print Merge command, Works prints all records in your selected database. When you select a specified page number in the Print Merge dialog box, Works prints those pages but prints all the records in the database. To print only a subset of a database, you must use selection or matching techniques. Use the ⌘-. (period) keyboard shortcut if you want to abort printing after starting it.

Choosing the Print command instead of the Print Merge command prints only the document shown in the word processor window. If you are displaying placeholders, Works prints one copy of the document with the placeholders in position. If you have selected Show Field Data in the Edit menu before choosing Print, only a single copy of the document prints, with data from the first record.

## Printing Mailing Labels

Using Microsoft Works, you can create two types of mailing labels: continuous labels (printing in one column) or multiple-column labels (printing in two, three, or more columns). The procedure involves making the appropriate choices in the Page Setup dialog box, preparing a merge document with the appropriate placeholders, and then executing a print merge.

### Printing Labels with an ImageWriter Printer

To set up the labels for printing, do the following:

1. Create a new word processor document and select the Page Setup command in the File menu.
2. Choose the Custom Size option.
3. Type the width of your label in the Paper Width box. When using a continuous label, type just the width of the single label. When setting up a multiple-column label merge, type the width of the entire page.
4. Choose the No Gaps Between Pages option.
5. Type the height of your label in the Paper Height text box. The label height is measured from the top of one label to the top of the next.
6. Set the margins of your paper in decimal fractions of an inch. For continuous labels, use a 0.25-inch left margin, 0.125-inch right margin, and top and bottom margins of 0. You may need to adjust the right and left margins, depending on the position of your labels in the printer platen.

To merge a label document, follow these steps:

1. Open the required database and select and match the records of interest. Sort them into the appropriate order.
2. Activate the word processor document you created for your labels, and format the mailing label appropriately. You may want to format the placeholders individually after you do step 3.

3. Choose the Prepare to Merge command from the Edit menu to insert the placeholders in the correct order.

4. To print your labels, select the Print Merge command, choose your printing options (number of copies, quality, and so on), and click the Print button.

At this point, you have a window that looks something like the top one in figure 13.22. Use the ruler to judge the width of your label. You may also want to choose Show Field Data to see what an individual label looks like, as was done in the lower window in figure 13.22. In order to see the bottom limit of your label, you should type enough carriage returns so that you can see the page break. Once you are set up to merge, you should remove the page break by deleting the additional carriage returns. Otherwise, Works inserts a blank label every other turn.

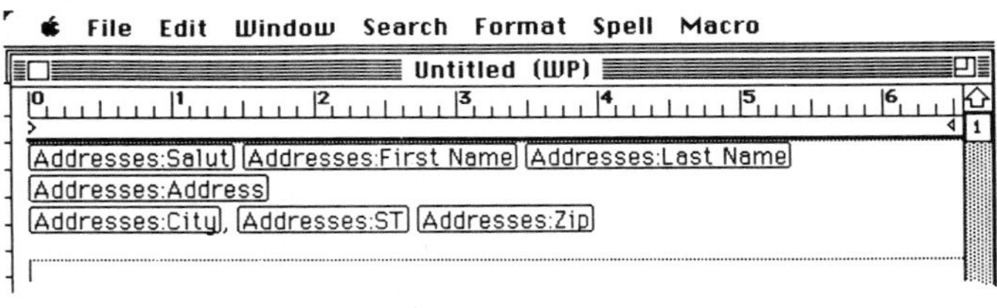


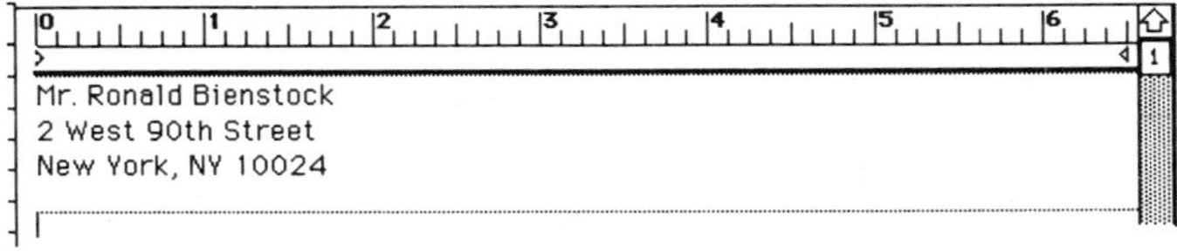


**Fig. 13.22**

*A merge label in both field name and field data forms.*

To create multiple-column labels, follow this procedure:

1. Open the required database, select and match records of interest, and sort the labels into the correct order.

2. Open a new word processor window, and format the text as necessary.

3. Choose the Page Setup command from the File menu, and fill in the label dimensions as before. Use the single label height for Paper Height, and the width of the label page as the Paper Width.

4. From the Format menu, choose the Spacing command and select the 6 Lines per Inch option.

5. Set manual left-hand tab marks on the ruler where each label should begin. You check this setup by measuring the label page (from the beginning of the left label to the end of the right label).

6. Using the Prepare to Merge command on the Edit menu, position the placeholders on the first line of the first label. You will find that working with the merge is easier if you select the Show Field Data command in the Edit menu.

7. Select the Multiple Labels command from the Edit menu.

8. Copy all the placeholders (now in data form), click after the placeholder, press the Tab key, and paste the information. To print three labels across the page, repeat this step. You are then at the stage shown in figure 13.23.

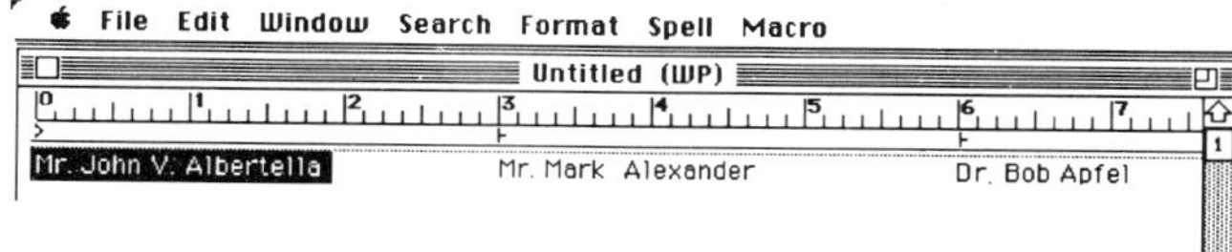


**Fig. 13.23** *Setting up the first line for printing multicolumn labels.*

9. On the second, third, and remaining lines, complete the first set of labels by repeating step 7.

10. Press the Return key until you have only one page break on-screen.

11. Copy the first row of labels, and paste them below the page break. At this point, your window should look like the one shown in figure 13.24.

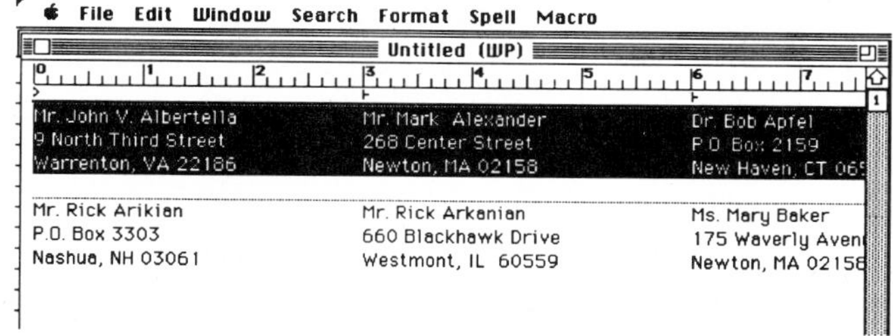


**Fig. 13.24** *Creating multiple-column labels for a page of labels by copying and pasting rows.*

12. Repeat steps 8-11 until you have exactly the right number of rows of labels for a page of labels.
13. Choose the Page Setup command from the File menu. In the resulting dialog box, change the Paper Height value so that it is the same dimension as the page of labels that you print.

You print your labels in a multicolumn label page in the same manner you use to print continuous single-column labels. Choose the Print Merge command with the appropriate database open. You may need to adjust your margins to align the labels in the printer correctly.

You can preview your multiple column labels by using the Print Preview feature in the Print dialog box, which is displayed when you choose the Print Merge command on the File menu.

**NOTE:** Works *spools* your labels when you perform a print merge operation. That is, the program collects the data and writes it to a place in RAM. You may experience a delay (as long as two minutes or more) while the program "thinks."

You will notice that Works downloads 128 labels at a time. The 129th label may be blank, with the next 128 labels correct. If your computer runs out of memory, Works issues an alert box. You may need to delete some files, freeing up some disk space. Then try printing one more time.

***Caution:*** With an ImageWriter printer, *never* roll your labels backward through your print platen to remove them. Always feed them through in the forward direction. Labels have a tendency to get stuck in the platen when reversed out, and removing them can be a devil of a job, if not impossible. The cost of a new platen and lost time is not worth getting a few more labels.

## *Printing Labels with a LaserWriter Printer*

To use a LaserWriter to print multicolumn labels, you must do the following:

1. Prepare your merge, using the same procedure you use for ImageWriters.
2. In the Page Setup dialog box, select the US Letter option.

3. Set the left and right margins at 0.5 inch, and the top and bottom margins at 1.0 inch.

4. Adjust these margins if needed, depending on the size of your labels.

5. Click the OK button, and the Print Merge is executed.

## *Using Merges for Database Reports*

The multiple-column feature of the Print Merge command gives you the opportunity to bypass the reports feature of the database module and create customized reports in the word processor module. Although the database window lets you print as many records as you can fit within the page margins, you can create a word processor document of any size, position your placeholders where you prefer, and type or draw any information that you want to display. Use the Multiple Labels and Print Merge commands, both in the Edit menu, to create your report.

You can use a database merge to create a report in exactly the same manner that you use database merges to create personalized forms by using the procedure outlined in the next section. Your report takes the place of the form and you use the Prepare to Merge command to place your field placeholders in whatever position you choose and on any size page.

# *Personalized Form Filling*

Chapter 5 discussed using the Works draw module to create various forms. And you know that you can create templates by using the Stationery feature, and even import forms as graphic images from scanned files. Using the Works merge feature, you can automate your business by using databases to produce direct mail pieces, mass correspondence, business expense forms, invoices, and statements. You have already learned all the techniques needed to perform these functions. This section summarizes the necessary steps.

When setting up a business form, you can type a single form just as if you were preparing it for an individual client or account. When you're done, go back and replace any names, addresses, or data with the correct placeholders from the database that contains the information. You can format the document with various fonts, type styles, colors, shapes, and lines to highlight important information.

To set up a form document, do the following:

1. Create a word processor document and design the form. Use the Page Setup command on the File menu to set the page size, and the Draw On command to add any graphic elements you want.
2. If you are working with a commercial form, you have the choice of either measuring the form with a ruler to determine where the fields go, or using a scanned image as a template. See "Using Stationery for Templates" in Chapter 5 for more information.
3. Open the appropriate database and then reactivate the word processor document.
4. Position the insertion point where you want your placeholders on the form to go.
5. Choose the Prepare to Merge command on the File menu and select the field(s) you desire.
6. Save your word processor document by choosing the Save command (press ⌘-S) in the File menu, or the Save As command. You can save the document either in normal format or as Stationery.
7. To merge print your personalized forms, follow the instructions in given "Printing Merged Documents," elsewhere in this chapter.

Figure 13.25 shows an example of a form created in this manner.

## *Making Works Desktops*

Whenever you quit Works, the program automatically saves a list of the files that were open on your desktop, including their window locations and window sizes, in a file called the Works Desktop. (You can find a picture of the Works Desktop file icon in fig. 1.3 in Chapter 1.)

Works 2.0 supports a feature that allows you to create a desktop file of your choosing, at any time, and save it with a new file name. The utility of this feature is that it allows you to open a set of files instantly with just one launch command. When you do a merge, you can bring all the needed files to the desktop with just a click of your mouse.

To create a desktop file, follow these steps:

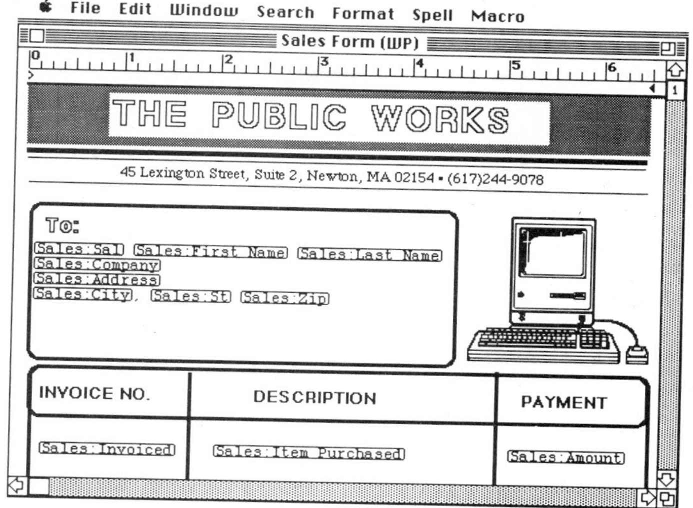


**Fig. 13.25**

*An automated statement form, created by using the merge feature.*

1. Open on your desktop all the files you want to include in your desktop file.
2. Close any unnecessary files.
3. Choose the Make Works Desktop command from the File menu. This command is available in all Works modules.
4. In the resulting Save As dialog box (SF Put), specify the new desktop file name (if desired). Figure 13.26 shows this dialog box.

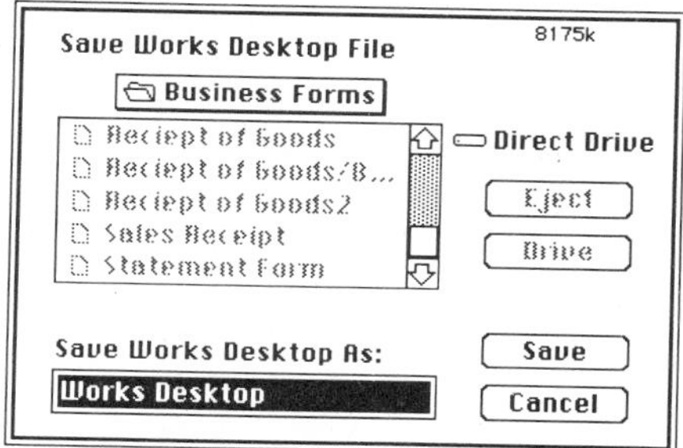


**Fig. 13.26**

*The Save As dialog box that appears after you choose the Make Works Desktop command.*

5. Navigate to the proper folder.
6. Click the Save button or press Return.

If you have an untitled file on your desktop, you must save it under another file name. Works alerts you if you try to make a desktop that contains an untitled document. The desktop file opens the original documents themselves. If you make subsequent changes to a document file that was part of a desktop set, your latest saved version appears when you launch the desktop file.

## Chapter Summary

Chapter 13 showed you that the Works modules are even more powerful when used in conjunction with each other. You can copy data from one module to another, use the Works merging capability to produce form letters, and print mailing labels. You learned how you can use Works to accomplish many different kinds of tasks.

# 14

# Using Works with Other Products

As powerful as Microsoft Works and your Macintosh are, you may want to augment them with other software and hardware products. Works has been designed to work with a variety of other programs, and a number of vendors have designed their programs with Works in mind. Because Works has become a bestseller, this trend will continue.

This chapter explores products that can be used with Works. Most of them you can find at your local Apple dealer, software retailer, or order through mail-order firms. If you need help obtaining them, refer to Appendix A for a list of the manufacturers' addresses and telephone numbers.

## *Other Graphics Packages*

You probably purchased your Macintosh partly because of its graphics power. Originally the Macintosh was sold along with MacWrite, MacPaint, and MacDraw. Over time the complexity and capability of these and other graphics products have increased substantially. Today the choice of graphics tools is almost overwhelming.

Works was designed to be compatible with many of the popular graphics products. You can capture most Macintosh screens as "paint files" and include them as bit-mapped objects in Works word processor or spreadsheet documents. If you can get a MacPaint-compatible image to your Clipboard or Scrapbook, Works can integrate that image with your document. Works 2.0 also allows the importation of MacDraw-compatible object-oriented graphics as well. Once a graphic has been pasted into a Works document, the graphic can be moved and resized.

## Paint Programs

A paint program is one that creates bit-mapped images, which were discussed in "Graphics and Design" in the Introduction. The first paint program for the Macintosh was MacPaint, initially sold bundled with the computer. The five intervening years have seen a proliferation of paint programs with advanced features. Some of the better paint programs include MacPaint 2.0 by Claris, Canvas 2.0 by Deneba, FullPaint by Ashton-Tate, and SuperPaint by Silicon Beach. DeskPaint by Zedcor is a desk accessory (DA), and Canvas offers a companion DA as well. This list is by no means exhaustive.

More recently, with the advent of the Macintosh II computer, 8-bit color paint programs like Pixel Paint 2.0 by SuperMac, Modern Artist 2.0 by Computer Friends, and Studio 8 by Electronic Arts have been introduced. These color programs offer the choice of 16.8 million colors from the color picker. You choose the color you want by using the Color program through the Control Panel. With an 8-bit video board, 256 colors can be on-screen at any one time. Currently, however, 24-bit color boards are on the market for Macintosh, and a 32-bit color QuickDraw is available. A 24-bit color system delivers photographic color on-screen.

Figure 14.1 shows a bit-mapped graphic object in a SuperPaint paint layer window. Notice the much larger collection of tools and patterns (not all are shown) that a full-featured paint program has. SuperPaint is one of several programs (Canvas is another) that contains both paint and draw layers together in the same program. To create many of the illustrations in this book, both MacPaint and SuperPaint were used.

## Screen Dumps

Have you ever wondered how writers create the sample screens used in operators' manuals and books like this one? A feature called a *screen dump* is the answer. The Macintosh offers a built-in screen dump capability, which creates a paint file that can be modified with programs like MacPaint, or used as is by Works.

To create screen dumps, you hold down three keys simultaneously: Shift-⌘-3. Works then creates a paint file that is an exact rendering of what's on-screen at the time you press the keys. Works automatically assigns each file one of ten names in the format *Screen n*, where n is a number from 0 to 9. When you have saved ten screens this way, you must rename them, move them to another disk, or trash them before you can create more.

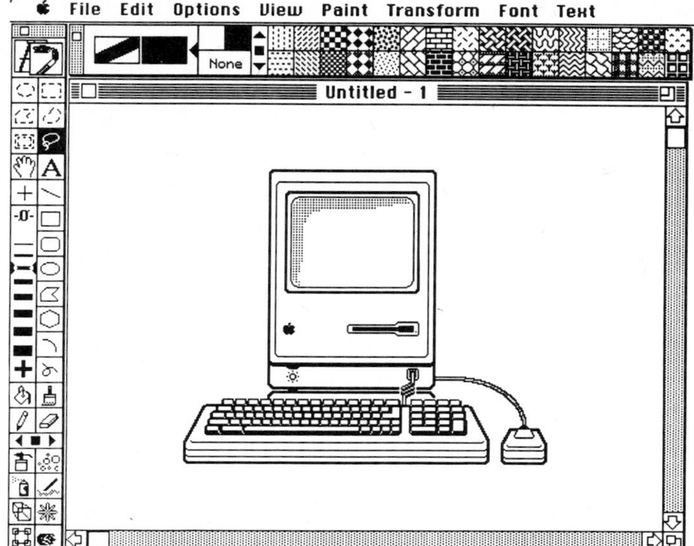


**Fig. 14.1**

*A SuperPaint paint window.*

The combination of Shift-⌘ and another key is called an *FKEY*, short for Function Key. Many shareware versions of FKEYS are available that do small convenience tasks, such as type the time or lock your screen. Check with the various users groups or find catalogs of companies that sell shareware programs.

If you have a Macintosh II with a color monitor, you may need to switch to the two-color characteristic setting on your Control Panel in order to do screen dumps. Often, screen dumps on a Macintosh II require a special shareware program to activate them, such as Scrn To Pict II, and the commercially available Capture.

Application programs sometimes prevent you from doing screen dumps with Shift-⌘-3. You cannot, for example, use this keystroke sequence to create a screen dump of the Works Greeting Screen. Macintosh Plus and SE users cannot generate screen dumps with the mouse button held down; therefore, capturing screens that show menus, for example, is impossible. Additionally, you cannot generally use the built-in screen dump with a Macintosh II.

Several companies offer desk accessories that get around these problems. One is Camera, a shareware accessory that enables you to take screen snapshots after a time delay that you set. This arrangement gives you time to invoke Camera, set up the screen that you want to capture, and even pull down and hold menus in place (see fig. 14.2). Macintosh Plus and SE users then can capture screens with the mouse button down. The program also gives you the option of hiding the pointer.

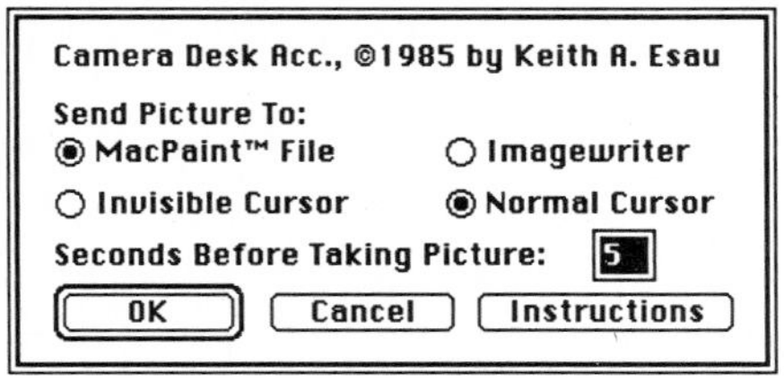

**Fig. 14.2**

*Using Camera to capture screen images after a time delay.*



Capture, from Mainstay, is a commercial product for doing screen dumps. Sold as an INIT, Capture works by creating a selection cursor that lets you drag the desired portion of the image on-screen. You can save it as a PICT file or copy it to your Clipboard. Capture works with all Macintosh models and supports full color PICT (as does the Clipboard).

## *Draw Programs*

In addition to bit-mapped images, you can import object-oriented graphics into Works. The draw layer in Works is object-oriented itself. For a more detailed discussion of manipulating objects, see Chapter 4, "Drawing," and Chapter 5, "Graphics and Design."

The first draw program offered with the Macintosh was MacDraw, which supports the standard PICT format. The PICT (from "picture") format uses Apple's QuickDraw programming routines. The other commonly used draw format (PostScript) includes graphics saved in the PostScript programming language, commonly saved along with formatting information as Encapsulated PostScript (EPS). Works can import any of these formats.

Several excellent draw programs are on the market, including the following: Canvas 2.0 (also a paint program) by Deneba, Cricket Draw, DeskDraw (part of the DeskPaint package) by Zedcor, MacDraft by Innovative Data Designs, MacDraw II by Claris, and SuperPaint (also a paint program) by Silicon Beach. Canvas also offers a companion DA. These programs are mostly meant to work in PICT format, except for Cricket Draw, which is output EPS to LaserWriters. Figure 14.3 shows a window from Cricket Draw.

Several programs are specifically designed to work in PostScript format. The two most prominent examples are Adobe Illustrator and Aldus Freehand. Both programs do full color separation and can use several of the current color models (RGB, CMYK, and so on) and can match color to the standard Pantone ink color system. These programs contain a full set of object tools and Bezier curve drawing functions, along with autotracing bit-mapped graphics to EPS. SuperPaint also supports Bezier curves and has an excellent autotrace feature. These programs are really graphic designer tools.

**Fig. 14.3**

*A full-featured draw program—Cricket Draw 1.1.*

## Clip Art

If you're not feeling artistic, or if you're in a hurry, you can purchase other people's art work and include it in your Works draw layer. These ready-made graphics are called clip art, and are available in either PICT or EPS format. Clip art graphic images can be quite stunning in quality. Libraries of digital art are now available on compact discs, which can contain up to 550-600M of data *each*, or the equivalent of 250,000 pages of typewritten text. A number of companies offer Macintosh clip art, and thousands of free or low-cost drawings are available in the public domain through clubs and shareware publishers.

Many of these drawing collections are cartoon-like; others are quite realistic, as you can see in figure 14.4. This figure shows some clip art from Dubl-Click Software and the bundled Art RoundUp DA. Drawings of people, places, maps, flags, tools, borders—you name it!—are available. You can assemble and modify most drawings by using the programs described previously in this chapter. After the drawings are in a compatible format, Works can use them.

**Fig. 14.4**

*Clip art from the Wet Paint series viewed with the Art RoundUp desk accessory.*

The low-cost and free clip art collections are suitable for school publications, newsletters, bulletin board announcements, and so forth. The more expensive professional-quality collections of art work are used by graphic artists to design ads, company logos, forms, and so on. Table 14.1 lists a few of the many sources of clip art. Check Appendix A for the addresses and telephone numbers of the manufacturers; call or write them for current catalogs and pricing information.

**Table 14.1**
**Clip Art Sources**

| *Product* | *Type* | *Sold by* |
|---|---|---|
| ArtWare:Borders | EPS | ArtWare Systems |
| Click & Clip | EPS | Studio Advertising Art |
| ClickArt | EPS | T/Maker Graphics |

| | | |
|---|---|---|
| EPS Illustrations | EPS | T/Maker |
| Image Club | EPS, disk, CD | Image Club Graphics |
| Japanese Clip Art | PICT | Qualitas Trading |
| Mac Art Dept. | PICT | Simon & Schuster |
| MacGraphics | PICT, 10 Megs | GoldMind Publishing |
| Post Art I | EPS | Olduvai |
| WetPaint | PICT | Dubl-Click Software |

If you store a lot of clip art to disk, you may want to look into using Curator by Solutions International and PictureBase by Symmetry. Both programs enable you to create catalogs of your art and label them by name or key word for later search and retrieval. Curator supports PICT, TIFF, EPS, and so on and can convert between format types.

## *File Conversion Utilities*

The proliferation of graphic file formats has led to programs that can read and convert between different formats. The two most prominent packages are Open It! from TenpointO and SuperGlue II from Solutions International.

SuperGlue II (a replacement for SuperGlue) contains two programs. One, SuperImageSaver (an INIT; see the top box in figure 14.5), is selected through the Chooser DA, and redirects to a disk file any output that would go to your printer. This redirected printer output is always stored as a series of QuickDraw commands, regardless of whether you have sent text, graphics, or both to the disk. You can use SuperImageSaver to capture items that otherwise are unavailable to the Works word processor feature, such as complete database reports. Choosing the Print command with Super ImageSaver selected brings up the SuperImageSaver Print dialog box (the middle box in figure 14.5). If you click OK, you are prompted via the Save Image As dialog box (bottom of figure 14.5) to name the Image File you are about to create, and to choose the appropriate format.

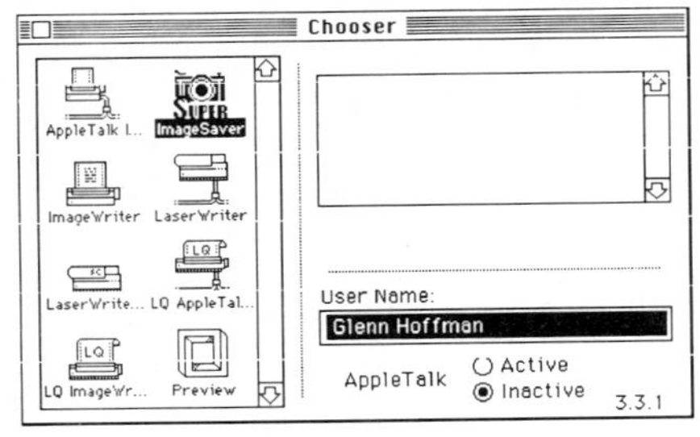


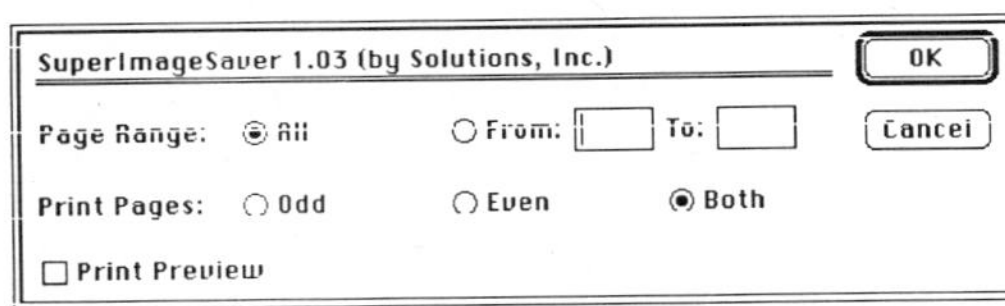


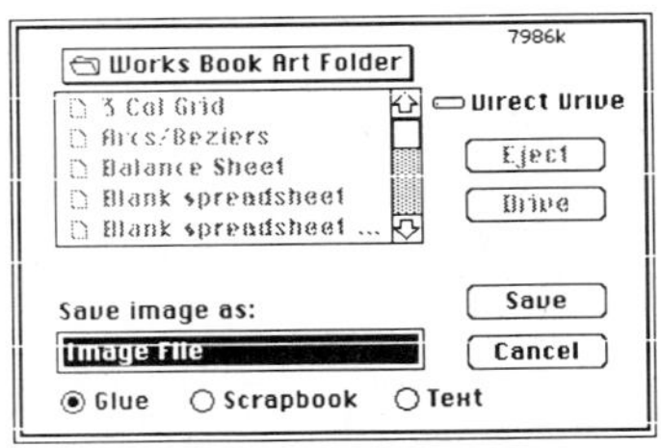


**Fig. 14.5**

*Using SuperGlue to convert print files to disk files.*

After you save the image you created with SuperGlue, you can view and modify the image by using the second program in the SuperGlue package: Viewer. Viewer enables you to see the contents of the Super ImageSaver files you have created. You also can print the files, convert them to PICT files, or save them as a Scrapbook or Text file. You can capture images larger than the screen, even if your paint or draw program will not let you copy them directly to the Clipboard.

With Works you cannot copy database reports directly to a word processor window. If you use SuperGlue to send a report to a bit-mapped file, however, you can import the report into a Works word processor window as a bit-mapped object. You can resize the report, draw lines, and so on. Remember, however, that the report is a graphic, so you cannot use Works to edit the text in the report. In figure 14.6, for instance, a Works report has been pasted into a Works word processor document, and the Works draw feature was used to add a box around part of the report. Then the Line Draw feature was used to add "drop shadow" lines at the bottom and to the right of the box.

CONFIDENTIAL KEY EMPLOYEE PHONE LIST

August 27, 1987

| LAST NAME | FIRST NAME | EXT | MSN | JOB TITLE | DEPARTMENT |
|---|---|---|---|---|---|
| Baxter | James | 5844 | 4321 | Director Personnel | Personnel |
| Baxter | Tammy | 5845 | 4321 | Assistant Director | Personnel |
| Berfel | Ferd | 0987 | 99 | Pull Tab Inspector | Test Lab |
| Flushland | Johnathon | 4324 | 543 | Cleaning Associate | Maintenance |
| Goldberg | Rubin | 7655 | 45 | Director, Engineering | Engineering |
| Gunlatch | Raymond | 0001 | 001 | President | Corporate |
| Gunlatch | Nancy | 0002 | 001 | Assistant to the President | Corporate |
| Makit | Willie | 3345 | 21 | Production Supervisor | Production |
| Mi | Sue | 7654 | 45 | New Product Development | Engineering |
| Norcross | Oliver | UNL | UNL | Sales | Sales |
| Quickcloser | John | 6543 | 43 | Inside Sales | Sales |
| So | Mi | 6543 | 43 | Inside Sales | Sales |
| Winston | Doc | 3456 | 565 | Sr. Sardine Eye Closer | Production |

**Fig. 14.6**

*A report pasted as a picture into a word processing window and enhanced with the Works drawing function.*

SuperGlue II offers a text-extraction mode that lets you capture reports as text (ASCII) and then paste the text into word processing windows for normal editing. A complete description of the Glue and SuperGlue programs is beyond the scope of this book.

Open It! provides several functions that overlap with those of SuperGlue and SmartScrap and the Clipper. Open It! provides a print-to-disk function, preview of documents on-screen, import and export of various graphic file formats, and an intelligent, full-featured Scrapbook.

## *Graphs*

Although the Works spreadsheet module provides five types of graphs, it contains very little capability for manipulating the data within the graph or for adding many of the niceties, such as error bars commonly found in scientific graphs. Cricket Graph offers professional graphing with 12 different graph types linked to a spreadsheet. Color is supported, as are data sets of up to 100 X 2,700 elements. A wide import and export file compatibility is supported by Cricket Graph.

With the recent advent of highly graphical presentation spreadsheets such as Trapeze by Access Technologies, Wingz by Informix, Full Impact by Ashton-Tate, and Excel by Microsoft, it is also possible to generate high quality graphs by exporting spreadsheet data to one of those programs.

# *Graphic Scanners*

*Scanners* are devices that convert images to digital form, creating bit-mapped images your Macintosh can store and manipulate. Scanners vary in terms of the number of *bits per pixel* they store. More than two bits can define shades of gray tones, and these scanners are typically called *gray-scale scanners*. Lower-priced scanners scan images at either 16 or 64 gray-scale. Some of the high-priced scanners that produce newspaper quality graphics deliver 256 gray-scale. The price of the scanners available ranges from $250 for ThunderScan by ThunderWare to as much as $6000 for some of the 256 gray-scale scanners. Apple sells the 16 gray-scale Apple Scanner with a HyperCard interface called HyperScan for $1,799. Typical 64 gray-scale scanners cost from $2,000 to $3,500 and deliver bit-mapped graphics at 300 dpi resolution—the same resolution as the LaserWriter printer. Most scanners can save their output in PICT (or PICT II) format, but the preferred format is TIFF, which contains more embedded information.

The ThunderWare scanner is an interesting low-price solution to scanning needs. It costs $250 and replaces the ribbon in an ImageWriter printer. (Note that ThunderScan works only with the ImageWriter II printer.) ThunderScan delivers reasonable quality scans, but the system is slow and susceptible to stair-stepping (jagged lines) if the paper is fed into your ImageWriter at the wrong angle. ThunderWare also sells a handheld scanner called LightningScan.

Scanners capture photographs, drawings, handwritten signatures, and other visual images. Some systems, such as Koala's MacVision, can even capture video images from a video camera or videotape player. The quality and resolution of scanner-captured images, which you import into the draw layer as you would any other graphic images, varies widely. The scanner field is changing very rapidly, and the Macintosh II series is becoming the platform of choice for a wide variety of digital imaging systems.

One software application that is quite exciting and in which the Macintosh has become the leading edge computer is digital image retouching. The two programs that accomplish this function are Image Studio by Letraset and Digital Darkroom by Silicon Beach. You use these programs to import scanned images (or any image) and by using a variety of tools, such as airbrushes, smudges, charcoal pencils, and selection tools, you can totally rework the digital image. The results can be quite astonishing. Small businesses have been set up to restore old photographs, and you can produce "science fiction-like" effects.

These programs are quite memory intensive, however, so you need to have a Macintosh with at least a 68020 CPU and 2M of RAM. Actually, you will find that you may require from 4-8M of RAM to be able to work adequately with some of these images. An 8 1/2-by-11 inch image created at 64 gray-scale can occupy from 1-2M of data.

Just around the corner are full color scanners (a few are now on the market) and color versions of digital image retouching software. The amount of memory required to work with 24 bit-per-pixel full color images boggles the mind (4-8M of RAM), and the pocketbook. Four megabytes of RAM used with virtual memory should be adequate.

# Fonts

We have discussed fonts and desk accessories at length in previous sections. For information on fonts, refer to the sections "Fonts, Printers, and Networks" in Chapter 1, "Adding Style to Your Documents" in Chapter 3, and "Following Some Basic Design Guidelines" in Chapter 5. For information on Desk Accessories, refer to "Using the Apple Menu and Desk Accessories" in Chapter 1.

Currently, a limitation of 15 DAs and 15 fonts is placed on Apple system software. Two third-party developers have created notable products to solve this problem: Suitcase II by Fifth Generation Systems and Master Juggler by ALSoft. Both products allow you to access suitcase files of fonts and DAs that you create by using Font/DA Mover (see "Fonts, Printers, and Networks" in Chapter 1) anywhere on your hard drive. You can use literally hundreds of fonts and DAs, as well as work with multiple FKEYs and sound resources. You should not own a hard drive without installing one of these two products.

The interface for Suitcase II is shown in figure 14.7. This utility (an INIT) installs as a DA and can be used to open any DA, Font, FKEY, and Sound in a suitcase for which you define a path. You also can examine the various styles of type in a font. With both Suitcase and Master Juggler you can compress your font files and resolve font identification number conflicts.

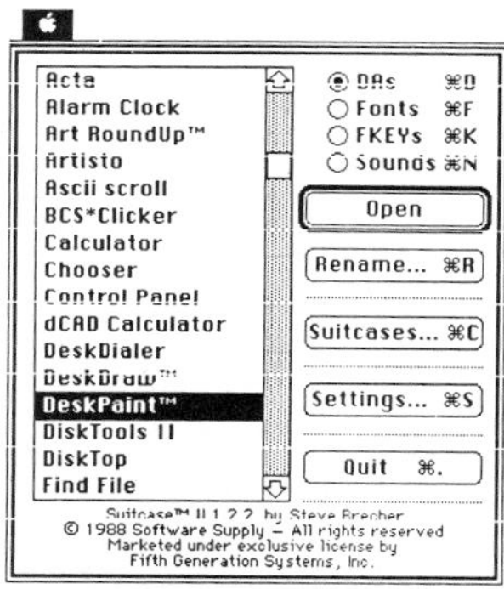


**Fig. 14.7**

*Using Suitcase II to manage multiple fonts and DA files.*

Many fonts in the public domain are distributed as shareware and freeware. Apple also supplies a set of fonts for use in system software. Commercial developers sell font families that can turn your Macintosh into a professional typesetting machine. Although the subject of type is beyond the scope of this book, there are a number of both bit-mapped and PostScript commercial fonts that you may want to investigate. Some of these fonts are listed in table 14.2

**Table 14.2**
**Commercial Fonts**

| *Product* | *Type* | *Manufacturer* |
|---|---|---|
| Adobe Type Library | PostScript | Adobe Corporation |
| MacFontware Typefaces | PostScript | Bitstream Corporation |
| Complementary Type | PostScript | Software Complement |
| Fluent Fonts | bit-map | CasadyWare |
| FONTastic Plus | bit-map | Altsys Corporation |
| FontSizer | Postscript | U.S. MicroLabs |
| LaserFonts | PostScript | Century Software |
| World-Class Fonts | bit-map | Dubl-Click Software |

# *Spoolers*

Works and most other programs usually force you to wait until your printer finishes printing before you can do anything else. If you have a slow printer and a long document containing graphics and fancy fonts, the wait can seem eternal. Printer manufacturers have begun including microprocessors and memory within printers to alleviate the problem; for example, a Motorola 68020 chip with 2 to 8M of installed RAM is built into a LaserWriter NTX. Printers like the LaserWriter SC, ImageWriter II and LQ, and most QuickDraw-based printers, however, rely on the Macintosh to supply the instructions needed to drive the printer. This reliance on the computer is what slows down and ties up your computer.

Two basic techniques can work around this problem. One involves buying a hardware device, similar to a disk cache, that downloads the print information. An example of this approach is the Proteus Double Buffer and Data Switch *print buffer*, sold by Computer Friends, Inc.

Another approach implements the solution by means of software. These programs are called *print spoolers* (which comes from the words "simultaneous print operators on-line") and they solve this problem by writing print instructions out to a print file. As you are working on another project, your print spooler steals small amounts of computer time to send information out to your printer. This method is not true multitasking because the spooler is not sending data all the time. Because your printer is so much slower than your computer, however, this technique works fine.

Apple includes a print spooler called Background Printing for spooling data to a LaserWriter printer. (Note that Background Printing is available only under MultiFinder. In System 7.0, however, all printers will be supported.) Other manufacturers, notably Infosphere's LaserServe and SuperMac Software's SuperSpool (for ImageWriters) and SuperLaserSpool (for both ImageWriters and LaserWriters), supply print spoolers. These utilities enable you to put the documents to be printed in order by priority, and create and work with a print queue (see figs. 14.8 and 14.9).

Spoolers are often built-in on a network. If you work in a group environment with your Macintosh, using AppleTalk or AppleShare (by Apple), or TOPS ( from "Transcendental Operating System") by Sun Microsystems, you can be sure that the network contains spoolers. Check with your network manual or computer dealer for more details.

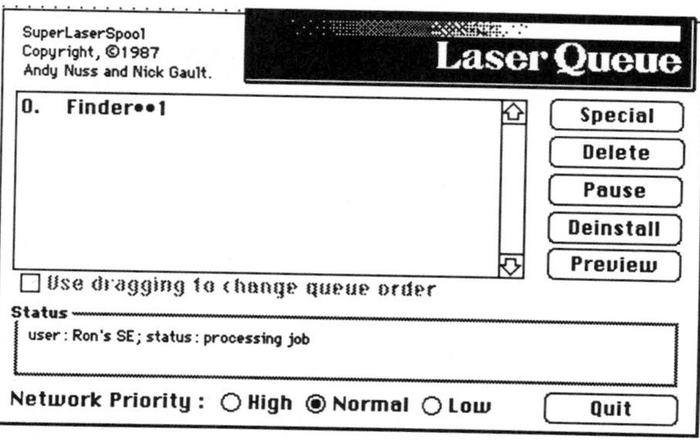


**Fig. 14.8**

*Using a spooler so that you can work on the Macintosh while your printer prints.*

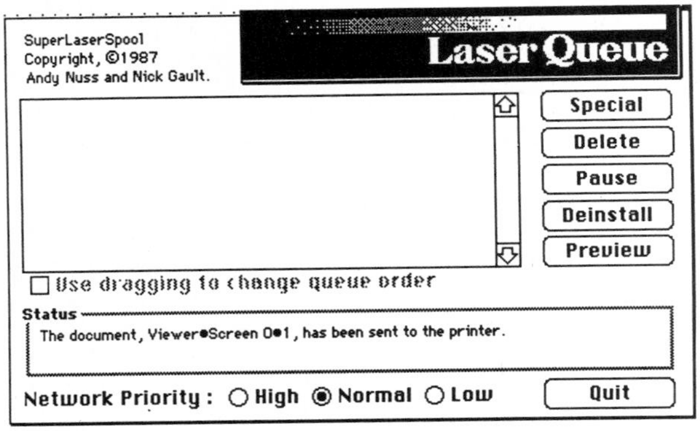

**Fig. 14.9**

*Printing-in-progress message from spooler.*

# *Templates and Canned Databases*

Setting up a new spreadsheet or database takes time; and entering the data, proofing it, and perfecting the spreadsheet can take even longer. Not surprisingly, some people decide not to undertake major new projects because of these time constraints.

If you're one of these people, consider purchasing the time and talents of others. A number of Works owners have spent time creating spreadsheets and databases in order to balance checkbooks, keep auto expense logs, perform mortgage calculations, do business planning, do engineering tasks, and so forth. For a small fee, these users will share their work with others. They've created spreadsheets called templates and collections of data called canned databases.

## *The WorksXchange*

Heizer Software acts as a commercial clearinghouse for tutorials, templates, and databases that independent developers have written in Works. The library of Works programs is called "The WorksXchange," and the company's offerings are vast and amazing. Among the current bestsellers are (program names are capitalized): a Schedule C Accounting System, model Business Plans, a Stock Portfolio Guide, a Mutual Fund Reinvestment Program, the NAIC Stock Selection Guide, a set of Works Payroll Templates, a Check Book template, a Personal Financial Planner, an All-Purpose Mortgage Calculator, federal and (some) state Tax Templates, and a set of Works Tutorials that offer a guided tour of the program. Space does not permit a full description of all the listings; some are whimsical, some are informative, and some defy characterization.

## *BAKERForms*

Baker Graphics sells a complete accounting solution called BAKER-Forms, which uses Microsoft Works as its engine (the software used to run another application). Designed for small businesses, you use it to prepare checks, invoices, and purchase orders on your Macintosh. Output is to an ImageWriter printer. The company distributes both the software and the forms needed to operate the system.

# *Information Exchange Devices and Software*

In an ideal world, you could take any word processing document, database, or spreadsheet created on your computer, and use that file on any other machine, regardless of make or model. But the world is far from ideal. As the number of computer brands and models increases, system compatibility and file compatibility become major stumbling blocks to the exchange of information.

Manufacturers routinely select incompatible disk drives, file storage techniques, graphics standards, operating systems, and other design approaches that are beyond the scope of this book. The result is an almost numbing array of compatibility problems. Sometimes the manufacturers do this deliberately.

Recently, computer hardware manufactures, software developers, and conversion specialists have started addressing this problem. They are doing so for two reasons. First, they are eager to have their new products coexist with today's massive "installed base" of computer hardware and software. Second, users are demanding a simple way to upgrade to fewer products and share information among themselves. Because a version of Works operates on PC-compatible (MS-DOS) computers, it is not surprising that Works now provides methods to facilitate such exchanges.

## *Hardware Issues*

If you need to exchange Works data with dissimilar machines (PCs, for example), things can be a bit tricky, because the disk drives probably are incompatible. The recent Apple FDHD drive can read MS-DOS formatted 3 1/2-inch floppy disks. To read a 5 1/4-inch disk, you need to consider purchasing a special disk drive and controller. Apple sells one of those as well.

Modems can help in these situations. If the dissimilar machines are in close proximity, you may be able to "hard wire" them by using a simple cable, thereby eliminating the need for modems and telephone lines. Another way to accomplish the exchange is to use a local area network that can accommodate both types of machines.

## Compatibility Issues

Getting information from one machine's disk to another's does not solve the more serious software compatibility problems. Program files rarely run on dissimilar systems. For instance, you cannot copy Microsoft Works (the Macintosh version) to an IBM PC disk and then use the IBM PC to run the Works program. Files containing data, such as word processor text and database records, frequently can be used by different machines. But the files must first be "converted" or cleaned up (usually, but not always). The Apple File Exchange program can reformat files in a number of different ways. For more information about this program, refer to your Apple System software (utilities) manual.

Some types of files, designed to be exchanged, work with little or no modification. The rest of this chapter deals with specific exchange and conversion procedures.

## Data Exchange Standards

When two products (such as Works and Excel) create files that use the same standard, exchanging accurate data is much easier. A number of data exchange standards have evolved over time. Works supports several standards, including the following:

- ❑ SYLK (for "Symbolic Link")
- ❑ ASCII (also sometimes called text files)
- ❑ Tab-separated fields within Return-separated records
- ❑ Multiple-space-separated fields within Return-separated records

Standards are loose definitions at best. Most vendors, for example, have their own "dialect" of ASCII. They usually can agree on how to represent letters and numbers electronically; but exchanges of special symbols, underscore instructions, commands for boldface printing, and so on, are more complicated. Because of these problems, more and more companies are offering conversion programs, which act as intermediaries in the exchange process.

# Works Conversion Features

Microsoft Works has some specific features that enable you to import information from selected non-Works programs. These features let you upgrade from a word processing package like MacWrite to the power of Works, without retyping all your frequently used MacWrite documents. You also can export items created by Works to programs like PageMaker and similar desktop publishing programs. Moreover, you can exchange Works spreadsheets with many of today's popular stand-alone spreadsheet programs, such as Excel.

Although compatibility issues sometimes arise, the exchanges listed in table 14.3 are relatively easy to make.

**Table 14.3**
**Ways Works Information Can Be Converted**

| *From* | *To* |
|---|---|
| Microsoft Word | Works word processing |
| MacWrite | Works word processing |
| Most ASCII word processing files | Works word processing |
| Works word processing | Most desktop publishing programs |
| Works word processing files | Most ASCII word processors |
| Excel spreadsheets | Works spreadsheets |
| Multiplan spreadsheets | Works spreadsheets |
| Works spreadsheets | Excel spreadsheets |
| Works spreadsheets | Multiplan spreadsheets |
| Most ASCII databases | Works databases |
| Works databases | Most ASCII databases |

## Importing Word Processing Text

You can import non-Works text files easily for use in a word processing window from the following word processors:

- ❑ Microsoft Word for the Macintosh Versions 1.0, 3.0, and 4.0
- ❑ MacWrite, all versions through Version 5.0
- ❑ Any application producing ASCII output
- ❑ Any word processing application that creates a Rich Text Format (RTF) file. This group includes Word 3.0 and 4.0, and versions of Word for the PC, and page layout programs like PageMaker.

Before you begin a conversion, print a copy of the document you intend to convert, using the original word processing software (Word, MacWrite, and so on). You can refer to that hard copy to see what the finished conversion should look like.

To import a Word, MacWrite, ASCII, or RTF file to the Works word processor, follow these instructions:

1. Choose the Open command on the File menu, which brings up the Open (SF Get) dialog box.
2. Click the Word Processor icon.
3. Click the Import File box. You see lists of ASCII files and folders containing ASCII files.
4. Double-click the desired file.
5. Works opens an untitled window with your file in it.

**NOTE:** Do not open SYLK files from the word processor because the conversion will not proceed correctly. If you do open a SYLK file by mistake, simply close the file and open another.

If all goes well, the resulting text file should be usable. You may need to reformat it, change margins, add tabs, adjust page endings, and so on. Figure 14.10 shows a file immediately after importation. Figure 14.11 shows the "fixed" file. You also may need to change fonts, add underscoring, and make other stylistic adjustments.

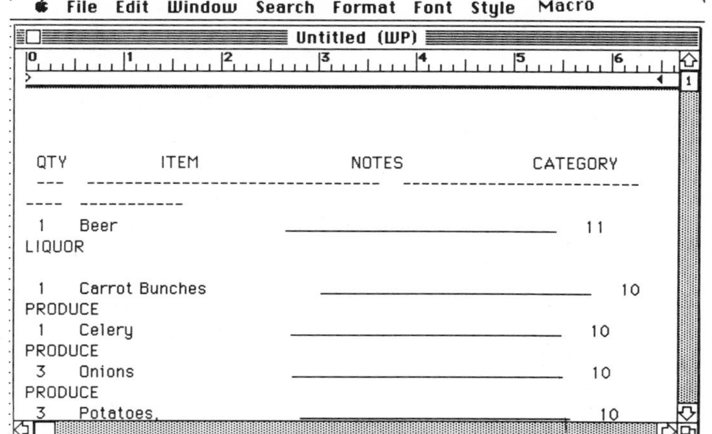


**Fig. 14.10**

*Part of an imported file with a few problems.*

File Edit Window Search Format Font Style Macro

Untitled (WP)

| QTY | ITEM | NOTES | | CATEGORY |
|---|---|---|---|---|
| 1 | Beer | ________ | 11 | LIQUOR |
| 1 | Carrot Bunches | ________ | 10 | PRODUCE |
| 1 | Celery | ________ | 10 | PRODUCE |
| 3 | Onions | ________ | 10 | PRODUCE |
| 3 | Potatoes, | ________ | 10 | PRODUCE |
| 1 | Bologna - Turkey | Louis Rich | 9 | MEAT |
| 1 | Chip Dip | ________ | 9 | DAIRY |

**Fig. 14.11**

*The fixed file.*

Sometimes imported documents are a mess, as shown in figure 14.12. Either this file was not really an ASCII document to begin with, or it's a nearly unusable dialect of ASCII. In such cases, you can delete the unwanted characters; however, if the document is large, that process may be more trouble than it's worth.

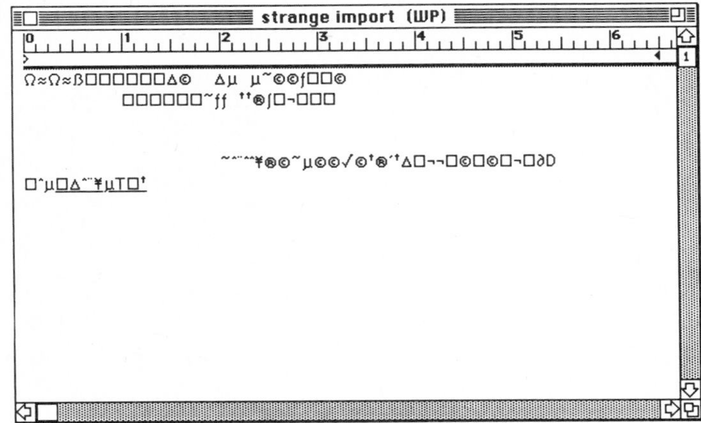


**Fig. 14.12**

*An imported file with big problems.*

# *Exporting Word Processing Text*

Most word processing software packages, such as MacWrite, Microsoft Word, and WriteNow, can import ASCII (or text only) documents. Many desktop publishing packages also can accept ASCII text. But if you save the file as ASCII text, you lose all your formatting information except tabs and carriage returns. Many programs can read files in the RTF format, however. Whenever possible, you should try to work with such compatible programs. Now, for example, you can export directly to Aldus PageMaker (using PageMaker's Place Text command) in RTF.

To export a Works word processing document, follow these steps:

1. Select the Save As command on the File menu, which brings up the Save (SF Put) dialog box.
2. Click the Export box and name the file. For an RTF file, click the Export as Rich Text Format box.
3. Click the Save button.

**NOTE:** Some of Apple's special characters may not be compatible with those of the importing system, if these characters are saved in your ASCII file at all. Be sure to proofread carefully the results of your exports and imports.

## Converting Spreadsheets

Plenty of good reasons for converting spreadsheets exist. For example, a friend or associate may have developed (on a dissimilar computer system) a template that you want to use. Or you may want to buy a template that is available only for Excel or Multiplan. Or you may use a stand-alone spreadsheet program at home and use Works in the office. Whatever the motivation, you need to keep in mind several points.

First, no two spreadsheet packages are identical, even if they're sold by the same company. For example, Works and Excel both come from Microsoft, but they offer different features. If the spreadsheet you plan to convert uses features (or functions) not supported by the destination product, problems arise. Sometimes you can work around them by redesigning the source spreadsheet or by using one technique on the source spreadsheet and a different approach on the destination spreadsheet.

This process can be confusing and time-consuming. Developing a new spreadsheet from scratch may be quicker than converting and testing one. This factor is particularly true if you want to convert a complex spreadsheet created on a feature-rich product like Excel for use with Works.

Second, Works represents numeric values differently from the way many other spreadsheet programs do. Works, for example, ignores the formatting of values contained in SYLK files and treats all numeric values as if they were in General format. Works also treats Date and Time imports as serial numbers.

Third, Works, Excel, and Multiplan all treat error values differently; and Works supports fewer operators than Excel or Multiplan. Specifically, Works doesn't support union, concatenation, or intersection operators.

Finally, computations containing or resulting in extremely small and extremely large numbers may produce slightly different results from package to package. The three programs also handle logical values (And, Or, True, False, and Not) differently. As for special functions, Works sometimes treats them differently or doesn't support them at all.

### Importing and Exporting Spreadsheets

You can import non-Works spreadsheets to Works by using one of two standards: SYLK or Text with Values/Formulas. If the source spreadsheet supports SYLK file formats, use that method of exchange. Microsoft Excel and Multiplan both create SYLK files for export to Works. SYLK files contain the labels, values, equations, formats, type attributes, and so forth.

The second spreadsheet importing option, Text with Values/Formulas, is useful when the source spreadsheet program creates files with cell contents separated by tabs, and row endings indicated by Return characters. Works always loads these files beginning in cell A1.

To import SYLK or text files to the Works spreadsheet, use the following procedure:

1. Select the Open command on the File menu, which brings up the Open (SF Get) dialog box.
2. Select the Spreadsheet icon.
3. Click the Import File box, and Works shows any SYLK or text files on disk.
4. Click the Open button, which results in a dialog box that requests you to specify whether the file is in SYLK or Text format (see fig. 14.13).
5. Make the appropriate choice in step 4, and click the OK button.
6. Works opens an untitled spreadsheet window.

**NOTE:** If Works loads a SYLK file with an unknown formula, the formula becomes text and a quotation mark is inserted in front of it. Make changes as need. Works warns you of conversion problems with an alert box.

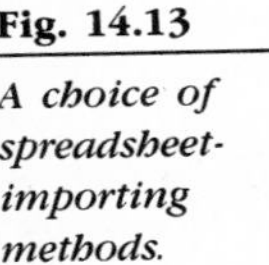

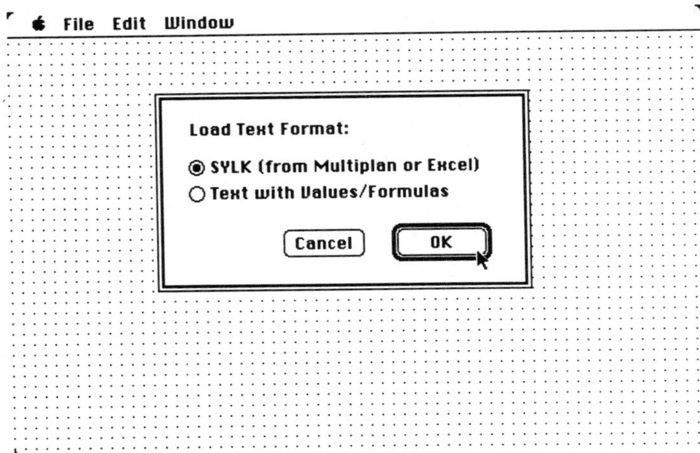


**Fig. 14.13**

*A choice of spreadsheet-importing methods.*

> **Caution:** A spreadsheet may convert without any warning message from Works or it may look all right after conversion takes place, but still not perform properly. You should subject the imported spreadsheet to all the testing you perform on any new design.

You can export Works spreadsheets for use by Excel, Multiplan, and other spreadsheet packages. And you can export text versions of spreadsheets for use in word processing packages. To access the SYLK, Text Only, and Text with Values/Formulas options, you click the Export File box in the Save As dialog box. Your choice will vary according to how you plan to use the exported file. If you plan to load the file into Excel or Multiplan, you should use SYLK to obtain the best results. If you choose the Text with Values Only option, Works creates an ASCII file that most text editors and desktop publishing systems can use.

# Exchanging Databases

On the surface, database conversion looks straightforward when compared to spreadsheet conversion. Either the source data arrives properly or it doesn't. But data must be used after it's converted, and for this reason database conversion requires some forethought.

Before you convert big database files, do some quick testing. Enter a few records manually to see whether Works (or any other destination database package) can handle your application. Large data conversions take time, and working for hours only to find that you need a feature not provided by the destination database is frustrating.

You also need to consider available memory. Works stores databases entirely in memory, but some (not all) other database programs use the disk for working storage and can frequently hold more records than Works. A big database may need to be divided into several smaller ones if Works is to use it, and this procedure is not practical. You also need to understand something about the way the source database exports or imports information.

## Using Popular Database Exchange Formats

Works can import database files of the following types:

- ❑ Tab-separated fields in records separated by return characters. These fields are used by Microsoft File as text files.

- Fields separated by two or more spaces, records separated by return characters.
- Field count, each field within a record separated by a return character, with a fixed number of fields per record. You tell Works the number of fields per record.

### Tab-Separated Fields

Many Macintosh database packages use fields separated by tabs and contained in records separated by returns. As you may recall, this method is used to prepare a word processing document for conversion to a database.

### Fields Separated by Multiple Spaces

Using fields separated by multiple spaces is a risky way to import data because a simple typo anywhere in a field can ruin the rest of the conversion. Works simply looks for any occurrence of two contiguous spaces anywhere in the database and starts a new field. If the spaces are accidental (or intentionally typed within the contents of the field), the conversion is flawed. Use other conversion methods whenever possible.

### Fixed-Field Formats

Some databases can export a specific number of fields per record, regardless of whether the fields are empty or not; these databases are sometimes called fixed-field formats. You simply tell Works how many fields to expect from each record. The rest is automatic—providing, of course, that the source file always contains a fixed number of fields per record.

## Importing Databases

Before importing a database, you may want to print it. You can then use this hard copy to see what the finished conversion should look like. To import a database, follow these instructions:

1. Invoke the Open command on the File menu to bring up the Open (SF Get) dialog box.
2. Click the Data Base icon, and click the Import File box. Works then displays ASCII files and folders containing ASCII files.

3. Double-click or highlight the appropriate file and click the OK button.

4. A new dialog box appears (see fig. 14.14). Select the appropriate import method, and Works then imports the data. If you are uncertain of the correct format, try different options. Save the document only when you find the correct format.

5. Rename, rearrange, and resize the fields, if necessary.

6. Works opens an untitled database, with field names labeled "Field 1," "Field 2," and so forth. In some data conversions, the field names are imported as the entries in the first record.

**NOTE:** Do not open SYLK files in the database mode, because they will not convert correctly. If you open one by mistake, close it and open a file of the correct format.

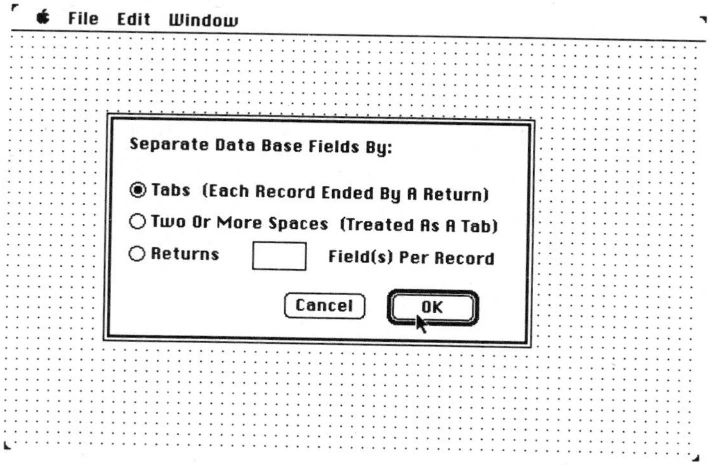

File Edit Window

Separate Data Base Fields By:

Tabs (Each Record Ended By A Return)

Two Or More Spaces (Treated As A Tab)

Returns Field(s) Per Record

Cancel OK

**Fig. 14.14**

*Choosing a database import method.*

## *Exporting Databases*

You can export entire Works databases for use by other database packages, or you can export only selected records. To access these options, use the Save or Save As (SF Put) dialog box (see fig. 14.15) to create a text file. Field names automatically become the entries in the first records of the text file. Works exports records separated by return characters; the fields within those records are separated by tabs.

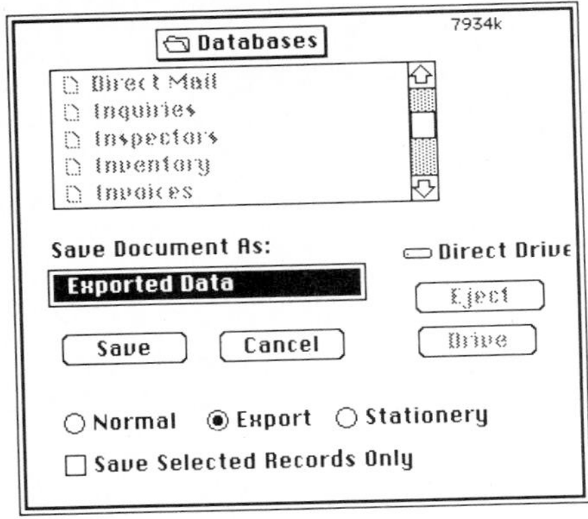


**Fig. 14.15**

*Using the Export button to export a database file.*

To export a database file, do the following:

1. Rearrange the order of the fields, if necessary.
2. Define selection criteria, if appropriate, using the selection methods explained in Chapter 9.
3. Choose Save As from the menu, and save as a text file.
4. Click the Export button.
5. Click the Save Selected Records Only box, if appropriate.
7. Name the destination file, and click the OK button.

Each database package you import to uses a slightly different technique to load and use imported files. You need to find out the details for your particular application or ask for experienced help.

## *Importing AppleWorks Files*

If you have files that you have created on the Apple II with the AppleWorks program, you can import them into Microsoft Works by using Apple's File Exchange Program on the Macintosh. Apple File Exchange will convert your Apple ProDOS files by using the Works-Works Transporter file.

In order to read these files, you must have them on a 3 1/2-inch floppy disk. To copy information from a 5 1/4-inch disk to a 3 1/2-inch disk, use an Apple IIe, Apple IIc, or an Apple IIGS that has both a 3 1/2-inch and 5 1/4-inch disk drive. Start AppleWorks and save the file by using the standard AppleWorks commands.

To convert your AppleWorks file to a Macintosh file, follow these steps:

1. Place a copy of the Works-Works Transporter file in the Apple File Exchange Folder.
2. Double-click the Apple File Exchange icon (in the Finder) or click once and choose the Open command (refer to your Macintosh Utilities user's guide for more information).
3. Put the AppleWorks disk in the Macintosh disk drive.
4. Select the Works-Works Transporter file.
5. In the list of the File Exchange dialog box, select the file you want to convert.
6. Click the Transfer button. Your Macintosh converts the file.
7. Choose the Quit command on the File menu to return to the Finder.

**TIP:** You also can have AppleWorks print to disk, then transfer the resulting text file by using Apple File Exchange (AFX) standard text transfer. Next, import the file to whatever application you want.

File Exchange converts AppleWorks formats as follows:

- Word processor text to Monaco 9-point type with all style and justification intact. Margins become paragraph indents, and indents become first-line indents. Headers and footers become text items in the body of the document.
- Database category names become field names. Record data become field entries, but if you convert a single record database you see a form window. Multiple records convert as a list window.
- Spreadsheet labels, formulas, and values are transferred to the correct cell.

## *Beyond Works*

You are probably wondering how it is possible to outgrow a program like Works! You probably also are wondering how you filled up your 80M disk drive. Answers to questions like these are always obvious in hindsight. Really the question is what programs to consider when you feel you need more functionality than Works provides.

Several full-featured word processors exist for the Macintosh market today. These word processors are Microsoft Word 4.0, Nixsus by Paragon Concepts, FullWrite Professional by Ashton-Tate, MacWrite II by Claris, WordPerfect by WordPerfect, WriteNow for the Macintosh by T/Maker, and Write by Microsoft, roughly in order of preference by users. The last two choices do not offer any additional value over the Works word processor. Basically, the major difference in the word processors mentioned is that they offer convenience features like outlining and improved layout capabilities.

If you need a more powerful database, you can choose from several good ones. Fourth Dimension from Acius, FoxBase+/Mac from Fox Software, Double Helix II from Odesta, Omni 3 from Blythe, Reflex Plus from Borland/Analytica, and dBASE Mac from Ashton-Tate are the choices in relational databases. For flat file databases, the choices are FileMaker II by Claris and Multiplan from Microsoft. It is unlikely that you will want to upgrade to another flat file from Works. You should instead consider one of the relational databases.

Foxbase reads dBASE files and is very fast; Fourth Dimension, Omni 3, and Double Helix are quite graphical and full featured.

For spreadsheets, the current choices are Microsoft Excel, Wingz from Informix, Full Impact from Ashton-Tate, and Trapeze from Access Technology. All these spreadsheets are considered presentation spreadsheets, because they have considerable graphing and representation capabilities.

The favored dedicated communications programs include Red Ryder from Freesoft, MicroPhone II from Software Ventures, VersaTerm-Pro from Peripherals, Computers & Supplies, and Smartcom II by Hayes.

## Conclusion

That's it! If you have read this entire book, you have learned about a fascinating and powerful tool that enables you to organize your professional and personal life while adding some fun and style to even the most boring tasks. No doubt you will discover new applications, techniques, and shortcuts as you use Works.

A

# Resources

The following is a list of products discussed in this book and the vendors that supply them. To obtain reviews of these products, check the current issue of *MacUser* (Ziff-Davis Publishing Co., One Park Avenue, New York, NY 10016). Check the MiniFinders section at the back of the magazine for capsule reviews and the Updates section for the current program versions. The Updates section is generally found just before the MiniFinders section.

For more recent information, and as an alternative source for program and vendor information, see *The Macintosh Buyer's Guide* (Redgate Communications Corporation, 660 Beachland Boulevard, Vero Beach, CA 32963).

**3G Graphics**
Suite 6155
11410 NE 124th Street
Kirkland, WA 98034
(206) 823-8198
Images With Impact!

**Access Technology**
6 Pleasant Street
South Natick, MA 01760
(508) 655-9191
MindWrite, Trapeze

**ACIUS**
20300 Stevens Creek Blvd.
Suite 495
Cupertino, CA 95014
(408) 252-4444
4th Dimension

Acta from Symmetry

**Adobe Systems**
1585 Charleston Road
Mountain View, CA 94039
(415) 961-4400
Illustrator, Laser Fonts, PostScript

**Affinity Microsystems**
Suite 425
1050 Walnut Street
Boulder, CO 80302
(800) 367-6771 or (303) 442-4840
Tempo

**Aldus**
411 First Avenue South
Suite 200
Seattle, WA 98104
(206) 622-5500
Freehand, PageMaker

**ALSoft**
Box 927
Spring, TX 77383
(713) 353-4090
DiskExpress, Master Juggler

**Apple Computer**
20525 Mariani Avenue
Cupertino, CA 95014
(408) 996-1010
Macintosh computers; fonts; CD drive; HyperCard; ImageWriter and LaserWriter printers; LocalTalk, AppleTalk, and AppleShare networks; Apple Scanner

**Ashton-Tate**
20101 Hamilton Avenue
Torrance, CA 90502
(213) 329-8000
dBASE Mac, FullPaint, FullWrite

**Baker Graphics**
204 Court Street
Box G-826
New Bedford, MA 02742
(800) 338-1753 [(617) 996-6732 in Mass.]
BAKERForms

**Berkeley System Design**
1700 Shattuck Avenue
Berkeley, CA 94709
(415) 540-5536
Stepping Out II

**Blyth Holdings Inc.**
1065 East Hillsdale Blvd.
Suite 300
Foster City, CA 94404
(415) 571-0222
Omnis 3

**BMUG** (formally the Berkeley Macintosh Users Group)
Suite 62
1442 A Walnut Street
Berkeley, CA 94709
(415) 849-HELP or (415) 549-BMUG
Public domain and shareware disks

**Borland International**
4585 Scotts Valley Drive
Scotts Valley, CA 95066
(408) 438-8400
Reflex Plus, Sidekick

**Boston Computer Society**
Macintosh Users Group
48 Grove Street
Sommerville, MA 02144
(617) 625-7080
Public domain and shareware disks

Canvas from Deneba Software

Capture from Mainstay

**CasadyWare**
Box 223779
Carmel, CA 93922
(408) 646-4660
Fluent fonts

**Century Software**
2306 Cotner Avenue
Los Angeles, CA 90064
(213) 829-4436
LaserFonts

**CE Software**
801 73rd Street
Des Moines, IA 50312
(515) 224-1995
DiskTop, MockWrite, QuicKeys, Vaccine

**Chesley, Harry R.**
1850 Union Street
San Francisco, CA Packit III

**Claris**
440 Clyde Avenue
Mountain View, CA 94043
(415) 962-8946 (customer relations)
(800) 544-8554 (upgrades)
(800) 334-3535 (U.S. dealers)
Claris CAD, FileMaker, MacDraw, MacPaint, MacProject, MacWrite

Click Art from T/Maker

The Clipper from Solutions International

Complementary Type from Software Complement

**CompuServe**
Box 20212
5000 Arlington Centre Blvd.
Columbus, OH 43220
(800) 848-8199 [(614) 457-8600 in Ohio]

**Computer Friends**
14250 NW Science Park Drive
Portland, OR 97229
(503) 626-2291
Modern Artist, print buffers, ribbon re-inkers

**Connectix Corporation**
125 Constitution Drive
Menlo Park, CA 94025
(415) 324-0727
Virtual

**Cricket Software**
40 Valley Stream Parkway
Malvern, PA 19355
(215) 251-9890
Cricket Draw, Cricket Graph, Cricket Presents

The Curator from Solutions International

dBASE Mac from Ashton-Tate

**Deneba Software**
Suite 202
7855 NW 12th Street
Miami, FL 33126
(800) 6-CANVAS or (305) 594-6965
Canvas, Comment, Spelling Coach

Desktop Express from Dow Jones

**Diehl Graphsoft**
8370 Court Avenue
Suite 202
Ellicott City, MD 21043
MiniCad

Digital Darkroom from Silicon Beach Software

Disk Express from ALSoft

DiskFit from SuperMac Technologies

DiskTop from CE Software

Double Helix from Odesta

**Dow Jones News/Retrieval**
Box 300
Princeton, NJ 08543
(609) 452-1511

**Dubl-Click Software**
18201 Gresham Street
Northridge, CA 91325
(818) 349-2758
WetPaint (clip art), World Class Fonts

**Dyna Communications**
Fifth Floor
50 South Main Street
Salt Lake City, UT 84144
(801) 531-0600
Dyna File MS-DOS to Mac conversion drives

**Electronic Arts**
1820 Gateway Drive
San Mateo, CA 94404
(415) 571-7171
Studio 8, DiskTools Plus

Excel from Microsoft

**Farallon Computing**
2150 Kittredge Street
Berkeley, CA 94704
(415) 849-2331
MacRecorder, PhoneNet, StarNET

**Fifth Generation Systems**
1322 Bell Avenue
Tustin, CA 92680
(714) 259-0541
FastBack, PowerStation, Suitcase

File from Microsoft

FileMaker from Claris

Findswell from Working Software

**First Aid Software**
42 Radnor Road
Boston, MA 02135
First Aid Kit HFS, Anti-Virus Kit

Fluent Fonts and Fluent Laser Fonts from CasadyWare

Font/DA Juggler from ALSoft

4th Dimension from ACIUS

**Fox Software**
118 West South Broadway
Perrysburg, OH 43551
(419) 874-0162
FoxBase+/Mac

**The FreeSoft Company**
10828 Lacklink
St. Louis, MO 63114
(313) 423-2190
Red Ryder

FullPaint from Ashton-Tate

FullWrite from Ashton-Tate

**GEnie**
Dept 02B
Rockville, MD 20850
voice: (800) 638-9636 data: (800) 638-8369

GOfer from Microlytics

GraphicWorks from Mindscape

HD Backup from Apple Computer

**Heizer Software**
1941 Oak Park Blvd.
Suite 30, P.O. Box 232019
Pleasant Hill, CA 94523
(415) 943-7667 [Orders: (800) 888-7667]
WorksXchange, Excellent Exchange, Stack Exchange

Helix from Odesta

HFS Backup from PCPC

**HJC Software, Inc.**
P.O. Box 51816
Durham, NC
(919) 490-1277
Virex

HyperCard from Apple Computer

**Image Club Graphics**
2915 19th Street NE
Calgary, Alberta
Canada T2E 7A2
Image Club

Image Studio from Letraset

Images With Impact! from 3G Graphics

**Infosphere**
4730 SW Macadam
Portland, OR 97201
(503) 226-3620
MacServe

**Innovative Data Design**
Suite A
2280 Bates Avenue
Concord, CA 94520
(415) 680-6818
MacDraft, Dreams

**International Typefaces Corporation**
2 Hammarskjold Plaza
New York, NY 10017
(212) 371-0699
Licensed laser fonts

LaserFonts from Century Software

**Lau, Raymond**
100-04 70th Avenue
Forest Hills, NY 11375
NYMUG: (212) 645-9484
GEnie: RAYLAU
CompuServe: 761742617

**Letraset**
40 Eisenhower Drive
Paramus, NJ 07652
Image Studio; Ready,Set,Go!; Ready,Set,Show!

**Lundeen and Associates**
Box 30038
Oakland, CA 94604
(800) 233-6851 or (415) 893-7587
WorksPlus Command, WorksPlus Spell

MacDraft from Innovative Data Designs

MacDraw from Claris

MacPaint from Claris

MacWrite from Claris

**Mainstay**
5311-B Derry Avenue
Agoura Hills, CA 91301
(818) 991-6540
Anti-Toxin, Capture, TypeNow

**MCI Mail**
1900 M Street NW
Box 10001
Washington, DC 20036
(800) 624-2255

**MicroCAD/CAM**
5900 Sepulveda Blvd.
Suite 340
Van Nuys, CA 91411
MGMS: Professional CAD for Macintosh

MicroPhone from Software Ventures

**Microscape**
3444 Dundee Road
Northbrook, IL 60062
(800) 221-9884 [(800) 654-3767 in Ill.]
GraphicWorks

**Microsoft**
16011 NE 36th Way
Box 97017
Redmond, WA 98052
(800) 882-8088
Excel, Flight Simulator, Microsoft Basic, MS-DOS, File, Mail, Multiplan, Word, Works

Modern Artist from Computer Friends

MORE from Symantec

MultiFinder from Apple Computer

Multiplan from Microsoft

**Odesta**
4084 Commercial Avenue
Northbrook, IL 60062
(800) 323-5423 [(312) 498-5615 in Ill.]
Double Helix

Omnis 3 from Blyth Software

Packit III from Harry R. Chesley

PageMaker from Aldus

**Paragon Concepts**
4954 Sun Valley Road
Del Mar, CA 92014
(800) 922-2993 [(619) 481-1477 in Calif.]
Nixsus advanced word processor

**PCPC** (Personal Computer Peripherals Corporation)
6204 Benjamin Road
Tampa, FL 33634
(800) 622-2888 or (813) 884-3092
HFS Backup

PhoneNET from Farallon Computing

Pixel Paint from SuperMac Technologies

PostScript from Adobe

PowerStation from Fifth Generation Systems

**Quark**
Suite 100
300 South Jackson
Denver, CO 80209
(800) 543-7711 or (303) 934-2211

Xpress

QuicKeys from CE Software

Ready,Set,Go! from Letraset

Red Ryder from FreeSoft

Reflex Plus from Borland International

**Silicon Beach Software**
Box 261430
San Diego, CA 92126
(619) 695-6956
Digital Darkroom, Silicon Press, SuperCard, SuperPaint, Super3D

Silicon Press from Silicon Beach Software

SmartScrap from Solutions International

**Software Ventures**
Suite 220
2907 Claremont Avenue
Berkeley, CA 94705
(415) 644-3232
MicroPhone

**Solutions International**
Box 989
Montpelier, VT 05602
(802) 229-0368
SmartScrap, The Clipper, Curator, SuperGlue II

Special Effects from Century Software

Spellswell from Working Software

StarNET from Farallon Computing

Stepping Out II from Berkeley Systems Design

Studio 8 from Electronic Arts

Stuffit from Raymond Lau

Suitcase II from Fifth Generations Systems

SuperGlue II from Solutions International

**SuperMac Technologies**
295 North Bernado Avenue
Mountain View, CA 94043
(415) 964-8884
DiskFit, Pixel Paint, Sentinel, SuperLaserSpool, SuperSpool

SuperPaint from Silicon Beach Software

SuperSpool (and SuperLaserSpool) from SuperMac Technologies

**Symantec**
10201 Torre Avenue
Cupertino, CA 95014
(408) 253-9600
(800) 441-7234
(800) 626-8847 (California)
MORE II, Symantec Utilities for the Macintosh (SUM)

**Symmetry**
761 East University Drive
Mesa, AZ 85203
(800) 624-2485 [(602) 884-2199 in Ariz.]
Acta, HyperDA

Tempo from Affinity Microsystems

ThunderScan from ThunderWare

**ThunderWare**
21 Orinda Way
Orinda, CA 94563
(415) 254-6581
ThunderScan, LightningWare

**T/Maker**
1973 Landings Drive
Mountain View, CA 94043
(415) 962-0195
ClickArt, WriteNow

**TOPS**
2560 Ninth Street
Berkeley, CA 94710
(800) 222-TOPS or (415) 549-5906
TOPS

Trapeze from Access Technology

**VersaCad**
2124 Main Street
Huntington Beach, CA 92648
(714) 960-7720
VersaCAD

Virex from HJC Software

Virtual from Connectix

WetPaint from Dubl-Click Software

Word from Microsoft

Word Finder from Microlytics

**Working Software**
Suite H
321 Alvarado
Monterey, CA 93940
(408) 375-2828
Findswell, Lookup, Spellswell

Works from Microsoft

WorksPlus Command from Lundeen and Associates

WorksPlus Spell from Lundeen and Associates

WorksXchange from Heizer Software

World Class Fonts from Dubl-Click Software

WriteNow from T/Maker

Xpress from Quark

B

# Macintosh-Related Bulletin Boards

Commercial BBSs provide access to information on a variety of subjects, such as news, sports, new shareware and freeware programs, perhaps even a round-table discussion of rumors and technical issues. You can subscribe to a bulletin board on a time-billed basis, or you can use the many free BBSs.

Internationally, there are thousands of BBSs, and they focus on everything from developers working with Acius's 4th Dimension relational database to users who are interested in the Macintosh as a platform for doing graphics work. Bulletin boards of this type can come and go with amazing speed.

Of course, many more bulletin boards exist than could possibly be listed here. Your local user group is a good source for locating other BBSs, both locally and nationally.

## *Commercial Services*

This appendix lists the major commercial services. Because they are commercial, they tend to be stable and long lasting.

### *BIX*

BIX is a highly technical BBS run by *BYTE* magazine. BIX attracts developers from major Macintosh companies who participate in round-table discussions. Many software companies maintain open lines on this board to allow you to register complaints or ask questions. Contact:

BIX, One Phoenix Mill Lane, Peterborough, NH 03458, (800) 227-2983, (603) 924-7681 (in New Hampshire).

## *CompuServe*

CompuServe is perhaps the most popular information service. You register by purchasing the CompuServe Starter Kit ($40), which includes local phone numbers, a log-in code, and instructions. Your on-line time is billed to your credit card. This service contains an extensive listing of public domain software and an excellent Macintosh round-table group. Contact: CompuServe, Box 20212, Columbus, OH, 43220, (800) 848-8199, (614) 457-8600 (in Ohio).

## *Dow Jones News/Retrieval*

Dow Jones provides news and financial listings, and you can use this service to follow the stock market in real time. Access to Dow Jones costs from $12 to $72 per hour, depending on the information you use. (See the MCI Mail listing for information.) Contact: Dow Jones, Box 300, Princeton, NJ, 08543 (609) 452-1511.

## *GEnie*

GEnie is very similar to CompuServe, but GEnie's rates are somewhat lower.

## *MCI Mail*

MCI Mail creates an electronic mailbox that allows you to send E-Mail (Electronic Mail) at relatively low cost to other MCI Mail, CompuServe, or Telex users. You also can use MCI mail to access the Dow Jones News/Retrieval database. You are given an in box, an out box, and a desk file for messages in progress or those you have read.

You are charged for using the Dow Jones services. For receiving mail, however, the only cost is for the phone call. MCI Mail has local phone numbers in most cities. The basic service costs about $18 per year, with charges for messages above a certain number. Contact: MCI Mail, 1900 M St. NW, Box 1001, Washington, D.C., 20036, (800) 624-2255.

## FidoNet

Nearly 5,900 bulletin boards are listed by FidoNet. Write to The International FidoNet Association, P.O. Box 41143, St. Louis, MO 63141, or call (314) 576-2743. The International FidoNet Coordinator may be reached by modem at the BBS number (602) 235-9653.

## Miscellaneous

Other commercial services that you might want to explore are Delphi and The Source. Both contain round-tables and file areas for downloading. Western Union EasyLink and AppleNet are two more E-Mail systems worthy of consideration.

# User Group Bulletin Boards

Many user groups maintain their own bulletin boards. This section lists a few of these BBSs, and you can use them to find others in your area.

| Name | Coordinator | Location | Phone |
|---|---|---|---|
| Ann Arbor MUG | Rod Ganiard | Ann Arbor, MI | (313) 663-5388 |
| Anchorage MUG | Nevin McClintook | Anchorage, AK | (904) 561-4732 |
| Apple Eye | Michael Rumelt | St. Louis, MO | (314) 569-2762 |
| Apple Pickers | David Herren | Indianapolis, IN | (317) 924-2784 |
| Arizona MUG | David Beginski | Gilbert, AZ | (602) 926-2080 |
| Atlanta MUG | Jerry Harris | Norcross, GA | (404) 448-1568 |
| BMUG | BMUG | Berkeley, CA | (415) 849-2684 |
| Boulder Macintosh Mtg | Ed Glassgow | Boulder, CO | (303) 494-7186 |
| Boulder Mac Maniacs | Ed Fenner | Boulder, CO | (303) 666-7543 |
| Boston Computer Soc. | BCS MAC | Sommerville, MA | (617) 625-7080 |
| Capitol City MUG | George Kent | Waddy, KY | (502) 223-1508 |
| Capital MUG | George | Silver Springs, MD | (301) 585-4262 |
| Check-In | Dave Game | Miami, FL | (305) 232-0393 |

| Name | Coordinator | Location | Phone |
|---|---|---|---|
| Clubmac (Europe) | K. Leslie | West Germany | 06583 1371 |
| Club Mac Midwest | William Davis | Des Moines, IA | (515) 276-2345 |
| Desk Toppers | Randy Bennett | Chicago, IL | (312) 356-3776 |
| East Bay MUG | Steve Usler | Pinole, CA | (415) 653-6849 |
| Gateway Area MUG | Eric Friedman | St. Louis, MO | (314) 361-1800 |
| Hawaii MUG | Ron Letson | Honolulu, HI | (808) 235-4609 |
| Hughes Aircraft | Bud Grove | Long Beach, CA | (213) 549-9640 |
| Intermountain MUG | Pam Simister | Salt Lake City, UT | (801) 485-6341 |
| LaserBoard | Stuart Gitlow | New York, NY | (212) 348-5714 |
| MUG | David Sanders | Los Angeles, CA | (415) 278-LAMG |
| Mac Atlanta | Herb Theisz | Marietta, GA | (404) 971-8216 |
| Mac Boston | Steve Garfield | Boston, MA | (617) 262-9167 |
| Mac Circles | Pat O'Connor | Pleasanton, CA | (415) 484-4412 |
| Mac Club ITALIA | A. Toscanini | Italy | 05 536 8730 |
| MacExplorers | Steve LeClair | Phoenix, AZ | (602) 932-5300 |
| MacFido Tribune | Vernon Keenon | Palo Alto, CA | (415) 923-1235 |
| Maclub Israel MUG | Yariv Nachshon | Tel Aviv, Israel | 2231925/249998 |
| Mac Orange | Robert Ameeti | Santa Ana, CA | (714) 542-9753 |
| The Mac Pac | Terry Duke | Richardson, TX | (214) 387-3632 |
| Mac SIG | Mike Carlson | Minneapolis, MN | (612) 866-3441 |
| Mac Valley UG | Ruth Steven | Burbank, CA | (818) 848-1277 |
| Mac U. of Del. (MUD) | Larry | Rockland, DE | (302) 656-1884 |
| The MUG U.K. | John Lewis | Oxford, England | 44 865-58027 |
| MACropedia | Dave Alpert | Chicago, IL | (312) 295-6926 |
| MacQueue I | Leo Laporte | San Francisco, CA | (415) 661-7374 |
| MacQueue II | Leo Laporte | San Francisco, CA | (415) 753-3002 |
| MacWichita | Jerry Copeland | Wichita, KS | (316) 522-6085 |
| Madison MUG | Steve Greenberg | Madison, WI | (608) 262-5896 |
| M.A.G.I.C. | Steve Sande | Denver, CO | (303) 791-8732 |
| MAGIS | Keith Elkin | Stockholm, Sweden | 46 673568 |
| Mass. Mac & Electric | Barr Plexico | Saugus, MA | (617) 231-2872 |
| Miami Apple MUG | Steven Kramer | Miami, FL | (305) 866-5507 |

| | | | |
|---|---|---|---|
| Nashville MUG | Clark Thomas | Nashville, TN | (615) 327-1757 |
| Newfoundland MUG | Randy Miller | Mt. Pearl, NF, Can. | (709) 368-3528 |
| New Orleans MUG | R. Collins | Metairie, LA | (504) 833-0189 |
| NY MUG | Leon Ablon | New York, NY | (212) 473-YMAG |
| N. Illinois C.S | Bill Gronke | Arlington Hts., IL | (312) 394-4274 |
| O-Mac | Richard Herbst | Orlando, FL | (305) 299-0021 |
| Omaha MUG | Gretchin Binns | Omaha, NE | (402) 592-1831 |
| Ottawa MUG | Ted and Susan | Ottawa, ON, Can. | (613) 824-4888 |
| Portland MUG | Neil Wolf | Portland, OR | (503) 232-PMUG |
| San Diego MUG | Diane Kelley | La Jolla, CA | (619) 566-3939 |
| San Gabriel MUG | Bill Viahos | Pasadena, CA | (818) 354-0496 |
| Sea/Mac | Jim Creighton | Seattle, WA | (206) 725-6629 |
| SEMCO | Jim Rarus | Detroit, MI | (313) 467-1321 |
| Stanford MUG | John Agosta | Stanford, CA | (415) 497-1496 |
| Sydney MUG | Ed Cox | St. Mary's, NSW, Aus. | 02 673 3236 |
| The Rest of Us | Terry Hueser | Chicago, IL | (312) 642-5920 |
| Tokyo MUG | Takashi Ohtsuka | Tokyo, Japan | 3-404-0593 |
| UNC MUG | Jane Stein | Chapel Hill, NC | (919) 929-1614 |
| Univ. MUG | John Lewis | Austin, TX | (512) 471-5569 |
| UH MUG | William Linsley | Houston, TX | (714) 749-4551 |
| Victoria's MUG | Michael Dlugos | Victoria, BC, Can. | (604) 381-5667 |
| Yale MUG | Philip Rubin | New Haven, CT | (203) 776-9120 |

# Index

## A



## B

## C

## D

## E



## F

## G

## H



## I

## J



## K



## L

## M

## N



## O

## P

## Q–R



## S

## T

## U



## V

## W



## X–Z

# Computer Books From Que Mean PC Performance!

## Spreadsheets

|  |  |
|---|---|
| 1-2-3 Database Techniques | $29.95 |
| 1-2-3 Graphics Techniques | $24.95 |
| 1-2-3 Macro Library, 3rd Edition | $39.95 |
| 1-2-3 Release 2.2 Business Applications | $39.95 |
| 1-2-3 Release 2.2 Quick Reference | $ 7.95 |
| 1-2-3 Release 2.2 QuickStart | $19.95 |
| 1-2-3 Release 2.2 Workbook and Disk | $29.95 |
| 1-2-3 Release 3 Business Applications | $39.95 |
| 1-2-3 Release 3 Quick Reference | $ 7.95 |
| 1-2-3 Release 3 QuickStart | $19.95 |
| 1-2-3 Release 3 Workbook and Disk | $29.95 |
| 1-2-3 Tips, Tricks, and Traps, 3rd Edition | $24.95 |
| Excel Business Applications: IBM Version | $39.95 |
| Excel Quick Reference | $ 7.95 |
| Excel QuickStart | $19.95 |
| Excel Tips, Tricks, and Traps | $22.95 |
| Using 1-2-3, Special Edition | $26.95 |
| Using 1-2-3 Release 2.2, Special Edition | $26.95 |
| Using 1-2-3 Release 3 | $27.95 |
| Using Excel: IBM Version | $29.95 |
| Using Lotus Spreadsheet for DeskMate | $19.95 |
| Using Quattro Pro | $24.95 |
| Using SuperCalc5, 2nd Edition | $29.95 |

## Databases

|  |  |
|---|---|
| dBASE III Plus Handbook, 2nd Edition | $24.95 |
| dBASE III Plus Tips, Tricks, and Traps | $24.95 |
| dBASE III Plus Workbook and Disk | $29.95 |
| dBASE IV Applications Library, 2nd Edition | $39.95 |
| dBASE IV Programming Techniques | $24.95 |
| dBASE IV QueCards | $21.95 |
| dBASE IV Quick Reference | $ 7.95 |
| dBASE IV QuickStart | $19.95 |
| dBASE IV Tips, Tricks,and Traps, 2nd Ed. | $24.95 |
| dBASE IV Workbook and Disk | $29.95 |
| R:BASE User's Guide, 3rd Edition | $22.95 |
| Using Clipper | $24.95 |
| Using DataEase | $24.95 |
| Using dBASE IV | $27.95 |
| Using FoxPro | $26.95 |
| Using Paradox 3 | $24.95 |
| Using Reflex, 2nd Edition | $22.95 |
| Using SQL | $24.95 |

## Business Applications

|  |  |
|---|---|
| Introduction to Business Software | $14.95 |
| Introduction to Personal Computers | $19.95 |
| Lotus Add-in Toolkit Guide | $29.95 |
| Norton Utilities Quick Reference | $ 7.95 |
| PC Tools Quick Reference, 2nd Edition | $ 7.95 |
| Q&A Quick Reference | $ 7.95 |
| Que's Computer User's Dictionary | $9.95 |
| Que's Wizard Book | $ 9.95 |
| Smart Tips, Tricks, and Traps | $24.95 |
| Using Computers in Business | $22.95 |
| Using DacEasy, 2nd Edition | $24.95 |
| Using Dollars and Sense: IBM Version, 2nd Edition | $19.95 |
| Using Enable/OA | $29.95 |
| Using Harvard Project Manager | $24.95 |
| Using Lotus Magellan | $21.95 |
| Using Managing Your Money, 2nd Edition | $19.95 |
| Using Microsoft Works: IBM Version | $22.95 |
| Using Norton Utilities | $24.95 |
| Using PC Tools Deluxe | $24.95 |
| Using Peachtree | $22.95 |
| Using PFS: First Choice | $22.95 |
| Using PROCOMM PLUS | $19.95 |
| Using Q&A, 2nd Edition | $23.95 |
| Using Quicken | $19.95 |
| Using Smart | $22.95 |
| Using SmartWare II | $29.95 |
| Using Symphony, Special Edition | $29.95 |

## CAD

|  |  |
|---|---|
| AutoCAD Advanced Techniques | $34.95 |
| AutoCAD Quick Reference | $ 7.95 |
| AutoCAD Sourcebook | $24.95 |
| Using AutoCAD, 2nd Edition | $24.95 |
| Using Generic CADD | $24.95 |

## Word Processing

|  |  |
|---|---|
| DisplayWrite QuickStart | $19.95 |
| Microsoft Word 5 Quick Reference | $ 7.95 |
| Microsoft Word 5 Tips, Tricks, and Traps: IBM Version | $22.95 |
| Using DisplayWrite 4, 2nd Edition | $24.95 |
| Using Microsoft Word 5: IBM Version | $22.95 |
| Using MultiMate | $22.95 |
| Using Professional Write | $22.95 |
| Using Word for Windows | $22.95 |
| Using WordPerfect, 3rd Edition | $21.95 |
| Using WordPerfect 5 | $24.95 |
| Using WordPerfect 5.1, Special Edition | $24.95 |
| Using WordStar, 2nd Edition | $21.95 |
| WordPerfect QueCards | $21.95 |
| WordPerfect Quick Reference | $ 7.95 |
| WordPerfect QuickStart | $19.95 |
| WordPerfect Tips, Tricks, and Traps, 2nd Edition | $22.95 |
| WordPerfect 5 Workbook and Disk | $29.95 |
| WordPerfect 5.1 Quick Reference | $ 7.95 |
| WordPerfect 5.1 QuickStart | $19.95 |
| WordPerfect 5.1 Tips, Tricks, and Traps | $22.95 |
| WordPerfect 5.1 Workbook and Disk | $29.95 |

## Hardware/Systems

|  |  |
|---|---|
| DOS Power Techniques | $29.95 |
| DOS Tips, Tricks, and Traps | $24.95 |
| DOS Workbook and Disk, 2nd Edition | $29.95 |
| Hard Disk Quick Reference | $ 7.95 |
| MS-DOS Quick Reference | $ 7.95 |
| MS-DOS QuickStart | $21.95 |
| MS-DOS User's Guide, Special Edition | $29.95 |
| Networking Personal Computers, 3rd Edition | $24.95 |
| The Printer Bible | $29.95 |
| Que's Guide to Data Recovery | $24.95 |
| Understanding UNIX, 2nd Edition | $21.95 |
| Upgrading and Repairing PCs | $29.95 |
| Using DOS | $22.95 |
| Using Microsoft Windows 3, 2nd Edition | $22.95 |
| Using Novell NetWare | $29.95 |
| Using OS/2 | $29.95 |
| Using PC DOS, 3rd Edition | $24.95 |
| Using UNIX | $24.95 |
| Using Your Hard Disk | $29.95 |
| Windows 3 Quick Reference | $ 7.95 |

## Desktop Publishing/Graphics

|  |  |
|---|---|
| Harvard Graphics Quick Reference | $ 7.95 |
| Using Animator | $24.95 |
| Using Harvard Graphics | $24.95 |
| Using Freelance Plus | $24.95 |
| Using PageMaker: IBM Version, 2nd Edition | $24.95 |
| Using PFS: First Publisher | $22.95 |
| Using Ventura Publisher, 2nd Edition | $24.95 |
| Ventura Publisher Tips, Tricks, and Traps, | $24.95 |

## Macintosh/Apple II

|  |  |
|---|---|
| AppleWorks QuickStart | $19.95 |
| The Big Mac Book | $27.95 |
| Excel QuickStart | $19.95 |
| Excel Tips, Tricks, and Traps | $22.95 |
| Que's Macintosh Multimedia Handbook | $22.95 |
| Using AppleWorks, 3rd Edition | $21.95 |
| Using AppleWorks GS | $21.95 |
| Using Dollars and Sense: Macintosh Version | $19.95 |
| Using Excel: Macintosh Version | $24.95 |
| Using FileMaker | $24.95 |
| Using MacroMind Director | $29.95 |
| Using MacWrite | $22.95 |
| Using Microsoft Word 4: Macintosh Version | $24.95 |
| Using Microsoft Works: Macintosh Version, 2nd Edition | $24.95 |
| Using PageMaker: Macintosh Version | $24.95 |

## Programming/Technical

|  |  |
|---|---|
| Assembly Language Quick Reference | $ 7.95 |
| C Programmer's Toolkit | $39.95 |
| C Programming Guide, 3rd Edition | $24.95 |
| C Quick Reference | $ 7.95 |
| DOS and BIOS Functions Quick Reference | $ 7.95 |
| DOS Programmer's Reference, 2nd Edition | $29.95 |
| Oracle Programmer's Guide | $24.95 |
| Power Graphics Programming | $24.95 |
| QuickBASIC Advanced Techniques | $22.95 |
| QuickBASIC Programmer's Toolkit | $39.95 |
| QuickBASIC Quick Reference | $ 7.95 |
| QuickPascal Programming | $22.95 |
| SQL Programmer's Guide | $29.95 |
| Turbo C Programming | $22.95 |
| Turbo Pascal Advanced Techniques | $22.95 |
| Turbo Pascal Programmer's Toolkit | $39.95 |
| Turbo Pascal Quick Reference | $ 7.95 |
| UNIX Programmer's Quick Reference | $ 7.95 |
| Using Assembly Language, 2nd Edition | $29.95 |
| Using BASIC | $19.95 |
| Using C | $27.95 |
| Using QuickBASIC 4 | $24.95 |
| Using Turbo Pascal | $29.95 |

For More Information,
Call Toll Free!

**1-800-428-5331**

*All prices and titles subject to change without notice. Non-U.S. prices may be higher. Printed in the U.S.A.*

## Using Excel: Macintosh Version

*by John Annaloro*

Complete with an introduction to Excel worksheets and macros, this combination of tutorial and reference shows readers how to create spreadsheets, databases, and graphics with this powerful Macintosh spreadsheet program. Covers the latest version of Excel!

**Order #1031**
**$24.95 USA**
**0-88022-494-0, 650 pp.**

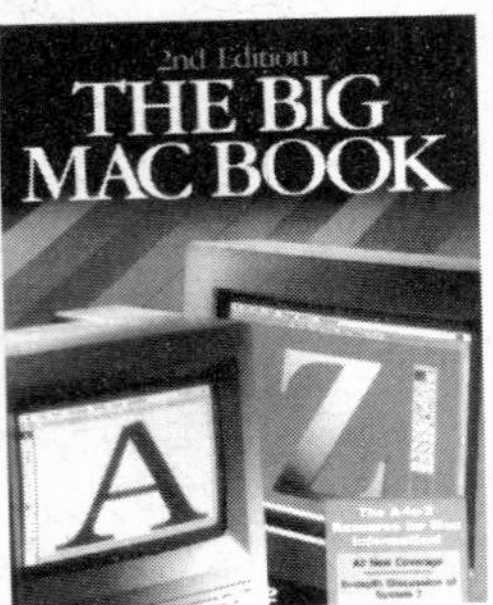


## The Big Mac Book, 2nd Edition

*by Neil J. Salkind*

This is the all new introduction to Macintosh computing! Compares Macintosh applications, discusses desktop publishing basics, graphics, and networking. Plus, the book includes a Troubleshooting section, user group directories, bulletin boards, and on-line services.

**Order #1258**
**$27.95 USA**
**0-88022-648-X, 700 pp.**

## Using PageMaker: Macintosh Version, 2nd Edition

*by C.J. Weigand*

This is the complete and updated practical guide to professional-quality newsletters, flyers, catalogs, and other documents. Packed with examples and advanced production techniques!

**Order #1195**
**$24.95 USA**
**0-88022-607-2, 450 pp.**

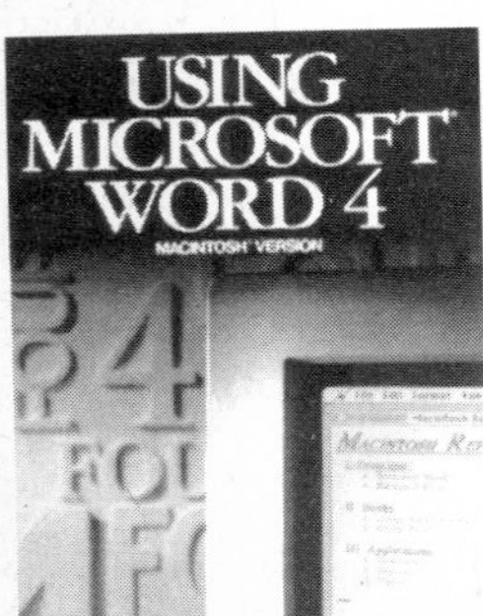


## Using Microsoft Word 4: Macintosh Version

*by Bryan Pfaffenberger*

Word processing expert Bryan Pfaffenberger leads users step-by-step from Word basics to the program's advanced features. Ideal for beginning and intermediate users of the Macintosh version of Microsoft Word.

**Order #987**
**$24.95 USA**
**0-88022-451-7, 500 pp.**

Que Order Line: **1-800-428-5331**

All prices subject to change without notice. Prices and charges are for domestic orders only. Non-U.S. prices might be higher.

NO POSTAGE
NECESSARY
IF MAILED
IN THE
UNITED STATES

BUSINESS REPLY MAIL
First Class Permit No. 9918 Indianapolis, IN

*Postage will be paid by addressee*

11711 N. College
Carmel, IN 46032

NO POSTAGE
NECESSARY
IF MAILED
IN THE
UNITED STATES

BUSINESS REPLY MAIL
First Class Permit No. 9918 Indianapolis, IN

*Postage will be paid by addressee*

11711 N. College
Carmel, IN 46032